Urban Spaces No. 2

The Design of Public Places

Edited by
John Morris Dixon, FAIA

Designed by
Harish K. Patel

Visual Reference Publications, New York

Urban Land Institute, Washington, DC

Visual Reference Publications, Inc.
302 Fifth Avenue
New York, NY 10001

Distributors to the trade in the United States and Canada
Watson-Guptill
770 Broadway
New York, NY 10003

Distributors outside the United States and Canada
HarperCollins International
10 East 53 Street
New York, NY 10022-5299

Book Design: Harish Patel Design Associates, New York

Library of Congress Cataloging in Publication Data:
Urban Spaces No.2
Printed in Hong Kong
ISBN: 1-58471-023-3

Contents

Contents by Project Type

Introduction

The Evolving Tradition of Urban Spaces

In the past century, our world has been transformed by such innovations as airplanes, television, and computers. In the field of urban development, our environments have been radically changed by such developments as the skyscraper and the shopping mall, air conditioning and the curtain wall, zoning regulations and freeways.

Yet all of these new devices have not replaced age-old ways of doing things, just added to them. In the age of e-mail and cable TV, we still gather to learn, to attend performances, to socialize, to eat. We move around in our environment by walking—though not as much as we should—and we want to enjoy doing it. Atriums, food courts, and airport concourses have been added to our stock of urban spaces, but we still have a demand for theaters, museums, and courthouses, as well as hospitable streets, parks, plazas, and promenades.

During the last century, we learned that some apparently rational modern planning concepts just don't work. "Tower in the park" developments initiated with great pride usually turned out to be towers in wastelands. Isolating pedestrians from cars, we found, was not always a good idea. Nor was there always any benefit in separating housing from commerce or public development from private investment. We're learning as well that suburbs, too, need well-designed urban spaces. Crucially, we learned that no development is successful as an isolated event, but only as part of a broader community fabric.

As a result, the projects in this book show a recognition that ancient urban development practices are not necessarily obsolete and that new ideas and old can be mixed effectively.

There's a consensus about what kinds of urban spaces we need, and a lot of public and private resources are going into developing them. Debate is still very active, however, about what architectural forms these should embody. Many believe that comfortable public places should include traditional elements such as cupolas, arches, wrought iron, and historically accurate lamp posts. Opponents call such design element merely nostalgic and call for geometries and materials in synch with today's art and technology. Partisans on both sides claim to be following the only true path, but many of us simply see a broader range of acceptable design approaches.

Another, related, issue involves theming. We're accustomed to restaurants and hotels with historical or exotic décor, but should an office park recall a Southern plantation, a shopping complex replicate a New England fishing village, a ski resort a Swiss mountain hamlet? One side says, "Why not, if it makes the users happy," and if, as is often the case, it comes at little or no additional cost. Detractors say this theming is a symptom of escapism. It could well be argued, however, that theming—like escapism—is an integral part of today's hectic, cosmopolitan societies.

As you peruse the accomplishments documented in this book, I hope you will evaluate them not on whether they are Modern or traditional, themed or not, but on how well their spaces serve their intended uses—and on ageless criteria such as proportion, color, texture, lighting, density of detail, contrast, harmony, and sequence. Ultimately, is each of these projects a place you would like to be, and why?

John Morris Dixon, FAIA

Because two firms contributed substantially to its design, one project is featured twice in this book: the U.S. Courthouse and Federal Building in Sacramento, a collaborative accomplishment of HLM Design (p.. 158) and ROMA (p. 254).

We are pleased that some projects shown as designs in the first Urban Spaces volume are included as finished works in this book: Elkus/Manfredi Architects' CityPlace in West Palm Beach (p. 90) and Sansom Common in Philadelphia (p. 94); ROMA's Mid-Embarcadero Open Space and Transportation Projects in San Francisco (p. 250)

ELS's Pioneer Place Pioneer Place in Portland, Oregon, shown completed in the earlier book, is followed here by the completed Pioneer Place, Phase II.

Preface

Richard M. Rosan, FAIA
*President,
Urban Land
Institute*

Once again ULI—the Urban Land Institute —is pleased to cosponsor *Urban Spaces*. These high-quality books provide an excellent opportunity to bring together some of the best examples of the innovative, creative design and development of urban spaces around the world.

Many believe that there is now a new search for meaning in our physical spaces, particularly in those that function as gathering points. Designers and developers of urban spaces are focusing attention on the elements of space that contribute— symbolically and literally—to bringing a sense of community to the urban form. Witness the increased interest in the notion of place making, the creation of a memorable experience that brings people back time and again for the sheer pleasure of being in the space.

ULI has nearly 17,000 members around the world who are involved in shaping and reshaping our environments. And the more ULI expands its global outreach, the more we discover that countries around the world share many of the same urban development concerns—most relating to the quest for livability and making places that people can love. We know place making can establish and revive areas because it brings people together.

Place making helps to restore a sense of community, a sense of belonging, to our neighborhoods—be they intensely urban or bucolically suburban. In the United States, place making has become part of a fundamental shift in neighborhood design —a shift away from single-family, segregated use, low density, auto-dependent design to communities that offer a great range of options. This shift in design is part of an overall effort by our metropolitan areas to find solutions to urban sprawl.

Without question, sprawl is taking a terrible toll on our citizens' quality of life. It has been well documented that work commutes are getting longer, bridges are crumbling, public schools are more crowded, and affordable housing less available. We're stuck in traffic, stuck in temporary trailer classrooms, and stuck on airport runways.

Improving livability and creating successful urban spaces are among the top priorities of our urban areas, our regions, and many of our states. These efforts require many elements to come together in a synergistic way—design, scale, materials, location, market, function, access, and many others. High on the list of elements, though, is high quality design—a central component of successful spaces. The firms and their projects represented in this book offer models for how to balance all the elements essential to delightful and usable urban places.

A. Epstein and Sons International, Inc.

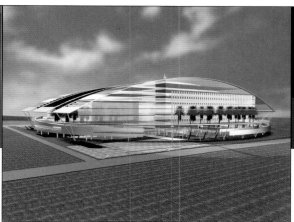

600 West Fulton Street

Chicago

Illinois 60661.1199

312.454.9100

312.559.1217 (Fax)

www.epstein-isi.com

ametter@epstein-isi.com

Los Angeles

Tel Aviv

Tokyo

Warsaw

A. Epstein and Sons International, Inc.

Comverse Network Systems Campus
Ra'annana, Israel

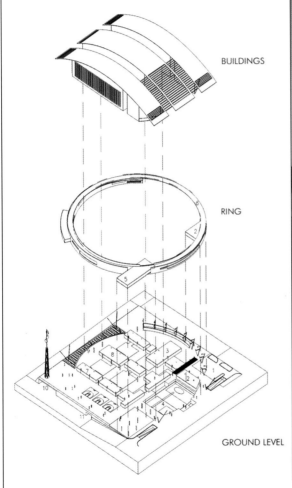

BUILDINGS

RING

GROUND LEVEL

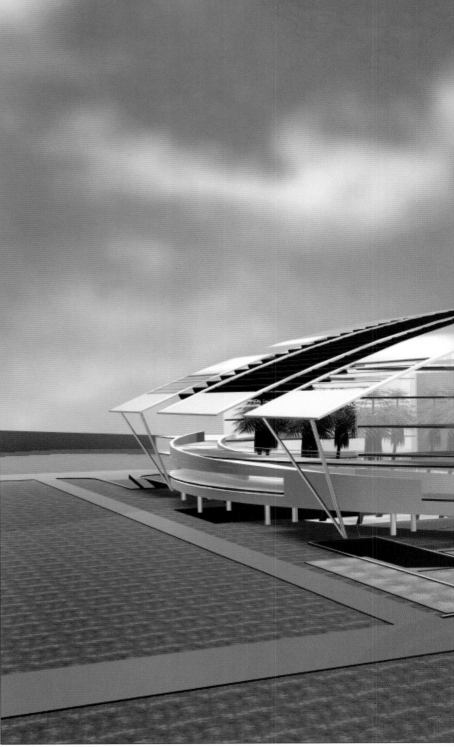

Above: Principal layers of complex.
Center: View from approach (east) side.
Right: Model viewed from west side.
Far right: Model view from south.
Photography (models): Andrew Metter.

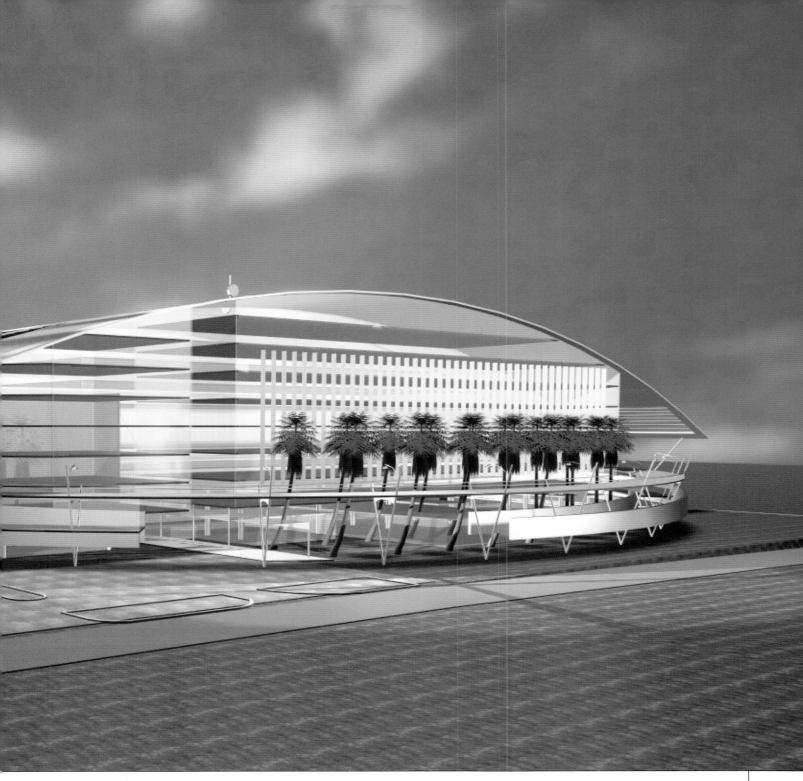

This 3-million-square-foot campus integrates the office and manufacturing activities of a major network systems company. The complex is organized in layers, with four underground parking levels, a below-grade manufacturing and warehouse level, and a cluster of distinct structures above grade. The first level below grade (-6 meters, about –20 feet) contains the production and storage facilities, along with a restaurant, an indoor swimming pool, and recreation courts. Natural light is introduced to this level through the courts, sky-lights, and extensive glazing on the north side, where the grade drops off. Escalators in a central spine connect all levels. Three linear office structures rise on columns above the large-ly open ground level, with separate lobbies for various departments. Two of these structures,

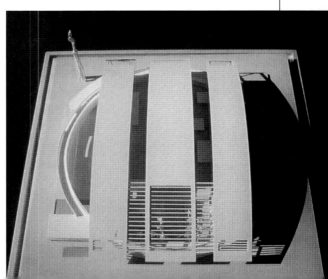

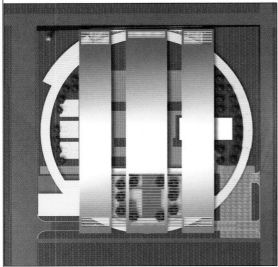

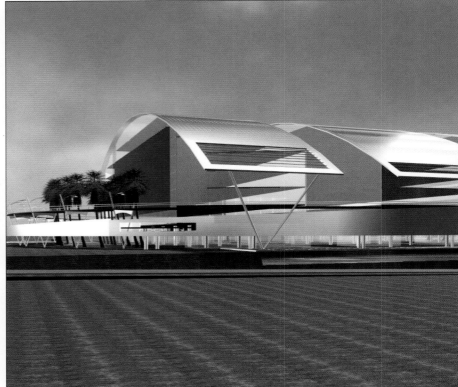

with 60,000 square meters (600,000 square feet) of floor area, will be built in Phase I. The third to be added later will bring the office total up to 90,000 square meters. Encircling the complex at 5 meters (about 16 feet) above ground is a ring that unifies it visually and serves as its prime communal and recreational element. It ties in to all the office blocks at mezzanine level and includes outdoor deck space, lounges, meeting and conference areas, and the fitness center. Atop the ring is a sports track that serves runners, in-line skaters, and even cyclists. At the entry court, it operates as a gateway. Above the whole complex will be the roof canopies, rising from the three-story level, where they face adjoining properties, to nine stories high at their peaks. Completing the composition is a communications tower that coordinates many requirements in one architecturally coherent element.

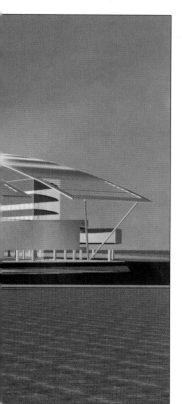

Above: *Four views of employee amenities: ring track, restaurant, lounge, and outdoor court.*
Left: *View from northwest corner, with communications tower in foreground.*

A. Epstein and Sons
International, Inc.

Renishaw
Hoffman Estates,
Illinois

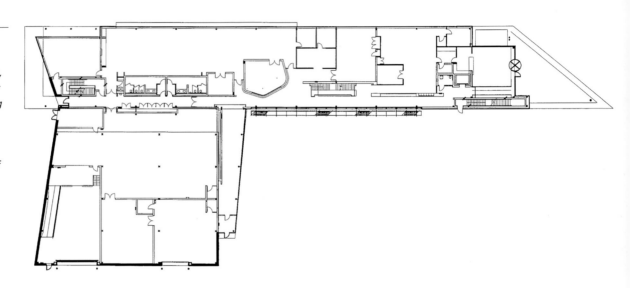

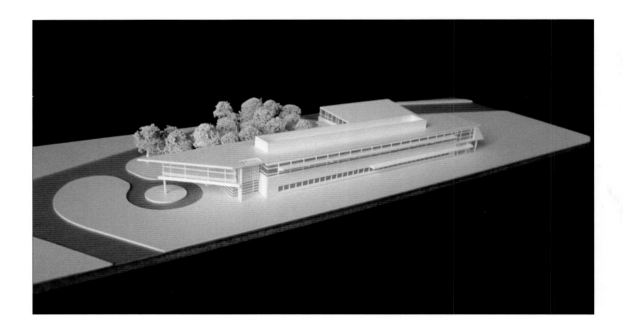

The North American
headquarters of
Renishaw, an English
manufacturer of laser
measuring devices, is
located in the Prairie
Stone office park in the
suburbs of Chicago. The
five-acre site includes the
only stand of mature
trees in this develop-
ment, and the building is
designed to preserve
them and underscore
their value. The 40,000-
square-foot structure is
intended for sales and
service of the company's
precision devices, with a
long two-story bar of
offices, labs, and a client
demonstration area jux-
taposed to a one-story,
high-bay receiving and
warehousing block. The
design presents a maxi-
mum façade exposure
toward the street, with
parking and truck access
to the rear. The 50-foot
width of the office/lab
element assures views of
the attractive landscape
from virtually all work-
stations. A single-loaded
corridor along the south
wall serves as a thermal
buffer, shielding workers
from direct sunlight
(with the trees providing
a further barrier much of
the year). At one end of
the linear structure is a
second-floor extension
that shelters the entry; at
the other end a can-
tilevered terrace opens
from the lunch room.
The building is steel
framed with white
metal panel cladding,
along with generous
areas of glass.

A. Epstein and Sons International, Inc.

Factory Façade Renovation
Schaumberg, Illinois

The design challenge was to redesign the façade of a 1970s industrial building on a budget of $150,000. The strategy was to develop a kit of parts, with frame and infill elements that could be clipped to the old walls. At the same time, the entry was reoriented toward the parking lot to one side. Design inspiration came from nearby industrial buildings from the 1930s, where old curtain walls had been altered by inserting various opaque panels to form effective mosaics. In this case, the pattern is composed of translucent glass panels and rectangular areas of aluminum grating.

Right: *Exploded view, showing kit of parts including clip-on steel framing, panels of translucent glass, rectangles of aluminum grating, and a louvered entrance canopy.*
Center right: *View of wall at entry.*
Bottom: *Preliminary façade pattern studies.*

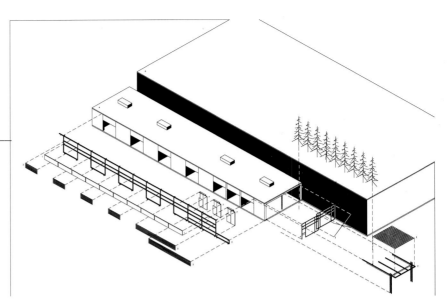

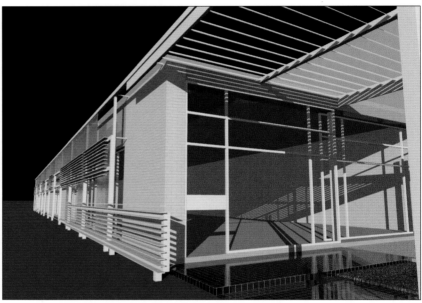

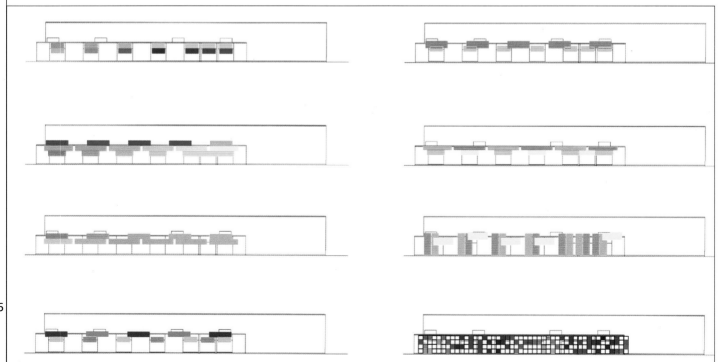

Altoon + Porter
Architects LLP

444 South Flower Street

48th Floor

Los Angeles

California 90071

213.225.1900

213.225.1901 (Fax)

www.altoonporter.com

apa@altoonporter.com

Altoon + Porter Architects LLP

Kaleidoscope
Mission Viejo, California

Right: Central court with upper-level covered walks.
Below: Court in evening, with strings of lights in tradition of Mediterranean plazas.
Photography: Erhard Pfeiffer.

Right: Trellises over walkways, soon to be vine-covered.
Below right: Rotunda framework and lighting.
Bottom right: Rotunda as seen from outside complex, serving as symbol and invitation to enter.

The site for this 215,000-square-foot shopping-entertainment center offered little inherent appeal. A leftover tract in the Mission Viejo master plan, it was surrounded by the 40-foot embankments of two freeways and the back of a strip mall. On this unpromising terrain, the architects built a three-story complex, including shops, restaurants, and a 10-screen cinema, focused inward on a simple but distinctive rotunda. Rising 65 feet from a 50,000-square-foot upper-level "town square" the fabric-covered rotunda serves as a beacon for the Mission Viejo business district. The project's central space can be used for dining or community events; restaurant ter- races overlook it from the center's top level. Night lighting, including illumination of the fabric canopy and strings of bare bulbs, establishes an atmosphere of unpretentious festivity.

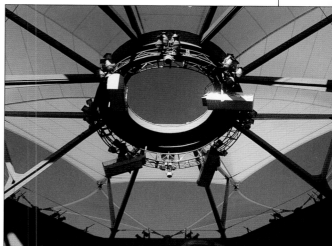

19

Altoon + Porter Architects LLP

The Gardens on El Paseo
Palm Desert, California

Building an open-air shopping complex in this desert climate "might be seen as either courageous or foolhardy," say the architects. Though temperatures can exceed 115 degrees Fahrenheit in the summer and drop well below freezing in winter, experience shows that residents enjoy the fresh desert air, as proven by the area's 70-plus golf courses. Surrounding a central garden, with secondary gardens, courts, and paseos, the two-story complex includes a 40,000-square-foot Saks department store, 117,000 square feet of shops, and 50,000 square feet of restaurants – all served by a 1,000-car parking structure. Open to the street, the project serves as the centerpiece for its upscale district. Landscaping includes both formal green areas and natural desert plantings, with high walls, trellises, pools and misting systems moderating the climate. Special landscaping measures include second-level pavers set in sand, which can be wet down in the morning, absorbing moisture that then evaporates to mitigate midday temperatures.

Top: Desert garden that acts as rainwater retention area.
Above: Palm fronds and trellises for patterned shade.
Right: Saks façade above symmetrical garden area.
Photography: Erhard Pfeiffer.

Above: *Night-lighted trellis.*
Left: *Water channel on axis of gateway trellis.*
Right: *Formal lawn and fountains.*

Altoon + Porter Architects LLP

Warringah Mall
Brookvale, Sydney,
Australia

Right: Portal to
Jacaranda Court.
Below: Circular bal-
conies and taller arcades
meeting at central court.
Photography: Stuart
Curnow.

Located in a northern suburb of Sydney, the existing Warringah Mall had a friendly beachside ambiance, but its disjointed layout and disparate, tired-looking buildings were liabilities in a competitive market. A relaxed but comprehensible order was generated by developing new "mall neighborhoods," created by building additions to the sides and top of existing structures. Way-finding for visitors is enhanced by the series of covered linear passages that define these neighborhoods. All of them are linked to a spacious central court, which serves as a civic space and accommodates events and performances. The use of glazed arcades, skylights, translucent fabric roofs, and trellises provides a variety of lighting conditions, all admitting day-

light in some form to the shopping environment. Light-colored materials, exposed metal, and lattice-like shadow patterns all reinforce the seashore atmosphere. Various parts of the complex are conceived as abstractions of the beaches, hills and valleys of this scenic peninsula district. A portion of the 16-hectare (40-acre) site is preserved as a habitat for the peninsula's native species to meet the environmental requirements of the wetlands site.

Above: Taller roofs suggesting silhouettes of local hills.
Left: Fabric canopies lending seaside atmosphere to enclosed arcade.
Bottom: Detail of main staircase and trellis structure at Garden Crescent.

Anthony Belluschi/
OWP&P Architects

111 West Washington Street
Suite 2100
Chicago
Illinois 60602.2714
312.332.9600
312.332.9601 (Fax)
www.belluschi-owpp.com
abelluschi@owpp.com

3101 N. Central Avenue
Suite 770
Phoenix
Arizona 85012
602.294.6500
602.294.6565 (Fax)

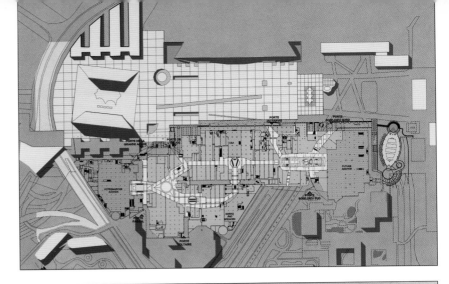

Anthony Belluschi/
OWP&P Architects

Les Quatre Temps
Paris, France

Top: *Plan of shopping center adjoining main plaza of La Defense (shops in rose, major stores in blue, public circulation in yellow).*
Right: *Skylighted eastern court.*
Below: *Main entry from La Defense plaza.*

A 20-year-old shopping center in the La Defense satellite business district of Paris is to be transformed through a $75-million renovation and expansion program. The architectural commission for the project was awarded through an international competition to Anthony Belluschi/OWP&P as design architects; and Saubot-Rouit & Associés Architectes as architect of record. Expanded to 1.8 million square feet (162,000 square meters) in area, the center is extremely complex, with many levels and multiple entrances. It will include enlarged retail areas, a new food court, a relocated multiplex cinema, and extensions of its entrance lobbies and façades, along with expansion of several terraces and landscape features. The project had to meet strict building volume and design guidelines administered by the La Defense district. Glass and steel extensions of the original concrete structure will contribute to an updated image of lightness and transparency. To reinforce the center's identity program, the design represents the four elements of earth, water, air, and fire, expressed in rich materials, graphics, lighting, and thematic details.

Anthony Belluschi/ OWP&P Architects

MetroCity Office/Retail/Residential Complex Istanbul, Turkey

Left: *Balcony overlooking Rotunda.*
Below left: *Multimedia environment of Tivoli Court.*

Right: *Section showing levels of MetroCity from underground parking and transit link through four levels of retail to office tower (right in drawing) and paired apartment buildings; plan indicating sequence of distinct shopping, dining, and entertainment settings.*
Bottom: *Fabric skylights over The Galleria.*

Located in the prestigious Levent district of Istanbul, this mixed-use complex includes 500,000 square feet of retail on four levels, a 28-story office building, and two 26-story apartment towers, above five levels of parking. Organized on a narrow site, the project is articulated into several distinct interior neighborhoods. Anthony Belluschi Architects designed the plaza and the retail and residential interior architecture. The Entry Court provides a transition from the East Entry Plaza to the formal Rotunda Court, where glassed elevators and a water feature rise from a geometrically patterned floor toward a fabric dome. Along the East and West Galleries, varied storefronts are arrayed under fabric roofs. At Tivoli Court, a wide range of entertainment, food, and retail options are offered in a multimedia environment. The two Millennium towers, while integral to MetroCity, assert their distinction as residential addresses. Completion of the complex is scheduled for 2001.

Hall at Tivoli Court   Tivoli Court   Gallery West   Gallery East   Rotunda   Entry Court   Plaza

Anthony Belluschi/
OWP&P Architects

Park Meadows Retail Resort
Littleton, Colorado

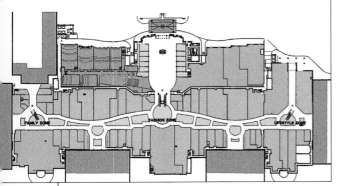

Above left: Upper level plan, with entrance at top, leading into cinema and entertainment zone (blue and orange) to shops along curved internal street; five department stores (brown) are accessed from interior courts.

Above: Porte-cochere.

Left: Seating area at Nordstrom Court.

Right: Exterior lighting detail.

Located some 15 miles south of Denver, this 1.7-million-square-foot shopping and entertainment complex designed by Anthony Belluschi Architects recalls the atmosphere of a Colorado mountain lodge. Traditions of the region's resort architecture are reflected in the local quarried stone, timber-and-steel framing, and copper roofs. Patrons arrive at a distinctive heavy timber porte-cochere. Inside the entrance is a 10-tenant "Dining Hall" of grand proportions flanked by a multiplex cinema and a large music, video, and entertainment store. Shops are laid out along the curving edges of an interior street, daylighted through high monitors and punctuated by distinctive courts ranging in mood from elegant to playful to rustic. All use a palette of natural wood—fir for columns, cherry, maple, and oak for other surfaces. Interior gathering areas feature large stone fireplaces, oversized furniture, and lodge-style lighting fixtures. Courtyards feature fractured stone and trickling water. Landscaped plazas and outdoor dining areas include native trees and shrubs. The complex occupies 100 acres of a 160-acre site, the remainder of which was planned for other commercial uses.

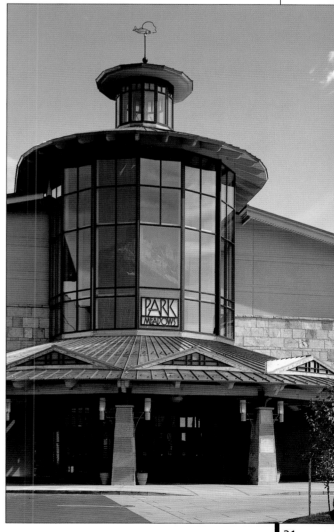

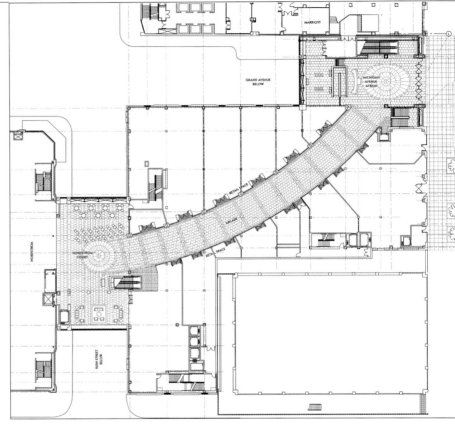

Anthony Belluschi/
OWP&P Architects

North Bridge
Chicago, Illinois

A four-story retail arcade traces a sweeping curve from a 90-foot-high, glazed Michigan Avenue atrium to an enclosed bridge over Rush Street that forms the entry to Nordstrom's department store. This arcade connection designed by Anthony Belluschi Architects is the gateway to a new retail development called North Bridge, on Michigan Avenue's "Magnificent Mile." A new 19-story office building is clad in 4,500 pieces of limestone reconstructed from the dismantled McGraw-Hill Building, a 1929 Art Deco landmark that stood on this site. Above the project's four retail levels is a 310-room luxury hotel. Below the retail arcade is the main entrance to the hotel, as well as retail shops lining Rush and Grand Streets.

Above right: Neighborhood plan, showing curved arcade linking Nordstrom's to Michigan Avenue.
Right: Building plan at Michigan Avenue level.

Right: Retail complex topped by hotel, seen from Rush Street level, with enclosed bridge and Nordstrom's to right.
Far right: Michigan Avenue atrium and arcade entrance adjoining new office building with reconstructed historic façade.

Burt Hill Kosar Rittelmann Associates

270 Congress Street
Boston
Massachusetts 02210
617.423.4252
617.423.4333 (Fax)

650 Smithfield Street
Suite 2600
400 Morgan Center   **Pittsburgh**
Butler   **Pennsylvania 15222**
Pennsylvania 16001   412.394.7000
724.285.4761   412.394.7880 (Fax)
724.285.6815 (Fax)

1735 Market Street   **1056 Thomas Jefferson Street NW**
53rd Floor   **Washington, DC 20007**
Philadelphia   202.333.2711
Pennsylvania 19103   202.333.3159 (Fax)
215.751.2900
215.751.2901 (Fax)   www.burthill.com

Burt Hill Kosar Rittelmann Associates

WHYY Technology Center
Philadelphia, Pennsylvania

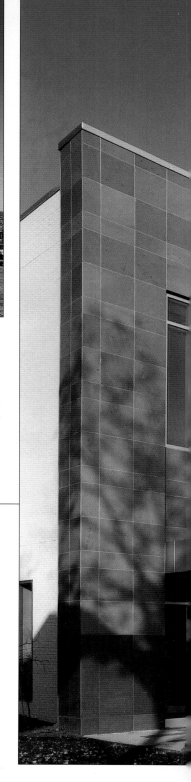

Facing Independence Mall, this new building for a public television station presents the image of a visible, accessible, cutting-edge operation. The façade, with its sweeping overhang and tilted glass wall, invites the public in to observe and participate in the station's operations. An 80-foot-long electronic tickertape flashes continuous news, and broadcasting studios can be viewed from the lobby. The front plaza and a forum space inside the building serve as settings for televised discussions and other events. Open office spaces promote staff collaborations. Electronically equipped conference rooms are available to businesses and the public for teleconferencing. This building is Phase I of an incremental program to replace WHYY's quarters, originally an exhibit hall for the 1975 Bicentennial. The success of this phase has attracted funding to speed up the rebuilding schedule.

Left: Lobby, with video monitors and windows for viewing operations. **Above:** Entry canopy and plaza facing Independence Mall. **Photography:** Matt Wargo.

Above: Large-scale elements giving façade presence on Independence Mall.
Right: Stair with high-tech details, including perforated metal, typical of interior.

Burt Hill Kosar Rittelmann Associates

Minuteman Place
Andover, Massachusetts

This 102-acre campus is being developed to include six new buildings ranging in size from 129,000 to 260,000 square feet. At full build-out the site will house 1,380,000 square feet of offices and 4,600 surface parking spaces. Occupancy will be primarily by offices and high-technology research and development facilities. A network of pedestrian and bike paths will connect buildings to foster an integrated campus environment. For each of the buildings, the project team developed a layout with flexibility to accommodate single or multiple tenants, as requirements fluctuate. The first of the new buildings, 50 Minuteman, includes 150,000 square feet housing offices, R&D facilities, and a customer service center. It is organized around a 2,700-square-foot atrium. The 200,000-square-foot 200 Minuteman building was custom designed to house the engineering functions of a technologically intensive service company. It is laid out with a central three-story atrium and two separate service courts. All buildings have sophisticated cabling and phone networks. The buildings of various configurations are unified by a common vocabulary of reflective glazing in mosaic patterns of blues and greens.

Above right: *Exterior and fountain pool, 50 Minuteman.*
Right: *Stairs and common areas in 50 Minuteman.*
Far right: *Atrium in 50 Minuteman.*
Photography: *Richard Mandelkorn.*

Burt Hill Kosar Rittelmann Associates

The Wanamaker Building
Philadelphia, Pennsylvania

Designed by Daniel Burnham and opened in 1911, the Wanamaker Building set a new benchmark for opulence in department stores. Retail operations still continue at this city-core location, facing Philadelphia's exuberant City Hall, but much of the two-million-square-foot building has been converted into office space, with the Lord & Taylor store occupying five floors as the lead tenant. The renovation of the upper floors had to be carried out without interrupting store operations. A new three-story office lobby has been created, with access to 21 new elevators. A 660-space garage has been developed in the building's underground volume. Up-to-date electrical, mechanical, vertical transportation, and life safety systems have been installed throughout. On the upper floors, a light-well above the store's Grand Court has been converted to an atrium providing views and daylight for surrounding offices. The 22,000-square-foot Crystal Tearoom has been preserved as a meeting place for office tenants. The project has served as a model for other major department store conversions in various cities.

Above: Restored exterior with new lighting.
Right: New atrium on upper office floors.
Facing page: Restored retail space.
Photography: Hedrich Blessing.

Burt Hill Kosar Rittelmann Associates

300 Park Avenue
Atlanta, Georgia

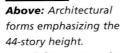

Above: *Architectural forms emphasizing the 44-story height.*
Top right: *Porte-cochere at entry.*
Above right: *Lobby.*
Photography: *Brian Gassel.*

A 44-story sheer tower with streamlined curves is designed to attract high-end residents in Atlanta's Buckhead neighborhood. With 726,000 square feet of floor area, it offers its 124 condominium owners amenities such as function rooms, exercise facilities, a pool, a wine cellar, and private elevators. All of the units have broad balconies and panoramic views. A two-story lobby features full-height mirrored walls that create the illusion of an even more expansive space.

Design Collective, Inc.

100 East Pratt Street
14th Floor
Baltimore
Maryland 21202
410.685.6655
410.539.6242 (Fax)
www.designcollective.com
parti@designcollective.com

Design Collective, Inc.

The Can Company
Baltimore, Maryland

This 100-year-old former cannery has been turned into a new town center for Canton, three miles east of Baltimore's renowned Inner Harbor. The $26-million project consists of 75,000 square feet of retail, 125,000 square feet of high-tech office space, a 60,000-square-foot NASA-sponsored emerging technology incubator, and structured parking for 200 cars. As a brownfields development in a populated urban area, the project had to satisfy environmental requirements and community concerns. As a historic adaptive reuse, it was designed in conformance with Federal rules to qualify for tax credits. Brick walls 80 to 105 years old were restored following exhaustive research to duplicate the characteristics of existing mortar. Virtually all of the factory's distinctive rooftop stacks, ventilators, and monitors have been restored. Inside, natural light has been maximized by reglazing the original steel sash with single-thickness clear glass (following preservation guidelines). New night lighting emphasizes the site's transformation from a long-term "black hole" to a safe, productive part of the urban fabric.

The project's rapid leasing officially launched the municipality's "digital harbor" initiative, which is now sparking other, larger developments. The Can Company has created 700 permanent new jobs, effectively replacing all those lost when the factory closed over a decade ago.

Left: Aerial view of "Gateway" complex.
Right: Lily pond at new office entry.
Photography: Jeff Katz (left), Ron Solomon (right).

Design Collective, Inc.

Maple Lawn Farms
Howard County, Maryland

This 500-acre mixed-use community near Baltimore is a model of sustainable growth. It combines 1,200,000 square feet of commercial development with 1,116 residential units. A mix of uses within each neighborhood ensures a range of activities and promotes a pedestrian-oriented environment. A network of small-scaled streets also helps reduce dependence on the automobile. The local approvals process allowed for project-specific regulations drawn up by the planner/ designer covering architectural design standards, building heights, lot sizes, setbacks, street widths, and landscape design. The plan includes four residential neighborhoods, each with a distinct center and diverse housing types. Each residential neighborhood and the Workplace District have distinctive central greens or "gathering places." A higher density with civic and mixed-uses, at the center, transitions to lower density toward the edge of each neighborhood. The urbanization of Howard County, between Baltimore and Washington, has been widely discussed ever since James Rouse broke ground for the planned community of Columbia 30 years ago. Maple Lawn Farms is the county's first Traditional Neighborhood Development (TND) with an integrated mix of uses, so responds to the Maryland legislature's call for "smart growth" development. The county's relatively educated, affluent populace will be invited to learn about new development patterns arguably preferable to the present ones.

Far left: *Public greens taking the place of front yards.*

Left: *Front porches to encourage socializing.*

Above: *Garden neighborhood overview.*

Left: *Plan showing four residential neighborhoods around Workplace District.*

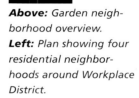

Far left: *Hillside neighborhood overview.*

Left: *Neighborhood green spaces.*

Above: *Workplace District, planned to have (with future phases) 1,200 residents within a 5-minute walk.*

Above right: *Village center, with retail, restaurants, public and religious facilities within 10-minute walk for residents.*

Design Collective, Inc.

Harborview
Baltimore, Maryland

Left: *Address.*
Bottom left: *"Before" view of site.*
Right: *Tower with historic Domino Sugars sign.*
Photography: *Ron Solomon.*

A 42-acre tract of former industrial and shipyard facilities has become the site of a $70-million complex with 224 residential units, a ballroom, a fitness center, an indoor swimming pool, a conference/community center, a yacht club, a dockmaster's office, retail, and structured parking for 1,600 cars. The need to preserve view corridors toward the harbor for existing streets led to the residential tower's very narrow profile. To break down the building's mass and put each resident in proximity to vertical circulation, the plan has two elevator cores connected by a central corridor. In developing the site it was critical to preserve privacy for the residents while permitting access to eight acres of public waterfront space. The Harborview design has established the architectural standard for subsequent development on the site.

Right: *Lobby of residential tower.*
Below: *Yacht club and community center in foreground, residential tower beyond.*

Far left: *Photomontage of completed project on site.*
Right, top to bottom: *Public waterfront; indoor pool at base of tower; runners on harborfront promenade.*

Design Collective, Inc.

Health Sciences and Human Services Library
Baltimore, Maryland

The "signature" of the 25-acre University of Maryland Baltimore campus, this $32-million structure houses the second-largest medical library on the East Coast. Its 190,000-square-foot floor area houses 360,000 volumes, 2,300 periodicals, 1,500 data port connections, 40 study suites, a 37-station research and information commons, plus three computer labs, a historical collections suite, a "Great Room" for receptions, offices, and a 30-seat café. All this was designed to fit into a small urban site between a major highway and the student center. It had to conform, as well, to the campus master plan in terms of massing, setbacks, etc., while projecting its own identity. The library was designed in association with Perry Dean Rogers & Partners of Boston.

Top left: Stadium view.
Top right: Entry plaza.
Above: Library at entry to campus.

Left: Greene Street entrance.
Right: Main lobby.
Photography: Anne Gummerson.

DeStefano and Partners

445 East Illinois Street

Suite 250

Chicago

Illinois 60611

312.836.4321

312.836.4322 (Fax)

www.destefanoandpartners.com

info@dplusp.com

London

Naples, FL

DeStefano and Partners

Urban Infrastructures
Chicago, Illinois

Top: *Adams Street Bridge presents new face to highway.*
Above: *Walkway railing is similar to Madison Street's, but stronger.*

Left: *Abstraction of Puerto Rican flag, inspired by symbols seen in neighborhood, itself now depicted on T-shirts and such.*
Photography: *Hedrich-Blessing.*

The firm has designed some highly visible improvements along Chicago's roadways and has more underway.

Division Street Gateways

A waving Puerto Rican flag is the motif of two symbolic portals installed by the city to define the ethnic identity of a stretch of Division Street. Designed to withstand winds up to 100 mph, the pennants are fabricated of steel plate and steel pipe and supported by caissons sunk 33 feet down. Other concurrent street improvements include 45 sheet steel banners with various Puerto Rican symbols, mounted on existing utility poles, and 16 "plazitas" with bench/table groupings, special paving, and planters.

Madison Street Bridge

The 1996 revitalization of this key bridge has inspired a total of eight redesigned bridges along the Kennedy Expressway corridor.

Only major structural supports were retained in rebuilding this span, a nondescript 1956 structure with ramps that did not meet current traffic standards. The architects designed deep fascias to hide the structural clutter under the new roadbeds, curving these out at points to form overlooks along the walkways. Red balustrades display motifs derived from the four-star Chicago flag, and blue diode lights outline the structure for drivers.

Adams Street Bridge

This bridge, completed in 1999, is the true prototype for the remaining six to be remodeled through 2002. The Madison Street precedent is followed in the fascia and paint colors. The balustrade here has been upgraded to meet higher structural standards, while presenting a similar image.

DeStefano and Partners

Sears Tower 2000
Chicago, Illinois

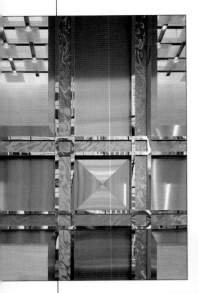

The conversion of the 110-story Sears Tower from one-tenant to multitenant use dictated reconfiguration of the original lobby, where elevator access at three different levels baffled visitors. Establishing a single lobby floor eliminated the notorious confusion and allowed two intermediate floors to be removed, yielding a 50-foot-high space appropriate to a world-class skyscraper. Stainless steel cladding celebrates the tower's hefty "bundled tube" structural framing. The Calder sculpture "Universe," once all but hidden on the mezzanine, is now placed where it can be enjoyed even from the street.

Outside, canopies were added at entrances to protect office staff and visitors from winds and falling ice, and a separate glass-walled entry pavilion was created with express elevators for visitors to the 103rd-floor observation deck. The once bare plaza was terraced and landscaped to form usable outdoor spaces. The $70-million project had to be accomplished without interrupting access for the building's 16,000 daily users or the many thousands who visit its popular viewing deck.

Above: *Stainless-steel detail from lobby.*
Right: *Lobby for visitors to observation deck.*
Photography:
Hedrich-Blessing.

Above: *Now-lofty lobby with Calder sculpture, "Universe."*
Left: *Fritted glass canopy at Wacker Drive entrance.*
Right: *Terrace outside observation deck lobby.*
Below left: *New Franklin Street curbside canopy at night.*
Below right: *Franklin Street lobby.*

DeStefano and Partners

Alliance Française
de Chicago
Chicago, Illinois

Right: *Former bank added to complex.*
Below right: *Steel and glass details of new link.*
Below: *Alliance's contemporary French furniture in serene setting.*
Bottom: *Fritted glass and tree shadows dissolving courtyard's edges.*
Photography: *Barbara Karant.*

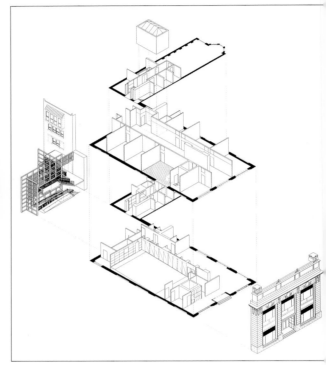

With programs bursting out of the 7,000-square-foot house it occupied, the century-old Alliance seized the opportunity to buy a 10,000-square-foot former bank abutting it at the rear garden and alley. Among the new facilities made possible by this expansion were a culinary instruction kitchen and a 150 seat auditorium sloped to accommodate subtitled movies. The architects had to create a linking structure and reorganize the old interiors so that the resulting complex not only func-tioned well but met codes for public occupancy. Aware of French skill at mixing period buildings with uncompromisingly Modern ones, the architects designed the link with exposed steel framing and fritted glass infill. Rising in a courtyard – and first seen from one of the Alliance's two old structures – the new element is reminiscent of the famous Maison de Verre in Paris, an early Modern glazed cage hidden away within a courtyard.

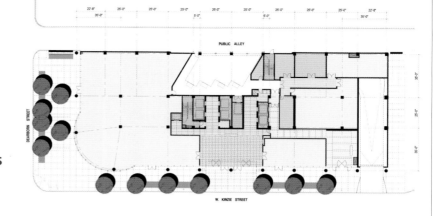

DeStefano and Partners

Dearborn Plaza
Chicago, Illinois

The site, measuring only 100 feet by 300 feet, posed a challenge for the design of an efficient 400,000 square-foot office building. But the location in Chicago's developing River North section was excellent. By devising a narrow core configuration, the architects were able to provide a marketable 37-foot depth on either side. The exterior envelope respects the city's office building tradition while demonstrating the architecture firm's commitment to cutting-edge technologies. A frame of limestone-colored concrete, with Chicago School proportions, is visually "clipped" over a silver metal curtain wall with clear glazing. This frame is deliberately held back at corners or wrapped beyond them to express the thinness of the plane. The wall planes engage a cylindrical volume at the intersection of two principal streets. Sun shades project off the frame on south and west elevations, shading the glass and affording definite mechanical benefits while allowing daylight deep into the office floors. The required 10-foot setback of the top floor was turned to advantage with trellises that effectively crown the structure.

Above: *Street floor plan.*
Right: *Office lobby.*
Below: *Cylindrical corner, with set back top floor and projecting sun shades.*
Below right: *Penthouse arcade.*
Photography: *Steve Hall, Hedrich Blessing.*

DeStefano and Partners

Greenwich Millennium Village
London, England

Planned by the London office of DeStefano and Partners, this proposal envisages over 1 million square feet (101,880 square meters) of mixed-use development for an 18-acre site on the Greenwich Peninsula. The scheme was drawn up for developers Hutchison Whampoa as an entry in a competition for the reconstruction of the area as an international showcase project. The competition brief called for a variety of residential units (including 25 percent social housing), plus supporting educational, health care, sports, community, and retail facilities. The adaptable urban pattern of Georgian London, with rowhouses arrayed around green squares, is the basis for the plan. Areas bordering the main traffic arteries and the waterside park would include taller residential and mixed-use structures. The Village Center would be laid out around a circular common near the center of the site, with a close link to the major park. A tower erected in the Thames itself would identify Millennium Village among the many landmark projects along the river.

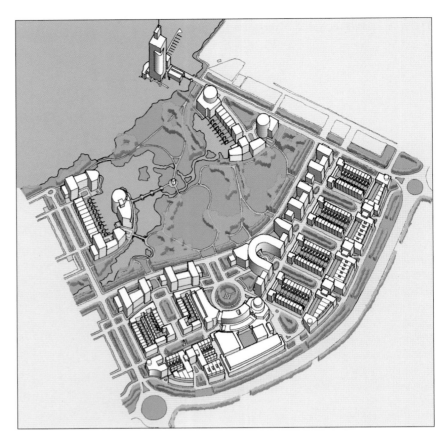

Above: The overall master plan of the village with low-rise zone and taller structures at the edges.
Left: Tall structures, including tower actually in the Thames, rising around riverfront park.

Development Design Group, Inc.

7 Saint Paul Street

Baltimore

Maryland 21202

410.962.0505

410.783.0816 (Fax)

www.ddg-usa.com

Development Design Group, Inc.

Cavendish Square
Cape Town
Republic of South Africa

Right: Entry façade.
Below left: Bold patterns and colors in food court.
Below right: Street view.
Bottom: Lively skylighted atrium.
Photography: Ronnie Levitan.

The renovation of Cavendish Square turned a forbidding, inward-focused shopping center that was in danger of failing into a reinvigorated three-level complex inviting visitors from the surrounding streets. An exterior facelift added display windows, distinctive torch-shaped street lighting, three-dimensional advertising panels, and bright graphic banners in gold, turquoise, and violet. A skylighted entrance and prominent canopies attract the public. Inside, a new atrium has been carved out of the middle of the structure, rising through the retail levels and three parking levels to a skylight. The amply lighted atrium ties together a complex that includes a department store, retail shops, a food court, and a 16-screen cinema. A garden surrounds the atrium at the lowest parking level. The character of the region is reflected in natural woods, indigenous plants, African colors and patterns, and warm tones throughout.

Development Design Group, Inc.
Cocowalk
Miami, Florida

Completed in 1990 as the first themed shopping center in America, Cocowalk helped define the genre. Its three U-shaped levels contain more than 40 shops, restaurants, nightclubs, and cafes, plus a 16-screen cinema. Parking under and behind the center offers direct access to shopping levels. Innovations include: making the cinema the project's anchor and locating it on the third floor to draw moviegoers past other merchants; reducing floor-to-floor heights to 4 meters (about 13 feet; roughly 2/3 the U.S. norm) to enhance intimacy and interaction between lev-

els. A palm-lined central court doubles as food court and entertainment venue. Boutique-lined verandahs surrounding the court open to public sidewalks so that visitors can walk in without the purposeful entering that shopping centers usually require. Tile roofs, stucco, and a variety of details create the impression of a Mediterranean village that has evolved over time.

Left: *Central court.*
Above: *Casual, welcoming street front.*
Right: *Stair to cinema.*
Photography: *Dan Forer.*

Development Design Group, Inc.

The Zone @ Rosebank
Johannesburg,
Republic of South Africa

For this high-tech 290,520-square-foot entertainment center in the inner suburb of Rosebank, two key features set the bold tone. One is the graphic power of electrified graphics, which take advantage of the location at the intersection of a major artery and popular pedestrian street. The exterior serves mainly as an armature for the contemporary expressions of the center's tenants, which include boutiques, high-tech arcades, Internet cafes, themed restaurants, a department store, and a 14-screen cinema. Rather than leave these graphics to chance, Development Design Group worked with tenants to ensure a high-energy, studiolike quality. The same graphic character is maintained in the interior, where tenants' advertis-

ing and merchandising are prominent. The second defining feature is the cone-shaped, skylighted volume that cuts through the cinema lobby at the center's core. The dynamism of the cone and the rose-petal pattern of the skylight draw attention and movement upward. Boldly lit columns carry the circle imprint of the cone down into the shopping levels. At cinema level, the cone surfaces double as projection screens for ads and movie trailers. At night, the cone serves as a beacon in the urban landscape.

Development Design Group, Inc.

Below: *Enclosed dining and entertainment mall in the form of a historic train station.*
Below right: *Concert on the village green.*
Photography: *Walter Larrimore.*

In this project, the New Urbanism approach to town design is applied in a 650,000-square-foot private development combining shopping with offices, entertainment, recreation, and other amenities. Designers adapted features of early 20th-Century Midwestern towns to contemporary uses. A bookstore is designed as a library, for instance, and a fitness center as a high school gym. The centerpiece is an enclosed mall in the form of a traditional train station, housing a 30-screen cinema and other entertainment-oriented tenants. A street grid allows cars to pass through the complex, but slows them for pedestrian safety with narrow rights-of-way and on-street parking. Stores and cafes line the streets, with offices on the second level. The Town Center is the first phase of a larger plan calling for additional commercial space, residential neighborhoods, and parks. Phase two is expected to add nearly 750,000 square feet of leasable area.

Right: *Play fountain in public plaza.*

Below: *Main square with enclosed mall in background, variety of stores and offices along side streets.*

Above: *Entrance to mall flanked by street-front tenants.*

Left: *Re-creation of c. 1940 downtown.*

Development Design Group, Inc. Robertson Walk
Singapore

Though its two residential towers are 10 stories high, several design features give this mixed-use development a human scale and orient it toward the street. The two-story retail-entertainment base adapts the indigenous Chinese "shop house" style with ground-floor arcades. A focal point of the 314,127-square-foot development is a central open court, with stone paving, banners, pushcart merchants, and lush landscaping. A pedestrian walkway with strong graphics and signage connects the complex to the nearby Singapore River. The two 90-unit residential towers are stepped back and tiered to reduce their apparent mass. Residents can enjoy amenities such as a rooftop garden, clubhouse, pool, and recreation facilities.

Top: Central court lined with two floors of retail and dining.
Above: Identifying campanile along street.
Left: Ten-story apartment towers stepping back from court.
Right: Court at night.
Photography: Tim Griffith.

Dorsky Hodgson + Partners

23240 Chagrin Boulevard

Suite 200

Cleveland

Ohio 44122

216.464.8600

216.464.8608 (Fax)

cleveland@dhp-arch.com

One Financial Plaza

Suite 2400

Fort Lauderdale

Florida 33394

954.524.8686

954.524.8604 (Fax)

ftlauderdale@dhp-arch.com

1250 24th Street

Suite 725

Washington

D.C. 20037

202.776.0400

202.776.9340 (Fax)

washingtondc@dhp-arch.com

www.dorskyhodgson.com

Dorsky Hodgson + Partners

Miromar Shoppes
Fort Myers, Florida

Right: Large fountain pool near main entrance.
Below right: Tropical plants and colonnaded shop fronts temper South Florida climate.
Below: Apse-like building feature complementing tiered fountain.
Photography: Philip Eschbach.

A Mediterranean village atmosphere was developed for this center to make it an appealing destination for its architecture, as well as its retail offerings. Two 180,000 sf phases of the project were completed in 2000, and a third phase of equal size is planned for the 60-acre site. A series of intimate, colonnaded walkways open into pleasantly scaled courtyards with a variety of fountains. Generous vegetation, including geometrically trimmed potted plants, is laid out formally to recall the traditions of Southern Europe. The steel framed buildings are clad with EIFS surfaces worked into simple variations of Classical detail, along with tile and metal roofing, metal balustrades and lanterns, shutters and awnings—all suggesting unpretentious Mediterranean towns rather than urban centers. Controlled design and placement of shop signs maintain the sense of a historical, unpressured locale. A variety of towerlike forms, highest at the main entrance and scaled down at the interior courtyards, serve as identifying markers. Arches and other distinctive architectural features further help to distinguish one area from another.

Above: *Piazza with fountain pool on axis of walkway and arched opening.*
Right: *Distinctive roof and column details along intimate walkway.*
Below: *Tower features of second floor walkways connect covered storefronts.*

Dorsky Hodgson + Partners

Winter Park Village
Winter Park, Florida

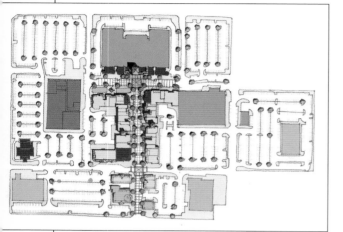

Left: *Main street plan of the 46-acre site.*
Below left: *Retail block facing landscaped plaza.*
Right: *Street fronts with characteristic cornices, balconies, and awnings.*
Below right: *Fountain and articulated storefronts.*
Photography: *Philip Eschbach.*

The architect responded to the design challenge by transforming an aging enclosed shopping mall into a "Main Street" environment, in the tree shaded Orlando suburb of Winter Park. Every existing structure on the 46-acre site was demolished except for the two-story department store anchor. The new plan creates two "Main Streets" accented at their intersection by a landscaped exterior piazza that links the center's anchors, and provides customer amenities including fountains and seating. The entrance element for the 20-screen cinema, reminiscent of several Classical architectural motifs, provides a focal point for the development. Other facilities in the 520,000 sf redeveloped center include professional offices, restaurants, a supermarket, apartments and a variety of retail shops. Throughout the complex, bold parapets and pediments above prominent second-story windows sustain the image of a traditional American townscape.

Left: *Cinema entrance scaled to provide a focal point at the end of street axis.*
Facing page: *Winter Park visitors refresh at a charming sidewalk café.*

Dorsky Hodgson + Partners

Urban Mixed-Use

South Boston Waterfront
Boston, Massachusetts
For a crucial harborfront parcel in the South Boston redevelopment area, Dorsky Hodgson + Partners in association with Arrowstreet, Inc. have designed the residential portion of a full-city-block complex that integrates a hotel, street-level retail, and underground parking. A total of 470 rental apartment units will be accommodated in structures that line the waterfront street and step up to a 21-story tower toward the rear of the block.

Right: Complex seen from water.

Downtown Hudson
Hudson, Ohio
For a town with an exceptional heritage of Early Nineteenth Century buildings in the New England tradition, the architects have completed a conceptual design of an 11-acre mixed-use development including retail, residential, and office functions. The buildings are divided visually into storefronts that are harmonious in scale, detail, and color with the existing town.

Right: Downtown Hudson, with store fronts recessed behind outdoor dining areas.

Rosedale Park
Bethesda, Maryland
A "living bridge" will connect two sites to unify a 252,000 sf residential development. The bridge will form a gateway from busy Wisconsin Avenue on one side of the site to the quiet, small-scaled East Bethesda neighborhood on the other side. The complex will include a health club, a party room, a pool on the roof, and a cafe and retail at street level.

Right: Wisconsin Avenue elevation, showing bridge and penthouse.

**The Waverly
Fort Lauderdale,
Florida**

Located in a mixed-use transitional zone, the project has to mediate between high-rise office towers on one side and single-family Victorian stylized residential community on the other. Variations in form and materials break down its scale. The 580,000 sf building will contain 320 apartments and 25,000 sf of retail, plus parking for 540 cars. The garages are concealed behind retail façades that simulate infill development.

Right: Main façade, showing small-scaled retail fronts in front of residential blocks.

**Acacia Shops
Lyndhurst, Ohio**

Architectural treatment reminiscent of an Eighteenth-Century French city will set the tone for this upscale, 125,000 sf "retail lifestyle center." Built on a constricted 13-acre site, adjacent to an established golf course, the center will have an attached hotel and conference center.

Right: Beaux-Arts architectural motifs evoking Continental luxury at Acacia Shops.

Below: Retail frontage, with existing overpass to left, office component in background.

**The Belcrest Center
Prince Georges
County, Maryland**

Organized around an existing Metro station, this 300,000 sf of offices, 290,000 sf of housing, and 225,000 sf of retail, including a multiplex cinema. An existing pedestrian overpass will be integrated into the project. Retail and entertainment uses will be located along the busy east-west highway, offices and pedestrian-scaled uses along Belcrest Road, and housing adjacent to an existing residential area.

Dorsky Hodgson + Partners

Sumner on Ridgewood
Copley Township, Ohio

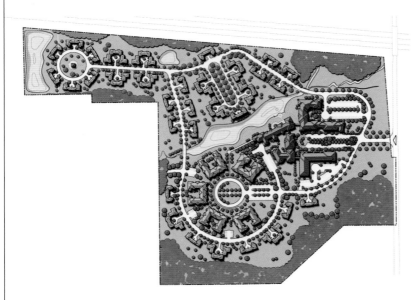

Top: *"Quartet" living units with English village image.*
Above: *Site plan balancing the formal order with the natural terrain.*
Below: *Picturesque structures around urban space at core of development.*

On this 64-acre site in Northeastern Ohio, near Akron, the architects have organized 260,000 sf of varied functions in a Continuing Care Retirement Community. The range of living space offered includes independent housing, assisted living, skilled care, and dementia care. Components of the complex include a 36,000 sf Manor House; 104,000 sf of garden apartments; 21,000 sf of four-unit "quartet" structures; 19,000 sf of two-unit "duet" buildings; a "catered living greenhouse" of 35,000 sf; and an "enriched care greenhouse" of 40,000 sf. The layout of the community combines casually curving streets with formally organized green spaces. Ponds and natural woodlands enhance the site. Service entrances to the central buildings are well concealed. The Tudor style of the buildings, with their prominent gables, tall hipped roofs, and facades of mixed materials, establishes a reassuring residential character throughout the development. The complex is to be completed in 2002 at a total cost of $52 million.

Duany Plater-Zyberk & Company

1023 Southwest 25th Avenue   Washington

Miami   Charlotte

Florida 33135   Berlin

305.644.1023

305.644.1021 (Fax)

www.dpz.com

Duany Plater-Zyberk & Company

Vermillion
Huntersville, North Carolina
www.vermillion-tnd.com

Right: Plan showing winding creekway, Bowman Square at top, triangular close above it.
Below: Townhouses on square.
Bottom left: Live/work units on square.
Bottom right: Single-family houses.

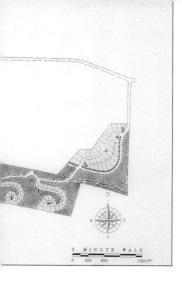

Beginning in the 1980s, the Bowman Development Group assembled several contiguous parcels at the edge of the historic town of Huntersville. In 1996 DPZ led a weeklong public charrette to create a master plan for a 400-acre community, integrated with the adjoining town. The rolling Piedmont terrain inspired a picturesque neighborhood and streetscape design. A creekway running through Vermillion is a central organizing element and connects to a county-wide greenway system. Public space along the creek forms a 1½-mile-long park ranging from 250 to 1,000 feet in width, with houses fronting on the parkside drives. The layout of the first 35-acre section focuses on William Bowman Square and a triangular close. The formally planned square is lined with townhouses, live/work units, a development office, and a pizza pub. The more casually designed triangular close is bounded by single-family houses and a community church. In all, there are about 180 residential units, including affordable apart-ments and houses sponsored by Habitat for Humanity. Almost all of the houses are served by rear alleys. Every resident is within a five-minute walk of a stop on a jitney bus loop that will connect to a planned regional rail system. Development plans include renovation of an old mill complex as a transit-oriented mixed-use development and construction of a school, a neighborhood swimming and recreation club, a small inn, offices, and additional retail. Further development is being overseen by a Town Architect office staffed by DPZ.

Duany Plater-Zyberk & Company

Middleton Hills
Middleton, Wisconsin

Right: Plan responding to rolling terrain, woods, and lakes.
Below: Street of houses with front porches and dormers in Bungalow Style tradition.
Bottom: Houses reflecting area's Prairie School design tradition.

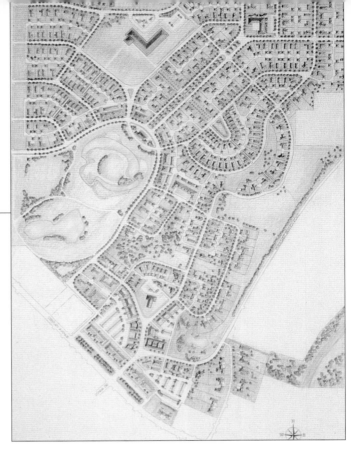

Located eight miles from the state capital, Madison, the 150-acre development will consist of 400 single-family houses, townhouses, apartments, and live/work units when completed. The emphasis is on intimate scale and friendly atmosphere. Comfortable looking houses with front porches and short setbacks line the streets. Garages, some topped by apartments, are tucked away on back alleys. Design controls require traditional building materials – no vinyl or aluminum siding. Ample green space nearby is available for hiking, bird watching, and recreation. Hills and trees, wetlands, and lake views have been preserved for community enjoyment. Small shops and businesses to sustain daily needs and provide local employment are a short walk from the houses. A major asset of

Middleton Hills is its physical setting, with the natural beauty of the local landscape, proximity to the city center of Middleton and the urban amenities of Madison and its University of Wisconsin campus. Designed in 1993 and growing in stages, Middleton Hills is being developed by Marshall Erdman and Associates, an architect-led design/build firm.

Above: Commercial
complex known as
Prairie Café Building for
its best-known tenant.
Right: Portion of com-
mercial area, with brick
and concrete detail
recalling area's Prairie
School architecture.
Photography:
Middleton Hills and Jeff
Speck.

Duany Plater-Zyberk & Company

The Village at Niagara-on-the-Lake
Niagara-on-the-Lake, Ontario

Voted "Canada's Prettiest Town" in 1997, Niagara-on-the-Lake is notable for its 18th- and 19th-century buildings, laid out on a traditional grid but with much variation in setbacks from the street. One objective for this 45-acre development was to mediate between the urban character of the adjacent historic core and a neighboring 1970's subdivision, with its typical loops and cul-de-sacs. The village plan takes advantage of a highway to its south by placing a curving main street, lined with mixed-use buildings, on its south edge. The curve terminates in a hard square for an open-air market and a prominent site at the tract's acute corner for a restaurant or pub. Mid-block parking serves the area. A narrow retail street running north leads to a triangular green, around which are sites for a hotel, a health club, live/work units, and an assisted-living facility. A post office and a library are planned for just north of the green. Residential units, including apartments, row-houses, single- and two-family houses, will have rear laneway access to garages.

Above: Plan (north at top) showing commercial area at southwest corner, street layout ranging from grid on west side to picturesque on east.
Below left: Houses in variety of traditional forms and materials.
Below: Small formal square.
Photography: Duany Plater-Zyberk; Tito Rivia.

Right: *Individual houses recalling 20th-Century revival styles.*
Below right: *Rowhouses near village center.*

Duany Plater-Zyberk & Company

Prospect
Longmont, Colorado

This 77-acre new town is located about two miles from downtown Longmont, in an area projected for intensive growth. Concerned about sprawl, area residents welcomed the opportunity to participate in a charrette planning process. Access from arterial roads to north and east was restricted. The charrette demonstrated that proposed conversion of the north artery to an expressway was unnecessary. The street layout on the flat site maximizes views toward four mountain peaks to the west. A variety of residential types includes rowhouses, live/work units, detached houses, and apartments over garages. Landscape regulations require indigenous plantings with low water requirements. The Rocky Mountain Institute is considering the neighborhood as a model for sustainable development.

Top left: *Plan, with streets converging on community and retail facilities to east.*
Above left: *Rowhouses facing park.*
Left: *Varied single-family houses.*
Above: *Detached and attached houses in a modernist style.*
Photography: *Ron Forth.*

EDSA
Edward D. Stone, Jr. and Associates

1512 E. Broward Boulevard
Suite 110
Fort Lauderdale
Florida 33301
954.524.3330
954.524.0177 (Fax)

www.edsaplan.com
info@edsaplan.com

301 W. Colonial Drive
Orlando
Florida 32801
407.425.3330
407.425.8058 (Fax)

3232-A Nebraska Avenue
Santa Monica
California 90404
310.315.1066
310.315.0916 (Fax)

EDSA

First Union Capitol Center
Raleigh, North Carolina

Below: Jets of central fountain, which can be enjoyed up close.
Below right: Street trees and planter at base of tower.
Bottom: Plantings programmed for year-round color.
Photography: EDSA.

The center's 28-story office tower was built to provide an upscale address for large business tenants, who would otherwise be forced to relocate in the suburbs. The site's adjacency to the Fayetteville Street pedestrian mall opened an opportunity to improve the mall while creating a high-quality urban plaza for the city. The developer's objective was to provide visitors to the building, the mall, and the State Capitol area with an experience of "quiet elegance." Public spaces have been shaped to provide a paved entrance court for the First Union Capital Center, an area suitable for outdoor art shows, and links to possible future developments on adjoining sites. The axis through the building lobby to the mall has been emphasized with annual plantings and flagpoles. The focal point of the redeveloped mall is a fountain with polished granite sitting walls and shade trees, designed to attract pas-sive activities away from the mall's main linear spine. Two forecourts with granite paving and seasonal plantings are provided, and raised planters with flowering trees and other plantings have been built to soften the transition from the public space to the office tower.

Top: *Statue of Sir Walter Raleigh sculpted by Bruno Lucchesi.*
Above: *Plaza used for circulation and for leisure.*

Museum of Anthropology
Xalapa, Mexico

As the official repository of cultural artifacts for the state of Veracruz, the museum contains one of the world's greatest collections of pre-Columbian art. It houses the famed Olmec head sculptures, up to 12 feet high and weighing as much as 10 tons, from the oldest known civilization in Mexico, dating from about 1200 B.C. To complement the 120,000-square-foot building, EDSA designed a fountain plaza, interior gardens, sculpture terraces, exterior terraces, and all planting on the site. The complex had to be completed in 16 months, before the end of a governor's administration, with site grading, construction, and planting carried out by hand. Managing a team of 450 local workers for

Below: Walled and trellised sculpture court.
Bottom: Unobstructed transition from sculpture court to outer grounds.

the landscaping allowed for an unusually high degree of craftsmanship and attention to detail. Paralleling the museum's galleries, a series of stone-paved terraces steps 40 feet down a slope, each curvilinear bed featuring a different tropical planting. The close integration of the walled sculpture courts with the building is made possible by Xalapa's ideal year-round climate, which makes air conditioning of the galleries unnecessary.

Orlando International Airport
Orlando, Florida

Recognizing that travelers to Orlando expect to be in a "tropical Florida environment," the airport authority gave EDSA major responsibilities in its Phase Two Passenger Terminal Complex and Expansion project. The firm provided complete landscape architectural services for three miles of airport access roads, a 450-room hotel, main terminal arrival areas, the seven-story Great Hall atrium shared by the terminal and the hotel, corridors of the above-ground transit between landside and airside terminals, terminal-top parking, and several smaller elements of the project. Landscaping in highly visible areas was designed to represent natural Florida environments and to mitigate the airport's hard surfaces. Some 50 acres of new lakes, created for the retention of storm water, are seen prominently by visitors. Plantings visible from roadways not only present a Florida image, but also screen back-of-

Right: "Florida theme" in planting, paving, and seating in Great Hall atrium.
Far right: Monorail connecting to terminal.
Photography: Andrew Allen.

Left: Great Hall atrium, focused on central fountain.
Right: Tropical planting extending up to Great Hall's balcony corridors.
Far right: Palm-surrounded fountain in intimate corner of Great Hall.

house operations from view. Cargo road overpasses crossing passenger access roadways were designed as gateways to Orlando. Plantings at remote parking areas soften the acreage of hardscape and enhance the pedestrian experience for users. Landscaping for the new Hyatt Hotel atop the landside terminal includes planting, fountains, and signage for its atrium, pool deck, and arrivals area.

Above: *Forty-five-foot fountain jet and computer-programmed fog system as focal point at airport entrance.*

Elkus/Manfredi Architects Ltd

530 Atlantic Avenue

Boston

Massachusetts 02210

617.426.1300

617.426.7502 (Fax)

www.elkus-manfredi.com

info@elkus-manfredi.com

Elkus/Manfredi Architects Ltd   CityPlace
West Palm Beach, Florida

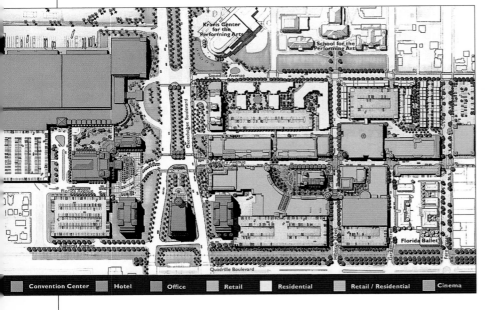

| Convention Center | Hotel | Office | Retail | Residential | Retail / Residential | Cinema |

Can a private development of almost 3 million square feet be integrated into a mid-sized city like West Palm Beach? The first phase of CityPlace, comprising just about half of the final build-out, shows how it can be done. Start with a thorough mix of uses: retail (78 shops totaling 350,000 square feet), restaurants (10, totaling 92,000 square feet), cinema (20 screens; 80,000 square feet); residential (586 units, 702,000 square feet), a performance hall (500 seats, 11,000 square feet), plus 188,000 square feet of retail arcades and other enclosed common areas. All of this is built along existing streets, in structures two to four stories high, that adjoin the existing downtown and extend its urban pattern. Many of the apartments, including 56 live/work units, are above street-front shops. Parking structures for 3,300 cars are inside the blocks or back up to main traffic arteries, behind broad landscaped bands. The keystone of the development is the reuse of a large Mediterranean style 1920's church at the center of the 72-acre area as a live-performance theater. A plaza developed around this landmark includes a large fountain pool that reinforces the drama of

Above: Plan, with first phase at right, centered on renovated church and plaza.
Right: Plaza and church, now The Harriet Himmel Gilman theater.
Below right: Street corner at theater.
Facing page: 2,500-sq-ft fountain in plaza.
Below: Palladium Plaza at night.

the space, in contrast to the relatively intimate qualities of the foliage-dappled streets extending from it. More than 900 trees, including 12 varieties of palm, shade the district's streets and public spaces. Balconies and upper-level gardened terraces further enhance the streetscape. The architecture of the deliberately varied buildings maintains the Mediterranean flavor of the old church and local landmarks by architect Addison Mizner, but is based as well on actual Italian townscapes. The second half of CityPlace will consist of larger-scaled buildings along broad Okeechobee Boulevard, the city's main artery, sensitively related both to the first-phase development and to the neighboring performing arts center. These will include three office buildings totaling 750,000 square feet, a 375-room hotel, and a 400,000-square-foot convention center

Elkus/Manfredi Architects Ltd   Sansom Common
Philadelphia, Pennsylvania

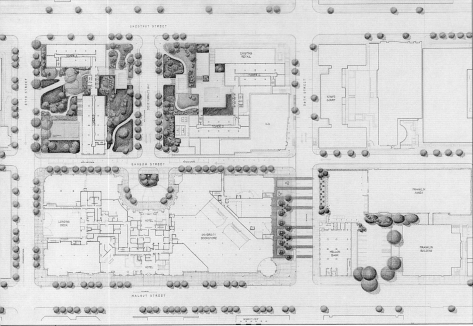

Encompassing six city blocks adjacent to the University of Pennsylvania, Sansom Common makes crucial connections between a hitherto inward-looking campus and its surrounding city. The primary strategy is to establish a critical mass of commercial facilities, oriented to university needs yet appealing to a broader public. A key component of the project's Phase One, now completed, is The Inn at Penn, a 259-room full-service hotel, including banquet and meeting rooms, a restaurant and bar, and the relocated university faculty club. Most of the six-story inn rises atop a podium of street-level retail shops. The anchor retail tenant is the 56,000-square-foot University of Pennsylvania Bookstore, which operates as a small department store. Other retailers include Urban Outfitters, Xando, and Eastern Mountain Sports. These buildings are designed to line the street edges and create active, pedestrian-friendly streets. Elkus/Manfredi's master plan included a new street, Steven Murray Way, which provides vehicular access to the main hotel entrance. The sidewalk of 36th Street from Walnut to Sansom has been widened to form a 50-foot-wide plaza, which not only accommodates commercial and public

Above left: Master plan, with hotel and retail in south blocks, housing sites to north.
Left: Hotel entrance at end of new street.
Above: Hotel entrance at night.
Right: Retail and new plaza along 36th Street.
Photography: °Peter Aaron/Esto.

uses, but serves as a forecourt for the existing Institute of Contemporary Art. Exterior materials, appropriate to commercial street fronts yet compatible with the campus, include molded Pennsylvania brick, cast stone trim, red granite bases, and aluminum storefronts. To enhance the area after dark, the exterior lighting includes generous retail windows, decorative sconces on the buildings, illuminated glass canopies, accent lighting on the focal tower, and historically inspired street lighting – all with warm-colored sources. Two small, informally landscaped courts will complement the 100 units of graduate student housing to be built in Phase Two of the development.

ELS
Architecture and Urban Design

2040 Addison Street

Berkeley

California 94704

510.549.2929

510.843.3304 (Fax)

www.elsarch.com

info@elsarch.com

Above: New Rotunda Building, with corner entrance.

Above right: Aerial view showing Pioneer Courthouse in foreground, Pavilion Building on next block, and Rotunda Building on block beyond that.

Right: Rotunda Building at night, showing lighting at corner and roof, bridge link to earlier Pavilion.

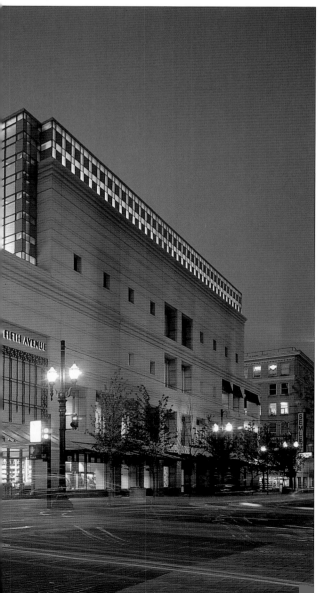

Phase II of this mixed-use development in downtown Portland adds one more city block to the two-block complex completed in 1990. That project included a 15-story office building above a two-story department store, with the three-story Pavilion building filling the second block. With its below-grade concourse, the Pavilion offers four levels of specialty shops arranged around a central, skylit atrium. It is carefully related in both scale and detail to the landmark Pioneer Courthouse on an adjoining block. The second phase, completed in 2000, is another atrium building called the Rotunda. It is another full-city-block mixed-use complex, with retail on below-grade, street, second, and third floors and a cinema on the fourth. Like the Pavilion, the Rotunda has prominent corner entrances and generous retail display windows on all frontages to enhance street activity. And like the original two blocks of the development, this one is linked to the rest of Pioneer Place both by a retail concourse below SW Fourth Avenue and by a third-floor bridge spanning the same street.

ELS
Architecture and Urban Design

Denver Pavilions
Denver, Colorado

The Denver Pavilions occupies two blocks along downtown Denver's 16th Street pedestrian-transit mall. This new open-air retail and entertainment center has rejuvenated a district once predominated by offices and vacant stores. The new complex contains 347,000 square feet of leasable area on four levels, and its tenants include a cinema, restaurants, night clubs, and retail shops. With its concentration of daytime, nighttime, and weekend uses, it provides a destination for residents of the region, downtown workers, and visitors to the city. The two-block project is bisected by Glenarm Place, which is bridged by a restaurant, a public walk, and the dramatic "Great Wall." Each of the two blocks, in turn, includes an outdoor arcade that opens from the 16th Street mall. The resulting four pavilion buildings are integrated into the downtown pedestrian environment and provide several prominent corner locations for major tenants. The forms and façades of the buildings harmonize with the scale and design characteristics of nearby historic structures. The design also accommodates the need for individual tenant identities while maintaining an overall unified character. The design of the Great Wall arose from a public art requirement and the desire to provide a unifying element for the project. The 360-foot-long, 30-foot-high perforated metal scrim forms the screen for computerized light shows and the backdrop for the 30-foot-tall letters that spell "Denver."

Right: Two-block project bridging Glenarm Place, with 30-foot-high "Great Wall" as signature feature.
Below left: Sensitively scaled pavilions seen along mall.
Below: 16th Street pedestrian-transit mall with project's pavilions at right, complementing old nearby buildings; state capitol in distance.

100

Right: Clean architectural forms and restrained details, respect design of 16th Street mall.
Photography: Andrew Kramer (bottom left); Timothy Hursley (all others).

Left: *By night, Denver Pavilions sign on the "Great Wall" and building façade lighting give coherence to the complex that includes many unique tenants.*
Above: *Project lighting merges effectively with public mall lighting.*
Photography: *Timothy Hursley.*

The Great Wall and the "Denver" letters, which make graphic reference to the area's historic cattle brands, serve as an icon for the Pavilions and for downtown Denver. Two levels of below-grade parking extend under Glenarm Place, providing for 800 cars; approximately 6,500 additional spaces are available within a two-block radius. The project is the outcome of a public-private collaboration between the Denver Pavilions Limited Partnership and the Denver Urban Renewal Authority.

Fox California Theater
San Jose, California

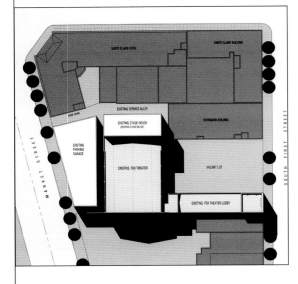

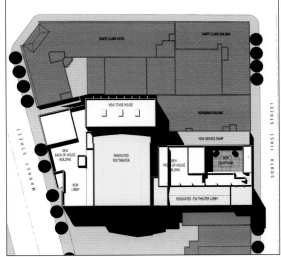

Left: *Before and after plans, showing new courtyard and ancillary spaces replacing garage on Market St., vacant lot on First St.*
Below: *Original lobby and courtyard entries on First Street.*
Bottom: *New wing and entry on Market Street, facing Convention Center.*

The theater renovation is part of a major revitalization of downtown San Jose's cultural and civic venues. In 1996-97, ELS assisted the Redevelopment Agency in planning for several projects in an Arts District Master Plan. Built in 1927, the theater will be recast as a mixed-use performing arts and film facility, complementing the adjacent Convention Center and nearby arts facilities. To accommodate the major tenant, Opera San Jose, as well as touring companies, a new stagehouse will be constructed with state-of-the-art technical capabilities. The historic

façade and interiors will be restored. Seating will be replanned to current standards, accommodating 1,120 (40 more when the new orchestra pit lift is raised). Two ancillary structures will be added to improve theater operation, a new entry courtyard will provide outdoor event space, and a two-story foyer will be built facing the Convention Center.

Fentress Bradburn
Architects Ltd.

421 Broadway

Denver

Colorado 80203

303.722.5000

303.722 5080 (Fax)

fentress@fentressbradburn.com

www.fentressbradburn.com

Fentress Bradburn Architects Ltd.

City of Oakland Administration Buildings
Oakland, California

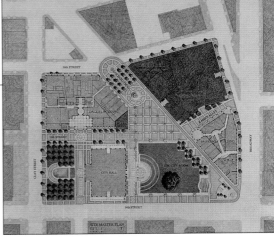

If Gertrude Stein could see her old hometown now, she could no longer say, "There is no there there." A carefully considered plan to "reweave the torn fabric" of downtown Oakland has produced an unforgettable "there" in a city striving for economic revival. Fentress Bradburn was the prime architect on a design-build team that won a national competition to consolidate city agencies on four city blocks centered on the historic City Hall. Seismic upgrades required in the wake of the 1989 Loma Prieta earthquake were included in the $94-million project. Besides a renovated City Hall, the total complex includes 444,000 square feet of offices in the new Dalziel Building – scaled and detailed in harmony with surrounding buildings —

and the Lionel J. Wilson Building created by remodeling and extending the flatiron-shaped Broadway Building. The focus of the traffic-free, 6.3-acre area is the 240,000-square-foot Frank H. Ogawa Plaza, with an amphitheater sited against the backdrop of the grand City Hall entry. Each of the two flanking city buildings also has a prominent, strategically placed entrance leading to a multistory lobby serving as an "indoor civic space."

Right: Model of complex, Dalziel Building to left of City Hall, Wilson Building to right.
Bottom right: Frank H. Ogawa Plaza, with Wilson Building at right, Dalziel Building at top center.
Below: Lobby entrance of Dalziel Building at dusk.
Photography: Ron Johnson (right, below right); Nick Merrick, Hedrich-Blessing (below).

Fentress Bradburn Architects Ltd.

1999 Broadway
Denver, Colorado

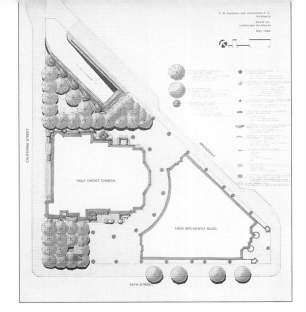

The challenge posed by the developer was to erect a 700,000-square-foot office building on the same small triangular block with historic Holy Ghost Catholic Church. The design response was to place a 44-story sheer tower hugging the sidewalk at one angular corner, carving out the side facing the church with an arithmetic spiral geometry wrapping around the church's apse. The architects note that the tower plan can be read as representing a dove, the traditional symbol of the Holy Ghost. The base of the tower is cut away to open up views of the church from surrounding streets and extend the public open space around it. The tower curtain walls are mini-mally detailed on the church side, in a shade of green to harmonize with the church roof. The street facades are more firmly delineated with limestone spandrels. Night lighting emphasizes the church as the focal point of the site. So much care was taken to minimize disruption from construction of the tower and the underground parking garage that not a single daily mass was missed during construction.

Top: Street-level plan, church at left.
Above right: Church seen through 50-foot columns at tower base.
Right and far right: Two views of faceted tower wall enfolding church.
Facing page: Evening view showing lighting of church, neon bands outlining tower.
Photography: Nick Merrick, Hedrich-Blessing (this page); Timothy Hursley (facing page).

Fentress Bradburn
Architects Ltd.

Ronstadt Transit Center
Tucson, Arizona

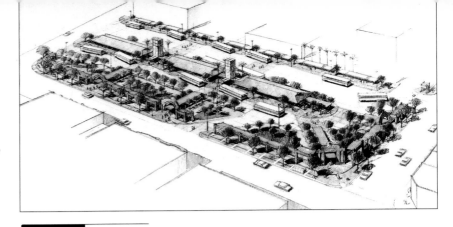

Above: Site, showing
18 bus berths.
Below: Brick arcades
surrounding center.
Photography: Nick
Merrick, Hedrich-Blessing.

Can a bus station handling 5,000 passengers a day be a good neighbor in a low-scale urban area? The city's challenge to the design team was to complement the neighborhood and provide a pleasant environment for passengers, while discouraging vandals and transients. A key step was to line the streets with pedestrian arcades, divided at the scale of individual building fronts and built of recycled brick from buildings demolished on the 2.7-acre site. Separated from the street by these arcades and generous planting areas are platforms accommodating up to 18 buses. Only 600 square feet had to be enclosed for ticket booths and restrooms, but much larger areas are shielded from the desert sun by roofs and canopies. Broad copper roofs reflect a regional tradition – and display one of Arizona's major natural resources. Benches are comfortable for waiting passengers, but too short for sleeping. Cooling towers, with technology developed at the University of Arizona Environmental Research Laboratory in Tucson, apply ancient chimney-effect techniques to cool areas under the shelters by as much as 10 to 15 degrees. As a setting for festivals and other community events, the center has been instrumental in neighborhood revitalization.

Top right: *Some of the center's 20,000 hand-made terra cotta tiles by artist Melody Peters.*
Center right: *Plantings and bus lanes inside arcade.*
Right: *Shelters with 50-foot air-cooling towers.*

Fentress Bradburn Architects Ltd.

Colorado Convention Center Expansion Denver, Colorado

Shrewd urban analysis won Fentress Bradburn the national design competition for Phase I, completed in 1990 at a cost of $85 million. The firm was chosen in 2000 to complete the project. With Phase II, the existing 1-million-square-foot structure will be expanded to nearly 3-million square feet. The ambitious $267-million scheme will create 600,000 square feet of contiguous exhibit space, a 5,000-seat auditorium, a 1,000-car parking facility, roof terraces and gardens.

Top right: Phase I west front against city skyline.
Center right: Soaring glazed entrance lobbies that set center's character.
Below right: Phase II roof terrace.
Bottom: Massing study for Phase II.
Photography: Nick Merrick, Hedrich-Blessing.
Renderings: Carl Dalio.

Field Paoli Architects

1045 Sansome Street

Suite 206

San Francisco

California 94111

415.788.6606

415.788.6650 (Fax)

www.fieldpaoli.com

architects@fieldpaoli.com

Field Paoli Architects

Paseo Nuevo
Santa Barbara, California

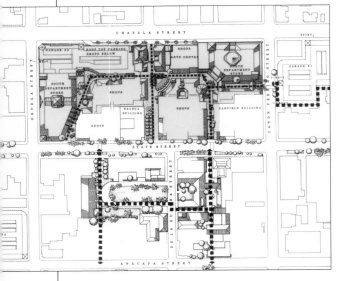

Above: *Plan of project (in blue), with landmark courthouse and other civic buildings on adjoining block.*

Above right: *Patio with distinctive details.*

Right: *Department store with paseo opening to its right, existing buildings along street to either side.*

114

Above left: Stair between levels.
Above right: Fountain courtyard.
Below right: Detail of stair.
Photography: Field Paoli Architects.

This 430,000-square-foot mixed-use infill development had to blend into the unique architectural character of downtown Santa Barbara yet meet the functional requirements of tenants. The complex includes shops, offices, and a performing arts center. In addition to adopting the district's required Spanish Colonial Revival architectural style, the project extends the pattern of pedestrian ways, known as paseos, established in the 1920s. Inviting gateways from surrounding streets open into circulation networks enhanced by plantings and fountains. Woven between existing buildings, the development includes a department store at each end, with shops and performing arts facilities between and offices above them. Marketed as Santa Barbara's "most intrigu-

ing shopping experience," Paseo Nuevo has triggered the revitalization of an area around historic State Street. It represents a joint effort of private developers and the city's redevelopment agency. The project won a 1995 ULI award.

Field Paoli Architects

Downtown Pleasant Hill
Pleasant Hill, California

With 350,000 square feet of new construction on 35 acres, this mixed-use development aims to bring new activity and identity to a hitherto anonymous Bay Area suburb. It integrates retail facilities, townhouses, offices, and a 120-room hotel with the Civic Center designed by Charles Moore to give the community a new focal point. The urban design framework is constructed to reinforce the pedestrian experience. A curving street called Crescent Drive links shops and mid-market anchor tenants with plazas, restaurants, parking, and a multiscreen theater complex. Sidewalks along the drive are linked by landscape walkways to a large interior-block plaza, to the Civic Center, and to parking areas behind the shops. The challenge of integrating large anchor tenants in a pedestrian setting was met by locating them off the shop-lined street, adjoining the midblock parking areas. Buildings are clad largely in EIFS and tile, with tilt-up concrete for some of the larger tenant structures. The overall development goal was for the local community to adopt this private project as their public downtown. Judging from experience since opening day on July 4, 2000, this has been achieved.

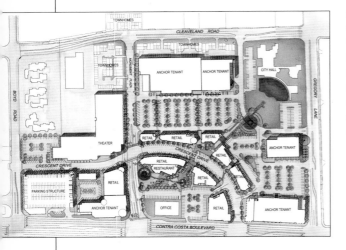

Above left: Small plaza opening onto Crescent Drive.
Left: Plan, with townhouses at top, Civic Center at top right.
Right: Shops along Crescent Drive.

Right: Interior-block plaza opening to Crescent Drive, with Civic Center in background.
Below left: Walkway to Civic Center.
Photography: Allan Geller.

Field Paoli Architects   The Shops at Riverwoods
Provo, Utah

For a growing residential district at the northern edge of Provo, an area without a well-defined community focus, this retail center reintroduces the concept of the main street. Existing streets and waterways on the 16-acre site have been realigned to permit a traditional cross-axis downtown plan, with a stream running along a green area between the development and adjacent arterial thoroughfares. Angled parking along the two internal streets is supplemented by parking lots at the perimeters of the site. A classical circle at the intersection of the two streets provides a sense of community and a space for gatherings. A plaza adjoining the circle extends out to the bank of a pond along the stream. The retail buildings are treated in a variety of forms, with polygonal volumes at key points and vaulted roofs distinguishing larger tenant spaces. Varied buildling materials include rustic stone, stucco, and pre-cast concrete. Striking views of the nearby mountains were considered in the planning of the site and the design of its buildings.

Facing page, top: Plan, showing crossing internal streets.
Facing page, bottom: View from central circle.
Top of this page: Varied building forms and materials.
Above: Colorful plantings in tradition of region.
Right: Storefronts with crisp steel details.
Photography: David Wakely.

Field Paoli Architects

Draeger's Market
San Mateo, California

This project establishes a new prototype for food marketplaces in downtown locations. Instead of presenting the windowless box long typical of such markets, Draeger's assembles an unprecedented variety of uses and makes them visible to the community. The 62,700-square-foot structure encompasses a deli, a sushi bar, a wine tasting room, a cookery school, a cookbook library, a cookware sales area, a bakery, a restaurant, and a sidewalk café, all under one roof. Balconies and display windows energize the street with views of activities such as the café and the second-story restaurant. Architectural treatment of street-front doors, windows, and balconies gives the building appealing human scale, while broad bracketed cornices and a central vault express its identity at a larger, urban scale. The project has stimulated business activity in downtown San Mateo.

Top left: *Sidewalk café.*
Above: *Boldly massed street front.*
Right: *Various uses around interior court.*
Photography: *David Wakely.*

Ford, Powell & Carson
Architects & Planners, Inc.

1138 East Commerce Street

San Antonio

Texas 78205

210.226.1246

210.226.6482 (Fax)

www.fpcarch.com

info@fpcarch.com

Ford, Powell & Carson
Architects & Planners, Inc.

Southern Pacific Depot
Historic District
San Antonio, Texas

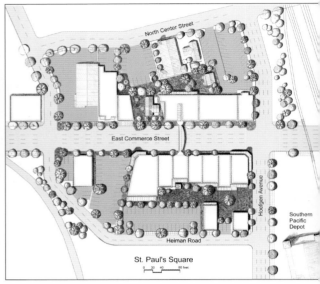

Top right: *Sunset Station on renovated square.*
Above: *East Commerce Street, with lighted pedestrian bridge (photo by D. Clarke Evans).*
Above right: *Area plan, showing depot, new plazas behind commercial buildings, and pedestrian bridge spanning East Commerce Street.*
Right: *Dining verandah outside depot.*
Photography: *Greg Hursley.*

122

Right: Detail of depot verandah.
Below left: Depot façade.
Below right: Depot interior.
Bottom: Detail of 1902 lighting and focal stained-glass window.

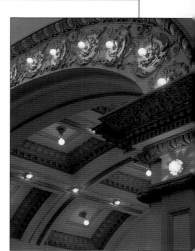

Completed in 1902, the Southern Pacific Railroad Depot faces a public area lined with low-rise commercial buildings. From the 1950s on, as railroad travel declined, the area deteriorated. Beginning in the 1970s, Ford, Powell & Carson collaborated on a master plan, then more detailed design criteria, for the station district. Then the 1980s saw the rehabilitation of some of the commercial buildings, including one occupied by the architects' offices. Façade renovation was accompanied by construction of a pedestrian bridge across East Commerce Street, which became a symbol of the area's revitalization. In 1997, the firm was commissioned (in a joint venture) to restore the station, now known as Sunset Station, in recognition of the transcontinental Sunset Limited train that used to stop here. Work on the depot included restoration of ornamental cast stone and plaster work, period lighting, and stained glass windows. In two warehouse buildings on the site, delicate wood roof trusses were again exposed. The whole complex now functions as an entertainment and retail center, drawing local residents and tourists. Streetscape improvements included paving, tree-planting, and development of stone and brick-paved plazas on the interior of each block.

Ford, Powell & Carson
Architects & Planners, Inc.

Paseo del Alamo Water Garden
San Antonio, Texas

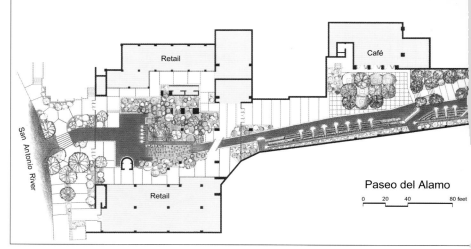

Retail

Café

San Antonio River

Retail

Paseo del Alamo

0   20   40   80 feet

Above: Water garden linking Alamo Plaza with river, passing under a major downtown street and through an hotel atrium.
Left: View from street viaduct toward Alamo Plaza end of garden.
Photography: Rick Gardner.

The paseo is an urban water garden that links San Antonio's two most visited attractions: the Alamo and the River Walk. An Urban Development Action Grant was used to clear the site for a new Hyatt hotel and this linear park. Beginning at the Alamo Plaza, the passage steps down 27 feet, past a series of pools and fountains, under a new viaduct that carries a major downtown street, and through the palm garden atrium at the base of the hotel to the river. During construction, excavations revealed caliche-block foundations of the Alamo mission's outer walls. The water descending through the paseo recounts metaphorically the water management of the Spanish settlers, attracted to this area in the

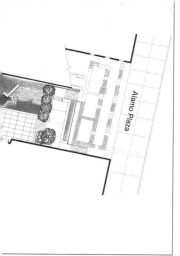

18th Century by its abundant springs. Diverted through small ditches known as acequias, the river water irrigated crops during Colonial times. Similarly, water here is impounded at various garden levels, at one point diverted through an aqueduct spanning the main path, with terraced planting beds representing agriculture of the past.

Though water appears to fall continuously through the garden to the river, the flow is divided into two recirculating systems.

Ford, Powell & Carson
Architects & Planners, Inc.

Downtown Tri-Party Street Improvements
San Antonio, Texas

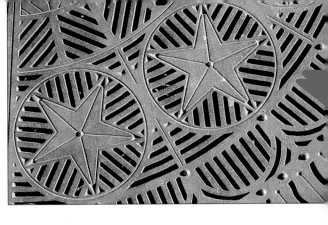

The City of San Antonio, Via Metropolitan Mass Transit, and the Downtown Owners Association retained three firms to redesign the streets of the 70-block Central Business District. Ford, Powell & Carson headed a team directing one $10.2-million portion of the total $40-million project. The work involved alignment and realignment of some streets and development of design standards for amenities such as bus benches and shelters, street lighting, paving, tree grates, telephone kiosks, drinking fountains, signage, and newspaper vending machines. Ford, Powell & Carson was also involved in design-related issues such as pedestrian lighting and traffic illumination and design of special lighting for bridges over the historic River Walk. The firm sought to develop standards applicable to all three projects, for the sake of continuity, and its design process included sophisticated consensus building and review-approval procedures. The major elements of Ford, Powell & Carson's design were widely adopted – with modifications in some cases – by the other two design teams for use in the overall project.

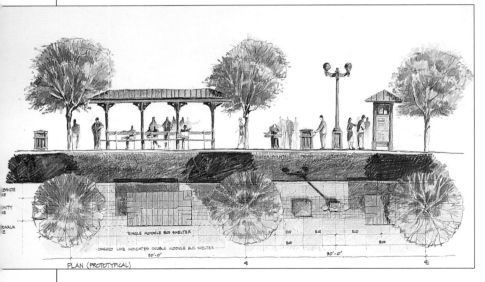

Top: *Tree grate with Lone Star theme.*
Left: *Plan and elevation of typical bus shelter and street furniture.*
Right: *Bench for area.*
Below: *Area map keyed to lighting design and street treatment.*

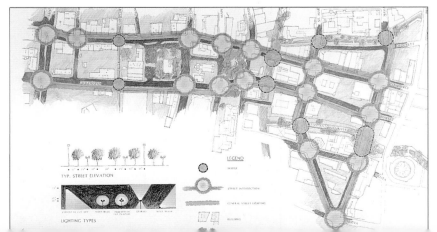

126

Ford, Powell & Carson
Architects & Planners, Inc.

Rivercenter Mall Turning Basin
San Antonio, Texas

In conjunction with the 3-million-square-foot private retail, hotel, office, and entertainment development, San Antonio's famous River Walk has been extended into the core of the retail complex. The 500-foot extension of the waterway and the public walkways around it occupy city property that was previously a parking lot. The additional waterway serves as a needed turning basin for river barges and water taxis plying this stretch of river. Spanning the newly created channel are a trussed Commerce Street bridge, a graceful footbridge (both designed by Ford, Powell & Carson) and a two-story Ponte-Vecchio-style wing of the mall. Like the new low-arched bridges, the walkways and landscaping around the basin echo the character of the original River Walk. A platform at the center of the basin serves as both dramatic boat landing and performance stage. Shops and restaurants face outward toward the turning basin rather than inward, as in the typical mall. An Urban Development Action Grant contributed toward the $6,860,000 cost of this public open space.

Top right: Design study for footbridge.
Above: Waterway passing under trussed street bridge, arched footbridge, and two-story portion of Rivercenter.
Right: Turning basin and public walkways at the heart of private mixed-use development.
Photography: Boone Powell (above); Greg Hursley (right).

Ford, Powell & Carson
Architects & Planners, Inc.

Lake Robbins Bridge
The Woodlands, Texas

The Woodlands, a planned community near Houston, needed to develop a new access link from the interstate highway to the east. The client wanted the link to be visible from the highway and to serve as a marker for The Woodlands—in particular for its waterway-related commercial and entertainment district. Working with CBM Engineering, the architects designed a symbolic arch spanning Lake Robbins between the divided roadway bridges. The arch structure is assembled of pipe sections with steel cables and compression struts, springing from forked concrete pylons.

Above: Bridge spanning lake.
Right: Vertical view of model.
Photography: George Gomes (above); Boone Powell (right).

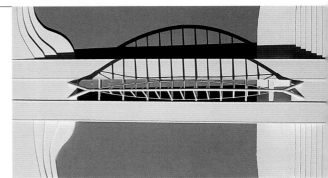

Fox & Fowle Architects

22 West 19th Street
New York
New York 10011
212.627.1700
212.463.8716 (Fax)
www.foxfowle.com

Fox & Fowle Architects

Commercial Projects

Right: Reuters building under construction.
Below: Industrial and Commercial Bank of China.
Below right: Bank's retail banking area.
Photography: Andrew Gordon, Luyun Studio.

The Industrial and Commercial Bank of China
Shanghai, China

Located in the burgeoning Pudong district across the river from the core of Shanghai, the tower comprises a solid slab, representing the bank's stability, joined to a curving, glazed slab representing dynamism and outward vision. The highrise structure acts as a foil for the curved banking pavilion and other smaller scaled program elements at the building's base.

The Reuters Building at Three Times Square New York, New York

To be finished in 2001, the building forms a pivot between Times Square and the revitalized 42nd Street entertainment district. A seven-story drum at the building's southeast corner marks the 42nd Street intersection, and its curve continues into a three-story lobby. At the northeast corner, facing the heart of Times Square, 30-foot-high video monitors will show Reuters programming, and a 14-story LED sign will display the Reuters Index.

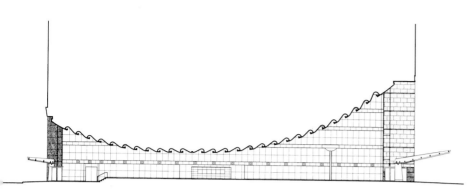

The Condé Nast Building at Four Times Square
New York, New York

The 48-story, 1.6-million-square-foot building is a crucial component of the master plan prepared by the 42nd Street Development Corporation, a public/private consortium created to promote the redevelopment of this traditional heart of Manhattan. While meeting the needs of the publishing company that is its major tenant, the building responds in sensitive ways to the various areas it faces. On the side facing Broadway, it takes on the character of Times Square, with active forms and lighted signs required on that front. On the side facing 42nd Street, east of Times Square, it takes on the more sober character of the Midtown business district. As the building rises, the collage of volumes and surfaces evolves into a unified shaft, with the same identity from all angles of view, culminating in a dynamic finial. At street level the Broadway frontage is reserved for retail, and the offices are reached via a lobby connecting entrances on 42nd and 43rd Street. The lobby ceiling descends and rises in a parabolic curve from one main entrance to the other. All building systems and construction technology meet or exceed state-of-the-art standards for energy conservation, indoor air quality, recycling systems, and sustainable manufacturing processes.

Top: Section through lobby from 43rd to 42nd Street.
Top right: Lobby, with aluminum-foil ceiling.
Left: 42nd Street entry, Times Square beyond.
Right: Tower seen from east along 42nd Street.
Photography:
Andrew Gordon,
Jeff Goldberg/ESTO.

131

Fox & Fowle Architects

Cultural Institution Projects

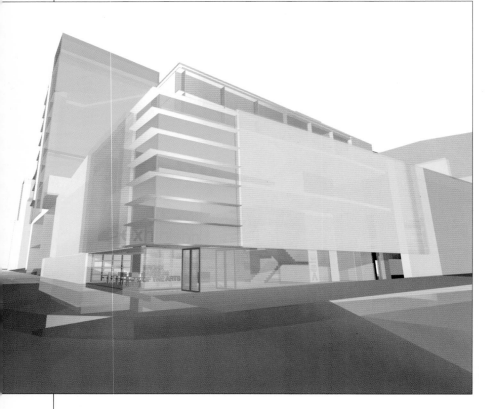

Bronx Museum
Bronx, New York

This project began with the identification of the museum's program needs. From these, a flexible master plan was developed to address both short-term code compliance issues and long-range opportunities to expand and better fulfill its mission to serve the community. The museum's 10-Year Master Plan is a pragmatic "road map" created to guide the institution through a series of physical changes in the coming years. Not an abstract vision, this document identifies development alternatives and phasing strategies to help guide decisions regarding physical improvements.

Queensborough
Community College
Port of Entry, Queens, New York

An addition to the existing Administration Building at the City University of New York's Queensborough Community College will create a visible and symbolic entrance to the campus. Sited at the top of a hill above the main gate and parking areas, the glass pavilion reaches out toward the site, welcoming students, faculty, and visitors to the school. The entry hall and adjacent courtyard areas will form a vital gathering place for the campus community. Interior renovations in the structure will include upgrading four classrooms for the college's Intensive English Language Development program, as well as new administration spaces to reflect current needs and technologies.

Top left: Port of Entry addition seen as welcoming lantern.
Top Right: New entrance enclosed largely with glass.
Above: Rendering of final Bronx Museum scheme.

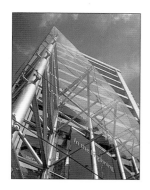

American Bible Society Renovation and Addition
New York, New York

To give the American Bible Society a renewed street presence, an all-glass pavilion projects toward Broadway from the original 1960's Modernist building. Designed not to diminish the architectural integrity of the original concrete structure, the pavilion sweeps in a grand curve through the first floor, engaging the bookstore, the concierge desk, and the entry, then out onto the plaza, where it leads the eye upstairs into the new gallery. The Society's message is conveyed through a multiscreen video system, projected images, and the words "In the Beginning" etched in 68 languages on the exterior glass. The 10 floors of offices above were also renovated, creating a model working environment that has dramatically increased employee productivity.

Left: *Pavilion seen against original façade.*
Right: *Media walls attracting passersby.*
Below: *Pavilion extending onto plaza.*
Photography: *Jeff Goldberg/ESTO.*

Fox & Fowle Architects

Transportation Projects

Hoboken Light Rail Station
Hoboken, New Jersey

Located on the Hudson River directly across from Midtown Manhattan, the arcing canopies of the Hoboken station of the Hudson-Bergen Light Rail Transit System will serve as visible gateways to New Jersey. Their cable-stayed light steel construction will complement the revitalized waterfront area. The light rail station will be the latest component of an intermodal transfer point that includes a trans-Hudson ferry, the underground PATH transit system, and commuter railroads operating from the old Erie Lackawanna terminal, which is now being restored. The new station will have two tall, canopied portions – one at the light rail platforms and one where it meets the old terminal – with a glass-covered walkway linking them.

Above: Hoboken Light Rail Station.
Below: Main entrance to Roosevelt Avenue Station.

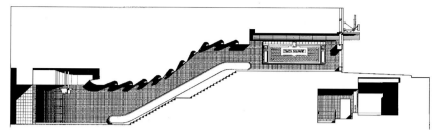

Roosevelt Avenue/ 74th Street Intermodal Station Queens, New York

The busiest New York City transit station outside of Manhattan, this transportation hub is a crucial transfer point between major elevated and underground lines, with bus connection to LaGuardia Airport and other Queens destinations. To replace the existing chaotic and run-down headhouse, the architects propose a new structure with exposed steel framing related to the cast-iron vernacular of the elevated tracks. The roof takes the form of a giant arcing fan. The adjoining bus depot will have a skylighted canopy and facades establishing continuity with neighboring retail buildings. A canopy will link the train and bus portions of the complex.

Times Square Subway Station Entrance New York, New York

This new entrance for New York City's busiest subway station captures the exuberance of Times Square. An undulating canopy topped with brightly lighted animated signs announces the subway's presence and orients passersby to the station's 11 subway lines. The "waved" canopy form continues into the station, becoming the ceiling over the token booth and turnstiles. On the track level, a marquée made of curved lighting and signage brings the flavor of Times Square into the heart of the station. To integrate the new entrance into the traditional station aesthetic, a well-preserved mosaic was relocated to the new street-level space, providing a touch of the old subway within the contemporary setting.

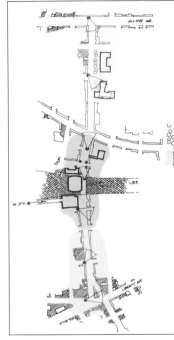

Fox & Fowle Architects

Planning/Urban Design Project

Jamaica Transportation Center Master Plan Queens, New York

The Port Authority of New York and New Jersey's proposal to construct a light rail system, or Airtrain, from JFK International Airport to the Long Island Railroad's Jamaica station will reinforce and expand the use of this busy station as an intermodal facility. In anticipation of this new transportation link, The Greater Jamaica Development Corporation has commissioned an area-wide transportation plan, a development plan, and an urban design plan for downtown Jamaica. The Airtrain will place this major commercial center within an eight-minute transit trip from the airport, closer than any comparable commercial center. The study examines the potential of accommodating future off-airport businesses and services in downtown Jamaica as part of a development strategy. The plan would strengthen commercial districts and buffer residential areas by clarifying zoning and enhancing streetscapes with appropriate landscape and urban design features.

Top Right: *Massing model of new airport-related business center to south of new Airtrain transportation center*
Right: *CADD rendering looking south towards transportation center.*
Far right: *Existing streetscape conditions in station vicinity.*
Below: *Downtown Jamaica CADD model, proposed new construction in green.*

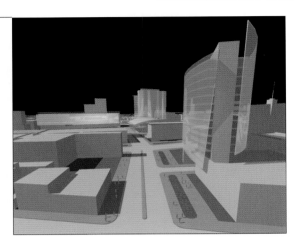

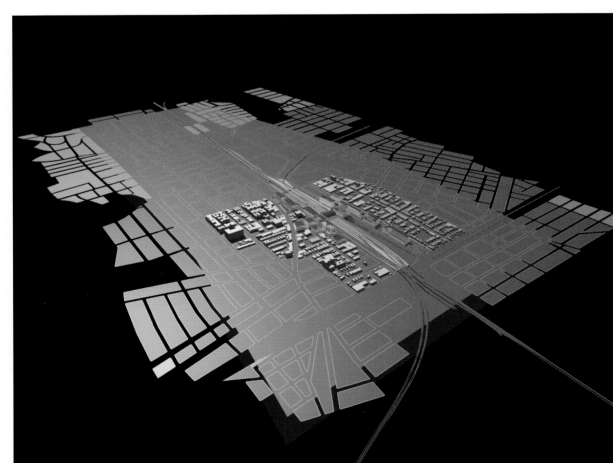

Gary Edward Handel + Associates

1995 Broadway

4th Floor

New York

New York 10023

212.595.4112

212.595.9032 (Fax)

www.gehany.com

gehany@bway.net

Gary Edward Handel + Associates

Lincoln Square Complex
New York, New York

Located just north of Lincoln Center, three high-rise mixed-use buildings establish a distinctive new transition zone between the performing arts mecca and Manhattan's Upper West Side. Completed in increments between 1994 and 1999, the projects include: Lincoln Square, a 47-story theater, health club, and residential building; Lincoln Triangle, a 32-story retail and residential block overlooking Lincoln Square Plaza; and Lincoln West, a 30-story residential and retail building connected to the renovated structure that houses a luxury, extended-stay hotel. A key innovation in these projects is the way typically suburban commercial facilities, such as big-box retailers and multiplex theaters, are integrated into the city by transforming them from closed to street-oriented volumes. The public realm is expanded by visually extending the sidewalk into the theater lobbies; health clubs are made transparent, lending animation to the street. Similar palettes of brick, metal, and glass – predominantly light in color – maintain an identity across several city blocks. In the Lincoln Square structure (designed in collaboration with Kohn Pedersen Fox Associates) a 400,000-square-foot base contains a 10-screen cinema, a health club featur-

Right: *Lincoln West tower rising on Broadway, with broad views of the city and Lincoln Center for the Performing Arts.*

Photography: *Aero Photo (aerial), Eduard Hueber (cinema front), George Corti (Phillips Club lobby), Skip Hine (Lincoln West exterior and lobby).*

Below: Lincoln Triangle lobby.
Facing page: Lincoln Triangle, offering exceptional unobstructed views.
Photography: Lily Wang (lobby), Andrew Gordon (exterior).

ing a 45-foot-tall climbing wall, plus a post office and retail; the 368-unit residential tower above includes a mix of condominium, short-term rentals, and corporate apartments. Lincoln Triangle includes a 65,000-square-foot Barnes & Noble store in its four-story retail base, with 23 stories of apart-four stories of penthouse units above. Lincoln West comprises a 27-story apartment tower above a four-story retail base that includes large Tower Records and Pottery Barn stores. Rising from the same continuous retail base is the ten-story, 109-unit Phillips Club, a luxury hotel and residential facility created by thoroughly renovating the former Chinese mission to the United Nations.

Gary Edward Handel + Associates

Sony Metreon
San Francisco, California

Completing the south edge of the Yerba Buena Gardens, the complex takes its place in the city's cultural district adjoining the Moscone Convention Center. As a unique flagship entertainment center, Metreon makes a transition between busy commercial streets and the institutions around the garden. The complex houses a 15-screen cinema, a 600-seat IMAX theater, and a variety of high-tech retail venues developed for Sony. On the city side, the building hugs the street line, with clear glazing on the lower floors. Several entries encourage circulation through to the garden. The potentially massive walls of the third-floor cinemas are relieved by subtle neon banding and lighted glass panels. A faceted wall of clear glass encloses the garden side of the 270-foot-long lobby, with a balcony offering broad views for cinema patrons. The project was a joint venture of SMWM and Gary Edward Handel + Associates.

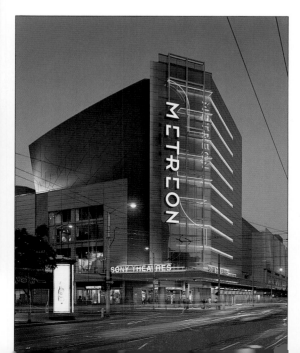

Gary Edward Handel + Associates

Projects in Construction

Four Seasons Tower
San Francisco, California

The 40-story tower rising above the corner of Market and Grant Streets will help link the Yerba Buena development to downtown. It will include a Four Seasons Hotel, residential condominiums, a health club, and 100,000 square feet of retail.

Millennium Place
Boston, Massachusetts

Two towers will define the south corner of The Common and form a gateway to the theater district and the neighborhood beyond. Each tower will rise from a podium compatible with neighboring buildings. The total of 1.8 million square feet will include a hotel, apartments, fitness facilities, theaters, retail, and below grade parking.

2200 M Street
Washington, DC

The 11-story building includes a luxury condominium, a hotel, and a sports club. Five levels below grade will house parking and hotel functions. There will be street-level retail on three sides. A 35,000-square-foot central landscaped court will cascade from the fifth floor to grade level as an amenity for residents and guests.

GGLO

1301 First Avenue

Suite 301

Seattle

Washington 98101

206.467.5828

206.467.0627(Fax)

www.gglo.com

gglo@gglo.com

Willows Lodge
Woodinville, Washington

The four buildings of Willows Lodge are strategically placed on the five-acre site to create a refuge for high-tech executives and weekend escapees from the city. The buildings accommodate 88 guest rooms, two restaurants, conference facilities, and a spa in 75,000 square feet of two-story wood-framed construction. To compensate for the lack of dramatic vistas from the low-lying site, a sequence of landscaped courtyards have been created between the buildings to provide a restful, natural inward focus. Buildings and plantings are arranged to divert attention from neighboring development – actual and potential. The buildings respect the Craftsman heritage of the Northwest and the architectural traditions of the Pacific Rim in buildings that are essentially

Modern in their spatial layouts, structure, materials, and details. The pervasive horizontality of the buildings, the repetition of structural bays, and the low-contrast palette of materials – many with natural finishes – sustain the atmosphere of rest and contemplation.

Left: Sculpture garden.
Above left: Dining room.
Top left: Central open space.
Above: Pool in sheltered sun pocket.
Right: Main entrance.
Photography: Bill Zeldis.

University Village
Seattle, Washington

Left: Trellises and potted plants along sidewalk.

Below left: Fountain in court defined by added structures.

Photography: Eckert & Eckert; Eduardo Calderon.

A 23-acre retail complex adjacent to the University of Washington campus, University Village was developed in the late 1950's as an open-air shopping center. In recent years, the present owners have commissioned a series of upgrades and additions. Site planning has been revised to elevate the role of the pedestrian over the automobile and re-create some of the atmosphere of a traditional Main Street. Canopies, lighting, and liberal landscaping enhance the project's internal pedestrian paths. On the periphery of the site, existing buildings have been reconstructed as one- and two-story retail spaces. A formerly isolated home improvement store at one corner of the tract has been given a pedestrian orientation by building four nearby pavilions that define a garden court, including an interactive fountain and seating. The added structures reach out toward the central retail buildings, to which they are linked by a short, tree-lined walk. Throughout the project, a feeling of solidity has been established with surfaces of cast stone blocks, hand-troweled stucco, and natural wood. Wide sidewalks and amenities such as bike racks and a variety of seating make the individual feel welcome.

Left: Welcome feeling created by signs, furniture, and awnings over generous windows.
Above: Building with top-floor garden center under retractable greenhouse roof.
Right: Canopy and window details.
Below right: Shadowbox store window.

Waterfront Landings
Seattle, Washington

Transforming an under-utilized section of Seattle's waterfront into a 234-unit residential development, the project links the heart of downtown to the harbor. Located at the base of the steep bluff, the development's three buildings had to counter a "black hole" perception of the site, plus an active railroad and a highway viaduct along its inland edge. An acoustical wall isolates the project from train and highway noise. The buildings are raised 3'-6" above a 450-car garage, giving the first floors a modest privacy separation from grade level. Buildings and open spaces are organized to take advantage of views yet respect view corridors through the site. A sense of security is assured by locating well-lit building lobbies and offices at street corners. Landscaped private courts are enclosed with open-rail fencing to offer appealing views for passersby. Architectural treatment of the three buildings ranges from relatively traditional at the south building to more contemporary at the north one, which has galvanized metal cladding that harmonizes with the new conference center and port offices nearby.

Top: Development sited on downtown waterfront.
Photography: Eckert & Eckert.

Above left: South building, with cornices and ceramic tile panels.
Above right: Project from water side, north building at left.

GGLO, LLC

The RD Merrill Building
Seattle, Washington

The RD Merrill Building is a 50,000 square foot office building located in the Eastlake neighborhood of Seattle across from Lake Union. The building contains three levels of office above a single underground parking garage containing 33 spaces. The building serves two tenants, the RD Merrill Company itself and a high-tech start-up company. The interior spaces are minimalistic with a focus on natural light and simple furnishings. The juxtaposition of old and new is featured in the lobby area where the company's original bank vault is placed amongst contemporary art. The lobby also acts as a gallery for the owners' extensive family art collection. GGLO Interiors designed 10,972 square feet of corporate office space within a newly built masonry shell. The client's extensive collection of art was incorporated throughout the building. A gallery space was created as an entry lobby to the building and again in an elegant reception area and boardroom. Art is displayed on a cherry stained wood wall that continues into the boardroom. An artisan commissioned conference table is on display through a transparent glass wall to the boardroom, with views overlooking Lake Union. An exposed structure with high timber ceilings combined with rich finishes make this space a combination of sophistication with an industrial feel.

Above left: *Southwest corner of the masonry shell building facing Seattle's Lake Union to the west.*
Top right: *Boardroom featuring company's art collections.*
Center right: *Company workstation area.*
Bottom right: *RD Merrill entrance and lobby,*
Photography: *Michael Shopenn.*

GGLO

4041 Central Plaza
Office Building
Phoenix, Arizona

The design team's commission was to reinvigorate an outdated 1970's plaza and upgrade the lobby and entries of the 20-story office building rising from it. In the redesigned plaza, circulation is directed to new main entries on the north and south faces of the tower. The revised layout allows for a visitor drop-off zone and a new location for deliveries. A new paint scheme, flagpoles, and architectural metalwork accent the tower's verticality. The two entries are distinguished by metal canopies, new signage, and attractive night lighting. The aging lobby has been replaced with two reconfigured lobbies, using light-colored materials and ample lighting.

Right: *Repainted tower and plaza greenery.*
Below right: *New canopied entry.*
Bottom right: *Entry at night.*
Below: *One of two new lobbies.*
Photography: *Alan McCoy.*

HLM Design

121 West Trade Street
Suite 2950
Charlotte
North Carolina 28202
704.358.0779
704.358.0229 (Fax)
www.hlmdesign.com
jcrossi@hlmdesign.com

Atlanta

Charlotte

Chicago

Dallas

Denver

Iowa City

Orlando

Philadelphia

San Francisco

Washington DC

HLM Design

Orange County Courthouse Complex
Orlando, Florida

Above: War memorial included in complex.
Right: Colonnade typical of low-rise wings.
Far right: Structures composed around central courtyard.
Below: Ceremonial courtroom.
Photography: Scott McDonald, Hedrich-Blessing.

"A strong symbol of justice in the community" was the design objective for this courthouse complex. The architects' comprehensive services for the project began with programming and the critical phase of site selection. The firm devised a method for weighing such factors as site size, cost impacts, and development potential. The midtown site that was chosen provided one 9.3-acre undivided parcel, in a high-density urban district, with only four property owners to negotiate with. The completed five-building, 965,000-square-foot complex includes a variety of courts and offices, plus a 750-car parking garage. The central high-rise structure provides an appropriate presence on the skyline, while surrounding lowrise buildings lined with colonnades are harmonious with surrounding historic and commercial districts. The tower is composed of three-story "sandwiches," in which one floor housing judges and holding areas is located between two courtroom floors, forming a series of self-contained "courts within a court."

Opposite page:
Skylighted entry rotunda at base of tower.

154

HLM Design   Arlington County Courthouse
Arlington, Virginia

Arlington's dense urban pattern and its tradition of NeoClassical architecture were strong influences on this design. Moreover, the new structure had to relate effectively to the existing detention facility on an adjacent site to form a cohesive justice precinct. The building's 285,000 square feet of floor area are necessarily stacked vertically, with the building façades forming a strong edge along the city's street grid. Façades are symmetrically organized, with setbacks and cornice lines adjusted to the volumes of the detention facility. Limestone-colored precast and carefully placed granite accents relate the building visually to the adjoining detention center and the city of Arlington. A formal public plaza between the new courthouse and its existing neighbor provides an axial view toward the Washington Monument, tying the complex visually to the nation's capital. Internally, the courthouse uses interstitial mezzanine floors to allow for two-story courtrooms and gracious public spaces, while maintaining standard floor-to-floor heights for offices. For more efficient use of space, courtrooms are not allocated to individual judges, like private property, but shared by several. The judges' offices are pooled at the top of the structure to take advantage of splendid Washington-area views.

Above: Ceremonial courtroom.
Below left: Courthouse seen from formal courtyard it shares with existing detention facility.
Below right: Courthouse, with detention building at left.
Photography: Scott McDonald, Hedrich-Blessing; Eric Taylor Photography.

Above: *Main lobby,
with detail recalling
NeoClassical tradition.*

HLM Design

United States Courthouse
Sacramento, California

This 740,251-square-foot courthouse and office complex was designed by a joint venture of Nacht & Lewis Architects, Sacramento, and HLM Design, San Francisco. As a large Federal facility, it had to fulfill complex programmatic needs, while serving as a visual representation of the American judicial system. To fit its tight urban site, the building is necessarily a high-rise, but the architects modulated its scale by clearly articulating its principal components in the exterior form. Entrance is by way of a low wing that strongly expresses its entry role while relating to the scale of the pedestrian and the generally low-rise fabric of Sacramento. The entry plaza is placed to recognize the nearby Southern Pacific train station and the proposed development around it. The orientation of the tower, with long sides to the north and south, minimizes adverse solar loading on the building. Visitors enter the low-rise block to find a soaring lobby crowned by a skylight that is visible on

Top right: *Portion of entry plaza with artwork.*
Center: *Sacramento from the river, with Federal Building and Courthouse at left.*
Right: *Plaza and entry block.*

the exterior. In the tower itself, the courts are organized in a highly efficient configuration, in which four magistrates or bankruptcy courts can be fitted in per floor, below three of the larger district courts. Two commissioned art works add to the impact of the entrance lobby: a set of twelve marble chairs by Rita Dove representing the members of a jury, inscribed with comments on the role of the individual in society; hanging above them, scales of justice by Larry Kirkland, with elliptical bowls that echo the lobby plan, surfaced in 23K gold to commemorate Sacramento's place as the locus of the California Gold Rush.

Above and right:
Elliptical skylighted lobby with sculptural scales of justice suspended above circle of marble chairs representing the jury.

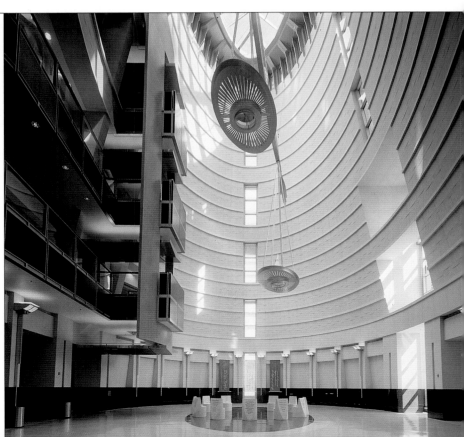

The HNTB Companies

HNTB Corporation

715 Kirk Drive

Kansas City

Missouri 64105

816.472.1201

816.472.4060 (Fax)

www.hntb.com

LDR International, Inc.

9175 Guilford Road

Columbia

Maryland 21046

410.792.4360

301.498.5070 (Fax)

More than 60 offices nationwide

HNTB Corporation

Lafayette Big Four Depot/Riehle Plaza
Lafayette, Indiana

When they could find no marketable uses for Lafayette's historic railroad station after the tracks were relocated, the architects and landscape architects recommended moving it four blocks to a site in the heart of downtown overlooking the Wabash River. Here it is the centerpiece of an intermodal transportation facility with a related community plaza, adjacent to the bridge that links the city to West Lafayette. The 112-foot-long, 547-ton station, with walls of brick and limestone up to 1-1/2 feet thick, was one of the largest structures ever moved. In its new location, it serves as a 6,000-square-foot meeting and special event space above a floor of transportation facilities serving Amtrak, Greyhound, and local buses. To meet Department of Interior preservation standards, the old depot had to retain its original one-story appearance, as it does from its new terrace. The new ground floor and the surrounding public spaces also follow national standards by being contemporary in design, while complementary to the old station. Restoration of the building included replacing asphalt roof shingles with slate to match its original appearance. The landscape architects also provided design services for the re-use of the Main Street Bridge as a pedestrian public space. Elevator towers required for access to the train platforms and the bridge were designed as identifying features of the development.

Above left: *Plaza, station, and pedestrian bridge.*
Left: *Public event on the station plaza.*
Facing page: *Prominent elevator tower as accessible alternative to fountain-centered stairway.*
Photography: *Dave Preston, Gary Quesada.*

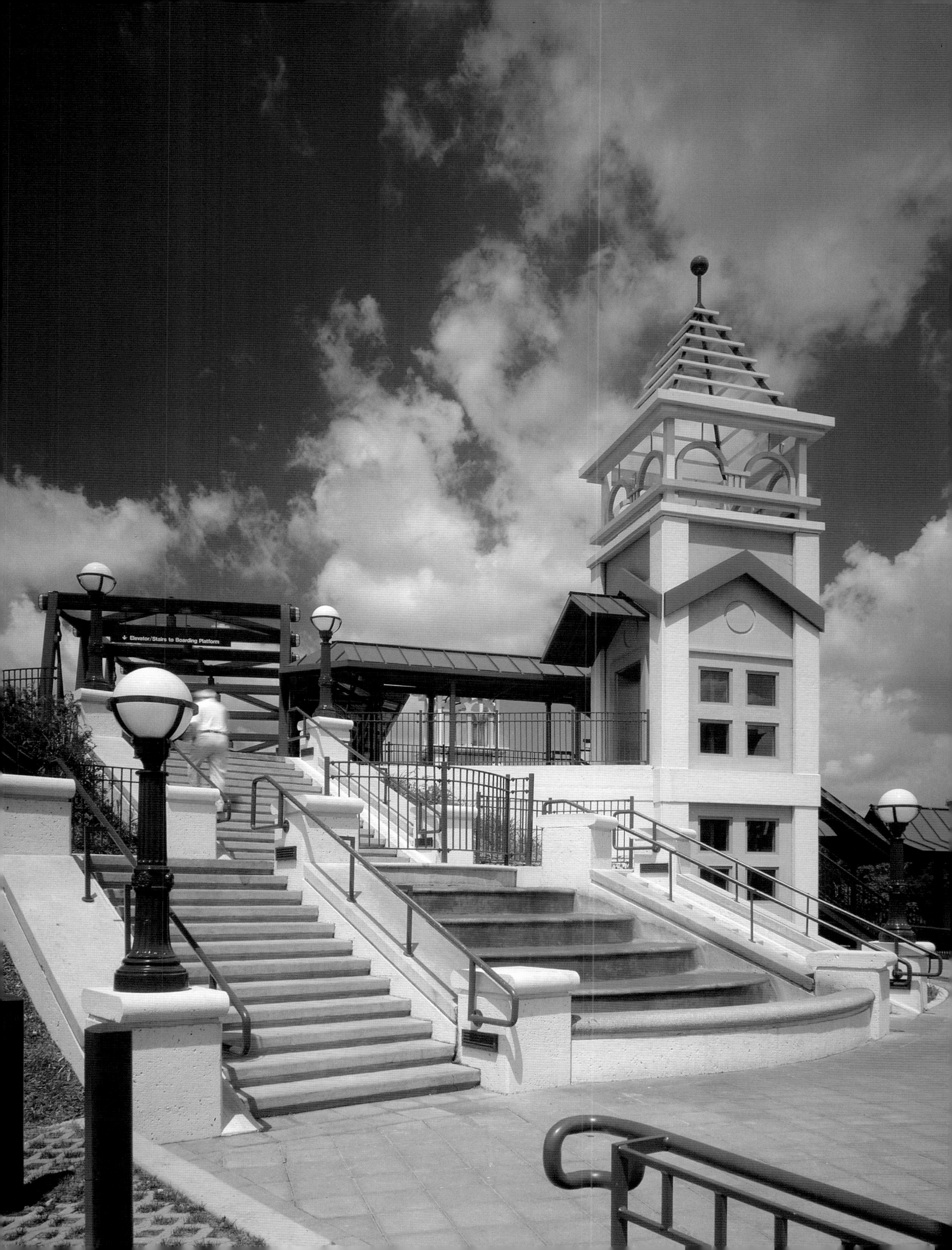
Elevator/Stairs to Boarding Platform

HNTB Corporation

Raley Field
West Sacramento, California

As the first component of a mixed-use redevelopment area, this minor-league baseball park is designed to stimulate and complement future development. Because of a "pinch" in the 16.7-acre tract, the seating for 11,500 fans "cradles" the playing field, in the manner of Yankee Stadium, rather than simply surrounding it. In its first season, in 2000, the field set a Pacific Coast League attendance record of 860,000.

Top: Seating "cradling" field in plan.
Left: Berm seating near scoreboard.
Above: Entrance and support buildings.
Photography: Douglas Johnson.

HNTB Corporation

Union Station
Kansas City, Missouri

America's second-largest railroad station, completed in 1914, sat empty from 1983 to 1999 despite a series of failed restoration proposals. Its vast halls are now occupied again as entry spaces to an intermodal transportation center (serving Amtrak and future light rail), restaurants, retail areas, and Science City, a much expanded version of the city's earlier science museum. Three theaters totaling 800 seats provide for integrated planetarium/laser/music/film presentations and live stage performances. The former Waiting Room is now a setting for banquets and other functions. Restoration work included the thorough refurbishing of three chandeliers, each 12 feet in diameter and weighing 3,500 pounds. A Tennessee Gray Marble quarry was reopened for the project. The adaptive reuse of the 800,000-square-foot building was made possible by Kansas City area voters' approval of a bi-state cultural tax that will raise $118 million.

Left: Restored facade.
Bottom: Waiting room beyond 6-ft-diameter clock.
Below left: Grand Hall ceiling, which absorbed much of $3.5-million plaster contract.
Photography: Roy Inman (exterior), Walter Smalling (interiors).

**LDR International, Inc.
An HNTB Company**

**Tubman Garrett Riverfront Park
Wilmington, Delaware**

Top left: Historic boats at park.
Top right: One of two brick and metal gates.
Above right: Computer view of park.
Left: Crowds along crescent walk.
Photography: Patrick Mullaly, Henry Alinger.

As part of a larger redevelopment of a once-industrial waterfront, LDR worked with the Riverfront Development Corporation and the city to design and construct this park "where downtown meets the Christina River." Adjacent to the Northeast Corridor train station, this formal open space creates a positive first impression for those arriving in the city. For residents, it provides a setting for seasonal festivals and events and a year-round place to enjoy the river's edge. The focus of the park is the space within a tree-lined crescent walkway. The originally flat site has been subtly regraded so that the crescent defines a grassy amphitheater facing a brick plaza that doubles as a temporary stage. Low black steel picket fences defining the park are marked by two prominent gateways. The use of red brick for the paving and gateway columns reflects the historic building material of Wilmington. Further development envisioned under LDR's plan includes retail and dining facilities and a new Riverfront Arts Center.

LDR International, Inc.
An HNTB Company

Savannah Parks
Savannah, Georgia

Above: *Gazebo in one of park squares.*
Right: *Axial walk and fountain in Forsyth Park.*
Below right: *Square as green oasis.*
Photography: *Cy Paumier.*

The development plan for Downtown Savannah identified six historically significant park squares to be restored in accordance with urban design plans prepared by LDR. In the uniquely far-sighted 18th Century plan for the city, these squares were intended as central commons and market-places for individual neighborhoods. Over the past century, the condition of these historic squares varied considerably. LDR worked closely with the Savannah Park and Tree Commission, the Historic Savannah Foundation, and neighborhood groups to draw up restoration plans. The restored squares have inspired preservation and revitalization efforts in their areas. LDR also prepared the master plan for Forsyth Park, a 32-acre multiuse park south of downtown. The plan protects and restores the park's 19th-Century gardens, exceptional central fountain, and Confederate war memorial, while providing active recreation facilities for nearby residents.

LDR International, Inc.
An HNTB Company

Downtown Lakeland
Lakeland, Florida

Recognizing its strategic location between the rapidly expanding metropolitan areas of Orlando and Tampa, Lakeland has made coordinated efforts to establish itself as a center for living, shopping, and conducting business. LDR worked with the Lakeland Downtown Development Authority to draw up an overall plan for the downtown, identifying key public and private projects vital to the city's future growth. Following completion of the Downtown Strategic Plan, LDR redesigned Munn Park, the primary public space in the city core. Detailed plans also were prepared for comprehensive streetscape improvements and enhancement of Lake Mirror Park and Promenade. The new amphitheater and lake-edge walkway create a pedestrian-oriented public amenity linked to the downtown by the Lemon Street Promenade.

James, Harwick+Partners, Inc.

8340 Meadow Road

Suite 248

Dallas

Texas 75231

214.363.5687

214.363.9563 (Fax)

www.jhparch.com

jhparch@jhparch.com

James, Harwick+Partners, Inc.

Treymore at Cityplace
Dallas, Texas

Right: Buildings hug streets, with parking inside block.
Below and below right: Roof forms, details, and materials in the tradition of Dallas houses.
Bottom: Central pool court.
Photography: Rion Rizzo/Creative Sources.

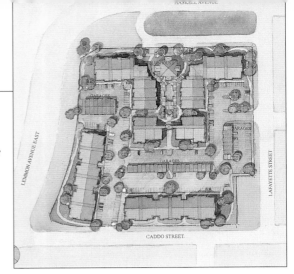

"This is a model for the nation," said HUD Secretary Andrew Cuomo at Treymore's opening ceremony. Built by Carleton Residential Properties, the 180-unit development includes 50 percent government-subsidized units for low-income families and 50 percent market-rate apartments and is funded through a combination of private investment, city funds, HUD programs, and tax credit bank financing. Its planning and design had to relate to a widely diverse set of neighbors: "big box" retail developments, a 40-story tower, the affluent Cityplace mixed-used development, and the impoverished 55-year old Roseland Homes public housing project — which has since been razed to make room for housing modeled after Treymore. Following New Urbanist principles, the complex is built out to adjoining streets, with parking internal to the block. Treymore's buildings relate in overall scale to large nearby structures, yet are divided visually into domestic-scaled elements. Materials and details recall the Craftsman style common in Dallas's single-family house neighborhoods.

James, Harwick+Partners, Inc.

The Enclave at Richmond Place
Tampa, Florida

Above right: Leasing office exemplifying development's design.
Right: Pavilion on landscaped site.
Below and below right: Details in Mediterranean tradition, with porches typical of Florida precedents.
Photography: Rion Rizzo/Creative Sources.

This 14-acre private development for Realty Development Corporation includes 280 apartments, leasing office, laundry/mail room building, 57 detached garages, tennis and volleyball courts, and a resort-style pool. Buildings are sited to take advantage of adjacent wetlands, reinforce the major street, enclose the project's amenity areas, and buffer adjoining single-family houses. To reinforce a sense of place and community in a fast-growing suburban area, the structures of varied scale are unified by consistent materials and details that recall the Mediterranean style characteristic of older residential developments in the Tampa area. Panels of broken tile provide distinctive, memorable features. Wood frame construction is clad and stucco, with concrete tile roofs

171

James, Harwick+Partners, Inc.

The Saulet
New Orleans, Louisiana

Right: *Area master plan, with Convention Center at upper right, the Saulet site at left.*
Below: *Leasing building, with retail/apartment buildings flanking its forecourt (upper left in site plan).*
Bottom: *The Saulet site plan by JH+P.*

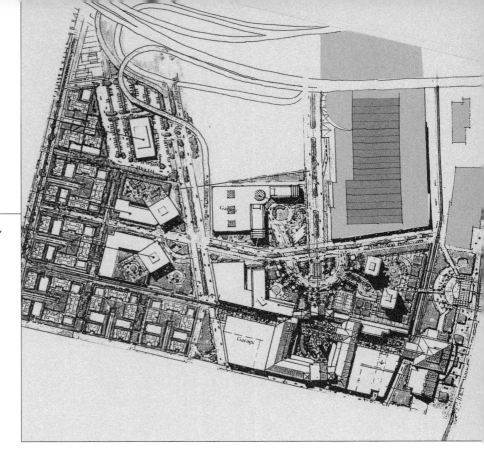

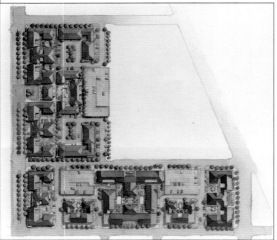

The historic fabric of New Orleans offers developers uniquely valuable architectural precedents, along with the challenge of reconciling today's functional needs with a very sensitive urban fabric. "One of the pitfalls," says Mark Wolf, AIA of JH+P, "is to get too nostalgic. We tried to take a cleaner, more contemporary slant, which was driven in part by the realism of the budget." Built for Greystar Capital partners on the site of derelict warehouses, the 13.5-acre development includes 708 living units, plus retail space for neighborhood services such as a dry cleaner, pharmacy, and corner deli. Some of the units are live/work combos, with street-level workspaces (permitted modest signs) connected by stairs to living spaces above. Urbanistically, the project had to make a transition from the residential Lower Garden District on one side to large-scale structures existing or planned around the city's Convention Center on the other. Building heights were limited to three stories along the street facing the Garden District, rising to four for the rest of the project. Parking facilities range from individual garages to small-scaled courts to parking structures. Building materials and proportions are used to differentiate between uses: retail areas include metal facade details, live/work units show variations on traditional wood fronts, and residential units are clad in stucco, with wood-framed porticos and galleries marking major axis and corners.

Above: View from outer corner of L-shaped site.
Right: Retail/housing structures and court in front of leasing building.
Below: Residential building fronts (left) and retail/housing fronts (right).

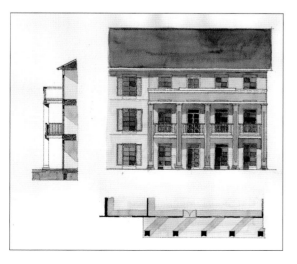

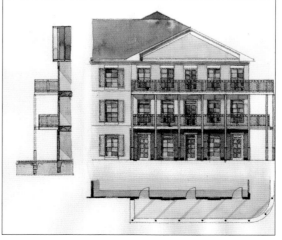

James, Harwick+Partners, Inc.

Courthouse Square Apartments
Fort Worth, Texas

A one-acre site in downtown Fort Worth, across the street from the historic Tarrant County Courthouse, is the setting for a development of 118 market-rate apartments. The location is within walking distance of the upscale Sundance Square development. A two-level parking structure covering most of the site serves as a podium for four stories of wood-framed apartments. Greenery, lattices, and robust balustrades provide appealing streetscape elements along the parking structure facades. Recalling the massing of the neighboring courthouse, the complex is symmetrical on all four frontages, with projecting central elements on two facades and deep courtyards over parking entrances on the other two sides. Corner pavilions are cut on the diagonal and stepped up in scale, with recessed balconies and metal-framed canopies adding further distinction. Stucco and brick facades are compatible with older buildings in downtown Fort Worth.

Above: Side street view, showing parking entrance and angular treatment of project's corners.
Below: Symmetrical entrance facade, with landmark courthouse beyond.

James, Harwick+Partners, Inc.

Summer Villa Apartments
Atlanta, Georgia

Located at the main entry to a corporate office development, this residential complex had to complement the architecture of an existing Tuscan style restaurant and includes some convenience retail space at ground level. Realty Development Corporation developed this project with 316 units on a 5.5-acre site. The project is dense, but it is surrounded by ample open green space. A four-level parking structure at the core of the development is hidden from public view by the four-story residential block. The planning and architecture of the complex had to win approval for rezoning and was also subject to intense review by the master plan developers. The commission was won by the design team in part for their deft handling of the view corridors from the existing landmark restaurant. The client also enjoyed the variation and texture of the building façades fronting into the main entry.

Top: Site plan, showing adjoining restaurant and park areas.
Above: Main entry, with local retail flanking central walkway.
Below: Apartments seen from restaurant.

James, Harwick+Partners, Inc.

Grand Bank
Dallas, Texas

This 37,000-square-foot structure was intended to anchor a vulnerable neighborhood with a strong institutional presence and present a strong image when seen from the adjacent freeway. A boldly geometrical half-barrel-vault skylight parallels the highway and lights a 200-foot-long banking lobby. Doubling as a pedestrian street, the lobby divides the one-story "officer functions" on one side from the lower-ceilinged "office functions," with second-story expansion space above them. Polished granite exterior cladding produces vivid reflections of building elements and landscaping. Many mature oaks on the 2.5-acre site were carefully preserved during the construction process.

Left: *Bold composition including dark skylight glazing and sheer polished granite walls.*
Above: *Tellers' counter facing tall skylighted lobby.*

JPRA Architects

31000 Northwestern Hwy.

Suite 100

Farmington Hills

Michigan 48334

248.737.0180

248.737.9161 (Fax)

www.jpra.com

info.jpra.com

JPRA Architects

Bay Harbor Marina District
Bay Harbor, Michigan

Replacing an old cement plant with a resort community is a bold effort, and JPRA took an unorthodox approach. They invented the tale of a 19th-Century resort that had fallen into disuse for the better part of a century until its recent rediscovery and restoration. An imagined lumber baron's fishing lodge at the center of the development became the site of varied shops, a "barnacled oyster bar," and a collection of restored guest rooms. Two other ostensibly 19th-Century structures along the harbor were conceived as if they had housed merchant vessel crews, with a large sailors' bar, a maritime repair shop, and a lighthouse-like lookout tower. The "historic" architecture was created as an eccentric version of Victorian resort architecture, influenced by the Northern forests. In real life, the Marina District is the commercial and entertainment core of a five-mile-long development of luxurious vacation retreats. It was developed on the site of the defunct cement plant and other lakefront industries after its sponsors assured local officials that the project would top out at only 800 affluent residents. They come here to enjoy the lake at their doorsteps and three nine-hole golf courses constructed over a 2-1/2-mile swath of limestone dust. Familiar with the world's most appealing urban environments, they are pleased with Bay Harbor's "new history."

Above: *Lakefront loft residential buildings.*
Left and right: *Victorian eccentricities, including irregular shingles, sculptured turrets, and copper cladding.*
Facing page: *Fancifully gated commercial-residential building.*
Photography: *Laszlo Regos.*

JPRA Architects

Arizona Mills
Tempe, Arizona

This 1.6 million square foot value retail and entertainment center in suburban Phoenix includes 175 stores in a single-level oval layout. It is divided into six shopping "neighborhoods," each with distinctive signage keyed to interior and exterior design motifs. Works of Southwestern artists are featured in the interiors and the unique sculptural entrances. Included in the $195-million project are such anchor tenants as a Virgin Megastore, a JC Penney Outlet Store, Saks Off Fifth, Nieman Marcus Last Call, Burlington Coat Factory, and American Wilderness Experience, along with a food court and IMAX and Harkins theaters. JPRA was responsible for the complete design, construction documents, and field administration, including architecture, structure, lighting, M/E/P engineering, environmental graphics, graphics, and interiors for all non-tenant areas.

Left: *One of center's sculptural entrances.*
Above: *Interior, with graphics identifying Neighborhood 3.*
Right: *Abstract sky symbols over the information desk.*
Photography: *Mark Delsasso@Visus Ltd.*

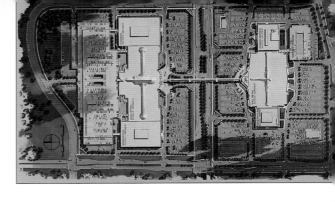

JPRA Architects

Somerset Collection
Troy, Michigan

The firm's work at the Somerset Collection, carried out over a period of several years, included the expansion of the existing Somerset Collection (South) to 220,000 square feet of leasable area and the construction of the new Somerset Collection (North) with 400,000 leasable square feet. The existing one level South building, was renovated, inside and out, and an entire second floor level of 113,000 square feet of G.L.A. was added. Anchor stores include an existing Saks Fifth Avenue and a new Neiman Marcus. A 40-foot-high entry court rotunda was created, with glass elevators. An existing central court café was redesigned and a new four-level parking deck was constructed, linked to the mall by a skylighted bridge. JPRA provided complete design services for this project, including engineering, environmental graphics and purchase of all interior furnishings. The cost was $36 million, including the parking deck, exclusive of site

Facing page, left: Interior of South building.

Facing page, top: Plan of the two-building complex, with North at left, skywalk spanning highway at center.

Facing page, middle: North building mall, with glass elevators.

Facing page, bottom: Bridge connection at South building.

Right: Skylighted central space, North building.

Photography: Balthazar Korab.

work and landscaping. The all-new, three-story North structure is anchored by a new Hudson's and Nordstrom store and includes a 4,000-car, four-level parking structure. The Peacock Cafes, a 500-seat, multilevel food court, is distinguished by continuity of wall surfaces for all of the food providers featuring stained wood, terra cotta tile and custom art tile. The project presented an opportunity to connect the North and South buildings by a 700-foot enclosed bridge, with moving sidewalks, spanning an eight-lane boulevard. Traffic on the road can see into the interior of both North and South buildings through the glass entry walls. JPRA Architects provided the same comprehensive services as noted on the South building project. The cost of the project was $80 million, including the skywalk, parking decks, site work, and landscaping.

Above: *Portion of North building interior.*
Right: *Peacock Cafes, North building.*
Above right: *Central space, North building.*
Photography: *Balthazar Korab.*

KMD Architects

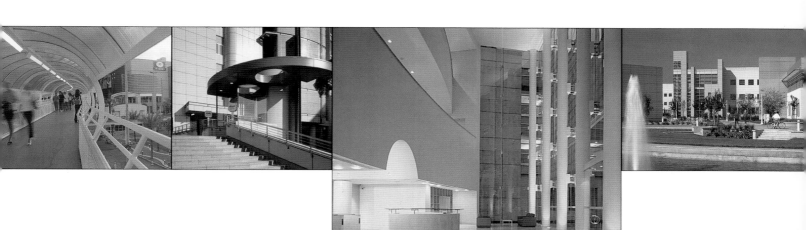

222 Vallejo Street
San Francisco
California 94111
415.398.5191
415.394.7158 (Fax)
www.kmd-arch.com
retail@kmd-arch.com

KMD Architects

Barra Entertainment Center
Rio de Janeiro, Brazil

This 300,000-square-foot entertainment center in southern Rio de Janeiro is located next to a large retail mall, alongside a major highway. As such, it represents an "outpad strategy" for the existing center. Creating an entertainment center on a portion of a retail mall site is becoming a popular and successful strategy in the U.S., as well as internationally. The Barra project includes a 18-screen cinema, a 50,000 s.f. international family entertainment center anchor, music and video stores, themed restaurants and cafes. The heart of the complex is a multistory open-air canyon sheltered from the sun by a vault-shaped fabric canopy. The pedestrian link between the entertainment center and other buildings in the development is a playfully serpentine steel-framed tube.

KMD Architects

Nadya Park
Nagoya, Japan

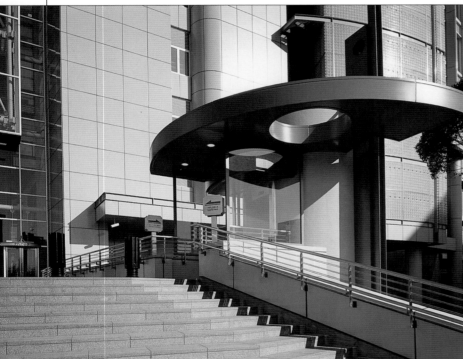

Above: Design Center and office tower, linked by atrium.
Left: Sculptural canopy at entrance.
Photography: Uemetsu-San (above), Isao Harukami (left).

As the first phase of Nagoya's ambitious downtown redevelopment, Nadya Park was the subject of an international design competition won by KMD. Intended to establish the city's emergence as a design capital, the 1-million-square-foot complex comprises a Design Center linked to an office tower by a 165-foot-tall atrium. The sculptural form of the 14-story Design Center houses a 300-seat multi-purpose hall, a design museum, a 700-seat theater, and educational facilities. The 23-story office building, with a seven-story retail and restaurant center at its base, has convex surfaces related to its neighbor. Topping the tower is an elliptical "crown" concealing mechanical systems. Joining the two buildings, the atrium is flooded with natural light and activated by irregular balconies, a glass elevator, and views into the flanking buildings, along with colorful sculpture and signage. A broad deck opening from the atrium provides pedestrian access to the adjoining Yaba Park and the city's center and allows events in the atrium to spill outside.

Top: Retail center lining one side of atrium.
Above: Convex walls with dominant verticals on tower.
Left: Several levels of shopping and dining accessible from atrium.
Photography: Uemetsu-San (above), Isao Harukami (top and left).

189

KMD Architects

3M Corporate Headquarters
Colonia Santa Fe, México

When the company decided to build a 300,000-square-foot suburban headquarters after 50 years in México, emphasis was placed on employee environment and operational flexibility. The traditional "director's floor" was rejected and executives dispersed among their departments. Column-free office floors with 3.66-meter (12-foot) ceilings offer all employees glare-free panoramic views and natural light through floor-to-ceiling windows. A spacious lobby 15 meters (50 feet) high greets prospective clients visiting the interactive product lab/showrooms, conference rooms, and 40-seat auditorium on the lower floors.

Above: Entry, with alabaster screen wall.
Right: Lobby screen wall as after-dark lantern.
Far right and facing page: Employee lounge balconies overlook tall lobby.
Photography: Hector Velasco Facio.

KMD Architects

Sun Microsystems
Newark, California

To accommodate Sun's explosive growth, KMD designed the new campus as part of a design/ build team charged with delivering a 635,000-square-foot facility within 18 months. The first R&D building was occupied just one year from the start of design. Buildings and extensive landscaping are intended to project a relaxed, campus-like image. Five structures are arrayed along an irregularly defined "Main Street," with "outdoor living rooms" and other special spaces along it. The low-rise building masses are punctuated by more playful, colorful vertical elements accommodating entrances, lobbies, stairs, conference rooms, and other support functions.

Right: One of varied structures along "Main Street."
Below: Several buildings overlooking fountain plaza.
Bottom: Portion of "Main Street."
Photography: Michael O'Callahan (right and below), Hensel Phelps (bottom).

Kaufman Meeks + Partners

16000 Memorial
Suite 100
Houston
Texas 77079

281.558.8787
281.558.3337 (Fax)
houston@kaufmanmeeks.com

20401 Birch Street
2nd Floor
Newport Beach
California 92660

949.756.0818
949.756.0817 (Fax)
newport@kaufmanmeeks.com

Dos de Mayo 25, 2-2
08190 Sant Cugat del Valles
Barcelona
Spain

www.kaufmanmeeks.com

barcelona@kaufmanmeeks.com

Kaufman Meeks + Partners

Diagonal Mar
Barcelona, Spain

Left: Two towers of Diagonal Mar's Phase I, overlooking new park.
Below left: Computer rendering of entire 84-acre project.
Bottom left: Unit balcony mock-up.
Bottom right: Phase I under construction.
Facing page: Phase I residential complex, with central recreation and pool area.
3D Imaging: Payne Rowlett.

At the end of Avenida Diagonal, where one of Barcelona's main thoroughfares meets the Mediterranean, U.S. developer Hines is constructing a $600-million mixed-use project on the site of a former railroad yard. The developer convinced the city to rezone the 84 acres to permit residential use and to build a half-mile-long wall, 200 feet deep, to keep the sea from seeping into underground garages. Diagonal Mar will include 940,000 square feet of retail (Spain's largest shopping center), 800,000 square feet of hotel and office space, a 35-acre park (Barcelona's third largest), a 7.5-acre site for a new convention center, and 1,634 luxury condominiums (2.2 million square feet). Phase One of the development's residential portion designed by KM+P, will include two 22-story buildings, a 10/12-story building, and a three-story building aligned on an axis perpendicular to Avenida Diagonal, facing both the sea and the city and defining a new edge for Barcelona. Visible from a long distance, the towers will be topped by shading devices, which will be illuminated by night, above the penthouse units. Phase I, to be completed in 2001, is located next to the retail center and overlooking the park. It will contain 321 apartment units plus eight penthouses, a heated swimming pool, a health club, two tennis courts, children's play areas, gardens, and plazas. Parking will be on two below-ground levels.

Kaufman Meeks + Partners Tierra Del Rey
Marina Del Rey, California

This 170-unit market-rate rental apartment development departs from local conventions by having its parking structure above grade. By building a freestanding multi-story garage, the developers saved time, compared to the typical sub-terranean parking levels, because both structures could go up simultaneously. A popular advantage with residents is the opportunity to park at the level on which they live, reached via bridges at each floor, rather than arriving by elevator from the basement. Completed in 1999, this was the first apartment project with above-ground parking that the architects completed in California. Now, several similar projects are under development across the nation. The architects recommend the scheme where the number of units per-mitted on the site leaves buildable area for such a garage. The apartments are in two adjacent buildings of 123 and 47 units on the 2.27-acre site. Resident amenities include a pool, two spas, a 3,600-square-foot clubhouse, exercise facilities, and a business center. The total cost of the development was $28 million.

Facing page, top: Courtyard façade.
Facing page, bottom: Street front, with variety of balconies.
Top right: Pool patio.
Above right: Clubhouse interior.
Right: Apartments overlooking pool.
Photography: Steve Hinds, except photo at right, Larry Falke.

Kaufman Meeks + Partners

Parkside at Clayton Park
Houston, Texas

Above: Parkside site, seen in center of photo.
Above right: Parkside's open space areas.
Right: Houses along cobblestone street.
Below: Porches making houses neighborly.
Photography: Steve Hinds.

The latest urban design concepts have been applied here to establish a new level of amenity for affordable housing. This gated community was designed to offer the look and feel of a 1940's or 1950's neighborhood. With a density of eight units per acre for the 26-acre area, the developers were able to market houses of 1,200 to 2,200 square feet for prices ranging from the $70,000's to the $100,000's. Because the lots are served by rear alleys and garages are located in the rear, the city granted two variations for 10-foot front building setbacks, instead of the 20-foot setbacks that are typically required by code. This allowed for 50-foot right of ways to become the main thoroughfares and the majority of the homes to front 18-foot cobblestone streets and/or parks. Open space in the development includes 3.5 acres of community park. Parkside has won numerous building industry awards, including a silver award for "best affordable community of the year" in 1999 from the National Association of Homebuilders. The architects see it as a prototype for other affordable housing developments.

Kaufman Meeks + Partners

Village at Museum Park
San Jose, California

Intended to revitalize downtown San Jose, the project restores residential activity to a site surrounded on four sides by uses ranging from commercial and industrial buildings to single-family houses that have been converted to professional offices. It accommodates 117 units (175,589 square feet) on its 3.38-acre property. Along the commercial edge, the development includes work/live stacked lofts with direct street access. On other block fronts are townhouses with step-up stoops and stacked flats. Along the streets, the project offers either 12-foot sidewalks or 6-foot-deep raised townhouse terraces. All units include direct access to one- or two-car garages. North/south and east/west mews through the site offer alternative pedestrian routes and access to internal open spaces.

Above: Pedestrian mews inside the block.
Right: Model of project.
Below right: Main street scene along Gifford Avenue.
Middle right: Corner of block, with live/work units to left, townhouse building to right.
Bottom right: Elevations of live/work and loft units.

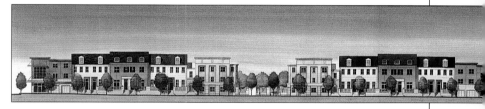

Kaufman Meeks + Partners

Cabot Bay at Bridgeport
Valencia, California

Located in the Neo-Traditional village of Bridgeport in Valencia, Cabot Bay comprises 76 townhouses on two irregularly shaped blocks, with a density of 15 units per acre. As the only attached housing for sale in an affluent neighborhood, the development was granted approval for its extensive use of tradi-tional architectural details such as porches and decks, shutters and dormers, with wood details and colors recalling East Coast precedents. Houses range in size from 1,300 to 1,575 square feet. Individual garages are reached via alleys and are a half-level below front entries. Every house has a 1-1/2-story living room inside the entrance, with other living spaces overlooking it. This lakeside village includes a 15-acre lake, 7,000 square foot Lake Club, future elementary school, parks and playing fields, paseo, and river trails.

Below left: Four-townhouse building seen from entry bridge.
Below: Dining area overlooking living room.
Bottom: Two-story porch in East Colonial style.
Photography: Jeffrey Aron.

Langdon Wilson
Architecture Planning Interiors

1055 Wilshire Boulevard
Suite 1500
Los Angeles
California 90017
213.250.1186
213.482.4654 (Fax)
asadkhan@earthlink.com
bsmith@langdonwilson.com

www.langdonwilson.com

18800 Von Karman Avenue
Suite 200
Irvine
California 92612
949.833.9193
949.833.3098 (Fax)
pallen@lw-oc.com

455 North Third Street
Suite 333
Phoenix
Arizona 85004
602.252.2555
602.252.2760 (Fax)
mschroeder@lwphx.com

Langdon Wilson
Architecture Planning Interiors

J. Paul Getty Museum
Malibu, California

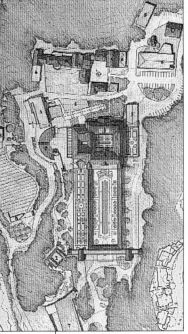

Top: *Rendering of expanded museum.*
Above: *Plan, with auxiliary buildings.*
Above right: *Main courtyard.*
Photography: *Robert C. Cleveland.*

202

Originally completed in 1970 by Langdon Wilson, the Getty's Malibu museum is now being remodeled and expanded by the same firm in association with Machado Silvetti. As a complement to the Getty complex in Los Angeles, this museum is now devoted to ancient classical art. The challenge, as before, is to re-create an ancient Roman villa, modeled after the Villa of the Papyri in Herculaneum, while meeting the demands and codes of a modern museum. The building includes 100,000 square feet, with two floors of galleries, one below-grade floor of offices, a research library, a photographic department, archives, and restoration facilities. The public is served by a bookstore, a cafeteria, and an auditorium for in-house and community programs.

Facing page, top: Main courtyard colonnade from approach drive.
Right: Internal atrium.
Far right: Inside main courtyard colonnade.

Center, above: Interior with characteristic Roman ornament.
Above: Sculpture hall.
Above right: Internal atrium garden.

Langdon Wilson
Architecture Planning Interiors

Phoenix City Hall
Phoenix, Arizona

Top: *Atrium serving City Hall and theater.*
Left: *Tower portion with varied sun baffles.*
Above: *Atrium entrance from new plaza, restored theater at right.*
Photography: *Timothy Hursley.*

This 550,000-square-foot complex consolidates offices formerly dispersed in 20 locations. The new structure shares a city block with the restored 1928 Orpheum Theater, and a new sky-lighted atrium serves both buildings. Public-contact departments on the large lower floors overlook the atrium. Energy-conscious measures include recessing windows behind the concrete building frame and installing exterior sunshades tailored to each exposure. A highly efficient central cooling plant on a lower-floor setback serves these and other public buildings nearby.

Langdon Wilson
Architecture Planning Interiors

World Plaza
Shanghai, China

Top: Lobby serving banking, retail, and offices.
Left: Tower rising over Pudong.
Above: Model of project.

The 48-story tower is the first steel-framed tower built in the new Pudong district of Shanghai. The octagonal form, the sequence of setbacks at upper floors, and the pyramidal roof reinforce the tower image. Polished granite cladding and stainless steel fins lend distinction. A sweeping curve on the lower floors addresses the major street intersection where it is located. The building houses 85,000 square meters (918,000 square feet) of banking, retail, and high-end office space.

La Jolla Commons
La Jolla, California

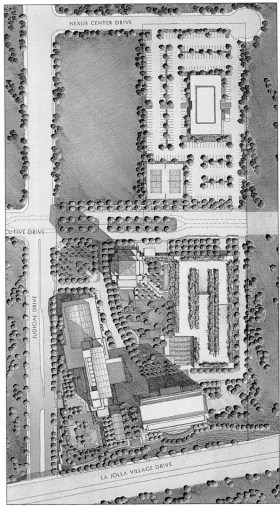

The project represents a unique opportunity to create a signature mixed-use development in northern San Diego County, at the east edge of University City. Prominently located, the project will anchor the business district along the 805 Freeway. The University City master-plan requires a mix of uses within projects of this scale to encourage a vibrant environment, offering residents, guests, and office staffs round-the-clock activity. The plan reserves right of way for a future light rail system and station, as well as future street extensions and widenings. Building limitations imposed by the Miramar Marine Corps Airstation also had to be considered. Planned structures include: a 20-story,

450,000-square-foot office building, a medium-rise 320-room hotel, and a 120-unit condominium tower. The area around and between the buildings will be developed as a series of memorably landscaped public spaces.

Facing page, left: *Aerial rendering with office building in foreground, hotel at left, residential tower beyond.*
Facing page, right: *Plan of project, showing parking structure with landscaped top level at right.*
Illustrations: *Michael Abbott & Associates, Peter Ropen.*

Langdon Wilson
Architecture Planning Interiors

Environmental Protection Agency Regional Headquarters
Kansas City, Kansas

Top: *West entry façade.*
Above: *Canopy at recessed entry.*
Above right: *Façade, showing wall details.*
Photography: *Erich Ansel Koyama.*

Close cooperation between the private developer, the Federal General Services Administration, the EPA, the architects, and the contractor has produced a paradigm of a "green building." The five-story, 220,000-square-foot structure, tailored to the needs of the EPA as tenant, has large floor areas laid out around a front-to-back terraced atrium, allowing light from the central skylight to penetrate the open office areas. Recessed windows with light shelves disperse light to the interior, reducing artificial lighting demand while minimizing solar heat gain. The stone cladding on the west-facing entry façade and precast walls on the other sides have high insulation values, as does the roof. Off-the-shelf environmentally responsible materials used include double low-e glazing with frit patterns, carpet made of recycled tires, and ceiling tile made with recycled slag. Deciduous trees on the entry plaza will block west sun in summer but allow solar warming in winter.

Loebl Schlossman & Hackl

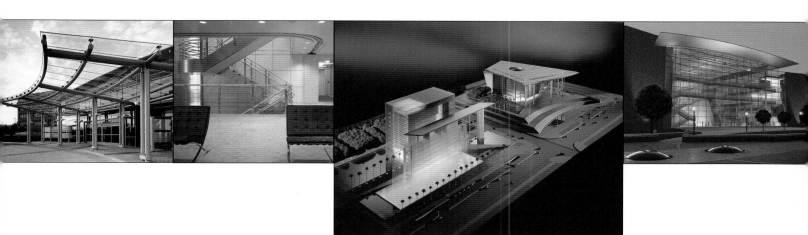

130 East Randolph Drive

Suite 3400

Chicago

Illinois 60601.6313

312.565.1800

312.565.5912 (Fax)

design@lshchicago.com

www.lshdesign.com

Loebl Schlossman & Hackl

Asian Projects

Shenzhen Cultural Center
Shenzhen, China

The project was intended to provide the burgeoning city of Shenzhen with a 2000-seat, world-class concert hall and a state-of-the-art four-million-volume library. Both buildings will face the public green space of the new Shenzhen Cultural Zone. Sharing a common language of materials and forms, the two structures reflect their distinct functions. The library expresses the physicality of book storage in a prismatic bookstack tower – solid within a translucent glass shell – while housing its digital storage and retrieval facilities in a transparent volume behind a computer-driven media façade. The concert hall enclosure is expressed as a polished wood volume behind the glass façade, reminiscent of a musical instrument, emerging within a metaphorical grove of columns that alludes to the park setting.

Luo-Hu Commercial Center
Shenzhen, China

This 47-story mixed-use complex totals 930,000 square feet (86,400 square meters) and includes commercial, hotel, office, and parking facilities. The tower's articulated volumes are clad in tinted, patterned fritted glass and stainless steel. The Sky Pavilion at the top, which accommodates dining, nightclub, and observatory functions, provides a soaring space between monumental steel trusses with clear glass cladding. It is reached by an elevator that transits the building's antenna mast. By day, the tower will appear ethereal and translucent. At night it will become a luminous beacon.

Loebl Schlossman & Hackl

South American Project

**Torre Paris Corporate Headquarters
Santiago, Chile**

The Galmez family commissioned this corporate headquarters to commemorate the 100th anniversary of their arrival in Chile and their success as retailers. The 22-story tower by Loebl Schlossman & Hackl with Jaime Bendersky Arquitectos of Santiago was the winning scheme in an international design competition. Its 200,000 square feet (18,600 square meters) include offices, retail spaces, and five levels of parking below grade. Each side of the building was designed according to the light it receives. Toward the top a keel-shaped glass volume emerges, with a composition of inclined planes and structural members rising to create a ship-like form seen against the city's sky.

Right: Sun visors and canopies adjusted to sun angles.
Below left: Main entrance which leads to commercial gallery.
Below right: Sculptural complex, with projecting forms at top suggesting a ship.
Photography: Guy St. Clair.

Loebl Schlossman & Hackl

Health Care Facilities

Right: Cappuccino bar, showing finishes representative of entire dining facility.
Photography: Bruce Van Inwegen.

Resurrection Medical Center
Dining Facility
Chicago, Illinois

Renovation of the 12,650-square-foot dining facility solved problems of overcrowding, delay, and noise levels and recognized current food-service trends. Seating was expanded to 395, using flexible arrangements of tables, booths, and banquettes. Fissured acoustic tile was installed to reduce noise, and a variety of hardwoods selected to reinforce the comfortable, reassuring atmosphere. The servery was expanded to almost three times its earlier size, with a scatter system reducing lines. A new bar for coffees and pastries was added, positioned so customers can bypass the servery.

Below: Glazed cancer center entry, with V-shaped roof.
Photography: James Steinkamp.

Gottlieb Memorial Hospital
Marjorie G. Weinberg Cancer Care Center
Melrose Park, Illinois

A freestanding building on a hospital campus, this 14,400-square-foot center is one of the most technologically advanced facilities for medical and radiation therapy. A key planning strategy was to place medical oncology areas along exterior glass walls to provide patients outdoor views during their lengthy treatments. Patients and families have the benefit of a large, airy waiting room, while private entrances are provided for non-ambulatory patients. The small building has been given strong identity with horizontally banded brick walls and a prominent glazed entry/lobby pavilion.

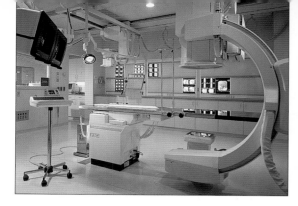

Resurrection Medical Center
Radiology Department
Chicago, Illinois

The first phase of a long-range plan to centralize the hospital's radiology facilities included 5,600 square feet of renovated space – mainly for office and storage functions – plus 8,350 square feet of new construction. For the first time, radiographic and specialized imaging functions are combined in one department. Phases II and III involved renovation of 6,200 square feet and 5,500 square feet, respectively. A two-story glazed atrium runs 50 feet along a main corridor to provide sky views for the internally located department. Interiors have been given a non-institutional atmosphere.

Above: Radiology facilities.
Right: Reception lobby, contemporary yet soothing.
Photography: Bruce Van Inwegen.

Cook County Hospital
Replacement Facility
Chicago, Illinois

The 87-year-old hospital, the nation's first public one, needed a 21st-Century facility for optimum patient care and financial performance. The eight-story, 1,185,000-square-foot facility provides 464 beds and comprehensive outpatient facilities. Patient rooms and medical/surgical suites are located on the upper floors. While incorporating the most advanced technologies and planning strategies, the complex is designed with patient dignity as a prime consideration.

Recognizing that English is not the primary language of all patients and visitors, the way-finding system combines alphanumeric signage with colors and graphic codes for universal communication.

Right: Model of 800-foot-long complex, with patient rooms articulated on upper floors.
Photography: James Steinkamp.

Loebl Schlossman & Hackl

Commercial Projects

Right: Slim tower divided into retail base, hotel middle, and office upper portion.
Photography: George Lambros.

Below left to right: Central fountain in a European courtyard; original design elements enhanced in water garden court; north mall addition.
Photography: Mark Ballogg.

City Place with Omni Hotel Chicago, Illinois
This 40-story, 482,000-square-foot structure accommodates a mix of uses on a site with only 78 feet of frontage along Michigan Avenue. A four-story base, sympathetic to neighboring structures, houses 32,500 square feet of retail. The next 21 floors include 347 hotel suites, conference rooms, and an executive health club. The top 13 floors are dedicated to office spaces with exceptional views, culminating in a sculptural penthouse. The variations in internal modules and fenestration are visible in the granite-and-glass-clad façades.

Old Orchard Shopping Center Skokie, Illinois
Completed nearly 40 years ago by the same architects, the center was an international prototype of the open mall. The current renovation added over 600,000 square feet, including two new anchor department stores, structured parking for 3,000 cars, and a seven-unit theater, for a new total of 1,850,000 square feet. The renovation retained the memorable design aesthetic of the original mall, while transforming its open spaces into distinct courtyards landscaped for year-round interest with various formal and informal themes.

Right: The new tower, located northeast of the insurance giant's original headquarters, filled a tall order, and provided a new identity for Prudential.
Below: Night view of shared plaza.

One and Two Prudential Plaza Chicago, Illinois

The commission included renovation of the 41-story One Prudential Plaza, completed in 1955, and the new 64-story, 1.2-million-square-foot Two Prudential Plaza. A one-acre plaza and a new 5-level underground garage add amenity and convenience for the entire area. The two buildings share a lobby and matching architectural elements at entrance level, where a pair of five-story atria connect them. The new tower's gray and red granite, chevron-shaped facades, and angular spire complement the slablike, stone-clad original building.

Right: New entrance.
Photography: Scott McDonald, Hedrich-Blessing (above left and right); Wayne Cable (right).

Loebl Schlossman & Hackl

Educational Facilities

Illinois State University, Science Laboratory Building Normal, Illinois

To provide state-of-the-art instructional and research labs for their chemistry and biological sciences departments, ISU commissioned a 130,000-square-foot building where the two disciplines can benefit from cross-fertilization. The building creates a campus focal point by providing a public plaza and a walkway connecting student activities. A daylighted four-story entry atrium connects the two departments occupying the building. Workspaces along the exterior receive natural light, and nearby interior spaces obtain "borrowed" light from them. Labs are laid out in repetitive modules, creating flexible areas that can be altered to meet research needs. They include 200 custom-designed see-through fume hoods that are being replicated in science labs all over the country.

Above: Plaza and entry atrium at campus focal point.
Right: Stairs in atrium.
Photography: Scott McDonald, Hedrich Blessing.

Left: Evening view of building front.
Below left: Central skylighted atrium.
Below right: View of front showing continuity of quad and skylighted atrium.

University Electrical and Computer Engineering Building

The new 180,000-square-foot facility is designed to consolidate a department now scattered at several campus locations. State-of-the-art facilities will reflect the reputation of the department and help attract top students and faculty.
The focal point of the structure is the expansive atrium entrance, with a full wall of glass overlooking the quad. Its glass ceiling brings in ample daylight and relates the space to the exterior environment, so that the movement of people in the space becomes a visual display. Facilities will include a suite of virtual classrooms, including two workstation laboratory theaters and a virtual reality theater for cutting-edge research. Large open ancillary areas provide spaces for students and faculty to exchange ideas freely.

MCG Architecture

200 South Los Robles Avenue

Suite 300

Pasadena

California 91101-2483

626.793.9119

626.796.9295 (Fax)

www.mcgarchitecture.com

Irvine

Las Vegas

San Francisco

New York

Long Beach

Cleveland

San Diego

Denver

MCG Architecture

Camino Real Marketplace
Goleta, California

Above: *Buildings with deep eaves, arcades, awnings, and traditional movie marquee embracing public plaza.*
Right: *Bold traditional architecture, with minimal detail and discreet graphics.*

This 82-acre project includes a 47-acre shopping center with 500,000 square feet of leasable retail and entertainment space, plus a community park and play fields. The total project cost of $50 million includes private developer costs and public contributions to the community recreation parts of the site. With such high-profile tenants as Home Depot, Costco, Comp USA, Borders Book Music and Café, and Metropolitan Cinemas, the designers were challenged to provide each tenant with a distinctive architectural identity within a coherent overall development. Commercial and public components of the plan had to be laid out to complement each other. Setback requirement of 40 feet and a location below a flight path influenced the layouts and forms of the buildings. Designed in an abstracted Mission style, the structures have been executed with concrete block and plaster, Spanish tile pavers, wood eaves, and traditional tile roofs. Intricately planned outdoor areas have interlocking pavers, with carefully placed drought-resistant plantings. MCG's full design services extended from initial studies in 1994 through through final design and coordination of tenant build-outs for a January 2000 openings.

MCG Architecture

Cathedral City Redevelopment and Entertainment Center
Cathedral City, California

Below: Aerial rendering of project, forming street wall along the primary entry.
Bottom: Partial elevation along boulevard.
Renderings: Lito Junio.

Plans have been developed for a mixed-use town center in the scenic Palm Desert area, where sprawl has been the prevailing pattern. When this project is completed, it will provide a walkable urban precinct combining public facilities, including a city hall, a police and fire station, and a jail, with privately developed retail, office, residential, cinema, and hotel components. The proposal calls for 68,000 square feet of civic buildings, 46,000 square feet of office, 221,000 square feet of retail, entertainment, and dining, a 350-room hotel, and a 2,900-seat cinema complex clustered around 103,000 square feet of public open space. Parking will be on the periphery of the 20-acre site to preserve the development's pedestrian environment. Each courtyard within the complex is designed as a desert oasis, with a central water feature, and each will have stone paving in intricate patterns recalling the weave designs of the local Cahuilla Indians. Planting will be limited to native species, including drought-resisant palms, in order to conserve water resources for the area's vast agricultural community.

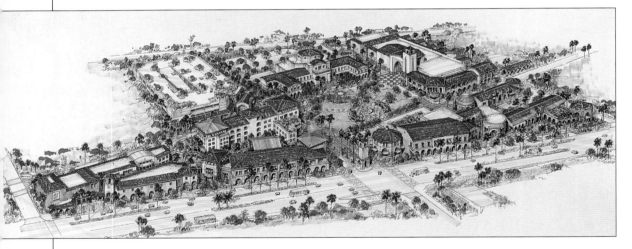

Above: *Sunsplashed courtyard with central fountain, trellises, arcades, and patterned paving.*

MCG Architecture

Galleria at Roseville
Roseville, California

Below: The mall's signature rotunda featuring rose-patterned floor and dome made of industrial metal parts.
Photography: Richard Reinsdorf.

Above: Lower "salon" of terraced outdoor space, with whimsical animal sculptures in central pool.

Left: Clock tower with exposed metal frame and simple light bulbs strung on wires allude to Roseville's farm town past.

The Galleria is meant to provide a sense of community, as well as needed retail facilities, for a Sacramento suburb that has grown from a small agricultural town to a city of 75,000. It introduces a new format for retail centers, with a balance between indoor and outdoor spaces for circulation and gathering. The scale of the complex, which houses 1,120,000 leasable square feet, is broken down by the use of fragmented volumes with a variety of distinct geometries. The idea of fragmentation is then carried further by juxtaposing fragments of traditional high architecture—prominent column capitals, cornices, and arches —with the exposed steel framing characteristic of agricultural buildings once prevalent in Roseville. Indoor and outdoor gathering spaces are conceived as "living rooms," underscoring the agrarian and suburban background of the locale. In the indoor mall, the four major tenants—Nordstrom, Macy's, JC Penney, and Sears—are approached through forecourts in the form of living rooms, with leather divans, plush chairs, rugs, and floor lamps. The 85,000-square-foot principal open space is divided into three "salons" on descending levels. The top salon is the "arts and amphitheater" patio, with a curved performance area and a central pool from which water tumbles to the lower areas.

The central salon has the most vivid "living room" image, with a grand staircase descending from the mall's second floor and a large fireplace symbolizing hearth and home. The final outdoor salon is the children's court, with small-scaled furniture and playground facilities. Tiles decorated by the town's children are embedded in the wall, allowing them to "put their stamp" on this public space.

Right: *Early Doric architecture with lively colors and forms are featured in the food court.*
Below: *Classical architectural details complement the exposed metal roof.*

McLarand Vasquez Emsiek & Partners, Inc.

1900 Main Street

8th floor

Irvine

California 92614

949.809.3388

949.809.3399 (Fax)

www.mve-architects.com

McLarand Vasquez Emsiek & Partners, Inc.

Lake at Las Vegas
Henderson, Nevada

Right: Lake separates resort development (on left) from primarily residential portion.
Below: One proposed hotel/casino complex.
Bottom: Yacht club in Southshore Community.

A four-square-mile tract of rugged land 10 miles from Las Vegas is being developed as a resort with nearly 2,000 residential units and more than 11,000 hotel rooms. Rights to develop this land, with a man-made lake, were assured decades ago, when its owners agreed to accept it as a swap for land submerged by construction of nearby Hoover Dam. The new 325-acre lake divides the project into from the Southshore Community, which is predominantly residential, and the Northshore Community, which will combine hotels, tourist facilities, and four championship golf courses (one completed). The Northshore will include six hotel/casino complexes (one completed), with emphasis on extended family vacations, recreation, and luxurious accommodations. Each includes a beach, several pools, and a marina. Electric boats will shuttle between the hotel marinas and the Southshore community, which will have its own 250-room "boutique" hotel and casino, plus a 200,000-square-foot retail village. The overall objective is to make guests feel they have come to "a place worth visiting."

McLarand Vasquez Emsiek & Partners, Inc.

Los Angeles County Metropolitan Transportation Authority Headquarters

Left: *MTA tower and plaza, tracks and station beyond.*
Right: *Lobby with mural by James Doolin.*
Below left: *Fence and sculpture by artists.*
Below: *Tower entrance.*
Facing page: *Plaza and tower.*
Photography: *Peter Malinowski.*

Long the backyard of the city's Union Station, the site had become a warren of low-intensity uses at the edge of downtown L.A. In the early 1990s, the station was restored as a hub for the renewed commuter rail system and the new subway, and a master plan was drafted for this site. As the first completed component of this plan, the MTA headquarters sets a tone, recalling the 1930s' Hispanic-Deco architecture of the station and other city landmarks. The new transit plaza extends the imagery of the station's revered gardens. The project's art program recalls the WPA efforts of the 1930s. The tower's three-story lobby anticipates links to further development, which calls for a third-level plaza and new buildings above the tracks. Some MTA functions are housed in lower buildings that compose an urban setting around the tower.

McLarand Vasquez Emsiek
& Partners, Inc.

The Water Garden
Santa Monica, California

Above: Glazed atrium-lobby linking pair of office buildings.
Right: Restaurant seating at middle of lake.
Photography: Eric Figge Photography, Inc.

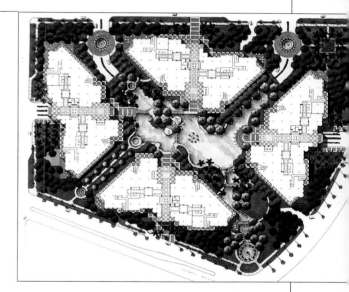

Above: *Promenades crossing lake to dining terrace and planted islands.*
Right: *Site plan, with four groups of paired office buildings.*

So impressed was the city council with the plan for this complex that they unanimously approved five-six-story construction on a site zoned for three-story structures. Office buildings totaling 1,257,000 square feet are laid out in four pairs around a 1.6-acre lake, with rental floors of 26,000 to 68,000 square feet, accommodating a wide variety of tenants. Promenades crossing the lake link the glazed building lobbies and the pavilions, shops, and arcades on islands and around the lake. Beneath the entire project is a three-level parking structure for 3,600 cars, organized for clarity in directing visitors to individual buildings. An on-site wastewater treatment plant reclaims water for irrigation and lake replenishment, a biofiltration system keeps the lake safe for fish, and the recycling of condenser water reduces the complex's water demand by 8,000 gallons per day.

McLarand Vasquez Emsiek & Partners, Inc.

Bridgecourt
Emeryville, California

Right: Core of complex.
Below: View from nearby park.
Bottom: Common room.
Bottom left: Street frontage.
Photography: Eric Figge.

Part of the redevelopment of a former industrial zone, this complex includes 220 residential units in three-story structures above ground-floor parking and retail. With complex financing involving revenue bonds, grants, and tax credits, the developers were able to reserve 91 units for below-market-rate rentals and devise a rent-to-own program that met local concerns about the transience of renters. Community workshops helped establish the types of retail uses and the project's aesthetics. The hard-edged architecture, with bold color accents and metal details, responds to surrounding industrial buildings, some of which are being transformed into artist's live work lofts.

PageSoutherlandPage

Austin

Dallas

Houston

Washington, DC

www.psp.com

PageSoutherlandPage

**Robert E. Johnson
Legislative Office Building
Austin, Texas**

Left: *Building enclosing courtyard, with typical downtown towers in background.*
Right: *Live oak preserved in courtyard.*
Below right: *View of building from street.*
Photography: *Greg Hursley.*

The design of this new state building in the Texas capital was an effort to propose a new pattern for this burgeoning city. Instead of the prevailing bulky building surrounded by parking lots and strips of meaningless landscaping, this complex is designed to provide users and visitors with well-defined courts, passageways, and arcades. Entry to the offices is from a through-building arcade, a kind of civic-scaled breezeway. The building's piers are of load-bearing local granite, recalling the precedent of the nearby capitol. Situated in the courtyard of the complex is the contrasting structure of a polygonal, zinc-clad conference center, with a covered porch overlooking the public open space. In the site planning and landscape design, care was taken to preserve existing live oaks and pecan trees; new cedar elms on the site extend the traditional landscaping of the capitol grounds.

Top of page: *View of courtyard from breezeway building entry.*
Above: *Newly planted cedar elms recall landscaping around capitol.*

Above: Ample daylight in concourse and boarding areas.
Right: Concrete sculptures by John Christensen in garden adjoining terminal.
Photography: Paul Bardagjy (above); John Edward Linden (right).

"We made a significant urban space of the airport terminal," say the architects, "by concentrating shops and food outlets in a central marketplace." This tall, liberally daylighted open space, where primary passenger paths converge, becomes an effective orienting device and a friendly, active place to see and be seen. This space is the heart of a $130-million, 560,000-square-foot expansion of the city's airport that includes restaurants, shops, five new boarding gates, and other airline facilities. Throughout the complex, an accessible, unpretentious character is maintained by exposing structural elements. Steel structural framing of a pragmatic, almost industrial variety is boldly revealed, as is the framing of other elements such as the retail cubicles. Three kinds of modern energy-conserving glass allow for generous daylight to be admitted, minimizing the need for artificial lighting, without unduly raising air-conditioning requirements. The project's extensive art program focuses on Texas themes, interpreted in styles that cover the range from abstraction to realism.

PageSoutherlandPage

Rough Creek Lodge and Conference Center
Glen Rose, Texas

The architects sought to create a friendly gathering place in a complex that includes a hotel, a restaurant, recreation and spa facilities, and meeting spaces. The 51,500-square-foot, $10.9-million center is situated on an 11,000-acre ranch about 50 miles from Fort Worth. A variety of porches, terraces, courts, and walkways at two levels encourages interaction among visitors and enjoyment of spectacular landscape views at all times of year. Structural systems are simply exposed throughout. Local limestone load bearing walls and piers characteristic of central Texas have concrete caps, lintels, and sills. Framing is of heavy timber with steel tension members. The vaulted, metal-clad roof of the main lodge building provides a huge sun visor against the usually cloudless skies. The complex won Texas and Austin Honor Awards from the American Institute of Architects.

Top: Upper walkways offer broad views of lake and plains.
Above left: Lodge structure with curving wood-framed roof that doubles as sun shield.
Far left: Two-story-high stone fireplace as centerpiece of lodge.
Left: Stone piers forming intimate colonnade.
Photography: Greg Hursley, Michael French.

PageSoutherlandPage

Austin Convention Center
Austin, Texas

Above: *Terraces along the back of the center, overlooking a tree-lined creekbed.*
Left: *Amply daylighted polygonal rotunda, which serves as main approach to ballroom.*
Photography: *Greg Hursley (above); Blackmon Winters (left).*

Too often just "big dumb boxes," architects aptly put it, convention centers *can* be active elements in the urban core. This $50-million, 410,000-square-foot structure, which occupies four city blocks, has been made a good neighbor by breaking down its scale into pavilions compatible with other downtown structures. Without a false theme-park effect, it presents the appearance of a group of buildings variously clad in stone, brick, and metal. Lobbies and prefunction spaces are located facing the street, with large glass areas and some outdoor terraces to make their activities visible to the public. To the back of the complex, the center's spaces open onto terraces overlooking a modest creek – a simple but humane gesture for convention-goers who are usually trapped in endless windowless spaces.

PageSoutherlandPage

Rice Lofts
Houston, Texas

From its opening in 1913 until it closed in 1977, the Rice Hotel was an indispensable part of Houston's heritage. After decades of indecision, the landmark was reincarnated as the Rice Lofts, opened in 1998. With a city housing agency as client, the architects carried out a $34-million restoration that transformed the massive structure into a 312-unit apartment building, which was a major step in Houston's downtown revitalization. Loft-type units were designed as desirable to the single professionals most likely to live downtown. A variety of one- and two-bedroom layouts were created – some with gourmet kitchens, for instance, and some with minimal kitchenettes; many have dens convertible to bedrooms for "weekend parents." The hotel's 7,000-square-foot ballroom was restored to its 1925 design, and the lobby's marble floors and walls refurbished. The basement swimming pool, long buried under a concrete slab, is now a feature of the on-site health club. An old annex was removed to make way for a 340-car parking structure. Original ink-on-linen architects' drawings were available, but many surprises from intervening years were found during the restoration, including some mezzanines that were incorporated into unconventional lofts.

Far left: Loft unit with stair to mezzanine.
Left: Lobby restored to original opulence.
Above: Rice Lofts with sidewalk canopy, once customary in Houston.

RTKL Associates Inc.

Baltimore	**Memphis**
410.528.8600	901.624.1600
Dallas	**Miami**
214.871.8877	305.461.3131
Washington	**London**
202.833.4400	44 (0) 20.7306.0404
Los Angeles	**Tokyo**
213.627.7373	81 (0) 3.3583.3401
Chicago	**Hong Kong**
312.704.9900	52.2166.8944
Denver	**Madrid**
303.790.4130	34 (0) 91.426.0980

www.rtkl.com

RTKL Associates Inc.

Shanghai Science
& Technology Museum
Shanghai, China

The new museum will occupy a site on the civic plaza of Pudong, the planned urban development across the river from Shanghai's existing core. Located axially across the plaza from the Pudong Government Complex, the curved roof of Shanghai Science & Technology Museum effectively encloses one side of the public space. The spiraling "wing" shape of the roof represents the trajectory of cutting-edge technology, while the egg-shaped hall directly on the axis stands for the incubation of life. The spherical glazed hall orients visitors, connecting to galleries, an adjacent research library, and administrative facilities. The main building curving around it houses five galleries dealing with the universe, living, intelligence, innovation, and the future. The overall design is intended to reflect the interrelationship between man, nature, science, and technology by symbolically incorporating the five essential elements of Chinese culture: metal, wood, water, fire, and earth. Lighting is designed to highlight the floating roof, with internal illumination making the glass walls less visible. The architects won the commission for the 957,600-square-foot complex through an international competition.

Top right: *Complex facing civic plaza.*
Above: *Main hall of gallery structure.*
Right: *Complex from opposite side.*
Facing page: *Inside central glazed egg.*

RTKL Associates Inc.

Miyazaki Station
Miyazaki, Japan

As a catalyst for center city redevelopment, the station provides an exuberant, high-tech image for this traditional honeymoon resort on Kyushu Island. Grand in scale, but not massive, the 97,000-square-foot structure comprises three distinct elements: a series of deep blue towers marking structural bays, a horizontally louvered frame that screens the train platform from winds, and a yellow canopy along the station's circulation-retail arcade. Principal exterior materials are perforated metal panels, porcelain-enameled panels, and glass. On the interior, ticket windows straddle the public concourse to allow free circulation between retail zones at either end; undulating forms, tropical colors, and light-colored materials underscore Miyazaki's resort character. The station gives the city a lively focal point that appeals to residents, commuters, and tourists.

Above left: *Train platforms.*
Left: *Central entry, marked by distinct façade pattern.*
Below left: *Station in city context.*
Facing page: *Light materials and bright colors expressing Miyazaki's resort role.*
Photography: *Hedrich-Blessing.*

245

RTKL Associates Inc.

Lalaport Shopping Center
Phase 3 Expansion
Minami Funabashi, Japan

A 350,000-square-foot addition brings Japan's first American-style shopping center, opened in 1981, to a total area of 1,850,000 square feet. A crucial element of the expansion was the creation of an open-air pedestrian street. To relieve the narrowness of this public space and minimize its apparent length, its flanking walls were divided into small, varied segments. Paving was given an undulating pattern and a circular space was developed at the end of the street as a gathering place. Indoor elements include a three-story skylighted mall for fashion retailers and a separate three-story restaurant building with 18 tenants.

Left: Outdoor promenades and stairs.
Right: Varied façades on pedestrian street running through development.
Photography: David Whitcomb.

Top left: Restaurant
building and express
escalator to third-floor
food court.
Above: Daylight flooding three-level mall.
Right: View of street
from upper level.

RTKL Associates Inc.

U.S. Capitol Visitor Center
Washington, DC

As the embodiment of the democratic system, the Capitol attracts more then 3 million visitors per year. The four basic goals of this project are security, visitor education, visitor comfort, and functional improvement. These objectives will be accomplished with an underground visitor center beneath a rebuilt East Plaza, which had to respect the historic Fredrick Olmsted landscaping. The granite-paved plaza with fountains, skylights, and plantings will enhance the relationship of the Capitol to its setting. Visitors will enter through symmetrically placed outdoor rooms notched into the Capitol Hill slope. Without obstructing the grounds, the center will provide educational exhibits, a 600-seat cafeteria, a gift shop, and restrooms. At its heart will be a great hall, 100 x 200 feet, with a skylighted 30-foot ceiling. A 450-seat auditorium will be available for visitors, Congressional meetings, and public events. Two 250-seat auditoriums will be used for orientation films. For security, the new center will be able to screen 3,800 visitors per hour. A monumental stair/escalator will move visitors into the Capitol itself.

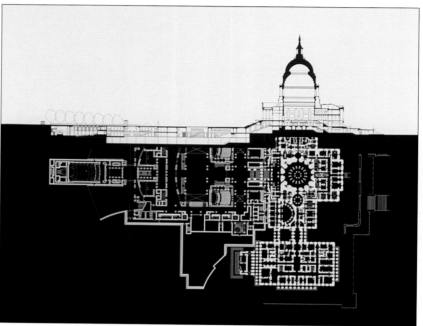

ROMA Design Group

1527 Stockton Street
San Francisco
California 94133
415.616.9900
415.788.8728 (Fax)
www.roma.com
roma@roma.com

ROMA Design Group

Mid-Embarcadero Open Space and Transportation Projects
San Francisco, California

Above left: *New transit stop in the Embarcadero Plaza illuminated at night by traffic, buildings, street lighting and the Millennium Lights.*
Lower left: *The Embarcadero Plaza is a place both of movement and repose.*

Facing page: *The Embarcadero Plaza area ia located at the foot of Market Street and adjacent to the landmark Ferry Building.*
Photography: *Ira Kahn and Herb Lingl.*

At the bay edge of the city on a site once occupied by the elevated Embarcadero Freeway, a series of large scale civic improvements have brought about a transformation of San Francisco's urban waterfront. Approximately twenty acres of land were liberated by the demolition of the Embarcadero Freeway and reclaimed as public space reuniting the city and its downtown waterfront. Located at the foot of Market Street and in front of the landmark Ferry Building, this historic threshold to the city continues to serve as a major cross-roads of travel by ferry, transit, foot, bicycle and private automobile. The design draws upon the traditional role of the area as a center of activity, and integrates complex functional requirements for a mixture of transportation modes. During the day and into the evening hours, the space pulses with movement, as platoons of pedestrians cross the area and move from the bay edge into downtown, as passengers alight from historic trolleys at the Embarcadero transit stop and as bicycles, buses and cars move north and south along the Embarcadero. Today, the space that once served a single transportation purpose is alive with the movement of people - on foot and on bicycles, and in trolleys, buses and cars. Most plazas balance movement with a sense of place. But, unlike the medieval parvis or Renaissance piazza surrounded by buildings in a tight urban pattern, the Mid-Embarcadero is a large open space only partially framed by structures representing vastly different periods in history and of dramatically contrasting scale and texture, ranging from 20th century high rise office buildings, to Gold Rush era boardinghouses. After the earthquake and at the outset of the design process, it became clear that a bold new vision would be required to knit this area back into the fabric of the city and to create a meaningful place out of what was once a freeway right-of-way and buffer lands. As a result, the space was dramatically reconfigured and reoriented to the water, utilizing a sweeping row of paired Canary Island palm trees, the stepping of the inland edge and the placement of two enormous "Millennium Lights" which would "ground" the Ferry Building and flank either side of its tower. Within the city, the Mid-Embarcadero has emerged as the premier place for public gatherings. Its scale and central

location make it an obvious choice for major civic events and activities, which include such annual affairs as the New Year's celebration, the Black and White Ball, the Bay to Breakers race and the Gay and Lesbian Pride Day parade. The space is large enough to be capable of accommodating all of the residents of the city and it is designed to enable one side of the split roadway to be closed to vehicular traffic, and for the trolley tracks to be used for an events "chassis". The tiered edge on the inland side provides built-in overlooks to activities within the plaza and along the roadway. Beyond, the bay itself presents a stage for aquatic activities and a reflective plane for water displays and fireworks. With the completion of significant development projects now underway around the Mid-Embarcadero, including the historic Ferry Building, the Downtown Ferry Terminal, Pier 1, and a new hotel, as well as the rehabilitation of existing office and retail uses, the area will change even further, expanding the population of the area and adding new meaning and layers of social activity. In addition, the Mid-Embarcadero is the "brooch" of a developing necklace of plazas, promenades and parks along the entire length of the urbanized shoreline, from China Basin to the Presidio. Together, this shoreline open space represents the modern-day equivalent of Golden Gate Park, both in the recreational opportunity that it creates, and in its contribution to the image and identity of the city.

Top: *View north, showing the curve of southbound lanes to create a center plaza in front of the Ferry Building.*
Middle: *Pedestrians, bicyclist and transit patrons in the center plaza, and the complex "weave" of granite paving.*
Bottom: *Lunchtime crowds are drawn to the Mid-Embarcadero from nearby office buildings in the downtown.*
Facing page: *View east to the Ferry Building and San Francisco Bay with the Millennium lights "grounding" the open space, the palm trees along the elevated "Malecon" edge and the north and south Ferry Terminal transit stops for the historic "F-line" trolleys.*
Photography: *Ira Kahn and Bob Swanson.*

ROMA Design Group

US Courthouse and Federal Building Plaza and Streetscape
Sacramento, California

Upper left: *Entry to the plaza from the historic rail station to the west.*
Upper right: *View to the new Federal Courthouse and main plaza.*
Bottom: *Patterned weave of paving and seat wall adjacent to fountain.*

Facing page: *View north to the Courthouse, showing plaza and streetscape improvements.*
Photography: *Bob Swanson and Pat Carney.*

ROMA prepared the master plan for the redevelopment of a 175-acre railyard adjacent to the State Capital District in downtown Sacramento. The Federal Courthouse is one of the first new projects to be constructed in the context of these plans. ROMA provided urban design guidance for the architectural design team on overall building massing and orientation, parking and access provisions, public space program, and pedestrian linkages. ROMA was also responsible for the final design and construction of all exterior public spaces on the courthouse site. The plaza provides a gracious entry from two sides of the site, connecting the courthouse to downtown and to the nearby historic rail terminal. It creates a gathering space for visitors, employees, and downtown patrons, as well as an attractive place to meet in small groups, eat lunch, or just sit and watch people go by. Seating is provided along a fountain wall, which emits cooling mists during warm summer months. The plaza space is defined by two prominent light pylons and pulled together by a distinctive pattern of granite paving.

ROMA Design Group

Downtown Ferry Terminal
San Francisco, California

Above: *Evening arrival at the San Francisco Downtown Ferry Terminal, the Millennium Lights ablaze in the night sky.*
Below: *View of the southerly boat basin at the Downtown Ferry Terminal with new breakwater pedestrian access pier.*
Illustrations:*Chris Grubbs.*

In San Francisco, the importance of the ferry system became evident in 1989 when the Loma Prieta earthquake damaged key elements of regional infrastructure, including the Bay Bridge, the Cypress Freeway and the Embarcadero Freeway. The Downtown Ferry Terminal Project was initiated not only to provide an alternative mode of travel, but also to take advantage of the resurgence of ferry travel, with growing patronage attributed to increasing congestion on the highways, the attraction and quality of ferry travel, and the new high speed catamarans that have significantly decreased travel time by water. The Downtown Ferry Terminal, located at the foot of Market Street and the Embarcadero and tied to the historic Ferry Building, represents a significant commitment to the future of ferry service within the Bay Region. It also places equal emphasis on public access and visibility of the shoreline, historic restoration of the Ferry Building (now underway by a private developer) and linkages between the water's edge and the necklace of parks and plazas beginning to emerge along the entire length of the San Francisco waterfront. The project includes the development of two boat basins to the north and the south of the Ferry Building tower for the ultimate berthing of twelve vessels. The new ferry landings incorporate traditional portals and modern mooring facilities to create a strong identity and an appropriate gateway to the city from the bay. In addition, a pedestrian promenade is being built along the shoreline, adjacent to the Ferry Building and extending out into the bay on the breakwater. The project capitalizes upon the exceptional bayfront site and provides new views and access to a portion of the shoreline that has been closed to the public for thirty years. The result is a fully improved harbor for ferries, a Ferry Building with restoration underway, and enhanced pedestrian areas, providing passengers with all of the modern efficiency of new ferry service with the urbanity of a great city.

Sasaki Associates, Inc.

64 Pleasant Street
Watertown
Massachusetts 02472
617.926.3300
617.924.2748 (Fax)
info@sasaki.com
www.sasaki.com

900 North Point Street
Suite B300
San Francisco
California 94109
415.776.7272
415.202.8970 (Fax)
sanfrancisco@sasaki.com

Sasaki Associates, Inc.

**Doosan 100-Year Park
Seoul, Korea**

To commemorate the 100th anniversary of one of Korea's largest business groups, a 1,000-square-foot park has been developed at one of Seoul's busiest intersections. Previously relegated to automobile parking, the site now provides a pleasant respite for pedestrians in an area that includes both historic monuments and increasing numbers of office towers displacing low-rise structures. With only four months to design and execute the park, the design team of landscape architects and several key consultants from Korea and abroad started by convening a charrette workshop involving intense consultation with client representatives. A design executed in three days had to be built in three months, with construction in this heavily trafficked area occurring only from midnight to 5 a.m. Required design elements included a representation of Doosan's original storefront quarters and its 27 subsidiary companies. Lighting was considered crucial—functionally and aesthetically—and the light tower became a prominent element of the design. Native stone and plantings were used throughout.

Above: Replica of Doosan's storefront 100 years earlier.
Right: Entire street-corner park and light tower.
Photography: Seung Hoon Yum.

259

Sasaki Associates, Inc.

Narragansett Landing
Providence, Rhode Island

Right: *Sinuous offshore boardwalk.*
Below: *Waterfront at central park, showing performance area, seawall promenade and boardwalk.*

In this plan for a 250-acre tract stretching more than a mile along the Providence River, old industrial uses are to be replaced by a new residential, business, and recreation district. Along the waterfront will be hundreds of apartments (some with their own boat slips) and a 500-boat marina. Some 4 million square feet of office buildings will be concentrated near Interstate 95. A system of public open spaces will include formal esplanades, boardwalks over the water, and paths winding through wildlife habitats; a 12-acre central park will accommodate festivals and cultural events, and a 20-acre greenway will link the existing Roger Williams Park to the waterfront. There will be new hotels at the marina and on the cen-tral park. Also fronting this park will be shops, restaurants, and a museum. On the promontory at the end of the marina will be the landmark Narragansett Bay Museum. Water taxis and ferryboat landings will enhance connections to points around the bay.

Above: Plan, with Interstate to west (left), central Allen Avenue spine, and river to east (right).
Right: Intimate cove and park at north end of site.

Sasaki Associates, Inc.

Charleston Maritime Center
Charleston, South Carolina

Top : *Plan of area, building in yellow.*
Above: *Structure seen from water.*
Bottom left: *Center with piers and public lawn.*
Bottom right: *Night view showing building transparency.*
Photography: *Greg Hursley.*

The fishing industry and the public will share the benefits of this new five-acre center and its 7,400-square-foot building. On a former industrial site bordering areas of residential and small-scale commercial buildings, the project reconnects the community to the water. The ground floor of the steel and glass structure is largely devoted to a fish-sorting room. Overhead doors provide access for fisherman from the waterside and trucks from the landside. Retail space for selling fish is at one end of this floor. On the second floor is a community room with kitchen, gift shop, and marina management offices. The design of the building draws on the steel framing and metal cladding of nearby industrial buildings and the pared-down components of shrimp boats and racing yachts moored outside. At the same time, it reflects the Charleston tradition of the "single house," typically one room wide with a two-story covered porch — or "piazza" — along one side. With precedents dating from the early 18th Century and showing West Indian influence, such houses are found in the adjoining neighborhood. Here the piazza becomes a viewing platform for waterfront activities. The lawn adjoining the building is a public gathering place for events such as yacht races and sport-fishing tournaments.

Sasaki Associates, Inc.

Dallas Area Transit Mall
Dallas, Texas

Below: Model showing transitway and downtown towers, set near typical canopied station.

Above: Stations along downtown block.
Below: Distinctive paving, lighting and signage towers, and street furniture.
Photography: Greg Hursley.

This 1.2-mile transitway through the heart of downtown Dallas had to be more than just a light-rail corridor in order to gain public acceptance. The landscape architects, who were prime consultants to the Dallas Area Rapid Transit Authority for the $48-million project, led a community outreach program to gain consensus and city approval for the design. While providing sleekly canopied stations, upgraded paving, planting, lighting, benches, trash receptacles, and banners, the project also had to meet Federal "value engineering" criteria and mesh for convenience and safety with existing pedestrian and vehicular circulation. The project has in fact promoted transit ridership and transformed two lifeless downtown streets into active corridors. Current development projects along the mall include two office buildings and a hotel.

Sasaki Associates, Inc.

Americas World Trade District
San Juan, Puerto Rico

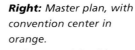

Right: Master plan, with convention center in orange.
Below: Model, with convention center at head of canal, arc of new boulevard to left, existing light-plane airport in foreground.

The government of Puerto Rico has proposed to increase the number of business travelers to the island by developing the first major convention center and world trade center in the Caribbean. The site is a 109-acre former military base at the heart of the San Juan area, adjacent to two desirable urban neighborhoods. As the prime consultants in collaboration with a local firm, the landscape architects led the development of a master plan and design guidelines. The process revealed adjoining derelict properties which created more viable redevelopment parcels and improved the quality of existing areas. The plan is organized around new canal park land, existing and new streets, and a boulevard. The canal connects the front door of the convention center with the other waterways and, ultimately, the ocean, enhancing the feeling of being on an island and allowing for boat links to hotels and other destinations.

Right: Canal-side development, convention center in background.
Bottom: Canal viewed from convention center.

Smallwood, Reynolds, Stewart, Stewart & Associates, Inc.

One Piedmont Center
3565 Piedmont Road
Suite 303
Atlanta
Georgia 30305
404.233.5453
404.264.0929 (Fax)

100 South Ashley Drive
Suite 350
Tampa
Florida 33602
813.221.1226
813.228.9717 (Fax)

83 Clemenceau Avenue #14-03
UE Square
Singapore 239920
Republic of Singapore
65.835.4355
65.835.4322 (Fax)

www.srssa.com
architecture@srssa.com
interiors@srssa.com

**Smallwood, Reynolds,
Stewart, Stewart
& Associates, Inc.**

**Corporate Square
Beijing, People's Republic of China**

Above: *Building mass
modulated by sculptural
variations in facades of
polished stone, enamel-
coated metal panels,
brushed aluminum, and
tinted glass.*
Photography: *John Nye.*

The design of this 90,000-square meter (969,000-square foot) office building integrates "a striving for innovation with the corporate need for an image of solid lasting quality and longevity." Occupying a prominent site at the south end of Beijing Finance Street, a new office district about three kilometers from Tiananmen Square, the structure had to balance a respect for the Beijing context with an expression of uniqueness and vitality. Constrained by a 1.48-hectare (3.66-acre) site and a 60-meter height limitation – with some discretion for penthouse elements – the 17-story building fills most of its allowable volume. Variations in façade treatment and subtle projections break up the overall mass visually. The tiered composition of the top floors further reduces the apparent volume, while increasing the number of corner offices. Three vertical cores serving different zones of the building are reached by a three-story-high atrium lobby. Car and bicycle parking are located below grade. DP Architects Pte. Ltd. were coordination/production architects, and Beijing Xingsheng Architecture & Engineering Design Co. Ltd. were architects of record.

Left: Generous metal and glass canopy at main entrance.
Above: Stone cladding and floors in three-story lobby, recalling traditional banking halls.

267

Smallwood, Reynolds, Stewart, Stewart & Associates, Inc.

Residential Projects

Stratford Court, Singapore

This luxury 25.7-hectare (63-acre) complex offers 268 condominium units organized around two distinctive landscaped courtyards. The east courtyard maintains a serene atmosphere, with formal landscaping featuring quiet fountains. The west courtyard provides an active environment, including swimming and wading pools, a spa, a children's playground, barbecue areas, tennis courts and fitness facilities. Tropical vegetation in both courtyards and bold white building masses with Regency-inspired detail recall turn-of-the-last-century resorts in the region. The two-to-four-bedroom living units include two-level maisonettes on the fourth floor with tall recessed balconies; ground-level units have private gardens behind balustraded walls. Canopied walkways lead from a large elliptical entrance court to the project's 16 elevator cores. A one-level below-grade garage accommodates 306 cars. Local architect for the project was Design Link Architects.

Left: Activity courtyard surrounded by four-story gabled structures.
Below left: Bold relief of white-painted walls as backdrop for formally landscaped courtyard.
Photography: Ng Hwee Yong.

Left: Condominium buildings surrounding Castle Green's spacious recreation courtyard.
Below left: Variegated skyline rising to 13 stories.
Photography: Ng Hwee Yong.

Above right: Apartment towers rising around a recreation area at Bishan North Street 24.
Photography: Ng Hwee Yong.

Castle Green Condominiums, Singapore

The castle-like appearance of this 664-unit condominium complex is established by the square building volumes, with finials at the corners and arched openings. The reinforced concrete structural frames are clad in an appropriately muted combination of tan brick and plaster. All of the two-to-four-bedroom units have open terraces. The buildings are arranged around a large central space for amenities including a swimming pool, a gym/fitness center, three tennis courts, two squash courts, a children's playground, and a jogging trail. The project is located in the northeast section of the island, overlooking the scenic Sungei Seletar Reservoir. Design Link Architects were the local architects.

Bishan North Street 24, Singapore

This 838-unit development of Singapore's Housing and Development Board is an ambitious public housing effort to house both adult professionals and their senior parents. Commissioned as the result of a design/build competition, the complex consists of six buildings, from 24 to 30 stories high, clustered in pairs around a park area with outdoor amenities. The central space includes an amphitheater, a children's playground, a central formal garden, and encircling terrace walkways. Each building has a circular, landscaped drop-off area at its public street front. The four 5-room apartments range from 105 to 120 square meters (1130 to 1300 square feet). A four-story adjoining garage can accommodate 838 cars. Playing courts and a fitness area adjoin the garage. Design Link Architects were the local architects.

Smallwood, Reynolds, Stewart, Stewart & Associates, Inc.

Millennium Tower
Kuala Lumpur, Malaysia

The assignment of Smallwood, Reynolds, Stewart, Stewart & Associates in this case was to redesign the exterior walls and roof treatment of a 25-story office tower that was already under construction. The objective was a distinctive corporate landmark that would introduce a mixed-use development in the Damansara suburb of the Malaysian capital, for which the firm is doing a master plan. The vertical dimension of the 61,500-square meter (662,000-square foot) structure is emphasized by a band of burnished stainless steel cladding rising from a five-story entrance arch to a similar arch at the top of the building. A copper-clad dome then caps the composition, with a pin-

Left: *Vertical band of sculptural stainless steel curtain wall from entrance canopy to rooftop, stressing building's height.*
Photography: *Ng Hwee Yong.*

Left: Main entry.
Above left: *Podium extension, with rooftop colonnade and domed belvedere.*
Above: *Entire tower, showing dome and cupola.*

nacled cupola marking its axis. Cubic sculpting of the envelope at the corners and upper floors reduces the tower's apparent bulk and recalls some of the historic architecture of Southeast Asia. In addition to the stainless steel, wall materials are polished and flame-finished granite, aluminum framing, and tinted glass. An extension of the five-story podium, topped with a trellised roof garden and buttressed by domed belvederes, provides an effective street frontage along the project's perimeter, related to the scale of pedestrians and neighboring buildings. Akitek Teknikarya collaborated in the work as the local architect.

Smallwood, Reynolds, Stewart, Stewart & Associates, Inc.

Hotel Equatorial
Yangon, Myanmar

This 359-room hotel marks a significant addition to visitors' accommodations in the growing city of Yangon. The design recalls the dignity of buildings from the British Colonial era. "Bookend" sections of the cement-plastered facades project toward the street, while the central portion is set back to accommodate a porte cochere and landscaping. At the angular intersection of two flanking streets, a stack of curved balconies adds visual interest. Among the hotel's amenities are three restaurants, a lobby bar, a disco/pub, a grand ballroom, conference rooms, a swimming pool, tennis courts, a fitness center, and retail shops.

Left: Main front with palm-shaded entrance.
Above: Distinctive curved balconies at angular street corner.
Right: Pool deck, recalling angles of abutting streets.
Photography: Ng Hwee Yong.

SmithGroup

SmithGroup JJR
110 Miller Avenue
Ann Arbor
Michigan 48104
734.662.4457
734.662.7520 (Fax)

SmithGroup
1825 Eye Street, NW
Suite 250
Washington, DC 20006
202.842.2100
202.974.4500 (Fax)
www.smithgroup.com

Ann Arbor
Chicago
Detroit
Los Angeles
Madison
Manila
Miami
Phoenix
Reston
San Francisco
Washington, DC

SmithGroup JJR

W.K. Kellogg Foundation Headquarters
Battle Creek, Michigan

Right, top to bottom:
Limestone slab terraces at river edge; waterfall and pool in Mill Race Park; headquarters from river; on city side, building redefining street corridor.

A 14-acre tract of fading downtown along the Battle Creek River has been transformed into a combination foundation headquarters and privately funded public space. The W.K. Kellogg Foundation committed to building its new headquarters in the heart of Battle Creek, where they could reconnect and celebrate the community and cultural heritage that made Kellogg great. SmithGroup JJR guided the Foundation in selecting a site that could establish the link between the commercial core and a rehabilitated stretch of the natural environment. Where a motley line of underutilized retail buildings lined once-prosperous Michigan Avenue, the brick facades of a 280,000-square-foot office structure and its adjoining parking garage now face landscaped sidewalks. Where a river was once hidden behind scrub growth, terraced lawns now step down to

an accessible stream. The new building is unified by the walls of same brick, limestone, and glass on all sides, but the geometry of the city side is clearly urban and that of the riverside relates to the re-created soft landscape. Across Michigan Avenue, Mill Race Park has been developed, with a waterfall commemorating the watercourse originally located there to power Battle Creek's lumber and cereal mills. Across the river, the W.K. Kellogg House has been relocated in a landscaped setting for use as a community meeting place and living quarters for an expert-in-residence program.

SmithGroup Civic Plaza Reconstruction
Phoenix, Arizona

SmithGroup transformed an uninviting 20-acre Symphony Hall Plaza into the "Civic Living Room" in the heart of downtown Phoenix. The new design is sensitive to the intense climate of the desert southwest and to the interface between the plaza and the urban context of metropolitan Phoenix. Permanent features such as a dandelion fountain, pergolas, and totem like light pillars, are designed to be complemented by temporary elements – canopies, a performance stage, and an exhibition hall erected for special events. Fabric structures are used throughout for shade, shelter and festive color. Walls and planters direct pedestrian circulation. Lighting is adaptable to various situations. Planting is limited to indigenous species of the Sonoran Desert.

Above left: Steel framing supporting fabric canopy.
Above right: Evening crowds gathering around performance stage.
Photography: Bill Timmerman.

Above: Christmas season festivities.
Left: Trellises provide spaces to assign for special events.
Right: Palms and paving patterns recognizing desert setting.
Photography: Bill Timmerman.

SmithGroup

U.S. Fish and Wildlife Service National Conservation Training Center Shepherdstown, West Virginia

Above: Campus at dusk.
Left: Informal and formal spaces offer room for dialogue, celebration and reflection..
Below right: Outdoor break-out areas provide opportunities for social interaction.
Below left: Central cluster of buildings shows "campus" configuration and network of quads and paths.
Photography: Prakash Patel.

278

The Conservation Training Center, located on a 540-acre farmstead tract along the Potomac River, is conceived as a community and educational gathering place. Designed as four multiple-building campuses linked by a network of paths and vistas, the Center applies the vocabularies of academic and civic placemaking to order and animate its wooded enclave. Distinct hierarchies of scale, form and material; strong axial relationships; a mix of formal and informal public spaces for dialogue, celebration, and reflection; quadrangles, "public squares" and a network of "streets" running through and between buildings create an environment of intensive social and communal interaction. The 345,000 square foot facility annually accommodates 10,000 students attending day to week-long sessions and a full-time staff of 200. Visually and ecologically harmonious vernacular building forms and materials, proven sustainability strategies, and responsible waste management and energy systems allow the project to rest lightly on the land.

Above: Vernacular forms and materials convey a strong sense of place.
Right: Long vistas communicate a clear relationship between buildings.

SmithGroup JJR

Stroh Riverplace
Detroit, Michigan

Above right: *Concept drawing of riverfront open space.*
Below right: *Landscaped entry walks to residential units.*
Below center: *Richly landscaped pockets of green.*
Below: *Patterned walks and custom lighting.*
Photography: *Paul S. Bednarski*

Revitalization efforts of Detroit's Riverfront began in 1977. The original Parke Davis campus designed by Albert Kahn was in need of upgrading to contemporary corporate standards. A non-profit planning corporation made up of the City of Detroit and Parke Davis Company developed the first redevelopment plan for this old industrial riverfront area. The eventual sale of the property to Stroh Brewery Company for its headquarters, resulted in a mixed-use development of office, residential and commercial uses called the Stroh Riverplace. A team of James Stewart Polshek & Partners and SmithGroup JJR worked collaboratively to preserve the spirit and character of this former industrial facility while adapting it to new and mixed uses.

The Stroh team developed building and site renovation plans, remaining conscious of the ultimate goal of providing improved riverfront access for residents, workers and visitors. A combination of public and private funds were used for upgrading the infrastructure of the site and developing detailed design plans for all pedestrian and landscape surfaces within the complex.

Today the project is one of the best examples of successful public and private *(joint ventures)* partnerships in the Great Lakes region. The development provides the eastern anchor to three miles of riverfront; Detroit's central business district provides the western anchor. Stroh Company and SmithGroup JJR also played a significant *(leadership)* role in getting the Detroit River, a historic international border, designated as an American Heritage River.

Thomas Balsley Associates

31 West 27th Street
New York
New York 10001
212.684.9230
212.684.9232 (Fax)
www.tbany.com
info@tbany.com

Thomas Balsley Associates

Gate City
Tokyo, Japan

Top: North garden, with kiosk and dining terrace.
Right: "Grove" sculpture on entry plaza's geometric paving.
Bottom right: "Phragmites" (reed) sculpture folly and bench.
Bottom left : "Carex" (grass) sculpture folly with illuminated glass block water runnel.
Photography: Thomas Balsley (below right); Kokyu Miwa (others on page).

Two landscaped spaces with sculpture provide unique entrance environments for this mixed office-retail-commercial development on the outskirts of Tokyo. The South Entry Plaza serves as the principal gateway, and a public garden on the north side affords a transition to the residential neighborhood. The strong geometrical patterns of the entry plaza relate to those of the Gate City buildings. A rectangular grove of poplar trees has been bisected by a diagonal entrance path. Each half is enhanced with stone monoliths, fog, water channels and bubbling pools to suggest to visitors and pedestrians a mountain and stream environment. A sculpture of tapered orange columns entitled "The Grove" offers a contrasting interpretation of the forest theme. The public garden to the north is connected to the adjoin-

Right: *South Entry Plaza from above.*
Below: *Lattice panels buffer the motor court.*
Below right: *Channels flowing into foamy basin.*

ing residential area by a bridge over a canal. Its open spaces and gentler geometries present a counterpoint to the entry plaza. Paving near the buildings accommodates events and café tables. Planting increases with distance from the buildings, becoming quite dense at the edge of the canal where organically shaped sculpture follies representing lilies, grasses, and reeds provide semi-private viewing sites for the garden's activity.

Thomas Balsley Associates

Progressive Insurance
Corporate Headquarters
Cleveland, Ohio

The siting of a one-million-square-foot office complex at the edge of a natural woodland inspired abstractions of existing landscape characteristics in the project's open spaces. The courtyard garden between the headquarters' two linear building masses recalls the site's ravine. A stream-like central path and partially buried precast retaining walls, take their cues from the natural shale ledges and the geometries of adjacent buildings. Some stretches of path are paralleled by a meandering gravel "dry streambed." Paved pods extend from the buildings into this landscape to serve as outdoor conference locations. A large outdoor dining terrace situated at a bend in the adjoining ravine provides a platform for viewing the natural site, as well as an exceptional dining experience at the edge of nature. Trees, shrubs, ground covers, and perennials provide seasonal displays of color and texture.

Thomas Balsley Associates

One Penn Plaza
New York, New York

The challenge was to revitalize a failed "bonus plaza," one of those urban spaces a developer provided decades ago in exchange for added interior floor area. The half-acre plaza, across the street from Madison Square Garden, had been shunned by office workers and relegated to drug dealers. After intensive research, the design team decided to add two café terraces to generate activity and to restructure access stairs to improve visibility from the street. The owner's request for a central fountain was transformed into a pyramidal fog sculpture. A dramatic form, placed for maximum visibility, the fog element remains appealing in winter and under windy conditions, while actually cooling air on hot days. A variety of seating, shade trees, evergreens, and perennials add to the plaza's appeal.

Top: Rough granite pyramid sculpture emitting fog.
Above: Raised garden with pyramid on axis.
Right: Central area with variety of seating.
Photography: Thomas Balsley.

Thomas Balsley Associates

Gantry Plaza State Park at Queens West
New York, New York

On a former industrial site, the park takes its name from the derelict gantries once used to transfer railroad freight cars on and off river barges. It is one component of a linear park that will eventually reclaim 1.5 miles of East River waterfront in Queens for public use. Planned in conjunction with the Queens West waterfront redevelopment, this park's design was critical in the acceptance of the larger project by the local community. Though the preserved gantries are the visual centerpieces of the park, it was essential not to take a theme park approach, but to provide a contemporary "common ground" for both existing and new residents. The park consists of three distinct spaces: a lawn promontory extending to the river's edge; an urban plaza with an arc of steps facing an adapted gantry to form a performance space; and an interpretive garden area within the ruins of industrial elements where natural forces are reclaiming the shoreline. Restored pier follies enhance the site's sweeping views. The park's remoteness as an outpost for future developments demanded durable materials such as granite, stainless steel, and tropical hardwoods, with rugged detailing – all of which tie the park appropriately to its industrial past.

Top: Fog fountain at future railroad workers memorial.
Center: Game tables.
Right and bottom: Stone blocks at shoreline; stargazer chaises.
Photography: Thomas Balsley (right); Betsy Pinover Schiff (others on page).

Thomas Balsley Associates

Peggy Rockefeller Plaza
New York, New York

Though confined in area, Rockefeller University has a tradition of fine landscape architecture by the renowned Dan Kiley. When new buildings produced an agglomeration of barren plazas over occupied facilities below, the university held a design competition for the redesign of the space. The winning scheme reconciles a variety of geometries and levels by focusing on a circular ginkgo grove with a fountain. The appeal of the space is further developed with amenities such as a café terrace, a performance lawn, and elevated terraces with spectacular river views. Stone ashlar walls and geometric paving patterns are imports from the main campus by Kiley. Two "Vortex" sculptures by the designers add memorable forms, plus welcome shade, to the upper terrace.

Top: Rendering from competition entry.
Right: Shade sculptures by Thomas Balsley and Steven Tupu.
Center right: Gardens introducing less formal landscape.
Bottom left and right: Two levels with circular features relate to curve of building atrium.
Rendering: Keith Crawford.
Photography: Betsy Pinover Schiff.

TVS/Thompson, Ventulett, Stainback & Associates

1230 Peachtree Street NE

Atlanta

Georgia 30309

404.888.6600

404.888.6700 (Fax)

www.tvsa.com

hhatch@tvsa.com

TVS/Thompson, Ventulett, Stainback & Associates

Atlantic Station
Atlanta, Georgia

Right: Site layout, with interstates to the east.
Below: *Development around oval lake, created from existing watercourse.*
Below right: *Entertainment center in high-density sector.*
Renderings: *Dan Harmon*

290

The largest "brownfield" tract in Georgia, the 138-acre site of a recently closed steel mill, is the subject of this ambitious master plan. The size of the tract and its situation in Midtown Atlanta make it a crucial extension of the city. The plan departs significantly from the automobile-oriented approach to development by providing for integrated living, learning, working, shopping and entertainment within the same district. Proposed for the site are 5,000 residential units, 6 million square feet of office space – including a research village for academic use – 1.5 million square feet of retail and entertainment, and 1,000 hotel rooms. All these had to be accommodated while minimizing environmental impact. It was essential to give the new community a unique sense of place, yet have it work effectively with surrounding communities, encouraging their revitalization. The plan places the highest density of development, with a full mix of uses, on the northeast portion of the site, close to the junction of two interstate highways. Lower-density residential

areas abut existing neighborhoods and extend their street patterns; some buildings fronting major streets have living units above commercial uses, with parking at the centers of blocks. Major streets form links to existing MARTA transit stations. A new bridge spanning I-75/85, designed to recall the site's steel-producing past, forms a symbolic gateway to central Atlanta while providing access to the site for public and private vehicles, cyclists, and pedestrians.

Top: Overall view with high density at the left, pond at the center, and lower density at the right.
Above: Major Boulevard within the site.

TVS/Thompson, Ventulett, Stainback & Associates

Long Beach Convention Center
Long Beach, California

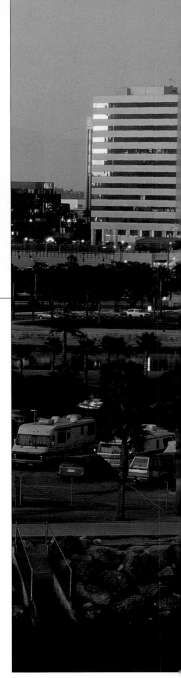

The main elements of this $80-million project include the expansion of an existing exhibit hall from 90,000 to 225,000 square feet and the addition of new lobby/prefunction space, meeting rooms, a 20,000-square-foot ballroom, support facilities, and parking for 1,500 cars. The design takes advantage of two unique site opportunities: first, the extraordinary 180-degree panorama of the Palos Verdes mountains and the Pacific; second, the chance to animate a windswept pedestrian promenade linking

downtown Long Beach to more recent waterfront development (including retail, a hotel, and a marina). Both of these opportunities were fulfilled by stretching a new, large-scaled, glazed concourse along the existing promenade. A construction challenge was to build over and around three existing structures as they continued to function. Stringent seismic requirements had to be met. Architectural imagery was influenced by the seaside location, the nearby marina, and the ocean liner *Queen Mary*, permanently

berthed at Long Beach. The main entrance is flanked by a pair of sculptural elevator towers, capped with dramatic lighting fixtures.

Above: Concourse walls, detailed to carry banners and pennants.
Right: Illuminated concourse as centerpiece of waterfront.
Below left: Access elevator towers at entry stair, topped by sculptural lighting (visible at center of photo to right).
Photography: Brian Gassel, TVS.

Left: Concourse, with outdoor wave-patterned walk above parking levels.
Right: In 50-foot-high concourse: carpet with wave motif, insulated "E" glass with frit patterns to control heat gain and glare.

TVS/Thompson, Ventulett, Stainback & Associates

Mall of Georgia at Mill Creek
Gwinnett County, Georgia

Above: View from Market street linking the village with the anchor.
Left: Food court with train station theme acts as the center piece to the village green and entertainment center.
Far left: Two views showing details along village streets.
Photography: Brian Gassel/TVS.

"A Walk Through Georgia" is the theme of this 1.7-million-square-foot shopping and entertainment complex, located northeast of Atlanta in one of America's fastest growing counties. With an ample 100-acre site, adjacent to an 80-acre nature park, the project was not constrained by the usual space limitations. It combines an indoor mall with an extensive outdoor village recalling the state's small town centers. Mall tenants are encouraged to provide streetlike fronts reflecting the character of Georgia's regions. Interaction between the mall and the village is achieved by the layout of the streets and the character of the entrances. At the center of the development is a 700-seat food court themed to recall Atlanta's old Union Train Station. Surrounding it are specialty retailers, restaurants and, overlooking the food court from the third level, a 20-screen cinema/IMAX entertainment complex.

294

Above: *Central food court recalling Atlanta's old Union Station.*
Left: *Main entrance to the village showing the bandshell and village green flanked by restaurants and enter- tainment retailing.*

TVS/Thompson, Ventulett, Stainback & Associates

Plaza Tobalaba
Santiago, Chile

The crescent configuration of this 300,000 sq. ft. complex embraces a large civic plaza that serves as both park and arrival court for the mall. The vaulted roof and glass walls of the food court combine with sculptural light towers to give the mall a dramatic presence. Large open stairways cascade down from the outdoor dining balcony, connecting the food court with the activity of the plaza and provide opportunities for people watching. The domed elliptically shaped center court punctuates the midpoint of the two level retail concourse and forms the interior arrival court of the exterior plaza.

Above: *Main entrance.*
Right, top to bottom: *Vaulted indoor court; plaza edge; main shopping rotunda.*
Photography: *Brian Gassel, TVS.*

Wallace Roberts & Todd, LLC

260 South Broad Street
Philadelphia
Pennsylvania 19102
215.732.5215
215.732.2551 (Fax)
www.wrtdesign.com

Coral Gables
305.448.0788

Dallas
214.220.2028

Lake Placid
518.523.0224

San Diego
619.696.9303

San Francisco
415.541.0830

Wallace Roberts & Todd, LLC

Canal Walk
Richmond, Virginia

Richmond's Canal Walk is a new pedestrian system that forges important connections, both real and symbolic. Reviving the city's forgotten canals, the project creates an important public amenity, reconnects the city to its history, and provides a catalyst for economic development. A partnership of the city with private developers has completed $30 million worth of public improvements, setting the stage for private office, hotel, residential, and retail development totaling over $240 million. A creative response to an unusual opportunity assured funding for the public portion: persuading authorities to locate a federally mandated combined sewer overflow system in the canal bed covered the cost of excavation and canal bed construction; landscaping and walkways were funded from other sources. Adjoining prop-

Above: Turning basin with downtown beyond.
Left: Iron bridge over canal dates from intervening railroad era.
Photography: Jim Barnett.

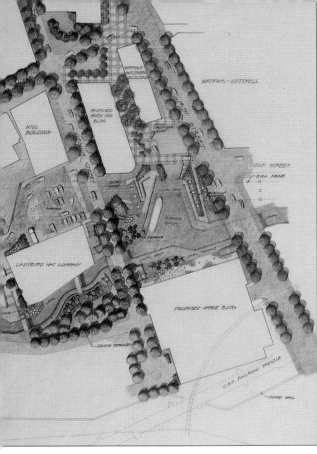

erty owners, participating in the Richmond Riverfront Development Corporation, agreed to site development and design guidelines drawn up by WRT. The plan identifies two zones: a lower canal zone that reflects the area's character in its 1840s heyday, with original canal wall stones and industrial light fixtures, and an upper zone that extends the architecture of the adjacent Shockoe Slip district. All private structures must have active retail along the canal, with historical interpretation required on key parcels. A historic ironworks has been restored as the National Park Service visitor center. Canal Walk has drawn large crowds since its opening in 1999, and plans are well under way for its development sites.

Top: Plan of canal and development parcels.
Above: Boarding a canal boat.
Above right: Building sites and existing structures along canal.
Right: Restored canal and tangle of highways that succeeded it.

Wallace Roberts & Todd, LLC

Washington Avenue Loft District Streetscape St. Louis, Missouri

Right: *"Plaza" portion, with stitch paving patterns echoed in overhead beads of light.*
Below: *Performing area with translucent canopy.*

A six-block area in a once nationally prominent garment district is the subject of this revitalization project. At a time when loft buildings are being rehabilitated for both residential and commercial uses, the city wanted to capitalize on this momentum by improving the area as a regional live/work/play destination. Key design steps toward this goal are the narrowing of the street from four lanes of traffic to two, the widening of sidewalks to facilitate outdoor dining and retail display, and the creation of a two-

block flexible "plaza" suitable for street festivals, performances, and celebrations. The plaza will be paved with interlocking pavers, in a pattern of contrasting colors evoking the stitching that was once the area's economic base. At another point, the south side of an intersecting street has been designed as an urban park, with a glass pavilion, artist-designed seating, and an interactive fountain. Enhancing the area's appeal will be street trees, distinctive graphics, and unique lighting. Indirect street lighting (through reflector panels) will be used to minimize glare on historic

building fronts; sidewalk lighting is provided by cut-off luminaires mounted on street poles, which also have special outlets accommodating speakers and stage lighting for special events. The poles are fabricated of four steel angles to form a cruciform section, inspired by the spare elegance of loft architecture.

Top: *Reduced traffic lanes and widened sidewalks encourage outdoor activities.*
Right: *Partial paving and tree-planting plan.*
Below: *Plan diagram indicating subdistricts and adjacencies.*

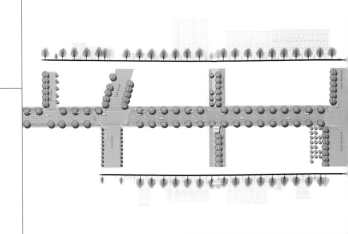

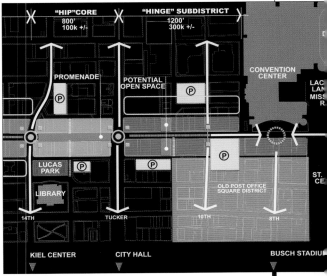

Wallace Roberts & Todd, LLC

**Renovations to South Beach
and Palisades Park
(Beach Improvement Group)
Santa Monica, California**

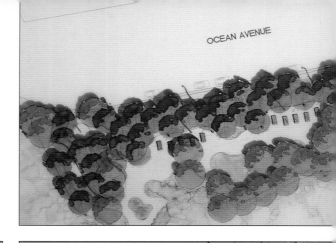

OCEAN AVENUE

Top: Portion of Palisades
Park plan.
Above: Site furnishings
at South Beach.
Left: South Beach prom-
enade.
Photography: Tim
Street-Porter.

WRT and artist Jody Pinto led an interdisciplinary team in the design of landscape, recreation, and infrastructure improvements along Santa Monica's 2.4 miles of oceanfront. Of the five interconnected sections comprising their plan, two key ones have been completed to date. South Beach and Palisades Park present two strikingly different sets of natural and cultural qualities, both identified with Santa Monica. Located adjacent to the famous Santa Monica Pier, South Beach is a 24-acre hub of human activity, home of Muscle Beach and Chess Park, its pedestrian promenade lined with hotels, concessions, and entertainment venues. The objectives of the $3.5-million improvements here were to enhance its unique characteristics with redesigned bicycle and pedestrian paths, a playground, signage, lighting, seating, and trash receptacles. Along the narrow, 1.5-mile stretch of Palisades Park, high on the coastal cliffs, the spectacle is mainly natural, with superb views of the Pacific and the coastal mountains. A lighter design touch here sets a subdued tone for joggers, picnickers, and those seeking relaxation and reflection. A rose garden, a pergola, and stone arches from the

Top: Wall detail showing native shells and beach rock embedded within concrete material.
Above: Path detail with native materials and thematic inset.
Bottom left: Drought tolerant native plantings at Palisades Park.
Below: Historic rose garden in Palisades Park.

Top: New restroom facilities at Palisades Park designed in collaboration with architect Maris Pika.
Center: Old pergola at edge of bluffs.
Right: New path along Palisades Park edge.

early 1900s have been restored and a new path system, lighting, drinking fountains, and fencing installed. Much of the $3.9-million cost of the Palisades section went for efforts to reduce impacts to the fragile bluffs; the land was regraded to drain away from the bluff faces, a water-on-demand irrigation system was installed to reduce soil watering, and some plantings were replaced with drought-tolerant varieties. The preservation of every existing tree in these areas was just one of many criteria established through extensive public participation, along with myriad approvals by government agencies, boards, and commissions.

Zimmer Gunsul Frasca Partnership

320 SW Oak Street
Suite 500
Portland
Oregon 97204   **Portland**
503.224.3860   **Seattle**
503.224.2482 (Fax)   **Los Angeles**
www.zgf.com   **Washington, DC**

Zimmer Gunsul Frasca
Partnership

Westside Light Rail
Portland, Oregon

Left: Washington Park
Station is the deepest
transit tunnel in the U.S.,
260 feet below the park
that includes the city's
zoo and major gardens.
Bottom: Glass block elevator towers identify
Sunset Transit Center,
where three million
square feet of develop-
ment is planned.
Right: Passengers at
Sunset Transit Center.
Photography: Eckert &
Eckert (left, below);
C. Bruce Forster (right).

Right, top to bottom:
Wall at Civic Stadium
Station. At Washington
Park: sculpture with tun-
nel borer traces; cylindri-
cal shafts at entrance;
260-foot core sample dis-
played in station.
Photography: Eckert &
Eckert (1,3); Strode
Eckert Photographic (2,4).

Based on the success of the earlier eastside light rail system, Portland area voters approved a tax measure for an 18-mile line to the west into the fast-growing area known as the Silicon Forest. Completed at a cost of almost $1 billion, the new line was Oregon's largest public project to date. Innovations on the new line include the first U.S. use of high-speed, low-floor light rail cars. Reducing the entry climb from 39 inches to a couple of inches has shortened loading time, thus increasing system capacity without requiring the construction of high boarding platforms, which would be obtrusive at outlying stops. The new cars are equipped with short ramps to accommodate the disabled. Other accessibility features include carefully designed access ramps to stations, Braille panels, raised maps, and accessible emergency walkways. The team approach to design involved artists from the outset, along with architects, engineers, and contractors. Working with local citizens, the design team set out to create distinctive individual stations within overall system design standards.

Zimmer Gunsul Frasca Partnership

California Science Center/Exposition Park
Los Angeles, California

ZGF was commissioned in 1989 to draw up a program and master plan for Exposition Park, a 160-acre public space on the south side of Los Angeles, adjoining the University of Southern California. Throughout its 120-year history, the park has been primarily a site for athletic and exhibition facilities, now including the Memorial Coliseum, the L.A. Sports Arena, the Natural History Museum, and the African-American Museum. At the heart of the plan was the renovation and expansion of the California Science Center, for which ZGF received the architectural commission. Phase I, completed in 1998, involved consolidation of eight existing buildings into one building, which includes an IMAX the-

ater, exhibition galleries, meeting facilities, offices, and retail. This phase also included landscaping improvements, expanded recreational facilities, and improved signage and lighting. Future plans for the park include expanded museum facilities, a new corner park and surrounding promenades.

Above: Restored 1913 façade of Science Center north wing, backdrop for park's historic Rose Garden.
Left: Ancient struggle in park.
Below: Exposition Park master plan.
Photography: Timothy Hursley.

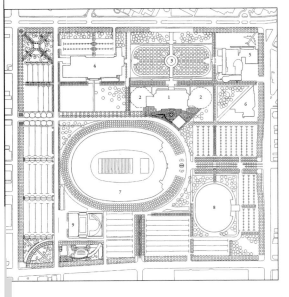

1. California Science Center
2. Future Expansion
3. Rose Garden
4. Natural History Museum of Los Angeles
5. Science Center School
6. African-American Museum
7. Los Angeles Memorial Coliseum
8. Los Angeles Sports Arena
9. Exposition Park Intergenerational Community Center

Above: *Inside entry pavilion, sculpture of 1,600 spheres and central granite bench depicting DNA cross section, both by Larry Kirkland.*
Left: *New recreation area.*
Right: *100-foot-diameter pavilion at Science Center entrance, both symbol and "front porch."*
Photography: *Timothy Hursley.*

Zimmer Gunsul Frasca Partnership

Everett Multimodal Transportation Center
Everett, Washington

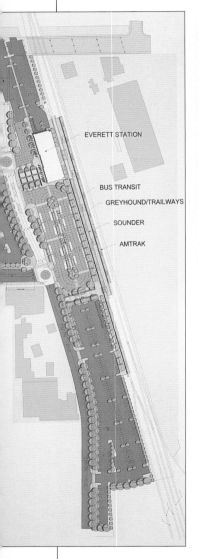

EVERETT STATION

BUS TRANSIT

GREYHOUND/TRAILWAYS

SOUNDER

AMTRAK

Above: Arched entry from city.
Far left: Site plan.
Left: Aerial view from southwest.
Below: Typical façade.
Photography: Chris J. Roberts.

On an 11-acre site, which the architects helped select, this $33 million project is conceived as a center for more than transportation. A 65,000-square-foot building will contain community meeting rooms, a career development center, and an 18,000-square-foot higher education center, offering degree programs from several regional colleges and universities. Transportation facilities provide for both Amtrak and commuter rail platforms, intercity and local buses, community transit, airport shuttles, taxis, and bicycles. Parking spaces for 1,600 cars are integrated with a composition of pedestrian and vehicular bridges, landscaped streets, gardens, and an entry plaza. The crossroads of the project will be the building's central hall, with arched openings facing the downtown area to the east and the Cascade Mountains to the west. A $300,000 public art program will help interpret Everett's history and diversity. Conceived as both a city gateway and a neighborhood centerpiece, the project promises to be a catalyst for redevelopment in its area.

Zimmer Gunsul Frasca Partnership

Bergenline Avenue and Vince Lombardi Stations
Hudson-Bergen Light Rail Transit System
West New York/
Union City and Ridgefield, New Jersey

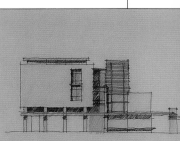

Above: Model of Bergenline Avenue Station, with elevator tower at right, bus platforms at left.
Left: Bergenline Avenue Station plaza.
Right: Preliminary sketch of headhouse.

Above: Partial model of Vince Lombardi Station, featuring referee-signal sculptures recalling coach Lombardi's career.
Photography: Rich Strode.

The light rail system planned for two densely populated counties just across the Hudson River from Manhattan will extend 20.5 miles, 9.5 miles of which opened in early 2000. Two stations designed for the final segment of the system respond to different contexts. At Bergenline Avenue, rail platforms 160 feet below ground use existing rail tunnels. A landmark shaft for high-speed elevators connects them to a headhouse, off-street bus bays, a public market, and a plaza that will form a neighborhood focal point. The architects worked with artist Alison Sky on art installations that reference the natural history of the site at the platform level, and the cultural history of the surrounding community on the surface. The Vince Lombardi Station will feature 300-foot elevated platforms with glass canopies that will be prominently visible from the busy New Jersey Turnpike; an adjacent five-level, 2,000-car garage will facilitate park-and-ride commuting. For this station, ZGF collaborated from the outset with artist Lisa Kaslow on elevator towers topped with sculptured hands symbolizing a referee signaling "touchdown."

Zimmer Gunsul Frasca Partnership

San Diego State University Tunnel Station
San Diego, California

A major intermodal station will be built on the 31,000-student SDSU campus as part of a 5.5-mile extension of the San Diego Trolley. In addition to improving connections between the campus and downtown, the station is intended to reduce the demand for parking on this commuter campus. The design organizes functions in layers, with the trolley platforms 50 feet below grade, a pedestrian mezzanine level opening to terraced green spaces that focus student activities on the campus, and bus stops at the top level on a continuation of Aztec Walk, the school's major pedestrian axis. In the process, the station connects the campus and an adjacent, developing community center on two levels.

Right, top to bottom: Model showing terraced garden, bus access at top; elevation of mezzanine-level arcade; circulation diagram; section through project; detail section showing trolleys, mezzanine, and elevator shafts.
Bottom: Plan of project.

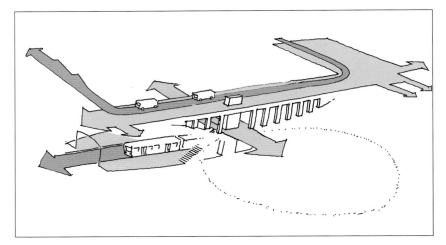

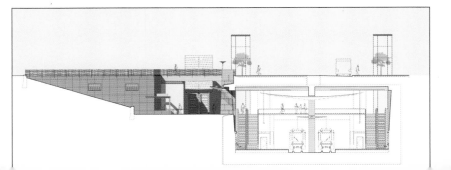

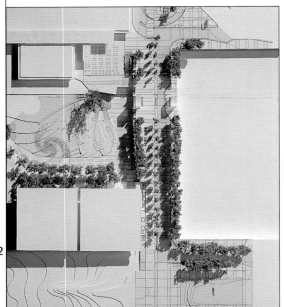

312

PROJECT CREDITS

A. EPSTEIN & SONS INTERNATIONAL, INC.

Comverse Network Systems Campus
Client: Comverse Corp.
Principal consultants:
A. Epstein and Sons International, Inc., architectural competition design

Renishaw
Client: Renishaw Corp.
Principal consultants:
A. Epstein and Sons International, Inc.

Factory Façade Renovation
Client: Gladston Group
Prinicipal consultants:
A. Epstein and Sons International, Inc.
Brickman Group, landscape

ALTOON + PORTER ARCHITECTS

Kaleidoscope
Client: Kaleidoscope Partners
Principal consultants:
Altoon + Porter Architects, LLP, planning, architectural design
ANF & Associates, structural engineer
Hall & Foreman, Inc., civil engineer
Store, Matakovich & Wolfberg, mechanical engineer
Integrated Lighting Design, Inc., lighting consultant
Rolf Jensen & Associates, Inc., code consultant
Stivers & Associates, landscape
Nikolakopulos & Associates, electrical engineers

The Gardens on El Paseo
Client: Madison Realty Partnership
Principal consultants:
Altoon + Porter Architects, LLP, planning, architectural design
Design Workshop, landscape architect
Snyder Langston Real Estate & Services, general contractor
Brandow & Johnston Associates, structural engineer
Store, Matakovich & Wolfberg, mechanical/plumbing engineer
Nikolakopulos & Associates, electrical engineers
Ralph Mellman & Associates, specifications
Patrick Quigley & Associates, specialty lighting design

Warringah Mall, Stage I
Client: Henderson Global Investors
Principal consultants:
Altoon + Porter Architects, LLP, urban master planning, architectural design
Thrum Architects Pty. Ltd., documenting architect
Hyder Consulting Australia Pty. Ltd., structural engineer
Norman Disney & Young, mechanical engineer
Barry Webb & Associates (NSW) Pty. Ltd., electrical engineering/lighting
Site Image, landscape architect
Rider Hunt, quantity surveyor
Birdair, Inc., fabric
Spacetech, fabric

ANTHONY BELLUSCHI / OWP&P ARCHITECTS

Les Quatre Temps Shopping Center
Client: Espace Expansion
Principal consultants:
Anthony Belluschi/OWP&P, awarded commission 2000 in design competition, all architecture, interior and exterior, renovation and expansion
SRA (Saubot-Rouit & Associés) Architectes, architect of record

MetroCity
Client: Gumussuyu Hall San AS
Principal consultants:
Anthony Belluschi/OWP&P, architectural, interior design of retail and residential and entry plaza
Dogan Tekeli - Sami Sisa, architects of record
Metrosite Insaat Musavirlik, Hizmet Ve Tic A.S., project manager
Fatin Uran, architectural consultant
Kate Friedman Design, graphic design
Yuksel Yapi Yatirim A.S., contractor

Park Meadows Retail Resort
Client: TrizecHahn Centers
Principal consultants:
Anthony Belluschi/OWP&P, planning, design development, development

construction documents, construction administration
Eskenazi & Farrell Associates, structural engineer
Civitas, landscape architecture
Communication Arts, graphics/amenities
Paller-Roberts Engineering, civil engineer
Store, Matakovich & Wolfberg, electrical engineer
Double "O" Engineering, mechanical/plumbing engineer
Nuhahn, Inc., contractor

The Shops and Hotel at North Bridge
Client: The John Buck Company
Principal consultants:
Anthony Belluschi/OWP&P, architecture and interior design of retail and hotel shell and core
TT-CBM Engineers, structural engineer
Environmental Systems Design, Inc., M/E/P
Kellermeyer Godfryt Hart, exterior wall
Schuler & Shook, Inc., lighting
Ambrosini Design, Ltd., graphics and signage
AMEC (formerly Morse Diesel), general contractor

BURT HILL KOSAR RITTELLMANN ASSOCIATES

WHYY Technology Center
Client: WHYY, Inc.
Principal consultants:
Burt Hill Kosar Rittelmann Associates, architecture, engineering
David Chou & Associates, structural engineering
Lisa Roth, landscape architecture
Lighting Design Collaborative, lighting design

Minuteman Place
Client: Brickstone Properties, Inc.
Principal consultants:
Burt Hill Kosar Rittelmann Associates, architecture, master planning
John Crowe Associates, landscape architecture

The Wanamaker Building
Client: Brickstone Properties, Inc.
Principal consultants:
Burt Hill Kosar Rittelmann Associates, architecture
Gilbane Building Company, construction manager
John Milner Associates, historical architecture
H.F. Lenz Company, mechanical/electrical engineering
O'Donnell & Naccarato, structural engineering
Environmental Planning & Design, landscape architecture
Lighting Design Collaborative, lighting design

(for Wanamaker Retail Store)
Ewing Cole Cherry Parsky, architecture, mechanical/electrical/structural engineering
E. Clifford Durrell & Sons, Inc., construction management
John Milner Associates, historical architecture
T. Kondos Associates, lighting
Walker Group/CNI, interior design
Long and Tann, Inc., slab impact specialists

300 Park Avenue
Client: Brickstone Properties, Inc.
Principal consultants:
Burt Hill Kosar Rittelmann Associates, architecture
Jack Adams, interior design
Hughes Good O'Leary & Ryan, landscape architecture

DESIGN COLLECTIVE, INC.

The Can Company
Client: Struever Brothers, Eccles and Rouse
Principal consultants:
Design Collective, Inc., historic adaptive reuse planning and design, architectural design, landscape architecture, interior architecture
Morabito Consultants, structural engineers
STV Incorporated, civil engineers
Betty Bird, architectural history and historic preservation

Maple Lawn Farms
Client: G & R Maple Lawn, Inc.
Principal consultants:
Design Collective, Inc., architect and town planner
Gutschick, Little and Weber, P.A., civil engineering
The Traffic Group, transportation

Harborview
Client: Parkway, Swirnow, IGB & Associates, USA, Ltd., now owned by Lubert-Adler, executing subsequent phases
Principal consultants:
Design Collective, Inc., design architects
Vlastimil Koubek, AIA, construction documents architects
M. Paul Friedberg & Partners, landscape architect
Whitman, Requardt & Associates, civil engineer
Mueser Rutledge, marine/geotechnical, geological engineer
Schnabel Foundations, geotechnical engineer
Frederick G. Hunt, P.E., marina and floating dock consultant
Silver Associates, Mechanical, electrical, plumbing engineers
Smislova, Kehnemui & Associates, structural engineers
Desman Parking Associates, parking consultant

Health Sciences and Human Services Library
Client: University of Maryland Baltimore
Principal consultants:
Design Collective, Inc., / Perry Dean Rogers & Partners, Joint Venture, architects and interior design
Smislova, Kehnemui & Associates, structural engineer
KCI Technologies, civil engineer
BR + A / Sullivan Partnership, mechanical/electrical/plumbing
Clark Construction, general contractor
Jay Lucker, library consultant
Kugler Associates, lighting consultant

DESTEFANO AND PARTNERS

Division Street Gateways
Client: City of Chicago Department of Transportation
Principal consultants:
DeStefano and Partners, architectural design, construction documents
McClier Corporation, associate architect
LeMessurier Consultants, structural engineer
Chicago Ornamental Iron Co., fabricator

Madison Street Bridge Revitalization
Client: City of Chicago Department of Transportation and Illinois Department of Transportation
Principal consultants:
DeStefano and Partners, architectural design and construction documents
Clark Dietz, Inc., engineers
Globetrotters Engineering Corp., engineers
Fisher Marantz Stone, lighting

Adams Street Bridge Revitalization
Client: City of Chicago Department of Transportation and Illinois Department of Transportation
Principal consultants:
DeStefano and Partners, architectural design and construction documents
HNTB Architects Engineers Planners, engineers

Sears Tower 2000
Client: The John Buck Company
Principal consultants:
DeStefano and Partners, architectural design
Skidmore, Owings & Merrill, structural engineer
Environmental Systems Design, Inc., mep/life safety engineer
Daniel Weinbach & Associates, landscape architect
David A. Mintz, Inc., lighting consultant
Jaros, Baum & Bolles Consulting Engineers, vertical transportation
Debra Nichols Design, graphics consultant

Alliance Française de Chicago
Client: Alliance Française de Chicago
Principal consultants:
DeStefano and Partners, architectural design
Tylk Gustafson & Associates, structural engineer
WMA Consulting Engineers, Inc., MEP engineer
Project Management Advisors, Inc., project management

Dearborn Plaza
Client: The Alter Group
Principal consultants:
DeStefano and Partners, architectural design
Uzun & Case, structural engineer
Environmental Systems Design, MEP engineer
Daniel Weinbach & Partners, landscape architect

Greenwich Millennium Village
Client: Hutchison Whampoa Properties Ltd.
Principal consultants:
Weintraub DeStefano and Partners, urban design and master planning/architectural design and coordination
Davis Langdon & Everest, quantity surveyors
Hyder Consulting Ltd., ecology, environmental services
Mott McDonald Ltd., infrastructure and engineering
CgMs Planning Consultants, planning
DTZ Debenham Thorpe, property consultants

DEVELOPMENT DESIGN GROUP, INC.

Cavendish Square
Client: Old Mutual Properties
Principal consultants:
Development Design Group, Inc., architects
Stauch, Vorster Architecture, local architects

Cocowalk
Client: Constructa Properties & Grand Oak Partnership
Principal consultants:
Development Design Group, Inc., architects

The Zone @ Rosebank
Client: Old Mutual Properties
Principal consultants:
Development Design Group, Inc., architects
LKA Architects, local architects

Easton Town Center
Client: Georgetown LTD/Steiner & Associates
Principal consultants:
Development Design Group, Inc., architects

Robertson Walk
Client: Centre Point Properties, Ltd.
Principal consultants:
Development Design Group, Inc., architects

DORSKY HODGSON + PARTNERS

Miromar Shoppes
Client: Miromar Development, Inc.
Principal consultants:
Dorsky Hodgson + Partners, master planning and architectural design
Taft Bradshaw, landscape architect
Stephen Feller, mechanical and electrical engineering
Case Contracting, general contractor

Winter Park Village
Client: Don M. Casto Organization
Principal consultants:
Dorsky Hodgson + Partners, master planning and architectural design
Reliance Engineering, structural engineering
Glatting Jackson Kercher Anglin Lopez Rinehart, landscape architect
Bovis Construction Group, general contractor
Stephen Feller, mechanical and electrical engineering

South Boston Waterfront
Client: Corcoran Jennison Companies/Cornerstone Real Estate Advisors, Inc.
Principal consultants:
Arrowstreet, Inc., project design architect
Dorsky Hodgson + Partners, architectural design of residential component

Downtown Hudson
Client: The Hudson Village Development Company
Principal consultants:
Dorsky Hodgson + Partners, master planning and architectural design
Neff & Associates, civil engineering

Rosedale Park
Client: The Magruder Companies
Principal consultants:
Dorsky Hodgson + Partners, architectural design
Dewberry & Davis LLC, civil engineering
Wells & Associates LLC, traffic consultants

The Belcrest Center
Client: Belcrest Center Associates (Taylor Development & Land Co.)
Principal consultants:
Dorsky Hodgson + Partners, architectural design, site concept design
Delon Hampton, civil engineer
Bovis Construction Group, pre-construction services

The Waverly
Client: ZOM Development
Principal consultants:
Dorsky Hodgson + Partners, architectural design
Burton Braswell Middlebrooks Associates, structural engineering
Tilden Lobnitz Cooper, mechanical and electrical engineering

Acacia Shops
Client: Snavely Development
Principal consultants:
Dorsky Hodgson + Partners, architectural design

Sumner on Ridgewood
Client: Sumner on Merriman
Principal consultants:
Dorsky Hodgson + Partners, architectural and interior design
GBC Design, Inc., civil engineering
David Toguchi, landscape architect
Hach & Ebersole, structural engineering
Scheeser Buckley Mayfield, mechanical and electrical engineering

DUANY PLATER-ZYBERK & COMPANY

Vermillion
Client: Nate Bowman
Principal consultants:
Duany Plater-Zyberk & Company, master plan, detailed plans, town architect, urban, architecture, land, and street regulations
Grenfell Architects
William Scott White Landscape Design
D. Turner Architects
J. Abrams Architect

Middleton Hills
Client: Marshall Erdman and Associates
Principal consultants:
Duany Plater-Zyberk & Company, site planning, code writing
Marshall Erdman and Associates, design/build

The Village of Niagara-on-the-Lake
Client: John Hawley and Bud Wright
Principal consultants:
Duany Plater-Zyberk & Company, site planning, code writing
Corbin and Goode, landscape architecture and urbanism
Engineering Concepts Niagara, electrical site servicing
Kerry T. Howe, site servicing engineers
Quartek Group Inc., working drawings and coordination for commercial buildings
Les Andrew, architect consultant for commercial buildings
TND Engineering, traffic, TND, transportation consulting
RGP Transtech Inc., traffic engineers

Prospect
Client: John "Kiki" Wallace
Principal consultants:
Duany Plater-Zyberk & Company, site planning, code writing
Samora Brown, landscape/park engineering, civil
Hobbs Design, graphics

EDSA, EDWARD D. STONE, JR. AND ASSOCIATES

First Union Capitol Center
Client: Southwind Development Corporation
Principal consultant:
EDSA/Edward D. Stone, Jr. and Associates (for the mall plaza and mall improvements, site plan approval assistance) full design services, contract documents for hardscape and landscape, construction administration

Museum of Anthropology
Client: State of Veracruz
Principal consultant:
EDSA/Edward D. Stone, Jr. and Associates, full service design, from schematic design through construction administration, including sculpture terraces, fountain plaza, interior gardens, main entry, exterior terraces, covered gallery patios, perimeter walls, grading, planting.
Edward Durell Stone Associates, architect

Orlando International Airport
Client: Greater Orlando Aviation Authority
Principal consultants:
EDSA/Edward D. Stone, Jr. and Associates, full service design from schematic design through construction administration, including arrival area, site signage, fountains, pool deck, sky atriums, theming, construction observation, full landscape design for interior and exterior areas
KBJ Architects, architecture
Irrigation Concepts, Inc., irrigation
Ken Martin & Associates, fountains
Janice Young and Associates, interior design
Matern Professional Engineering, electrical and mechanical engineering

ELKUS / MANFREDI ARCHITECTS LTD.

CityPlace
Client: CityPlace Partners, Palladium, Related Managing Partners
Principal consultants:
Elkus/Manfredi Architects Ltd, master planning, architectural design, landscape and streetscape design
Wolfberg Alvarez & Partners, architect of record and engineering
E&S Construction Engineers, Inc., mechanical engineering
Craven Thompson & Associates, Inc., civil engineering
Bradshaw, Gill & Associates, landscape architect of record
Sasaki Associates, Inc., landscape design architect
REG Architects, Inc., performance hall architect
Roger Fry AIA, residential architect
Mcbride Co., graphic design
Fisher Marantz Stone, lighting design
Art Assets, art consultant

Sansom Common
Client: University of Pennsylvania
Principal consultants:
Elkus/Manfredi Architects Ltd, master planning for six city blocks, complete architectural services for hotel and retail core/shell.
Jones Lang LaSalle, development manager/client rep
Williams Jackson Ewing, Inc., leasing agent
Antunovich Associates, bookstore interior architect
Brennan Beer Gorman Monk, hotel interior architect
Pennell & Wiltberger, Inc., m/e/p engineer
O'Donnell & Naccarato, structural engineer
Andropogon Associates Ltd., landscape architect
Barton & Martin Engineers, civil engineers
Grenald Waldron Associates, lighting design

ELS

Pioneer Place - Phase II
Client: The Rouse Company
Principal consultants:
ELS, architect
David Evans and Associates, Inc., civil engineer
KPFF Consulting Engineers, structural engineer
MacDonald-Miller Company, Inc., mechanical/plumbing engineer
B&R Electrical Services, Inc., electrical engineer
Sussman/Prejza & Company, Inc., signage and graphics
Fisher Marantz Stone, lighting
Charles M. Salter Associates, Inc., acoustics
Howard S. Wright Construction Company, general contractor

Denver Pavilions
Client: Denver Pavilions Limited Partnership
Principal consultants:
ELS, architect
L.A. Fuess Partners, Inc., structural engineer
Martin/Martin Consulting Engineers, civil engineer
Alfaro Slotka Associates, Inc., mechanical and electrical engineer
George Sexton Associates, lighting
Civitas, Inc., landscape architect
Rolf Jensen & Associates, Inc., life safety
Hensel Phelps Construction Company, general contractor
The Wells Partnership, construction management

Fox California Theater
Client: The Redevelopment Agency of the City of San Jose
Principal consultants:
ELS, architect
Auerbach + Associates, theater consultant
Charles M. Salter Associates, Inc., acoustics
A.T. Heinsbergen, historic finishes
Rutherford & Chekene, structural engineer
Guttman & Blaevoet, mechanical engineer
The Engineering Enterprise, electrical engineer
Auerbach + Glasow, architectural lighting
Brian Kangas Foulk, civil engineer
Tom Richman & Associates, landscape architect
Rudolf & Sletten, construction manager
Anthony Grand, renderer

FENTRESS BRADBURN ARCHITECTS LTD.

City of Oakland Administration Buildings
Client: City of Oakland, California
Principal consultants:
Fentress Bradburn Architects Ltd., site planning, urban planning, master planning, architecture, interior design, renovation, restoration, coordination of team of 41 sub-consultants
Hensel Phelps, contractor
Muller & Caulfield, associate architect
Gerson/Overstreet, associate architect
Y.H. Lee Associates, associate architect
KPa, structural
CMI, mechanical
Rosendin, electrical

Ronstadt Transit Center
Client: City of Tucson, Arizona
Principal consultants:
Fentress Bradburn Architects Ltd., feasibility study, building analysis, site analysis, site design, site planning, urban design, zoning review, code review/analysis, building systems evaluation, project management, conceptual design, schematic design, design review, design development, contract documents, contract administration, bidding, bid evaluation, negotiations, construction administration, cost estimating
Parsons Brinkerhof Quade & Douglas, civil engineering
Moy Nassar, structural
Acorn Davis, mechanical
Rogers Gladwin Rothman, landscape

1999 Broadway
Client: Lawder Corporation of Denver
Principal consultants:
Fentress Bradburn Architects Ltd., planning, architecture, interiors
Severud Perrone Szegeddy Sturm, structural
Herman Blum, mechanical/electrical
EDAW, landscape architecture

Colorado Convention Center
Client: City and County of Denver
Principal consultants:
Fentress Bradburn Architects Ltd., feasibility study, building analysis, site analysis, site design, site planning, land planning, urban design, zoning review, historic research, master planning, project management, architecture including conceptual design
Martin/Martin, structural engineer
M-E, mechanical, electrical, plumbing
Civitas, landscape architecture
Compositions, interiors

FIELD PAOLI ARCHITECTS

Paseo Nuevo
Client: Reininga Corporation
Principal consultants:
Field Paoli Architects, feasibility, site planning, architectural design
Fong Hart Schneider and Partners, landscape
Kraft Structural Engineers, structural
Montgomery & Roberts, mechanical

Downtown Pleasant Hill
Client: Burnham Pacific Properties, LLC
Principal consultants:
Field Paoli Architects, architectural design, construction administration
David Gates and Associates, landscape
KPFF, structural
Architectural Lighting Design, lighting

The Shops at Riverwoods
Client: Esnet
Principal consultants:
Field Paoli Architects, site planning, architectural design, construction administration
Mesa Design Group, landscape
Robinson Meier Jully Associates, structural
Lefler Engineering, mechanical
Architectural Lighting Design, lighting

Draeger's Market
Client: Draeger's
Principal consultants:
Field Paoli Architects, site planning, architectural design, construction administration
David Heldt and Associates, landscape
Dasse Design, structural
Charles & Braun, mechanical
Architectural Lighting Design, lighting

FORD, POWELL & CARSON ARCHITECTS & PLANNERS, INC.

Southern Pacific Depot Historic District
Client: San Antonio Redevelopment Agency/Sunset Station Group
Principal consultants:
Ford, Powell & Carson - St. Paul Square, master plan, architectural guidelines, bridge design; Sunset Station, historic restoration, preservation, and adaptive reuse, architecture
St. Paul Square: JV Architects; Haywood, Jordan McCowan
Sunset Station: Kell, Munoz, Wigodsky; JV Architects

Paseo del Alamo
Client: City of San Antonio
Principal consultants:
Ford, Powell & Carson, architecture and landscape architecture
TVS/Thompson Ventulett Stainback & Associates, associated architects

Downtown Tri-Party Street Improvements
Client: City of San Antonio, Via Metropolitan Mass Transit, and Downtown Owners' Association
Principal consultants:
Ford, Powell & Carson, urban design, including design of sidewalks and street furniture, tree grates; involved in design of pedestrian and traffic illumination and special lighting for historic bridge over Riverwalk
Pape-Dawson Engineers, Inc., civil engineer
Barton Aschman, traffic

Rivercenter Mall Turning Basin
Client: City of San Antonio Special Projects
Principal consultants:
Ford, Powell & Carson, architecture and landscape architecture
K.M. Ng & Associates, civil and structural engineering
Ray Pinnell, P.E., bridge design consultant

Lake Robbins Bridge
Client: The Woodlands, Texas
Principal consultants:
Ford, Powell & Carson, architectural design
Joe Colaco, P.E. of CBM Engineering, bridge engineering

FOX & FOWLE ARCHITECTS

The Reuters Building at 3 Times Square
Client: 3 Times Square Associates, LLC
Principal consultants:
Fox & Fowle Architects, architectural and sustainable design
Cosentini Associates, lighting
Severud Associates, structural engineers
Jaros Baum & Bolles, mep engineers
Tishman Construction Corporation, construction

Industrial and Commercial Bank of China
Client: Industrial and Commercial Bank of China
Principal consultants:
Fox & Fowle Architects, architectural design
East China Architectural Design Institute, construction

The Conde Nast Building at 4 Times Square
Client: The Durst Organization
Principal consultants:
Fox & Fowle Architects, architectural and sustainable design
Tishman Construction Corporation, construction
Cantor Seinuk Group, PC, structural engineers
Cosentini Associates, mechanical engineers

Queens Community College, Port of Entry
Client: Queensborough Community College, City University of New York
Principal consultants:
Fox & Fowle Architects, architectural design

The Bronx Museum
Client: The Bronx Museum
Principal consultants:
Fox & Fowle Architects, site selection, feasibility, architectural design

American Bible Society Renovation and Addition
Client: American Bible Society
Principal consultants:
Fox & Fowle Architects, programming, architectural and interior design
Weiskopf and Pickworth, structural engineers
Goldman Copeland Associates, mep engineers
Whitehouse & Company, graphics

Roosevelt Avenue Subway Station Rehabilitation
Client: New York City Transit Authority
Principal consultants:
Fox & Fowle Architects, architectural design
Vollmer Associates, structural and civil engineer
Cosentini Associates, mep engineer

Hoboken Light Rail Station
Client: New Jersey Transit 21st Century Rail
Principal consultants:
Fox & Fowle Architects, architectural design

Times Square Subway Station Entrance
Client: The Metropolitan Transportation Authority/NYC Transit Authority
Principal consultants:
Fox & Fowle Architects, architectural design
Morse Diesel, construction manager
Atkinson Koven Feinberg, mep engineers
Carlos Dobryn Consulting Engineers, structural engineers
Ann Kale Associates, lighting designer

GARY EDWARD HANDEL + ASSOCIATES

Lincoln Square
Client: Millennium Partners
Principal consultants:
Gary Edward Handel + Associates, coordinating architect
Kohn Pedersen Fox Associates, design architect
Schuman Lichtenstein Claman Efron Architects, architect of record

Lincoln Triangle
Client: Millennium Partners
Principal consultants:
Gary Edward Handel + Associates, design architect
Schuman Lichtenstein Claman Efron Architects, architect of record

Lincoln West
Client: Millennium Partners
Principal consultants:
Gary Edward Handel + Associates, design architect
Schuman Lichtenstein Claman Efron Architects, architect of record

The Phillips Club
Client: Millennium Partners
Principal consultants:
Gary Edward Handel + Associates, architecture and interior design

Sony Metreon
Client: Millennium Partners/WDG Ventures
Principal consultants:
SMWM / Gary Edward Handel + Associates, collaborating architects

Millennium Place
Client: Millennium Partners/MDA Associates
Principal consultants:
Gary Edward Handel + Associates, architect
Childs Bertman Tseckares, architect of record

Four Seasons Hotel
Client: Millennium Partners/WDG Ventures
Principal consultants:
Gary Edward Handel + Associates, design architect
Del Campo & Maru, associate architect

2200 M Street
Client: Millennium Partners/EastBanc
Principal consultants:
Gary Edward Handel + Associates, design architect
Shalom Baranes Associates, associate architect

GGLO, LLC

Willows Lodge
Client: Willows Lodge, LLC
Principal consultants:
GGLO, architecture
Wanzer Munizza, interior design
Walsh Construction Company, general contractor
I.L. Gross, structural engineers
Brumbaugh & Associates, landscape architect
David Evans and Associates, civil engineer

University Village
Client: University Village
Principal consultants:
GGLO, architecture and interior design
McCarthy, general contractor
Hart Crowser Inc., geotechnical
Sparling, Inc., electrical engineering
Skilling Ward Magnusson Barkshire, Inc., structural engineer

Waterfront Landings
Client: Intracorp
Principal consultants:
GGLO, architecture
RSP/EQE, structural engineer
Intracorp Construction, general contractor
Olympic Associates, waterproofing engineer
Portico Group, landscape architect
Brandt & Henderson, interior design
KPFF, civil engineer

4041 Central Plaza Building
Client: SSR Realty Advisors
Principal consultants:
GGLO, architecture
Skilling Ward Magnusson Barkshire, Inc., structural engineer
Lerch-Bates Associates, Inc., elevator consultant

HLM DESIGN

Orange County Courthouse
Client: Orange County Board of Commissioners
Principal consultants:
HLM Design, master planning, programming, courtroom planning and design, interior design, mechanical engineering, electrical engineering, structural engineering, civil engineering, fire protection, landscape architecture, construction administration
A/R/C Associates, Inc., roofing consultant
Acentech, Inc., acoustical consultant
Applied Research Engineering Services Inc., wind engineering consultant
Carter Gobel Associates Inc., correctional programming consultant
Freeport Fountain Design, site/water feature consultant
H.M. Branston & Partners Inc., special lighting consultant
Hanscomb Associates Inc., cost estimating consultant
James L. Cox & Associates, hardware consultant
LBN Inc., vertical transportation
Leming Associates Inc., fire protection consultant
Vanasse Hangen Baistlin Inc., parking design consultant
Morse Diesel Inc., project field superintendent
Harper Mechanical, mechanical contractor
Tri-City Electric, electrical contractor

Arlington County Courthouse
Client: County Board of Arlington
Principal consultants:
HLM Design, architecture, construction administration, structural engineering, mechanical engineering, electrical engineering, civil engineering, interior design, landscape architecture, environmental graphic design, site planning, security support design
Applied Research Engineering Services Inc., wind engineering consultant
Carter Gobel Associates Inc., correctional programming consultant
Gage-Babcock & Associates Inc., fire protection/life safety
Hanscomb Associates Inc., cost estimating
Sylvan R. Shemitz Associates Inc., lighting design
Testwell Craig Berger Inc., exterior wall consultant
Turner Construction Company, construction management
Joiner Consulting Group, acoustical consultant
Lerch, Bates & Associates, elevator consultant

United State Federal Building and Courthouse, Sacramento
Client: General Services Administration
Principal consultants:
NLA/HLM Architects (joint venture of Nacht + Lewis Architects and HLM Design), full design services and construction administration
Capital Engineering Consultants, mechanical engineering
Hanscomb Associates Inc., cost estimating
The Hoyt Company, transportation/parking
Lerch, Bates & Associates, vertical transportation
Omni-Group, Inc., programming
Paoletti Associates Inc., acoustical
Psomas & Associates, civil engineering
Rolf Jensen & Associates, fire/life safety consultant
ROMA Design Group, urban planning/landscape architecture
Middlebrook & Louie Inc., structural engineering
Lehrer McGovern Bovis, construction management
Morse Diesel International, general contractor (phase I)
John F. Otto, Inc., general contractor (phase III)
Heitmann & Associates, Inc., cladding
The Engineering Enterprise, electrical engineering/exterior lighting
The Schatz Consulting Group, finish hardware/security systems
Wallace Kuhl & Associates, Inc., geotechnical engineering
3D/International Inc., interior design
Door + Hardware Consultants, Inc., food service
Laschober & Sovich Inc., landscape architecture
Nishita & Carter Inc., landscape architecture

THE HNTB COMPANIES

Lafayette Big Four Depot/Riehle Plaza
Client: City of Lafayette, Indiana
Principal consultants:
HNTB Corporation, feasibility study, historic agencies coordination, landscape architecture, civil engineering, structural engineering, mechanical engineering, electrical engineering, building move coordination, interior design, construction administration
Blitch Architects, design consultation for pedestrian bridge, towers, and Main Street Bridge.

Raley Field
Client: River City Baseball Associates, LLP
Principal consultants:
HNTB Corporation, full architectural services, structural engineering, construction administration
FP&C Consultants, fire protection and codes
Peabody Engineering, civil engineering
Frank M. Booth, Inc., mechanical and plumbing design-build
Collins Electrical Co., electrical design-build, including sports lighting
Advance Sound and Electronics, sound and broadcast wiring design-build
Duray Equipment, food service design-build
HLA Group, landscape design
Weidner Architectural Signage, signage and graphics
J.R. Roberts Corp., design-build general contractor/cost estimating

Union Station, Kansas City
Client: Union Station Assistance Corporation
Principal consultants:
HNTB Corporation, architect of record, production architect in association with BNIM, CDFM2, Mackey, Mitchell Zahner Associate and Rafael Architects.
Ehrenkrantz & Eckstut/Keyes Condon Florance Architects, design architects
Oehrlein & Associates Architects, preservation architect
Structural Engineering Associates/Ysrael A. Seinuk, structural engineer
Boyd Brown Stude & Cambern (a Division of Transystems Corp.) and Taliaferro & Browne, civil and transportation engineers
HP Environmental and Woodward-Clyde, environmental/geotechnical engineers
Jeffrey R. Bruce & Co., production landscape architect
Ted Mather Lighting Design, lighting design

Tubman Garrett Riverfront Park
Client: Riverfront Development Corporation of Delaware
Principal consultants:
LDR International, Inc., overall riverfront planning, design services for
  key projects including Tubman Garrett Riverfront Park

Savannah Parks
Client: Park and Tree Commission, City of Savannah
Principal consultants:
LDR International, Inc., urban design plans for six park squares, master
  plan for Forsyth Park

Downtown Lakeland
Client: Lakeland Downtown Development Authority
Principal consultants:
LDR International, Inc., overall downtown plan, redesign of Munn Park,
  plan for Lake Mirror Park and Promenade

JAMES, HARWICK + PARTNERS, INC.

Treymore at Cityplace
Client: Carleton Residential Properties
Principal consultants:
James, Harwick + Partners, Inc., architect of record, site planning,
  architectural design, construction administration
Henkel Engineers, Inc., structural engineer
Perry Hescock & Associates, mep engineer
Enviro Design Landcape Planners, landscape architect
Carleton Construction, Ltd., general contractor

The Enclave at Richmond Place
Client: Realty Development Corporation
Principal consultants:
James, Harwick + Partners, Inc., architectural design
J.M. Flannigan & Associates, structural
Adams Davis & Partners, mechanical, electrical, plumbing
AVID Engineering, Inc., civil

The Saulet
Client: Greystar Capital Partners, L.P.
Principal consultants:
James, Harwick + Partners, Inc., architect
Greystar Development & Construction, L.P., construction
Schrenk & Peterson Consulting, civil engineer
SCA Consulting Engineers, structural engineer
Talley Associates, landscape architect
KAI, interior design
Eustis Engineering Co., Inc., geotechnical

Courthouse Square Apartments
Principal consultants:
James, Harwick + Partners, Inc., architectural design

Perimeter Summit Apartments
Principal consultants:
James, Harwick + Partners, Inc., site planning, architectural design
Browder-LeGuizamon, structural
Realty Construction Corporation - J. Lancaster Associates, civil
Brewer - SKAGA, mep
Greg Arnold Associates, landscape

Grand Bank
Principal consultants:
James, Harwick + Partners, Inc., architectural design
Tommy E. Hixson, structural
Trisha Wilson, interiors
Arjo, Inc., mep

JPRA ARCHITECTS

Bay Harbor Marina District
Client: Bay Harbor Company, LLC
Principal consultants:
JPRA Architects, complete design, planning, construction, documents and
field administration

Arizona Mills
Client: The Mills Corporation, Simon DeBartolo Group, and
  The Taubman Company
Principal consultants:
JPRA Architects, complete design, construction documents, and field
  administration for architectural, structural, lighting design,
  environmental graphics, mechanical/electrical/plumbing, selection of all
  interior furnishings for mall food court and project facilities

Somerset Collection
Client: Frankel/Forbes-Cohen Associates
Principal consultants:
JPRA Architects, complete design, construction documents, and field
  administration for architectural, structural, lighting design,
  environmental graphics, mechanical/electrical/plumbing, design of

parking structure, selection and purchase of all interior furnishings for
mall food court and project facilities

KMD ARCHITECTS

Barra Entertainment Center
Client: Grupo Multiplan
Principal consultants:
KMD Architects, architectural design, interior design, lighting design
Clovis Barros, construction documents
Joao Fortes Engenharia Ltd., general contractor

Nadya Park
Client: Toyoshi Nakano, Mitsubishi Trust Bank
Principal consultants:
KMD Architects, prime architect, architectural design
Daiken Sekkei, associate architect, engineer-of-record
Toda Construction Company, construction manager
Futaba Sekisan, cost consultant
Doubles Wave, retail marketing

3M Corporate Headquarters
Client: 3M Mexico S.A. de C.V.
Principal consultants:
KMD Architects, architect-of-record, design architect, prime architect,
  production architect
KMD Mexico, Carlos Fernandez del Valle in coordination with 3M interior
  department, interior design
KMD Mexico/Espacios Verdes, landscape architect
Alonso y Miranda Ingenieria, structural engineer
Rheinland Consultants International, mechanical engineer
High Tech Services, electrical engineer
IESSA, construction manager
Grupo Gut S.A. de C.V., general contractor

Sun Microsystems
Client: Sun Microsystems
Principal consultants:
KMD Architects, prime architect
Bottom Duvivier, associate architect
Jacobs Engineering, owner's representative
Ove Arup & Partners, m/e/p engineers
Rutherford & Chekene, structural engineers
Guzzardo & Associates, Inc., landscape architect
Hanscomb Inc., cost estimator
Treadwell & Rollo, geotechnical consultant
DPR Construction, general contractor

KAUFMAN MEEKS + PARTNERS

Diagonal Mar
Client: Hines
Principal consultants:
Kaufman Meeks + Partners, design architects for condominium complex
BST, Barcelona, collaborating architect, phase one
Tusquets, Diaz and Associates, Barcelona, collaborating architects for
  phase two and three
Enric Miralles of Barcelona firm Miralles/Tagliabue, joint designers of
  park
EDAW, joint designers of park

Tierra del Rey
Client: Legacy Partners
Principal consultants:
Kaufman Meeks + Partners, architectural design, land planning
HRP Landesign, landscape architecture
Faulkner Design Group, interior design
Psomas and Associates, civil engineer
Trical Construction, Inc., contractor

Parkside at Clayton Park
Client: Parkside
Principal consultants:
Kaufman Meeks + Partners, architecture, land planning
McDugald Steele Landscape Architects, landscape architect
Kathy Andrews Interiors, interior design
Brown and Gay Engineers, civil engineers

Village at Museum Park
Client: Legacy Partners
Principal consultants:
Kaufman Meeks + Partners, architectural design, land planning
Civil Engineering Associates, civil engineer
Daniel Silverie III, Inc., general contractor
Guzzardo Associates, landscape architect
Biggs Cardosa Associates, Inc., structural engineer

Cabot Bay at Bridgeport
Client: Greystone Homes
Principal consultants:
Kaufman Meeks + Partners, architectural design, land planning
The Collaborative West, landscape architect
Pacific Dimensions, Inc., interior design

LANGDON WILSON ARCHITECTURE

J. Paul Getty Museum, Malibu
Client: The J. Paul Getty Trust
Principal consultants:
Langdon Wilson in association with Machado & Silvetti, architects for restoration and new facilities
Denis Kurutz, landscape
Ove Arup, mechanical
Nabih Youssef, structural

La Jolla Commons
Client: Polygon Development
Principal consultants:
Langdon Wilson, master planning, architectural design
Joseph Wong Design Associates, Inc., hotel architect
Perkins & Company, condominium architect
Wimmer Yamada & Caughey, landscape
Paul Friedberg, landscape

Phoenix City Hall
Client: City of Phoenix
Principal consultants:
Langdon Wilson, programming, architectural and interior design, A/E documents, construction administration
Evans Kuhn, civil
Paragon, structural
Bridges & Paxton, mechanical/electrical
Carol Schuler, landscape

Environmental Protection Agency Regional Headquarters
Client: Koll Real Estate Group; Environmental Protection Agency (tenant)
Principal consultants:
Langdon Wilson, programming, architectural and interior design, A/E documents, construction administration
MHI, structural
Fred Brown, electrical
Tsuchiyama & Kaino, mechanical
Sylvan Lighting, lighting design
Koll Construction, general contractor

World Plaza
Client: Shanghai Ming Tai Real Estate Co.
Principal consultants:
Langdon Wilson, architects
Martin & Huang, structural
William Yang & Associates, mep

LOEBL SCHLOSSMAN & HACKL

Shenzhen Cultural Center
Client: Shenzhen Cultural Bureau
Principal consultants:
Loebl Schlossman & Hackl, design architect, master planning, programming, schematic design
Shenzhen University Institute of Architectural Design, associate architect
The Talaske Group, acoustical consultants

Luo-Hu Commercial Center
Client: Shang Long Investment & Development Company, Ltd.
Principal consultants:
Loebl Schlossman & Hackl, design architect, master planning, programming, schematic design
Shenzhen University Institute of Architectural Design, associate architect

Torre Paris Corporate Headquarters
Client: The Galmez Family of Almacenes Paris LTDA
Principal consultants:
Loebl Schlossman & Hackl, design architect, site planning, programming, space planning, schematic design, design development, interior design, construction documents
Jaime Bendersky Arquitectos, associate architect
Alfredo Fleischmann, electrical engineering
Arze, Recine & Associates, structural engineering
Empresa Construction Tecsa S.A., contractor

Resurrection Medical Center, Dining Facility
Client: Resurrection Health Care Corporation
Principal consultants:
Loebl Schlossman & Hackl, design architect, programming, space planning, schematic design, design development, construction documents, bidding and negotiation, construction administration, interior design, A.D.A. compliance, certificate of need

Dickerson Engineering, electrical engineering
Janows Design Associates, food service
Robert G. Burkhardt & Associates, m/e/p engineering
Power Construction Company, LLC, contractor

Marjorie G. Weinberg Cancer Care Center
Client: Gottlieb Community Health Services
Principal consultants:
Loebl Schlossman & Hackl, design architect, site planning, programming, space planning, schematic design, design development, construction documents, bidding and negotiation, construction administration, interior design, A.D.A. compliance
Paul Veit, landscape architect
Rittweger & Tokay Inc., structural engineering
SDI Consultants, Ltd., civil engineering
Robert G. Burkhardt & Associates, mechanical/electrical engineering
The George Solitt Construction Company, contractor

Resurrection Medical Center, Radiology Department
Client: Resurrection Health Care Corporation
Principal consultants:
Loebl Schlossman & Hackl, design architect, programming, space planning, schematic design, design development, construction documents, interior design
Robert G. Burkhardt & Associates, mechanical engineering
Dickerson Engineering, electrical engineering
Beer Gorski & Graff, Ltd., structural engineering
Power Construction Company, LLC, contractor

Cook County Hospital
Client: Cook County Bureau of Health Services
Principal consultants:
CCH Design Group-headed by Loebl Schlossman & Hackl, includes:
McDonough Associates, Inc., mechanical, electrical, structural engineering
Globetrotters Engineering Corporation, m/e/p engineering, fire protection
Henningson, Durham & Richardson, medical planning & design, programming
Loebl Schlossman & Hackl, master planning, schematic design, design development, construction documents, bidding and negotiation, construction administration, interior design, A.D.A. compliance
Walsh/Riteway: A Joint Venture, construction manager

City Place with Omni Hotel
Client: Fifield Companies, Ltd. and VMS Realty Partners
Principal consultants:
Loebl Schlossman & Hackl, design architect, site planning, programming, space planning, schematic design, design development, construction documents, bidding and negotiation, construction administration
Environmental Systems Design, mechanical, electrical engineering
McDonough Associates, Inc., civil engineering
Chris Stefanos Associates, structural engineering
Power/Perini Joint Venture, contractors

Old Orchard Shopping Center
Client: JMB Retail Properties Co.
Principal consultants:
Loebl Schlossman & Hackl, design architect, planning, schematic design, design development, construction documents, construction administration
Ives/Ryan Group, Inc., landscape architecture
Design Development Group, associate architect
Environmental Systems Design, engineering
W.E. O'Neil Construction Company, contractor

One and Two Prudential Plaza
Client: Prudential Plaza Associates and NLI Properties
Principal consultants:
Loebl Schlossman & Hackl, design architect, master planning, programming, schematic design, design development, contract documents, contract administration, landscaping, A.D.A. compliance
McDonough Associates, Inc., site and civil engineering
CBM Engineers, Inc., structural engineering
Environmental Systems Design, mechanical and electrical engineering
Garrison Inc., owner's consultant
Turner Construction Company, contractor, new tower
Pepper Construction Company, contractor, renovation

Illinois State University, Science Laboratory
Client: State of Illinois Capital Development Board
Principal consultants:
Loebl Schlossman & Hackl, design architect, site planning, master planning, programming, schematic design, design development, construction documents, bidding and negotiation, construction administration, interior design, A.D.A. compliance
Gordon Burns and Associates, associate architects
Beer Gorski & Graff Ltd, structural engineering
Henneman Raufeisen Associates, m/e/p consulting

Research Facilities Design, laboratory consulting
Diversified Buildings, Inc., contractor

University Electrical and Computer Engineering Building
Client: State of Illinois Capital Development Board
Principal consultants:
Loebl Schlossman & Hackl, design architect, site planning, master planning, programming, schematic design
Earl Walls Associates, laboratory consultants
Bard, Rao + Athanas Consultants, mechanical engineering
Bowman Barrett & Associates, structural engineering

MCG ARCHITECTURE

Camino Real Marketplace
Client: Wynmark Company
Principal consultants:
MCG Architecture, design studies, schematics, architectural design, color and materials selection, graphics, coordination with tenants, construction documents, construction administration
B3 Architects, master planning and landscape architecture

Cathedral City
Client: Palm Canyon Partners, LLC
Principal consultants:
MCG Architecture, urban plan, site studies, design studies, public spaces and sequencing, massing studies, architectural design, color and materials selection, graphics
Sarah Huie Design, environmental graphics, signage
IMA + Design, landscape architecture

Galleria at Roseville
Client: Urban Shopping Centers, Inc.
Principal consultants:
MCG Architecture, design studies, site studies, entitlement services, cost analysis, variations, architectural design, environmental design, landscape concept, artist collaboration
Sarah Huie Design, environmental graphics, signage
Lighting Design Alliance, lighting
MacKay & Somps, civil engineers
Shenberger & Associates, structural engineers
Syska & Hennessy, Inc., mep engineers
Code Consultants, Inc., code
Mesa Design Group, landscape architecture
John Hess & Associates, vertical transportation

MCLARAND VASQUEZ EMSIEK & PARTNERS, INC.

The Water Garden
Client: J.H. Snyder Company
Principal consultants:
McLarand Vasquez Emsiek & Partners, Inc., master planning, design, construction documents, construction administration
Robert Englekirk Consulting Structural Engineers, structural engineers
Tsuchaiyama & Kaino, mechanical engineers
Fredrick Brown Associates, electrical engineers
SWA Group, landscape architects
C.W. Cook Company, civil engineers

Lakes at Las Vegas
Client: Transcontinental Properties
Principal consultants:
McLarand Vasquez Emsiek & Partners, Inc., master planning
Jack Nicklaus, golf courses
Peridian Group, landscape architect

Los Angeles County Metropolitan Transportation Authority Headquarters
Client: Catellus Development Corporation/Los Angeles County Metropolitan Transportation Authority
Principal consultants:
McLarand Vasquez Emsiek & Partners, Inc., planning, design, construction documents, construction administration
Martin & Huang International, Inc., structural engineer
Tsuchiyama & Kaino, mechanical engineer
Levine/Seegel Associates, electrical engineer
The Mollenhauer Group, civil engineer
Olin Partnership, Ltd./Fong Hart Schneider & Partners, landscape architect
Charles Pankow Builders, Inc., contractor

Bridgecourt
Client: Catellus Residential Group
Principal consultants:
McLarand Vasquez Emsiek & Partners, Inc., planning, design, construction documents, construction administration
Guzzardo & Associates, Inc., landscape architect
KPFF, structural engineer
MHC, mechanical engineer
HCP, electrical engineer
Saddleback Interiors, interior design of clubhouse

PAGESOUTHERLANDPAGE

Robert E. Johnson Legislative Office Building
Client: General Services Commission, State of Texas
Principal consultants:
PageSoutherlandPage, programming and planning, architectural, mechanical, electrical, and civil engineering design, interior design
Jaster-Quintanilla & Associates, structural engineering
The Landscape Collaborative, landscape architecture
Project Cost Resources, cost estimating
Berkebile Nelson Immerschuh McDowell, sustainability consultants
ENSAR Group, sustainability consultants

Barbara Jordan Passenger Terminal Complex, Austin-Bergstrom International Airport
Client: City of Austin, Texas
Principal consultants:
PageSoutherlandPage, prime architect/engineer, with responsibility for planning, architectural and engineering design, interior design
Gensler, design architect
Lawrence W. Speck, FAIA, design architect
Cotera, Kolar, Negrete & Reed, associated architect
TCI - Landrum and Brown, aviation planners
Burns & McDonnel, associated engineers
Jaster-Quintanilla & Associates, structural engineers
Lozano Ortiz & Kent, associated engineers

Rough Creek Lodge and Conference Center
Client: J.Q. Enterprises
Principal consultants:
PageSoutherlandPage, planning, architectural and engineering design
Jaster-Quintanilla & Associates, structural engineers
Childress Engineers, civil engineers
Craig Roberts Associates, lighting
Site Planning Site Development, landscape architecture
H.G. Rice and Company, food service
Vivian Nichols Associates, interior design
Armstrong Berger, Inc., pool design
Accessology, Inc., accessibility specialist

Austin Convention Center
Client: City of Austin
Principal consultants:
PageSoutherlandPage, prime architect-engineer for 26-member Austin Collaborative Venture, responsible for site selection, planning and programming, public participation, architectural and mechanical, electrical and civil engineering design, and interior design, as well as development of district master plan and urban design guidelines for surrounding 40-block CBD area
Ellerbe Becket, structural engineering
Cotera, Colar, Negrete & Reed, associate architects
Boner Associates, acoustics and a/v
QTM Engineering, telecommunications
Johnson Johnson & Roy, landscape architecture
Archillume Lighting Design, lighting
H.G. Rice and Company, food service
Wilbur Smith, transportation engineering

Rice Lofts
Client: Houston Housing Finance Corporation
Principal consultants:
PageSoutherlandPage, architectural design, mechanical, electrical and plumbing design, interiors, landscape, urban design
Tribble & Stephens, contractor

RTKL ASSOCIATES INC.

Shanghai Science & Technology Museum
Client: Science & Technology Museum
Principal consultants:
RTKL Associates Inc., architecture, interior architecture
ID8 (division of RTKL), graphics
Shanghai Modern Architectural Design (Group) Co., Ltd., structural and m/e/p engineering

Miyazaki Station
Client: JR Kyushu
Principal consultants:
RTKL Associates Inc., planning, architectural design, interior design, graphics
Seibu Kotsu Architectural Office, associate architects

Lalaport Shopping Center
Client: Mitsui Fudosan Co. Ltd.
Principal consultants:
RTKL Associates Inc., architecture and environmental graphics
Mesa Design Group, landscape
Theo Kondos, lighting

U.S. Capitol Visitor Center
Client: Architect of the Capitol
Principal consultants:
RTKL Associates Inc., architecture, structural engineering, m/e/p engineering, landscape architecture
James Posey Associates, Inc., m/e/p engineering
Hughes Associates, Inc., fire science & engineering
Culinary Advisors, food service
Ralph Appelbaum Associates, Inc., exhibition
H.M. Brandston Partners, lighting
Auerbach & Associates, theater, auditorium, and audiovisual
Hanscomb, Inc., construction management
Weidlinger and Associates, constructability and structural engineering
David Volkert & Associates, civil engineering
The Care of Trees, arboricultural
Code Access, ADA compliance
Cerami & Associates, acoustical engineering
John A. Van Deusen & Associates Inc., vertical transportation
Sasaki Associates, Inc., hardscape

ROMA DESIGN GROUP

Mid-Embarcadero Transportation and Open Space Projects
Client: City and County of San Francisco
Principal consultants:
ROMA Design Group

U.S. Courthouse and Federal Building, Sacramento
Client: General Services Administration
Principal consultants:
ROMA Design Group, landscape architect
NLA/HLM, building architect

SASAKI ASSOCIATES, INC.

Doosan 100-Year Park
Client: Sisang Design Group
Principal consultants:
Sasaki Associates, Inc., architecture, urban design

Narragansett Landing
Client: Providence Redevelopment Agency
Principal consultants:
Sasaki Associates, Inc., landscape architecture, planning, urban design

Charleston Maritime Center
Client: City of Charleston, SC
Principal consultants:
Sasaki Associates, Inc., architecture, civil engineering, landscape architecture, planning, urban design

Dallas Area Transit Mall
Client: Dallas Area Rapid Transit Authority
Principal consultants:
Sasaki Associates, Inc., landscape architecture, transportation, urban design

Americas World Trade District
Client: Puerto Rico Tourism Company
Principal consultants:
Sasaki Associates, Inc., civil engineering, landscape architecture, planning
TVS/Thompson Ventulett Stainback & Associates
Conventional Wisdom
JRB Inc.
CSA
C.H. Johnson Consulting

SMALLWOOD, REYNOLDS, STEWART, STEWART & ASSOC., INC.

Corporate Square
Client: Guoco Properties Ltd.
Principal consultants:
Smallwood, Reynolds, Stewart, Stewart & Associates, Inc., design consultant
DP Architects Pte, coordination/production architect
Beijing Xingsheng Architecture and Engineering Design Co, local architect of record

Stratford Court
Client: First Changi Development Pte Ltd.
Principal consultants:
Smallwood, Reynolds, Stewart, Stewart & Associates, Pte Ltd., design consultant
Design Link Architects, local architect of record
Beca Carter Hollings & Ferner, m/e/p
DE Consultants, structural
Martin Lee Designs, landscape

Castle Green
Client: Allgreen Properties Ltd.
Principal consultants:
Smallwood, Reynolds, Stewart, Stewart & Associates, Pte Ltd., design consultant
Design Link Architects, local architect of record

Bishan North Street 24
Client/Design-build contractor: Sim Lian Construction Co, Pte, Ltd
Principal consultants:
Smallwood, Reynolds, Stewart, Stewart & Associates, Pte Ltd., design consultant
Design Link Architects, local architect of record
Engineers Partnership, structure
United Project Consultants Pte Ltd., m/e/p

Millennium Tower
Client: Hong Leong Property Management Co. Sdn Bhd
Principal consultants:
Smallwood, Reynolds, Stewart, Stewart & Associates, Inc., design consultant
Arkitek Teknikarya, local architect
PDAA Sdn Bhd, landscape
T.Y. Lin (SEA) Sdn, structure
Perunding Metrik Sdn Bhd, mechanical and electrical
Northcroft Lim Perunding, quantity surveyor

Hotel Equitorial Yangon
Client: Pidemco Land Ltd
Principal consultants:
Smallwood, Reynolds, Stewart, Stewart & Associates, Inc., design consultant
PDAA Design, landscape
Bescon Consulting Engineers, m/e/p

SMITHGROUP

W.K. Kellogg Foundation Headquarters
Client: W.K. Kellogg Foundation
Principal consultants:
SmithGroup JJR, landscape architecture/site design
Luckenbach/Ziegelmanl & Partners, Inc., architect
Walbridge Aldinger, construction manager
CMS Collaborative, water feature consultant
Steffy Lighting Design, lighting design
Greenscape Services, landscape contractor
Granger Construction, Mill Race Park contractor

Phoenix Civic Plaza Reconstruction
Client: City of Phoenix
Principal consultants:
SmithGroup, architecture, mechanical/electrical engineering, forensic structural analysis
Alpha Engineering, structural engineering
Cella Barr, urban planning
CF Shuler, landscape architecture

U.S. Fish and Wildlife Service National Conservation Training Center
Client: Federal Government
Principal consultants:
Oheme Van Sweden, landscape

Stroh's Riverplace Development
Client: Stroh's Riverplace Properties, Inc.
Principal consultants:
Polshek & Partners, architects

THOMAS BALSLEY ASSOCIATES

Gate City
Client: Mitsui Fudosan Co., Ltd.
Principal consultants:
Thomas Balsley Associates, schematic design through construction support services for landscape architecture and fountain design
Thomas Balsley and Steven Tupu, sculpture
Nikken Sekkei Architects, architect
LGA, lighting

Progressive Insurance
Client: Progressive Insurance Company
Principal consultants:
Thomas Balsley Associates, full site and landscape design services, from schematic to construction documents
William Bialosky Architect
H.M. Brandston & Partners, Inc., lighting

Gantry Plaza State Park
Client: Empire State Development Corp., Queens West Development Corp.
Principal consultants:
Thomas Balsley Associates in collaboration with Sowinski Sullivan

Architects and Lee Weintraub, master plan, public design approvals, cost estimates, final documentation and construction support services for Phase 1
Mueser Rutledge Consulting Engineers, engineers
212 Harakawa, graphics
Domingo Gonzalez Design, lighting

One Penn Plaza
Client: Helmsley-Spear, Inc., Metropolitan Life Insurance Co.
Principal consultants:
Thomas Balsley Associates, schematic and design development of plaza
Thomas Balsley, fountain sculpture
Beyer Blinder Belle, architect
Quentin Thomas, lighting
Lebowitz Gould, graphics

Peggy Rockefeller Plaza
Client: Rockefeller University
Principal consultants:
Thomas Balsley Associates, full design services from schematic through construction; first place in invited design competition
Thomas Balsley and Steven Tupu, sculpture
Weidlinger Associates, structural
Wendy Evans Joseph Architects, architect
H.M. Brandston & Partners, Inc., lighting

TVS / THOMPSON, VENTULETT, STAINBACK & ASSOCIATES

Atlantic Station
Client: Jacoby Development, Inc.
Principal consultants:
TVS/Thompson, Ventulett & Stainback, master planning, schematic design, design development, construction documents, construction administration
Ebbarc International, Inc., construction manager
Law-Gibb Engineering, civil, electrical, site remediation
Carl Walker, Inc., parking
EDAW, landscape architect
Moreland-Altobelli, traffic engineers

Long Beach Convention Center
Client: Long Beach Redevelopment Agency
Principal consultants:
TVS/Thompson, Ventulett & Stainback, master planning, urban planning, design architect, production architect, construction architect
TVS Interiors, interior design
Boner Associates, Inc., acoustics, audiovisual
Moffatt & Nichol, civil engineers
Schimmer Engineering, code compliance
Leonard Smith Associates, Inc., cost estimator
Hayakawa Associates Consulting Engineers, mechanical, electrical, plumbing, fire protection
FSA Design, food service
Law Crandall, Inc., geotechnical
Cumming Design Partnership, graphics
Waller Davis Associates, hardware
The SWA Group, Inc., landscape architect
PHA Lighting Design, Inc., lighting consultant
Electronic Systems Associates, security
John A. Martin & Associates, Inc., structural
PCL Construction Services, Inc., general contractor

Mall of Georgia at Mill Creek
Client: Simon Property Group/Ben Carter Properties
Principal consultants:
TVS/Thompson, Ventulett & Stainback, master planning, conceptual design, architecture, interior design, store design and planning
Communication Arts Inc., design consultant/environmental graphic designer
3D Group Environmental Graphic Service, graphics and specialty fabrication
Hardin Construction Group, construction manager and general contractor
E & S Construction Engineers, Inc., mechanical engineer
Stern & Associates, Inc., electrical engineer
Thornton-Tomasetti Engineers, structural engineer
Post, Buckley, Schuh & Jernigin, Inc., civil engineer
Code Consultants, Inc., code consultant and fire protection
T. Kondos Associates, Inc., lighting
Satulah Group/Brookwood Design, special consultants
Hughes, Good, O'Leary & Ryan, exterior landscape
MESA Design Group, interior landscape

Plaza Tobalaba
Client: Mall Plaza
Principal consultants:
TVS/Thompson, Ventulett & Stainback, architecture, master plan, schematic design, design development, design documents
TVS Interiors, interior design
Projectos Cooperativos, graphics
MESA Design Group, landscape architect
T. Kondos Associates, Inc., lighting

WALLACE ROBERTS & TODD, LLC

Richmond Canal Walk
Client: Richmond Riverfront Development Corporation
Principal consultants:
Wallace Roberts & Todd, LLC, planning and design
Greeley & Hansen, environmental engineers
Ralph Appelbaum, Inc., historic interpretation
Cloud & Geshen, signage

Washington Avenue Loft District Streetscape
Client: City of St. Louis Development Corporation
Principal consultants:
Wallace Roberts & Todd, LLC, urban design and landscape architecture
Kiku Obata & Company, signage and lighting
David Mason & Associates, Inc., surveying, civil engineering
Crawford, Bunte, Brammeier, traffic and transportation engineers

Santa Monica Beach Improvement Group
Client: City of Santa Monica
Principal consultants:
Wallace Roberts & Todd, Inc. (WRT practices as a corporation in CA; hence the variation in name), landscape architectural design - concept through construction observation
Jody Pinto, collaborating artist
T.Y. Lin, International, structural engineer
Maris Peika, AIA, architecture
Moore Iacofano Goltsman, community participation
Earth Mechanics, Inc., geotechnical engineering
Psomas & Associates, civil engineering
Storms & Lowe, mechanical and electrical engineering
Adamson Associates, cost management
Horton-Lees, Inc., lighting design
Sussman/Prejza & Co., Inc., graphic design and signage
Leslie Heumann & Associates, historical consultant
Valley Crest, contractor
Black & Veatch, construction management

ZIMMER GUNSUL FRASCA PARTNERSHIP

Westside Light Rail
Client: Tri-County Metropolitan Transportation District of Oregon
Principal consultants for Civic Stadium, Washington Park and Sunset Transit Center stations:
Parsons Brinckerhoff Quade & Douglas, Inc., prime engineer
Zimmer Gunsul Frasca Partnership, architect and urban designer for 12-mile segment from Portland to SW 185th Avenue including design of 11 stations, two maintenance facilities, street furniture and paving, and landscaping concepts
Otak, Inc., architect and civil engineer for six-mile segment from NW 205th to Hillsboro including design of nine stations
Parsons Brinckerhoff Quade & Douglas, Inc., civil, structural and mechanical engineer for Washington Park Station
BRW, Inc., trackway/civil engineer (except Washington Park Station)
LTK Engineering Services, electrical/systems engineer
KPFF Consulting Engineers, structural engineer (except Washington Park Station)
PAE Consulting Engineers, mechanical engineer (except Washington Park Station)
Elcon Engineering, electrical engineer
Murase Associates, Inc., landscape architect
Mayer/Reed, graphics/signage
Hoffman Construction, Kajima Engineering and Construction, Slayden Construction, Inc., Wildish Construction, general contractors
Artists: A total of 25 artists served on design teams for individual stations and above-ground improvements. Artists for the Civic Stadium, Washington Park and Sunset Transit Center stations include Norie Sato, Tad Savinar, Richard Turner, Mierle Ukeles and Bill Will

California Science Center/Exposition Park
Client: California Science Center/State of California
Principal consultant:
Zimmer Gunsul Frasca Partnership, prime architect
California Science Center consultants:
RAW International, consulting architect
Offenhauser/Mekeel Architects, historical architect
West Office Design Associates, exhibit design
Englekirk & Sabol, structural engineer
Tsuchiyama & Kaino, mechanical engineer
ENTEG, Inc., electrical engineer
Horton - Lees Lighting Design, lighting design
Debra Nicols Design, graphics/signage
Exposition Park consultants:
Peter Walker and Partners, landscape concept
Melendrez Babalas Associates, landscape development and implementation
Psomas and Associates, civil engineer
The Planning Group, community relations
Myra L. Frank & Associates, EIR consultant

Kaku Associates, traffic consultant
Keller Construction, general contractor
Turner Construction Company/Vanir Construction Management, construction manager
Hoberman Associates, Larry Kirkland Studio, artists

Everett Station
Client: City of Everett
Principal consultants:
Zimmer Gunsul Frasca Partnership, prime architect
LTK Engineering Services, rail engineer
INCA Engineers, Inc., civil engineer
Shapiro & Associates, Inc., environmental assessment
Exponent Environmental Group, Inc., environmental services
Skilling Ward Magnusson Barkshire, Inc., structural engineer
Path Engineers, LLC, mechanical/electrical engineer
Gibson Traffic Consultants, traffic consultant
Pacific Rim Resources, Inc., public affairs/communication
Mayer Reed, graphics
Milbor-Pita, geotechnical engineer
Lumena Lighting, lighting design
C3 Management Group, Inc., cost analysis/financial planning
Lerch Bates North America, Inc., elevator consultant
Bruck Richards Chaudier, Inc., acoustical engineer
Tad Savinar, public art consultant
Wilder Construction Company, Haskell Corporation, general contractors

Hudson-Bergen Light Rail Transit Station
Client: New Jersey Transit
Principal consultants:
Parsons Brinckerhoff Quade & Douglas, Inc., prime engineer
Zimmer Gunsul Frasca Partnership, architect for design of Bergenline Avenue and Vince Lombardi stations
Jambhekar Strauss PC, associate architect
Gannett Fleming, structural engineer
Sidhu Associates, Inc., mechanical/electrical engineer
Parsons Brinckerhoff Quade & Douglas, Inc., structural and mechanical/electrical engineer for Bergenline Avenue Station
HNTB, structural engineer for Vince Lombardi Station
YU & Associates, geotechnical engineer
Rolf Jensen & Associates, fire/life safety engineer
Wallace Roberts & Todd, landscape architect for Bergenline Avenue Station
John A. Van Deusen & Associates, elevator consultant
Twenty-first Century Rail Corporation, design/build contractor
Alisan Sky, Bergenline Avenue Station; Lisa Kaslow, Vince Lombardi Station, artists

San Diego State University Tunnel Station
Client: Metropolitan Transit Development Board
Principal consultants:
Zimmer Gunsul Frasca Partnership, architect for design of station, gardens and grade-level plaza
URS/BRW, Inc., prime civil engineer
Hatch Mott MacDonald, tunnel engineer
INCA Engineers, Inc., station structural engineer
Lloyd Lindley, ASLA, conceptual landscape design
Estrada Land Planning, landscape architect
Golder Associates, geotechnical engineer
Southland Geotechnical Consultants, geotechnical engineer
Wilson Ihrig & Associates, acoustical engineer
Lintvedt, McColl and Associates, wet utilities consultant
Randall Lamb, dry utilities consultant, station electrical engineer
Williams J. Yang & Associates, station mechanical/electrical engineer
Lerch Bates North America, Inc., elevator consultant
Anne Mudge, artist

The Inspired Reality of Great Public Space

Joe Brown, FASLA,
President/CEO
EDAW, Inc.

Like the magician's sleight of hand, there is more to the creation of a great urban space than meets the eye. A successful public space is always more than a collection of elements, no matter how dazzling the elements are in their own right. Tall buildings, active streets, sculpture, landscape, history, steel and glass — these are inherently sources of excitement, and, by extension, natural subjects to photograph. But what you see is not the same as what you experience. Nor can the benefit to the city as a whole — both as place and community — be ascertained in color images. I challenge you, as you read this book, to look for what you don't easily see, and to bring the same challenge with you when you observe urban spaces first hand. Set out to discern the spirit and thinking behind the scene.

What makes an urban space work? A successful urban space transcends ordinary experience. It is inspired reality, especially compared to the virtual reality of our brave new world. It generates a magnetic force, attracting and gathering people, providing venue and reason for human connection. It conveys information through story telling, and elements of the built environment that are symbols of our culture. It links neighborhoods by moving people from one part of the city to another, it channels buildings-full of individuals and their private aspirations into a shared experience in the public realm. A good public space fosters wonderment and pleasurable contact with society, a sense of belonging; complex and dynamic, it embodies the stimulation of urban life.

The landscape architects at EDAW have developed a palette of techniques that have been very effective in urban design and stimulating economic growth, and I'm happy to share the way we think about public spaces. First, we firmly believe in being place specific, in harnessing the power of place. The design must reinforce the spirit and identity of the locale. This confers substantial user satisfaction, and can be accomplished straight out by

physical, often playful, representations of local history. In exuberant Chattanooga, Tennessee, EDAW embedded the song "Chattanooga Choo-Choo" in bands of park paving. It puts bounce in your step! I have yet to encounter a city whose story and unique contributions were anything less than colorful when illustrated well, or a community that did not respond with enthusiasm to a lively rendition of its heritage. This can also be done by site planning and restoration that honor historic structures and weave old and new together in the urban fabric. A sense of place can be enriched by the use of characteristic local building materials and design vocabulary, by installing the work of resident artists, or by a catchy naming — or renaming — that injects the name of a plaza or park into common parlance.

We want to be appropriate, but we also want to be original. Is there a signature here? The site generates an esthetic language that, once established, must be kept consistent throughout the project. In judging a public space, ask yourself: does it look whole, or is it merely an amalgam of parts? Users sense and seek integrity.

Imagery, of course, is not everything. We insist that public spaces be comfortable. In order to attract people —and that, without question, is the prime requirement for successful public space —users must feel safe and well accommodated. Unless counteracted, all social problems in America tend to flow downhill into public spaces. There must be transparency into and across the space. We start by creating public space on grade where it can be seen. Sunken terraces and raised podiums are invisible and therefore uncertain. In an EDAW plaza or urban park, no ground surface is raised more than three feet or lowered more than eight feet: we protect a visual cone at human height so the user feels in control and at ease.

As the great sociologist of urban street life, William H. Whyte, divined, people tend to sit where there are places to sit, and they have the good sense, or instinct, to avoid the unpleasant. It's surprising that so many places that bill themselves as an "urban living room" are not designed for comfort. We are careful about ergonomics. We take particular care to position benches and seat walls for desirable amounts of warmth and shade, depending on the climate and sun angles, for protection from traffic noise and fumes, for respite, observation and interaction.

Another way to create populated space is to mesh with the existing circulation paths in a city. Public space must be part of urban form, and do something for it in return (impossible to deduce from a photograph in isolation). For example, at Centennial Olympic Park, a centerpiece of the 1996 Summer Olympics in Atlanta, Georgia, EDAW designed a grid of pathways in synch with city streets, a purposeful design based on known behavior to get people to use a brand new park in an unfamiliar part of town. According to my colleague Dennis Carmichael, the design of Centennial Olympic Park (Phase 1), helped knit together Atlanta's urban form. Another personal favorite is the Place Vendome in Paris, where the intimate size and scale are in keeping with the grandeur of that extraordinary city. From within, Place Vendome is experienced as a place apart, but when viewed on a city map — or from the rear seat of a careening taxi! — it is inextricable from the network of boulevards, monuments and squares.

There have been some notable changes in the approach to designing urban public space over the last decade or so. Complex problems are being tackled by collaborative teams of professionals. I believe that landscape architects are best suited to lead these teams. As a profession, we tend to be better listeners than our peers in architecture or engineering; we come without an agenda and put site and social needs first. In fact, our best collaborations are usually with the client and community.

Bear in mind that what we think of today as "urban public space" is not confined to traditional cities; it is also located in towns

and amorphous suburbs surrounding the urban core. These smaller cities and their surrounding ill-formed sprawl are undergoing a renewal of their own with the creation of new public space leading the charge. Happily, this is generating opportunities to create the kind of active gathering places once reserved for their denser, more populous counterparts.

We are increasingly asked to design urban space to support festivals and crowd-pleasing programmed events. Craft fairs, farmers' markets and ethnic celebrations have become a mainstay, so we outfit our projects with functional features on their behalf. For example, at Belvedere Plaza, in Louisville, Kentucky, EDAW created fabric-roofed, steel-framed pavilions that at first glance are elegant shade structures, but can morph into a vendor's shelter. Power and water outlets are installed right there for food and beverage service, as well as sanitary sewer lines for restaurant waste. Pull up a beer truck one weekend, an Italian sausage-mobile the next. Music performances are extremely popular (and a rousing way to bolster local identity), but there must be enough electrical power for elaborate sound systems (220 volt instead of 110 volt) and well planned outlets so you don't have to run 20,000 leagues of cable. For Dennis Carmichael, the European prototype of flexible, invigorated space is the Grand Place in Brussels. There, simplicity of the ground plane allows something different every day — a roundabout, a flower mart, an art show — all surrounded by the richness of gothic and baroque architecture.

A commitment to safety and security, as discussed above, has replaced dated notions of urban flight. Smart lighting is another design essential; at EDAW, we tend to theatrically over-light to enhance the perception of comfort, security and entertainment. Sometimes, at the client's request, a public space is officially closed at dusk, and fenced from entry in the evening to prevent encampments or abuse of the facility. This is usually counterproductive. Still, we can treat the fence as a design opportunity, integrated into the project, and hope that some day such interventions will not be necessary. Other clients engage police services to oversee park activity.

Another trend is the introduction of permanent commercial space into urban parks; while some object to this kind of thing as diminishing the open space, we regard the better examples, such as the bar and cafe at Bryant Park in New York City, as yet another way to draw in people, and sustain the park's operating budget.

Donations to support urban park development are also on the increase, whether via sale of 10,000 imprinted bricks to individuals at $30 each, or corporate support for a blockbuster fountain. Foundations are bullish on cities and urban open space, and want to be associated with public benefit. I congratulate the Heinz Endowments and the Mellon Foundation for multi-million dollar donations to riverfront parks in Pittsburgh.

Quality of place is more important than ever before, according to Richard Florida, guru of the new, knowledge-based economy. Knowledge workers "are young, very individualistic in dress and tastes, work intensely for long, unscheduled hours, prefer hard-edged environments (where wires look good on the floor)... They like to mix fun with work, to be close to stimulation from colleagues...More than 50 percent of knowledge companies are housed in central business districts. Knowledge workers like old buildings, authenticity, diversity, the efficiency of integrating work and play...They want quality of place that can accommodate their desired lifestyle." [in *The Town Paper* (Vol.3, No.1) December/January 2001] Florida maintains that skilled talent calls the shots. And skilled talent is after original, high-quality urban space.

Little wonder, then, that American cities, have come to view investment in urban space as a powerful economic development tool. Investment in public infrastructure pays. For example, with the success of Centennial Park in Atlanta, property value in the immediate area soared from two dollars a square foot in the early 1980s to $150 a square foot in the late 1990s. In Louisville, $100 million in private reinvestment followed a half-dozen park and streetscape projects, including the centerpiece Riverfront Plaza and Belvedere. As people return to city living, or spend longer work days downtown, we are becoming a much more cosmopolitan culture, learning how to enjoy urban squares and plazas as common ground. Perhaps soon, too, Americans will learn to maintain and repair our public spaces to a higher standard. With the investment we are making, it is illogical to do anything less.

Author Peter Harnik declares that we are in the midst of a City Revival movement. In his book *Inside City Parks*, published in 2000 by the Urban Land Institute, Harnik surveys 25 American cities and concludes they are spending $500 million a year on capital construction and reconstruction of urban parks, and more than twice that amount — about $1.2 billion a year — on day-to-day operations and programs.

Whyte, according to *The Town Paper,* once said in support of such enlightened investment in small urban spaces, "The multiplier effect is tremendous. It is not just the number of people using them, but the larger number who pass them and enjoy them vicariously, or the even larger number who feel better about the city for knowledge of them...For a city such places are priceless, whatever the cost."

Now I ask you to do this: go back and look at the photographs in this book a second time. Go out and experience a nearby urban space. Think fondly back to an urban space that made your heart sing. And ask yourself about them all: Is there an esthetic language here? Has it addressed the social challenge, the seriousness, the mission? Is there humor? Does it give back to the city? Have the sponsors invested adequately? Is it inspired? In the answers lies the measure of the project's success.

Acknowledgments

It is a pleasure to publish the second edition of *Urban Spaces*. The cosponsorship and the cooperation of the ULI once again made this book possible. Thanks especially to Rick Rosan, Rachelle Levitt, Lori Hatcher, Gayle Berens, Lloyd Bookout and Laura Templeton for their interest and input which contributed to the establishment and continuation of this series.

John Dixon's ability to identify and describe the most salient features of the over 175 projects in *Urban Spaces No. 2* made his commentary interesting and informative. His skill in interpreting the architects' goals and in communicating with the firms in the new edition expedited the exchange of copy and proofs.

We must also thank Harish Patel, our expert designer and photo editor, for choosing and presenting the best images to showcase the projects most effectively. His patience and knowledge in dealing with the various forms of graphic and electronic media we processed was remarkable.

Thanks also to John Hogan of VRP and Ken and Avan Lee of our printers who are the production professionals that were involved with the many details of creating *Urban Spaces,* from manuscript to finished book.

I was indeed fortunate to have my associates Larry Fuersich and Lester Dundes available to provide advice and direction.

We have Joe Brown, CEO of EDAW, to thank for providing a most inspiring and thought-provoking essay.

I was most happy to be able to work again with the 13 firms that participated in both editions of *Urban Spaces.* It was particularly relevant to have shown renderings of some projects in the first edition and then being able to view the completed projects in this edition. We also added 15 new firms to our *Urban Spaces* family. All the architects and marketing directors we met during the publication process were most cooperative and responsive. I made many new friends and enjoyed our numerous conversations.

Thanks again to all of you who played a part in the production of *Urban Spaces No. 2.*

Henry Burr,
Publisher

This book
belongs to

....

The CHILDREN'S
Factfinder

The CHILDREN'S Factfinder

zigzag

CONTENTS

CREEPY CRITTERS 8

Growers • Developers • Hunters and trappers
Rotters, tunnelers and burrowers • Suckers • Flyers
Crawlers and runners • Hoppers, jumpers, and skaters
Slitherers and wrigglers • Camouflagers • Tricksters
Flashers and warners • Singers and glowers • Carers

MONSTER ANIMALS 36

Monsters on land • Monsters of the sea • Monsters in the air
Hairy monsters • Scary monsters • Disgusting monsters
Fierce monsters • Fat monsters • Weird monsters
Deadly monsters • Masses of monsters • Rare monsters
Imaginary monsters • Extinct monsters

FANTASTIC SEA CREATURES 64

Coral creatures • Seashore creatures • Deep-sea creatures
Cool creatures • Microscopic creatures • Giant creatures
Coastline creatures • Clever creatures • Deadly creatures
Flying creatures • Scaly creatures • Strange creatures
Prehistoric creatures • Mysterious creatures

WARRIORS 176

INVENTIONS 204

SUPERNATURAL 232

OPTICAL ILLUSIONS 260

BALLET AND DANCE 288

INDEX 317

Young **scorpions** are carried on their mother's back.

Many young animals look like small versions of their parents. They simply grow into adults. Others look completely different. They develop into adults through stages.

Some young creatures that look like small adults, such as snails, grow very gradually. Others, such as insects, have a hard outer skeleton. They have to molt in order to grow.

They molt by making a new, soft skeleton beneath the hard one. The new skeleton is pumped up with air, and this splits the old skeleton. The young creature grows inside the new, hard skeleton.

Cockroaches lay their eggs in a hard purse-shaped case. When the young hatch, they look like small adults.

Cockroaches can produce 30,000 young in a single year!

Young **snails** look like miniature adults when they hatch from round, silvery-colored eggs. As they grow, more coils are added to their shells.

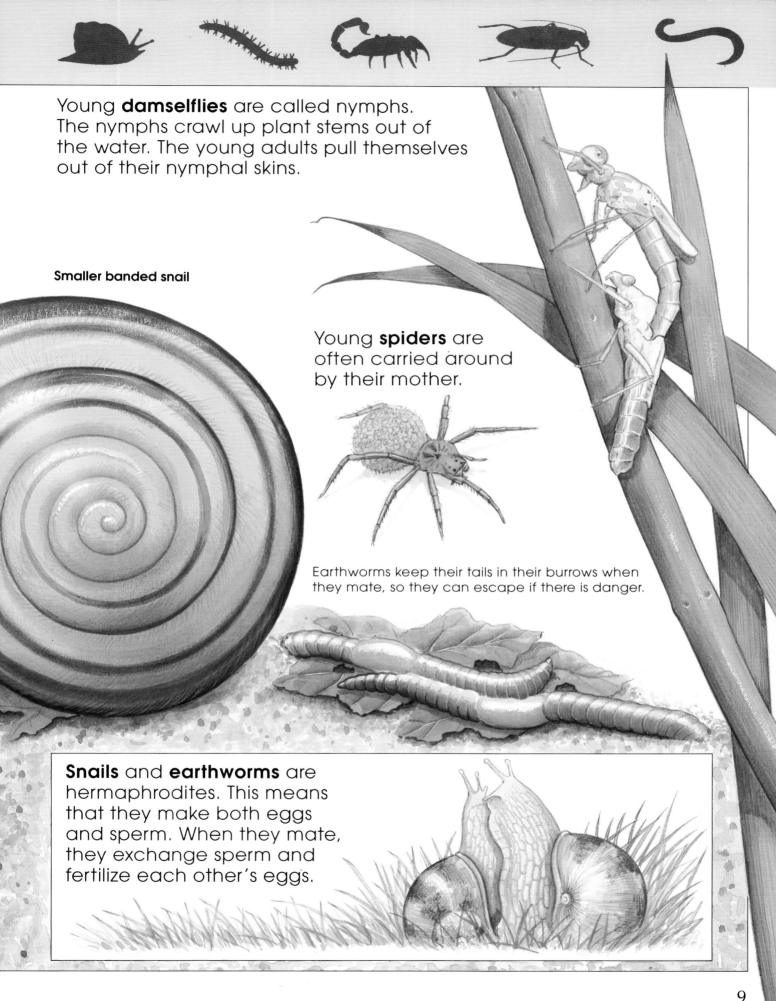

Young **damselflies** are called nymphs. The nymphs crawl up plant stems out of the water. The young adults pull themselves out of their nymphal skins.

Smaller banded snail

Young **spiders** are often carried around by their mother.

Earthworms keep their tails in their burrows when they mate, so they can escape if there is danger.

Snails and **earthworms** are hermaphrodites. This means that they make both eggs and sperm. When they mate, they exchange sperm and fertilize each other's eggs.

When they are born, many young creatures look completely different from their parents. They go through several stages to develop into adults.

The young that hatch from the eggs are called larvae. A larva feeds and grows. It eventually develops into a chrysalis, which is also called a pupa. Inside the chrysalis, the larva changes into an adult. After a time, the adult emerges from the chrysalis.

The development of a larva into an adult through these stages is called metamorphosis.

Lady bug beetles and their larvae feed on aphids.

Caddis fly larvae live underwater. They make homes to live in by sticking together pieces of plant, sand, shells and other material. They carry their homes around with them.

The larvae of **butterflies** and **moths** develop into adults through metamorphosis.

This egg has been laid by a **pasha** butterfly.

This **pasha** caterpillar will turn into a chrysalis.

A caddis fly larva develops into a chrysalis in its home. It then leaves its home and swims to the water surface to become an adult.

You can watch young caterpillars grow by keeping them in a jar with some food. You should ask an adult to make a hole in the lid of the jar. Cover the jar with greaseproof paper with tiny holes in it, and replace the lid. This will allow the caterpillars to breathe.

Black fly larvae live in streams and ponds. They attach themselves to rocks with the sucker on their rear.

Adult black flies suck blood. Some of them carry diseases which they inject when they suck the blood.

Inside the chrysalis, the **pasha** caterpillar changes.

The adult **pasha** butterfly emerges from the chrysalis.

Hunters and trappers

Small creatures have to find food to eat in order to grow. Some of them eat the leaves, shoots, flowers, fruits and roots of plants. Many creatures even eat other creatures!

Little creatures find their food in different ways. Some of them eat rotten plants or animals, while others suck juices from plants, or even blood from animals!

Some small creatures tunnel and burrow through the soil, while others hunt for a meal on the surface of the ground. Some minibeasts even make traps in which they catch their prey.

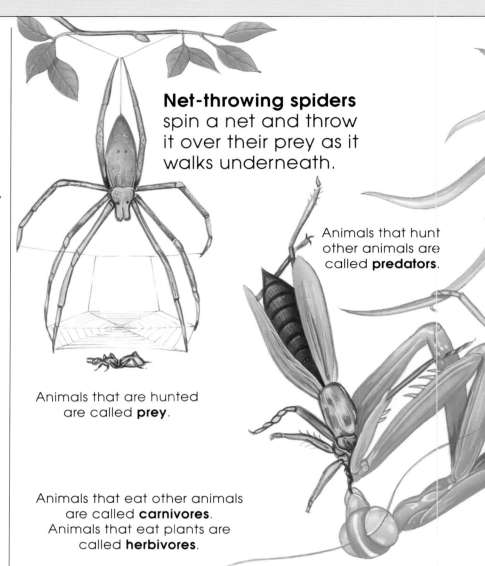

Net-throwing spiders spin a net and throw it over their prey as it walks underneath.

Animals that hunt other animals are called **predators**.

Animals that are hunted are called **prey**.

Animals that eat other animals are called **carnivores**. Animals that eat plants are called **herbivores**.

Long-jawed spiders are well camouflaged on grass as they wait for their prey to walk past.

Trap-door spiders hide in a silk-lined burrow with a trap door at the entrance. They throw open the trap door to grasp their prey.

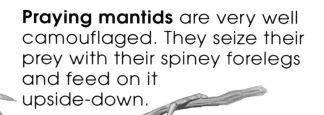

Praying mantids are very well camouflaged. They seize their prey with their spiney forelegs and feed on it upside-down.

Antlion larvae lie half-hidden at the bottom of a funnel-shaped pit. They flick sand at creatures that slip over the edge of the pit, so that the tiny creatures fall down to the bottom.

Blue-black spider wasps have a loud buzz which terrifies their prey.

Euglandina rosea attacking a *papustyla* snail.

Tiger beetles are fierce hunters. They use their strong jaws to kill and cut up their prey, which includes young lizards.

Snails sometimes attack and eat other snails. If the snail has withdrawn inside its shell, the attacker will drill a hole through the shell to eat the snail.

13

Rotters, tunnelers and burrowers

Nothing lives for ever. Plants and animals die and rot away. Many feed on rotting material, helping to break it down into smaller particles.

Some of these pass into the soil, and are eaten by burrowing creatures. The particles contain nutrients which help them to grow.

Mole crickets dig burrows with their large spade-like feet. They eat the roots of plants and other insects.

Scarab beetles make balls of dung, and bury them in a tunnel where they lay their eggs. The larvae discover a pantry full of lovely food.

Mites help to break down the remains of dead plants in the soil. Some of them feed on fungi, while others hunt other mites.

Dermistid beetles help to tidy up the remains of dead animals.

Many different kinds of small creatures can be found in compost heaps. To find them, place a handful of compost in a sieve and warm it gently with a lamp for two to three days. Remember to keep the tissue paper damp.

Stag beetle larvae live inside logs. They tunnel through the decaying wood for several years before they emerge as adult stag beetles.

Termites tunnel into wood or soil and build nests. These hang from trees, or are huge mounds rising from the ground.

Microscopic animals live inside termites. They break down the plant food that termites eat.

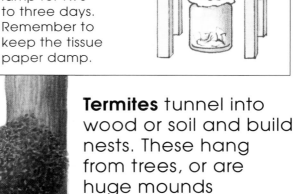

Millipedes tunnel through the soil. They eat particles of rotten material which are rich in nutrients. They also eat fallen leaves, breaking them down into smaller pieces.

Suckers

Some insects live on liquid food. They have extremely sharp mouthparts which they use to pierce the skin of an animal or the tissue of a plant.

They usually suck blood or plant juices through a sucking tube.

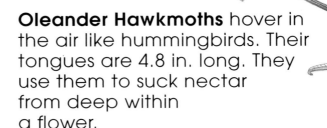

Oleander Hawkmoths hover in the air like hummingbirds. Their tongues are 4.8 in. long. They use them to suck nectar from deep within a flower.

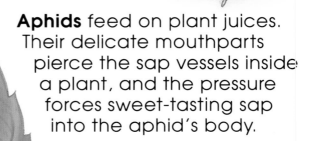

Fleas use the hooks and spines on their bodies to hold tightly on to the fur or skin of their hosts. Fleas can carry diseases which they inject into their hosts when they bite.

In the Middle Ages, the disease called the Black Death was spread by the rat flea. This disease killed millions of people.

Ticks are parasites. They sink their hooked mouthparts into the flesh of their host. As they suck the blood, their round, elastic bodies swell greatly.

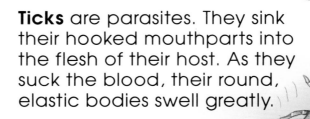

Aphids feed on plant juices. Their delicate mouthparts pierce the sap vessels inside a plant, and the pressure forces sweet-tasting sap into the aphid's body.

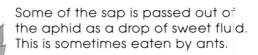

Some of the sap is passed out of the aphid as a drop of sweet fluid. This is sometimes eaten by ants.

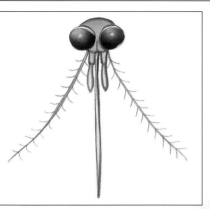

The long, needle-sharp mouthparts of a mosquito contain a sucking tube.

Mosquitoes feed on blood and plant juices. Female mosquitoes have a meal of blood before they lay their eggs. Male mosquitoes suck plant juices instead of blood.

Female mosquitoes bite humans. A person can lose over a pint of blood in an hour.

Jungle leeches suck blood. When they have had a blood meal, their body swells.

Animals that live and feed on other animals are called **parasites**. The animals that provide a home and food are called **hosts**.

Thrips are tiny "thunder-bugs." They have mouthpieces on one side of their mouth only, which they use to suck plant juices.

Thrips are pests, feeding on corn and other crops.

Robber flies catch and stab their prey with their sharp mouthpieces. Their victim is then sucked dry.

Cochineal bugs suck plant juices. They are used to make food coloring as they are dark red.

Small creatures have to get around in order to find food, a mate, and a new place to live. They also need to be able to escape from predators.

Insects use many ways of getting around. Some of them crawl and others run. Some of them jump and others wriggle. Some of them can even fly.

Most insects that fly have two pairs of wings which beat together.

Spiders are creatures that can fly but do not have wings!

A young **wolf spider** has released a long, silken thread. The wind will pluck the thread into the air, whisking the young spider away with it.

Beetles have two pairs of wings. The first pair is very tough and protects the delicate flying wings which are folded underneath when not in use.

Dragonflies chase other flying insects by rapidly beating their outstretched wings.

Emperor dragonfly

Damselflies fly by fluttering their wings. They catch other flying insects by grasping them with their legs.

Butterflies fly during the daytime. Most of them slowly flap their large, colorful wings.

The wings of the **Painted lady** warn other insects to keep away.

The wings of the **swallowtail** make a noise as they clap together.

Flies are the best acrobats of the insect world. They can even land upside-down on a ceiling.

Flies have only one pair of real wings. The rear wings are tiny bat-shaped objects which beat very fast.

Hover flies can hover, dart backward and forward, and even fly straight upward.

Midges have one of the fastest wing beats. Some beat their wings over 1,000 times a second.

Fairy flies have delicate, feathery wings. They are one of the smallest flying insects.

Cockchafers fly at dusk. They can fly over 3 miles in search of a mate.

Crawlers and runners

Many small creatures get around by crawling or running. Some of them have lots of short legs which they use to crawl about.

Other creatures have fewer legs, but they are usually quite long. Long legs allow the creature to run about quickly.

Pseudoscorpions can run backward as well as forward! They are active hunters that crawl among decaying leaves in search of a meal.

Pseudoscorpions have long sensitive hairs on their rear to help them feel where they are going.

Caterpillars usually have plenty of food around them. As they do not need to move far to find a meal, they have short legs.

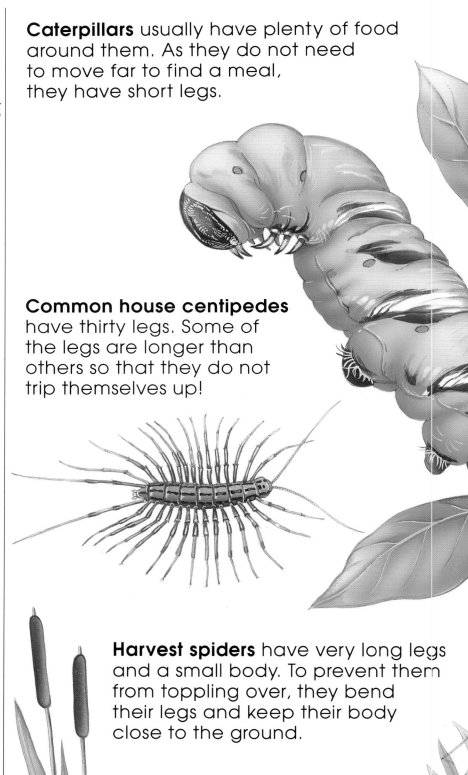

Common house centipedes have thirty legs. Some of the legs are longer than others so that they do not trip themselves up!

Harvest spiders have very long legs and a small body. To prevent them from toppling over, they bend their legs and keep their body close to the ground.

The legs of harvest spiders are not used for speed. The spiders crawl through the vegetation where they live.

Caterpillars have special suckers, called prolegs, on their bodies which keep them firmly fixed on to twigs and leaves, even in a strong wind.

Privet hawkmoth caterpillar

Millipedes have over one hundred pairs of legs which they use to crawl along the ground.

Jewel beetles scurry around in search of food. They have beautiful colored wing cases. In South America, they are used as living jewelery which is why they are called jewel beetles.

Huntsman spiders hide underneath the bark of a tree while they wait for their prey. They then race to catch it using their long legs.

Golden huntsman spider

Woodlouse-eating spiders have enormous jaws which are specially designed to catch woodlice.

All spiders have eight legs, which they use to run about.

Hoppers, jumpers and skaters

Some small creatures move around by hopping and jumping. Being able to jump suddenly is a good way to catch a meal, or to escape from a predator.

Some insects skate across the surface of water in search of food or a mate.

Raft spiders stand half on the water and half on a water plant. They race across the water surface to catch their prey, which includes small fish.

Grasshoppers and **crickets** have huge back legs. They use the strong muscles in these legs to catapult themselves high into the air.

Fleas have large back legs which allow them to jump very high - well over half a yard.

Fleas jump onto animals, such as cats, where they make their home.

Treehoppers hop from tree to tree in search of food.

Pond skaters have waterproof hairs on their feet which help them to float on the water surface.

Grasshoppers attract a mate by rubbing their back legs against their front wings to make a singing sound.

Springtails can spring suddenly into the air using their special "tail."

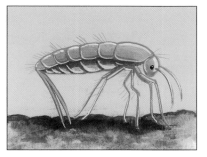

The "tail" is tucked under the springtail's body.

The "tail" straightens suddenly, making the springtail spring into the air.

Jumping plant lice have very strong back legs which means they can jump from plant to plant.

Click beetles have a peg on their bodies. When they lie on their backs and bend, the peg pops free with a loud click, and they jump into the air.

Apple suckers are jumping plant lice which live on apple trees.

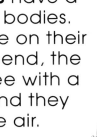

Whirligig beetles skate quickly across the surface of a pond in a zigzag pattern.

Jumping spiders have excellent sight. When they see a fly, they will leap into the air to catch it.

Slitherers and wrigglers

Legs can get in the way, so some creatures do not have any legs at all. They have soft bodies, and they move around by slithering along the ground or wriggling through the soil.

Earthworms make burrows which let air into the soil. They drag leaves into the burrows for food.

Leeches move along by using their suckers. They have two suckers on their bodies, one at the front and one at the rear. The one at the front has teeth as it is also their mouth.

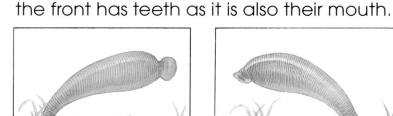

The rear sucker sticks to the ground and the body stretches forward.

The front sucker sticks to the ground and the body is pulled forward.

African giant snail

You can make a wormery by putting some earthworms and compost into a plastic bucket with small holes in the bottom. As the earthworms eat the compost, you will need to add some more to the bucket.

Earthworms burrow through the soil by eating it. They grip the soil with very small bristles along their bodies.

Slugs and snails are special creatures that slither along on a trail of slime using one foot. If you place a slug or snail on a piece of clear plastic and look at it from underneath, you will see ripples moving along the foot as the slug moves forward.

Hover fly larvae look like little leeches. They wriggle along in search of aphids which they eat.

Fly larvae hatch from eggs laid on dung. They have small legs, or no legs at all. To move about, they wriggle through their squidgy food.

Soil centipedes have up to 100 pairs of tiny legs which help them to grip the soil.

Nematodes are minute roundworms which live inside many animals and plants, and in soil. They move around by wriggling their tiny bodies.

Camouflagers

Some small creatures hide from predators or prey, while others display bright colours, make noises, or glow at night to attract attention.

Many use colors and shapes to disguise themselves. Some blend into their background, which is called camouflage. Others pretend to be fierce creatures.

Some animals use bright colors to frighten or warn their predators. Others use sound and light to "talk" to each other and attract a mate.

Assassin bug larvae look like the surrounding soil.

Peppered moths blend into the bark of the tree trunk on which they are resting.

Some peppered moths are darker. They hide on tree trunks which have been blackened by pollution.

African bush-crickets are perfectly camouflaged among the leaves.

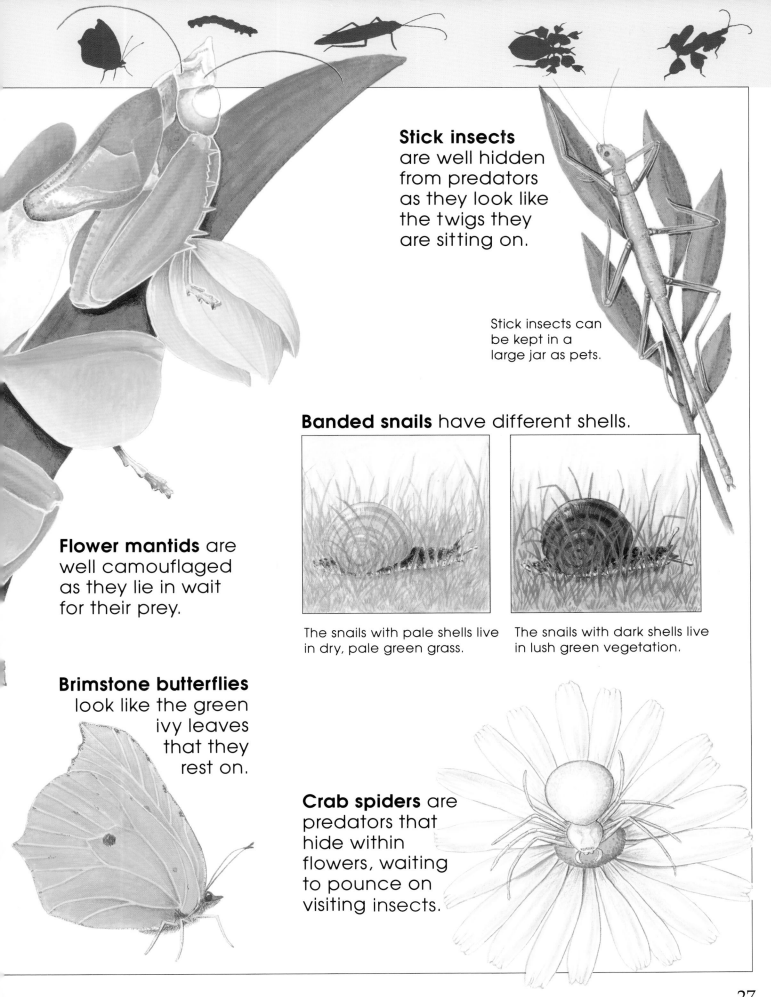

Stick insects are well hidden from predators as they look like the twigs they are sitting on.

Stick insects can be kept in a large jar as pets.

Banded snails have different shells.

The snails with pale shells live in dry, pale green grass.

The snails with dark shells live in lush green vegetation.

Flower mantids are well camouflaged as they lie in wait for their prey.

Brimstone butterflies look like the green ivy leaves that they rest on.

Crab spiders are predators that hide within flowers, waiting to pounce on visiting insects.

Tricksters

Many insects try to trick predators by using different disguises. Some of them have the same colors as creatures that are fierce or poisonous, so that predators will leave them alone.

Other insects let predators approach them, but then they give them a nasty surprise. A few even use false heads to confuse their predators!

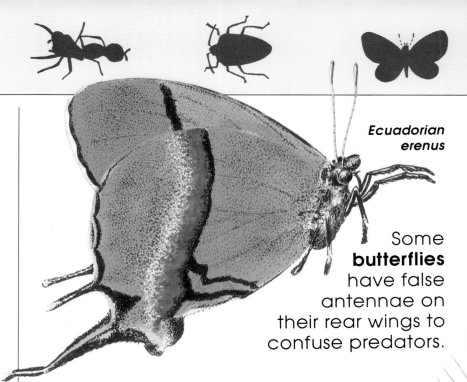

Ecuadorian erenus

Some **butterflies** have false antennae on their rear wings to confuse predators.

Tussock moth caterpillars have fine irritating hairs on their body which give predators a nasty shock!

Diadem butterflies are not poisonous but they trick their predators by flying with poisonous **African monarch** and **Citrus swallowtail butterflies**.

Citrus swallowtail

African monarch

Wasp beetles are not dangerous as they do not sting. They pretend to be wasps to trick their predators.

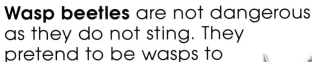

Copying the color of another creature is called **mimicry**. This helps to protect harmless insects from predators.

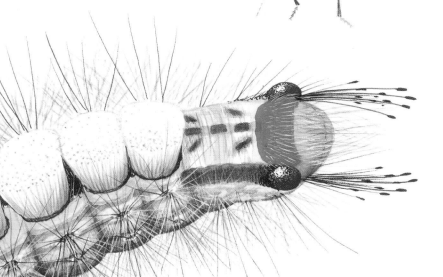

Some **jumping spiders** mimic mutillid wasps to protect themselves.

The jumping spider's rear looks like the head of a mutillid wasp.

Shieldbugs ooze a stinking liquid when they are in danger. This is why they are also called stinkbugs.

Golden-silk spiders have bright colors. At a distance, these break up the shape of the spider, making it difficult to see.

Diadem

Flashers and warners

Many creatures use bright colors to protect themselves. Some of them frighten their predators by suddenly flashing bright colors at them.

Some insects show their bright colors all the time. Predators learn that these are warning colors, telling them that the insect is dangerous.

There are only a few warning colors: black, white, yellow, red and brown. Creatures learn quickly that these colors warn of danger.

Peacock butterflies have large colorful eye spots on their wings.

Puss moth caterpillars shoot out long red tassles from tubes on their rear when they are frightened.

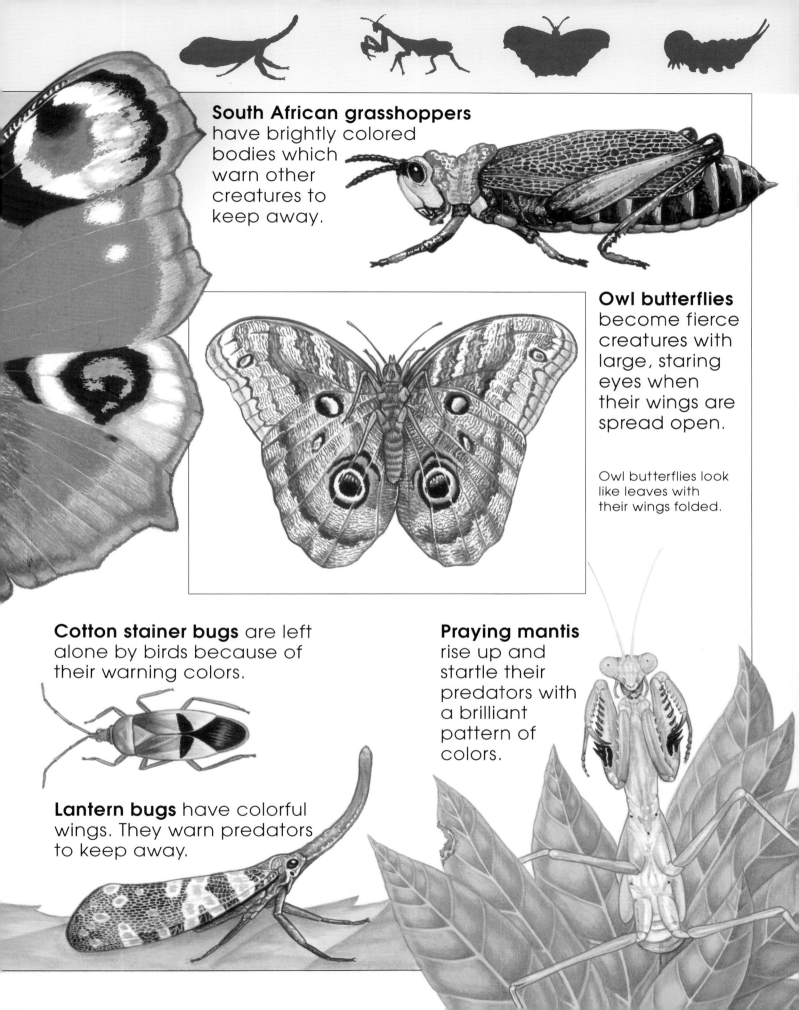

South African grasshoppers have brightly colored bodies which warn other creatures to keep away.

Owl butterflies become fierce creatures with large, staring eyes when their wings are spread open.

Owl butterflies look like leaves with their wings folded.

Cotton stainer bugs are left alone by birds because of their warning colors.

Praying mantis rise up and startle their predators with a brilliant pattern of colors.

Lantern bugs have colorful wings. They warn predators to keep away.

Singers and glowers

Many creatures use sound to attract a mate, or to warn off predators. Some of them make sounds during the day. If you walk through a field or a forest, you may hear all kinds of chirps and buzzes.

Many insects make sounds at night, while others use light to attract a mate. The males or females glow in the dark, and their mates are attracted to them.

Katydids sing their repetitive song "katydid, katydidn't" at night. They sing by rubbing their left front wing against a ridge on the right wing.

Katydids and other crickets have ears on their legs.

Tree crickets make thousands of piercing chirps without stopping. Some tree crickets can be heard 1 mi. away!

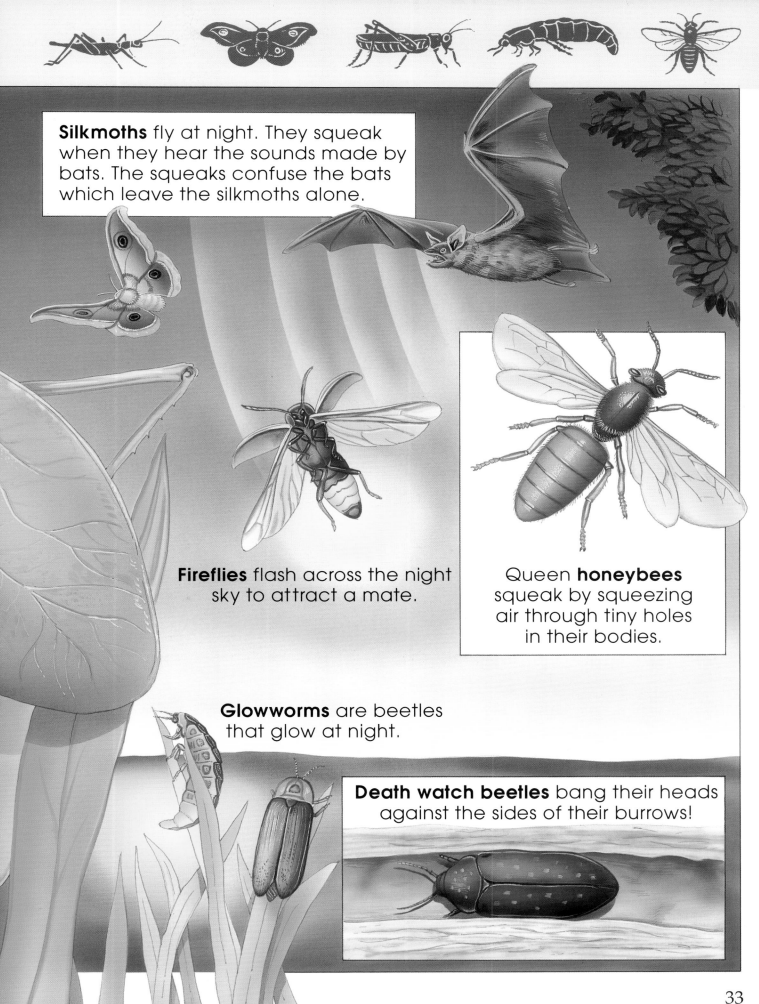

Silkmoths fly at night. They squeak when they hear the sounds made by bats. The squeaks confuse the bats which leave the silkmoths alone.

Fireflies flash across the night sky to attract a mate.

Queen **honeybees** squeak by squeezing air through tiny holes in their bodies.

Glowworms are beetles that glow at night.

Death watch beetles bang their heads against the sides of their burrows!

Carers

Most creatures leave their young to look after themselves. Many of the young starve to death, or are eaten by predators. To overcome this, many eggs are laid.

Some creatures care for their eggs and young, so fewer eggs need to be laid. Insects such as female ants or bees work together to provide shelter and food for their young, giving them a better chance of survival.

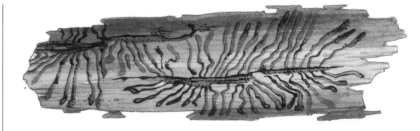

Look at the bark of fallen trees and see if you can find the tunnels of bark beetles.

Elm bark beetles tunnel under the bark of a tree where they lay their eggs.

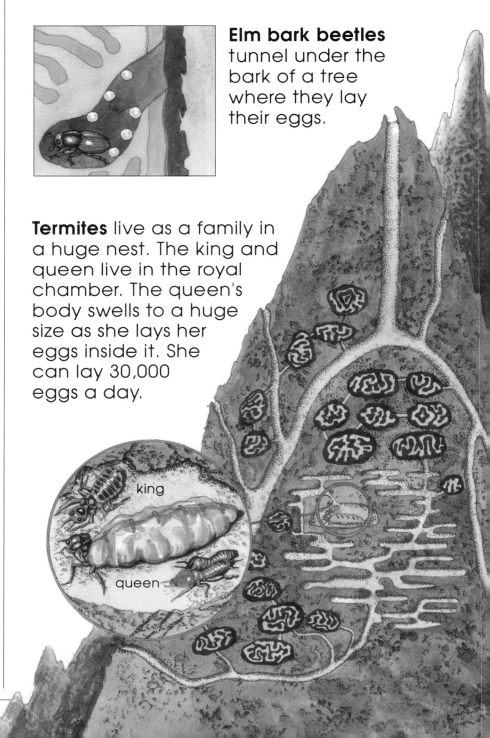

Termites live as a family in a huge nest. The king and queen live in the royal chamber. The queen's body swells to a huge size as she lays her eggs inside it. She can lay 30,000 eggs a day.

king

queen

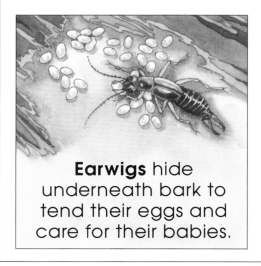

Earwigs hide underneath bark to tend their eggs and care for their babies.

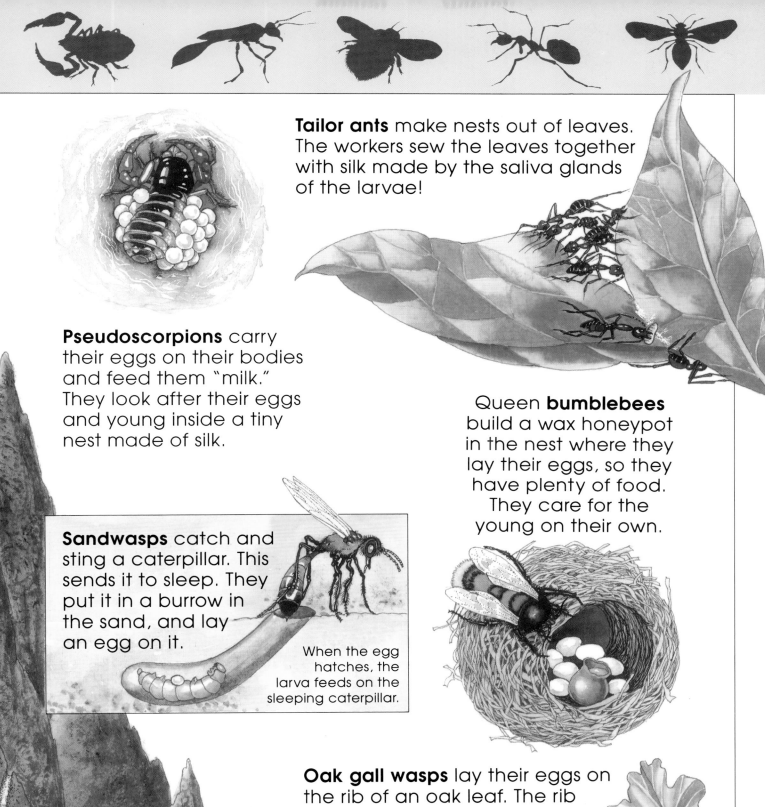

Tailor ants make nests out of leaves. The workers sew the leaves together with silk made by the saliva glands of the larvae!

Pseudoscorpions carry their eggs on their bodies and feed them "milk." They look after their eggs and young inside a tiny nest made of silk.

Queen **bumblebees** build a wax honeypot in the nest where they lay their eggs, so they have plenty of food. They care for the young on their own.

Sandwasps catch and sting a caterpillar. This sends it to sleep. They put it in a burrow in the sand, and lay an egg on it.

When the egg hatches, the larva feeds on the sleeping caterpillar.

Oak gall wasps lay their eggs on the rib of an oak leaf. The rib swells and forms a gall which is a safe home for the larvae that grow inside it.

Galls come in all shapes and sizes. The aleppo gall is used to make special permanent ink which is used by banks.

35

Happily there are few really monstrous large animals. Smaller monsters are much more common.

Pythons swallow their prey whole.

Giant **pythons** coil their powerful bodies around their helpless prey until they suffocate it.

Many large animals might look frightening, but usually they do not attack unless they are threatened.

The **elephant** is the largest land mammal. A full grown male (bull) African elephant can be over 10 ft. tall and weigh 9 tons.

This fierce lizard, nearly three metres long, will even attack people.

The enormous **Komodo Dragon** prowls through the forest on lonely Indonesian islands.

A **tiger** has huge, sharp teeth which grip and kill its prey.

The **giraffe** is the tallest mammal on Earth. However, it is not fierce and eats only leaves.

Grizzly bears tower a frightening 10 ft. when they stand upright on their hind legs. They have big, sharp claws for tearing at food.

Gorillas are the largest primates. When threatened, a male gorilla will beat his chest with his hands, roar and rush toward the enemy.

The **Goliath beetle** is a heavy weight champion of the insect world. It can carry a load 850 times its own weight. That is similar to a human carrying 67 tons.

Monsters of the sea

Some of the strangest monsters can be found swimming and living in the sea.

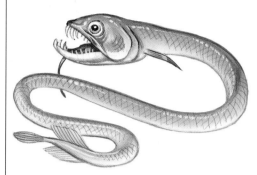

Large ones like the whales and sharks swim in the open ocean. Others, like giant sponges, hide deep down on the seabed.

Lurking at the bottom of the sea near Japan are **giant spider crabs**. With their claws outstretched they can measure nearly ten feet.

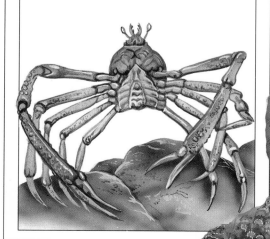

The suckers on a 50 foot **giant squid** measure 4 in. across. But sucker scars on whales have been seen as long as 18 in.!

Trailing deadly poisonous tentacles, **Arctic giant jellyfish** drift in the northern seas. Their tentacles can reach down over 100 feet.

Sharks can detect vibrations and electricity given out by injured creatures over long distances. Some can even taste blood

Loggerhead sponges can be a yard high and a yard across.

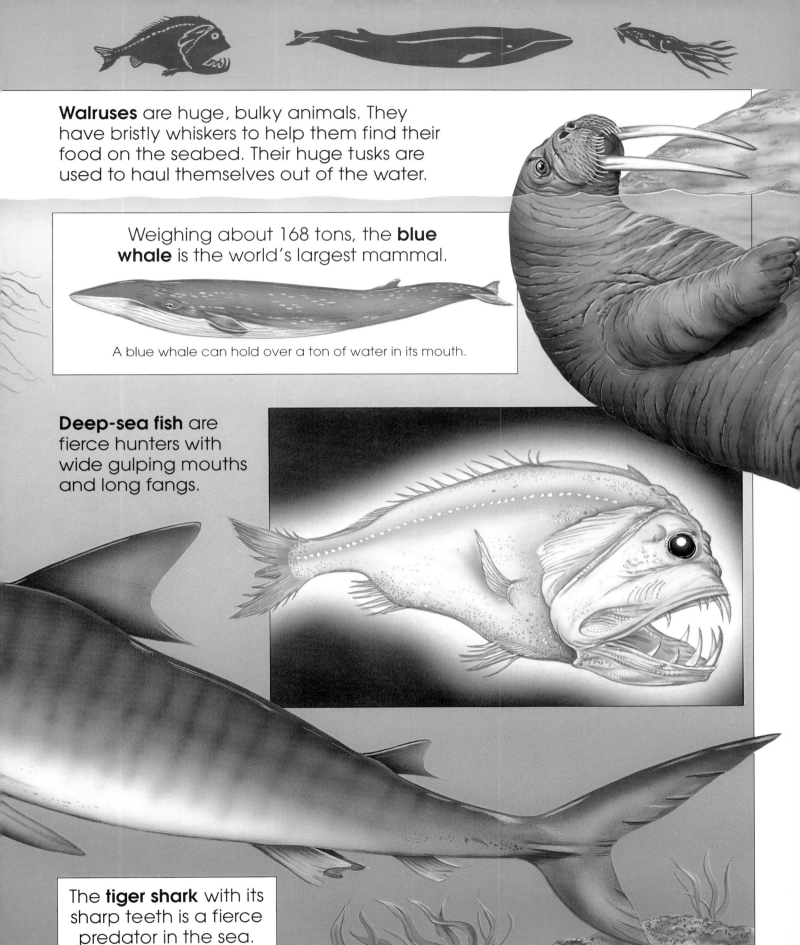

Walruses are huge, bulky animals. They have bristly whiskers to help them find their food on the seabed. Their huge tusks are used to haul themselves out of the water.

Weighing about 168 tons, the **blue whale** is the world's largest mammal.

A blue whale can hold over a ton of water in its mouth.

Deep-sea fish are fierce hunters with wide gulping mouths and long fangs.

The **tiger shark** with its sharp teeth is a fierce predator in the sea.

Monsters in the air

Birds, bats and insects all have wings and can fly. Some are fierce hunters in the air and can grow very large.

Others use their long, needle-sharp claws, called talons, to catch and kill.

Monstrous **robber flies** hunt other insects in the air, piercing them with sharp mouthpieces, and sucking out the contents of their bodies.

Bats are the only mammals that can truly fly. The largest bat is the **flying fox** which can have a wingspan of over 6 feet.

The **Andean condor** is the world's largest bird of prey and can weigh over 25 lbs.

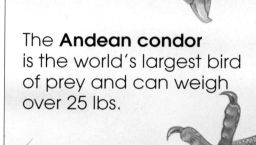

Albatrosses circle the Earth, only coming to land when they want to breed.

The wings of an **albatross** can span more than 10 feet. They enable it to fly hundreds of miles at a time.

The wingspan of the largest moth in the world, the **atlas moth**, is 10 in.

Pelicans dive to catch fish. Nearly half a yard long, their huge bills scoop up several fish at a time which they then swallow.

This evil-looking **wasp** has paralyzed another insect with its terrible sting.

Hairy monsters

Monster animals covered with hair can look very strange. They are hairy for many reasons.

Some live in very cold places and need to keep warm. Others use hair for camouflage.

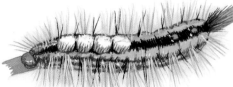

Poisonous hairs protect against attack. Hairs are even used to help some animals breathe underwater.

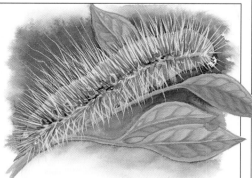

The hairs on this **Japanese Dictyoploca moth caterpillar** irritate and hurt any predator trying to eat it.

The body of a **porcupine** is covered with special hairs. When frightened the animal rattles these needle-sharp quills.

Some porcupines can even shoot quills out at their enemy.

The "old man of the forest," or **orang-utang**, has very long, golden red hair.

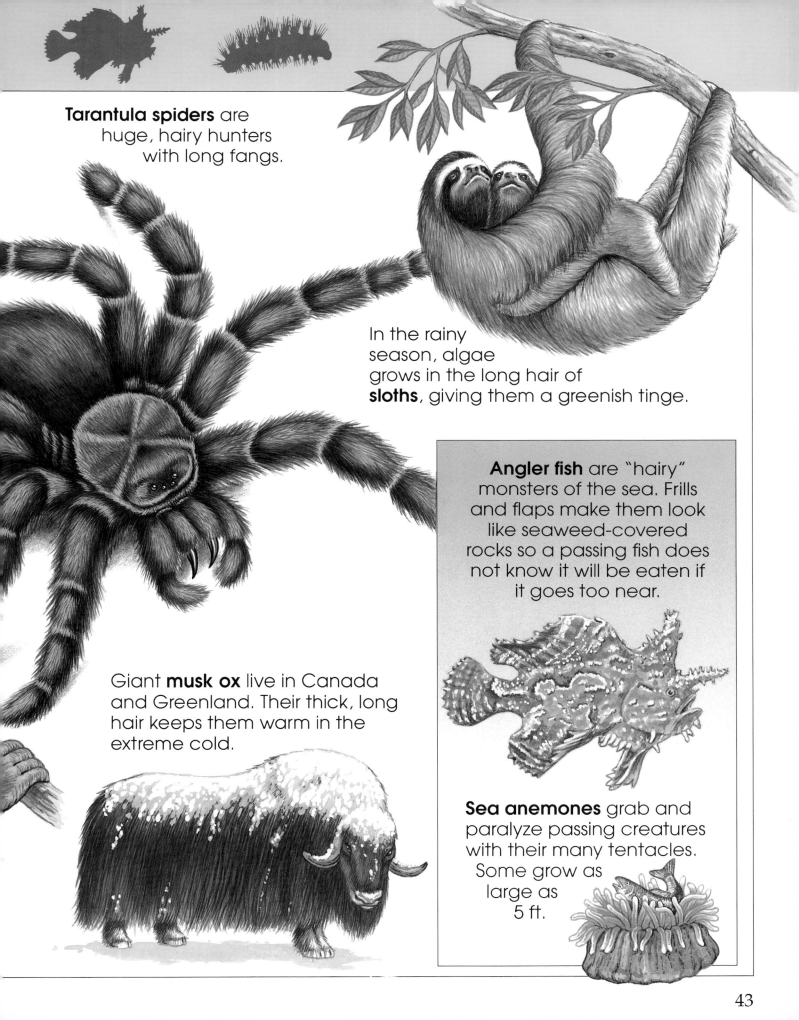

Tarantula spiders are huge, hairy hunters with long fangs.

In the rainy season, algae grows in the long hair of **sloths**, giving them a greenish tinge.

Angler fish are "hairy" monsters of the sea. Frills and flaps make them look like seaweed-covered rocks so a passing fish does not know it will be eaten if it goes too near.

Giant **musk ox** live in Canada and Greenland. Their thick, long hair keeps them warm in the extreme cold.

Sea anemones grab and paralyze passing creatures with their many tentacles. Some grow as large as 5 ft.

To protect themselves from being attacked or eaten, many animals are monstrous looking.

Some look frightening all the time, while others can make themselves scary when they have to.

Roaring and puffing up their bodies are just some of the methods used.

Death's head hawkmoths can enter beehives and steal honey without being stung.

The strange skull-like markings on the **death's head hawkmoth** give it a deathly appearance.

This is not a fierce prehistoric monster, but a **frilled lizard**. This harmless lizard puts on an impressive display when it is frightened.

Male **stag beetles** have huge, fearsome jaws. They cannot bite with them, but instead joust with other males over females.

Stag beetles use their huge jaws to try and flick their opponent over.

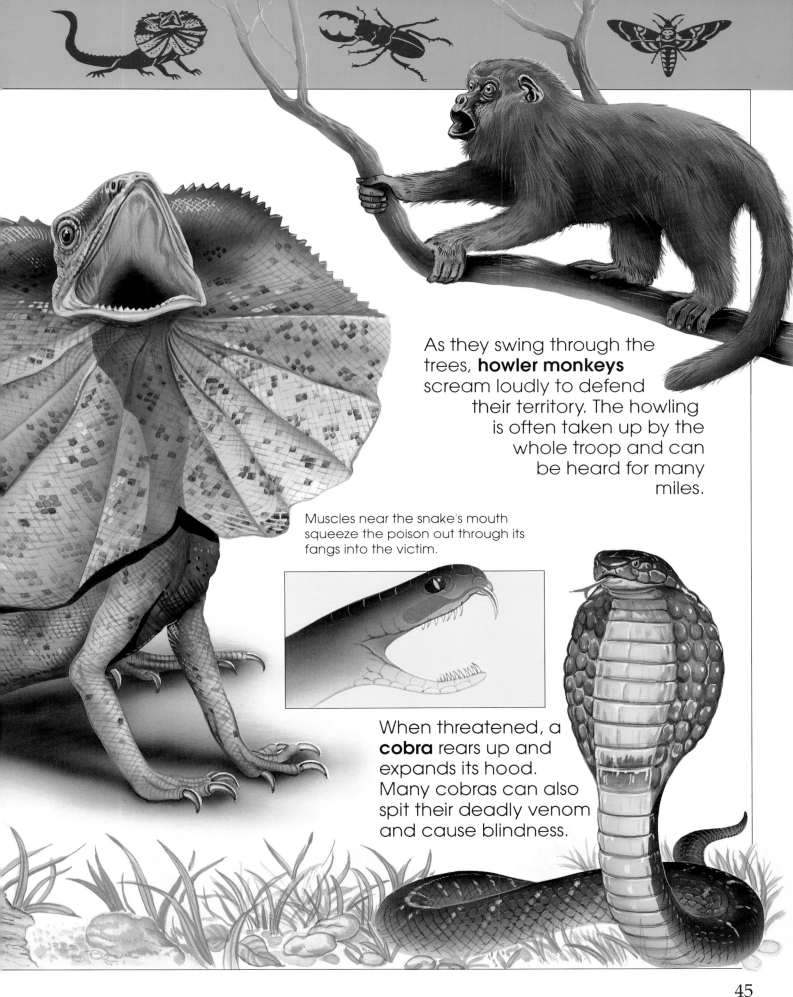

As they swing through the trees, **howler monkeys** scream loudly to defend their territory. The howling is often taken up by the whole troop and can be heard for many miles.

Muscles near the snake's mouth squeeze the poison out through its fangs into the victim.

When threatened, a **cobra** rears up and expands its hood. Many cobras can also spit their deadly venom and cause blindness.

Disgusting monsters

Some monster animals use horrid smells to frighten their predators.

Others live in smelly places or have disgusting habits.

Eating dung and rotting corpses is not particularly nice, but without these animals to clear up, the world would be even smellier!

Big **dung beetles** carefully roll dung into balls which they hide in tunnels underground for their grubs to eat.

When a **vampire bat** finds a sleeping animal, it bites into the skin with its razor-sharp front teeth and laps up the blood with its tongue.

Vultures have bald heads and necks. This stops them from getting too dirty with blood as they poke their heads inside a corpse to feed.

Lampreys cling to other fish with their strange circular mouths surrounded by hooks. They gnaw the flesh and even wriggle into their host's body.

Leeches attach themselves to animals and suck blood causing their bodies to swell. Some can grow as long as 8 in.

Flies are attracted to dead bodies where they feed and lay their eggs. Once hatched, the maggots help to break down the rotten flesh.

Phew! The pungent odor of a **skunk** is disgusting. Skunks spray their scent to mark their territory and put off attackers.

Fierce Monsters

Many animals are hunters, preying on other creatures. To catch and kill they have to be cunning, powerful and quick. Most have special teeth, jaws and stings to help catch, hold, kill and devour their victims.

Some of these fierce monsters are quite small. Others grow enormous and will even attack and eat people.

Giant **Colombian horned toads** are aggressive and will attack animals much bigger than themselves - they even bite horses!

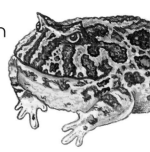

Over a thousand people a year are killed by the world's largest and fiercest crocodile, the **Indo-Pacific crocodile**.

A **scorpion** grabs its prey with sharp claws and then bends its tail with its deadly sting over its head and into the victim, killing it with the poison.

Using their razor-sharp pointed teeth, **killer whales** can snatch a seal from a beach by rushing on to the shore on a wave. People stranded on ice floes have also been tipped off and eaten.

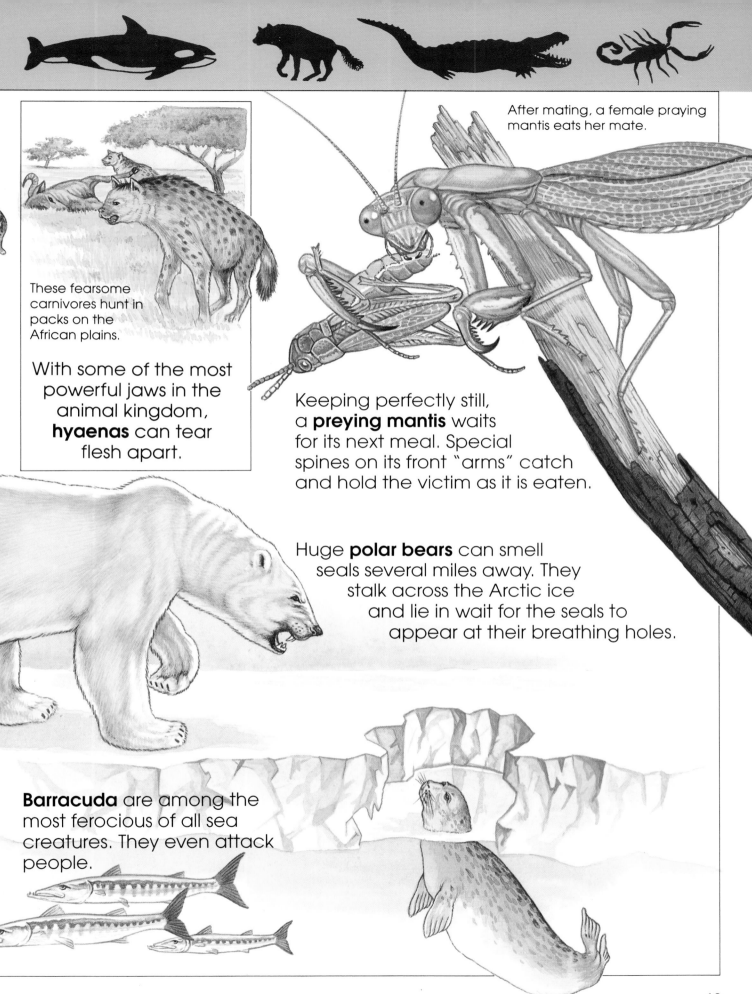

After mating, a female praying mantis eats her mate.

These fearsome carnivores hunt in packs on the African plains.

With some of the most powerful jaws in the animal kingdom, **hyaenas** can tear flesh apart.

Keeping perfectly still, a **preying mantis** waits for its next meal. Special spines on its front "arms" catch and hold the victim as it is eaten.

Huge **polar bears** can smell seals several miles away. They stalk across the Arctic ice and lie in wait for the seals to appear at their breathing holes.

Barracuda are among the most ferocious of all sea creatures. They even attack people.

49

Fat monsters

Some animals are monstrously fat. Many of them spend most of their time in the water where the weight of their bodies is supported.

Fat bodies can hold a lot of food for times when there is little food around. They can also be used to scare off attackers.

The fat **Vietnamese pot-bellied pig** is kept as a pet in some parts of the world.

Herds of **elephant seals** wallow on the beach. An adult male can weigh almost four tons. When males fight each other they often crush the babies on the beach.

Hippopotamus means "river horse." Although they look fat and clumsy on land, when they are in water they can swim fast.

Hippos use their large teeth for digging up water plants and fighting.

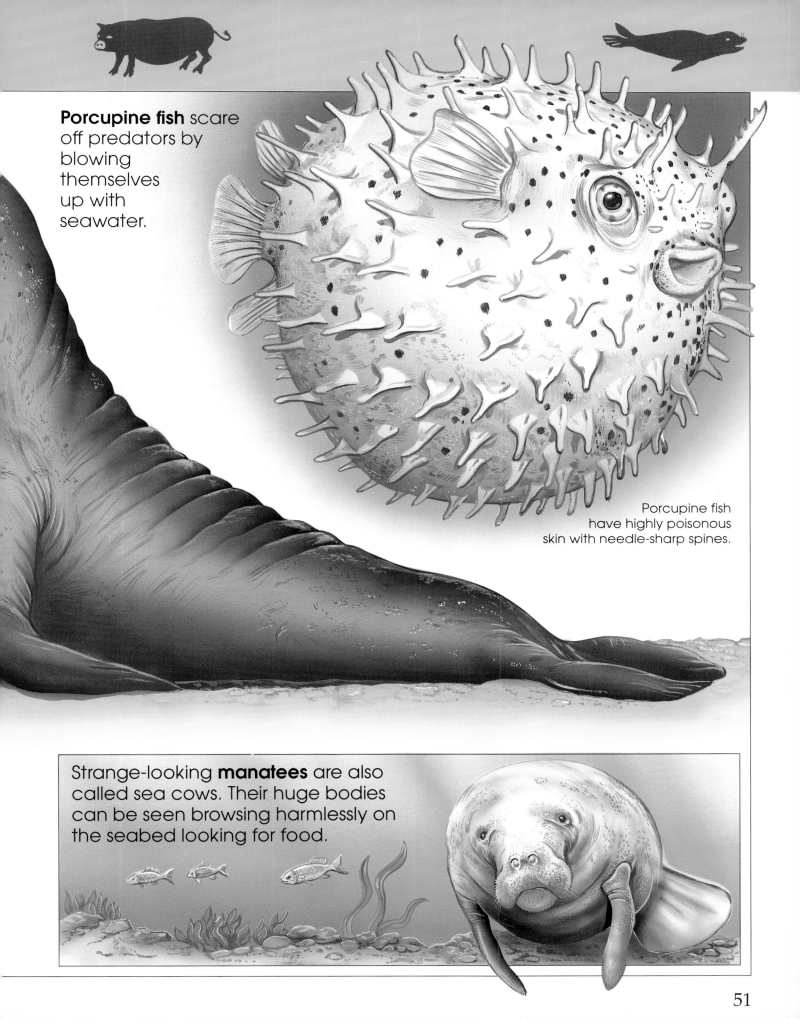

Porcupine fish scare off predators by blowing themselves up with seawater.

Porcupine fish have highly poisonous skin with needle-sharp spines.

Strange-looking **manatees** are also called sea cows. Their huge bodies can be seen browsing harmlessly on the seabed looking for food.

Weird monsters

Some animals are very strange-looking to us. But these monsters are usually the shape they are for a reason.

Everything is made so that it is suited to where it lives so it can survive.

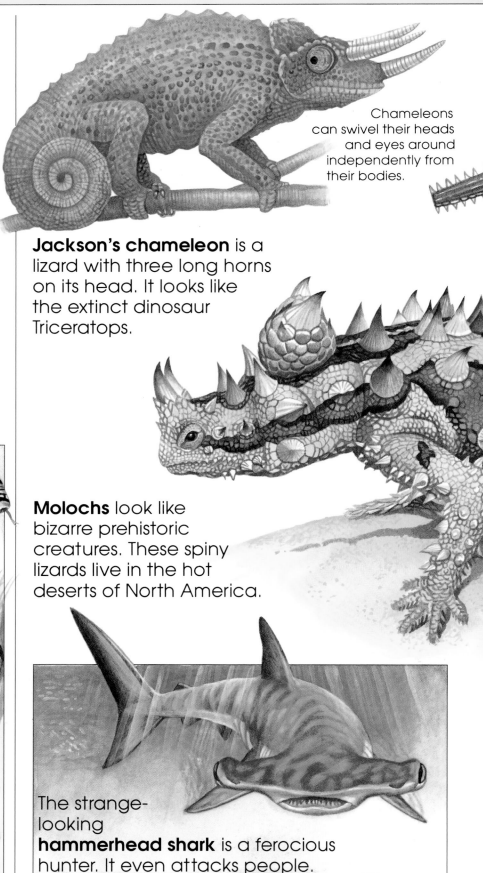

Chameleons can swivel their heads and eyes around independently from their bodies.

Jackson's chameleon is a lizard with three long horns on its head. It looks like the extinct dinosaur Triceratops.

Molochs look like bizarre prehistoric creatures. These spiny lizards live in the hot deserts of North America.

Animals do not usually have two heads, but sometimes they are born. This freak two-headed **kingsnake** was found in California.

The strange-looking **hammerhead shark** is a ferocious hunter. It even attacks people.

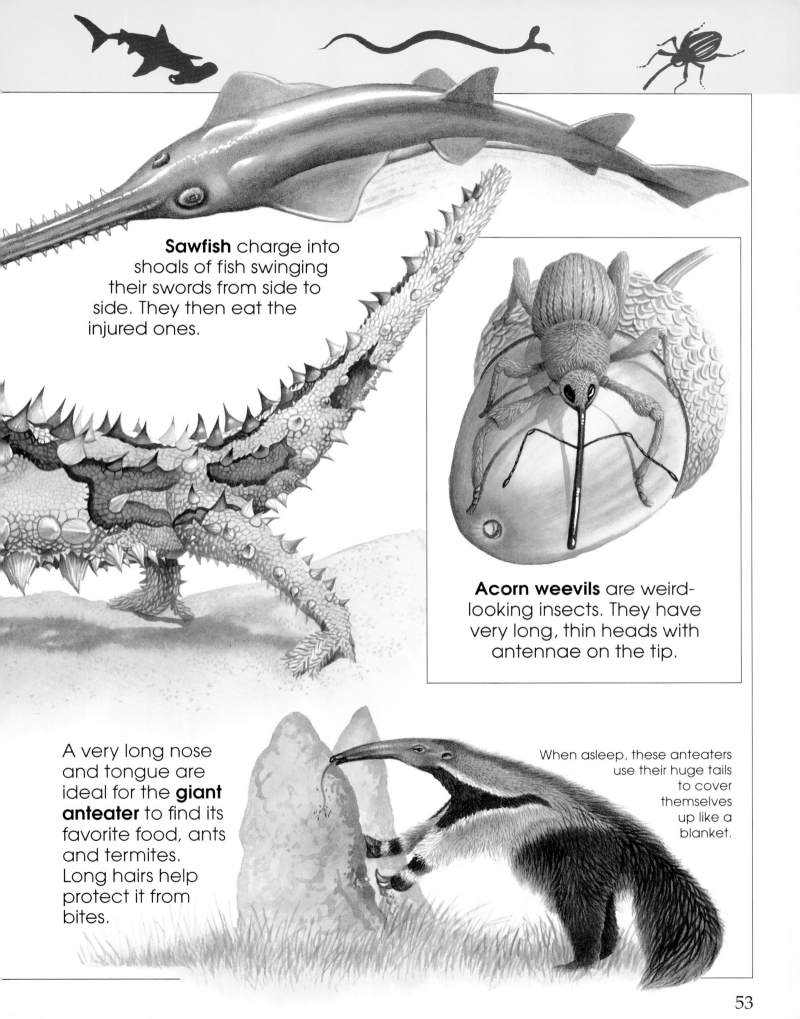

Sawfish charge into shoals of fish swinging their swords from side to side. They then eat the injured ones.

Acorn weevils are weird-looking insects. They have very long, thin heads with antennae on the tip.

A very long nose and tongue are ideal for the **giant anteater** to find its favorite food, ants and termites. Long hairs help protect it from bites.

When asleep, these anteaters use their huge tails to cover themselves up like a blanket.

53

Deadly monsters

Many animals protect themselves from attack by stinging or biting.

Some animals use poison to stun or kill their prey. Many of these deadly animals have ways of warning others to keep away!

The long trailing tentacles of the **Portuguese Man O'War jellyfish** are highly poisonous. Stinging cells shoot tiny barbed harpoons into anything that touches them.

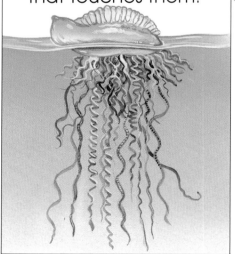

A **black widow spider** traps its prey in a web and then sucks out its insides.

Long, brightly colored spines cover the body of the beautiful but deadly **lion fish**. The sharp spines are coated with toxic mucus and cause terrible pain if touched.

The bright colors of **poison dart frogs** warn predators to leave them alone.

People living in the rainforests of South America smear their blow-pipe darts with the frog's mucus (slime) to poison their prey.

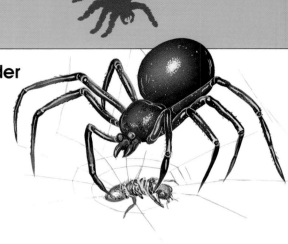

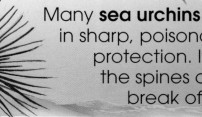

Many **sea urchins** are covered in sharp, poisonous spines for protection. If stepped on the spines can stab and break off in your foot.

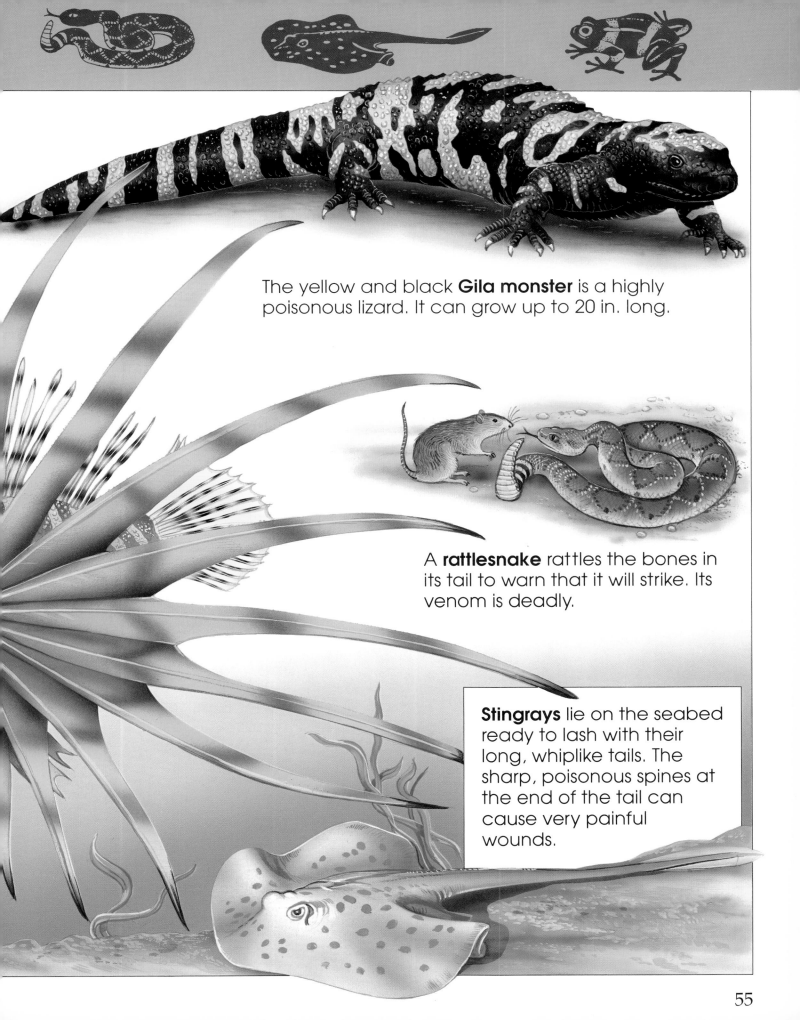

The yellow and black **Gila monster** is a highly poisonous lizard. It can grow up to 20 in. long.

A **rattlesnake** rattles the bones in its tail to warn that it will strike. Its venom is deadly.

Stingrays lie on the seabed ready to lash with their long, whiplike tails. The sharp, poisonous spines at the end of the tail can cause very painful wounds.

Masses of monsters

Some animals are only frightening and dangerous in large numbers.

Some, like bees, live together in groups to help each other. Others, like wolves, hunt in packs.

Some animals only group together in masses at certain times.

In some parts of the world, plagues of flying **locusts** can darken the sky, eating every green plant they land on.

Hornets live as a colony, nesting inside hollow trees. They use their huge jaws and deadly sting to hunt.

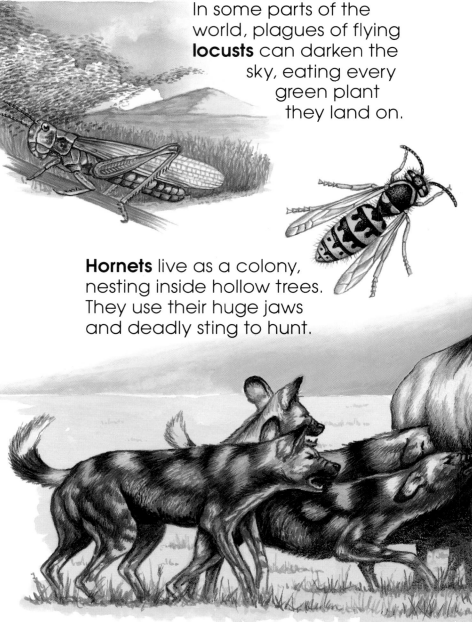

A colony of **army ants** marching through the forest will eat everything in its way - even small animals.

Millions of **mosquitoes** often breed together. The females must have a blood meal before they can lay their eggs. A person can lose nearly a pint of blood to these insects if they are not protected.

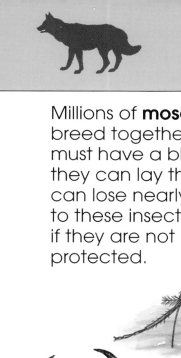

Swarms of African bees often leave their hive to find a new home. These **"killer bees"** are very aggressive and will attack anything in their way.

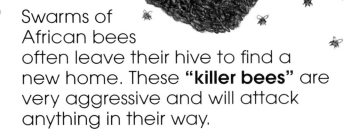

African wild dogs live in packs of up to 60. By circling their prey and dashing in and biting it, the victim is soon weakened and killed.

Hunting together in packs, **wolves** can catch and kill large animals. They usually attack the weak and sick, but rarely people.

Many animals are becoming rare. Some have already become extinct and will never be seen again outside a museum.

People kill animals for their skin, fur, feathers and horns. We also destroy the places where they live.

The largest **false scorpion** in Europe lives under the bark of dead trees. It is now extremely rare and only found in ancient forests.

On Maria Island in the West Indies lives the world's rarest snake, the **St. Lucia racer**. There are less than 100 left.

Racers are large, fast snakes which strike repeatedly with their heads when attacked, tearing the flesh.

Wildlife parks and zoos do important work trying to save animals from extinction. The last wild **Californian condor** was captured so it could breed under protection.

Trap door spiders in Southeast Asia are the rarest spiders. They use their jaws to dig holes, leaving a hinged lid at the entrance. When a victim comes near, the spider opens the lid, grabs its prey, and pulls it underground.

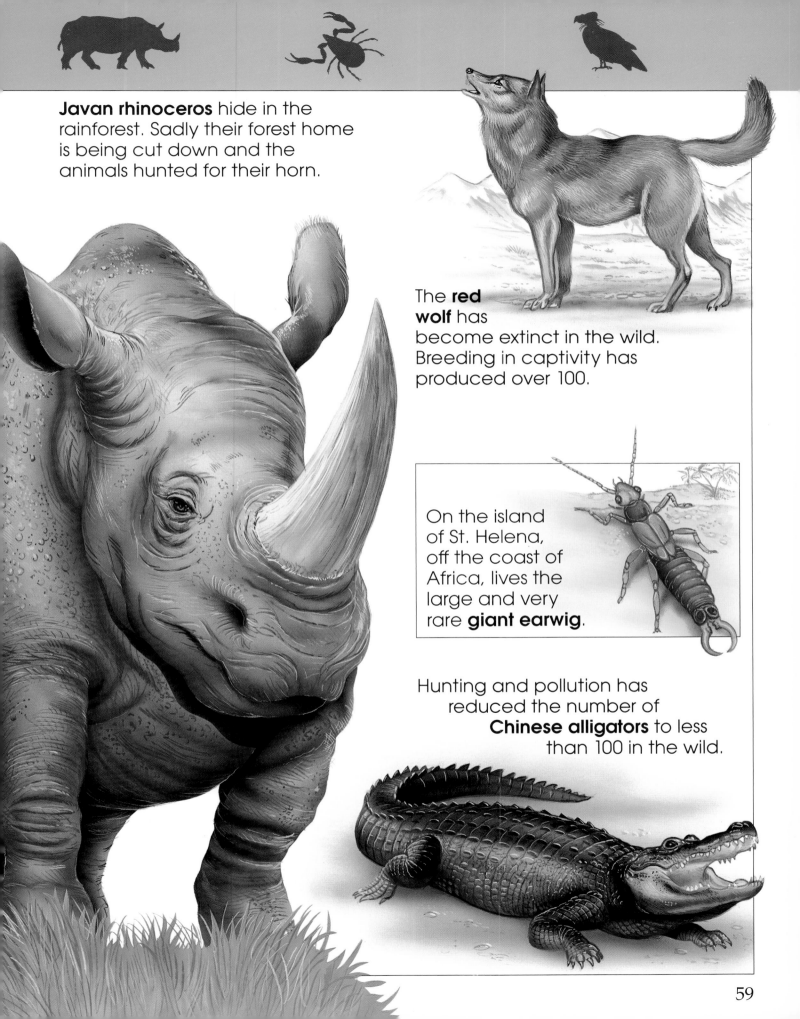

Javan rhinoceros hide in the rainforest. Sadly their forest home is being cut down and the animals hunted for their horn.

The **red wolf** has become extinct in the wild. Breeding in captivity has produced over 100.

On the island of St. Helena, off the coast of Africa, lives the large and very rare **giant earwig**.

Hunting and pollution has reduced the number of **Chinese alligators** to less than 100 in the wild.

Imaginary monsters

Superstition and fear have made people dream up all kinds of strange and imaginary monsters.

Some of these unnatural creatures were invented from stories of unusual animals brought back by travelers.

Other mythical monsters are based on actual living, and extinct, animals.

Some imaginary monsters might be real, we just do not know for sure.

Every year, thousands of people watch the water on Loch Ness in Scotland, hoping to see the **Loch Ness Monster**. Some believe that the monster could be a surviving plesiosaur, a prehistoric sea creature.

The **hydra** is a nine-headed beast of Greek mythology. It was very difficult to kill as each time a head was cut off it grew two new ones.

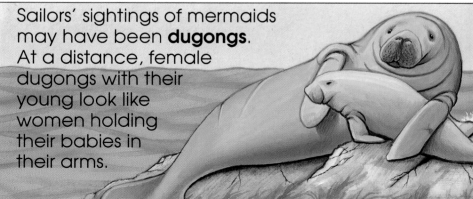

Sailors' sightings of mermaids may have been **dugongs**. At a distance, female dugongs with their young look like women holding their babies in their arms.

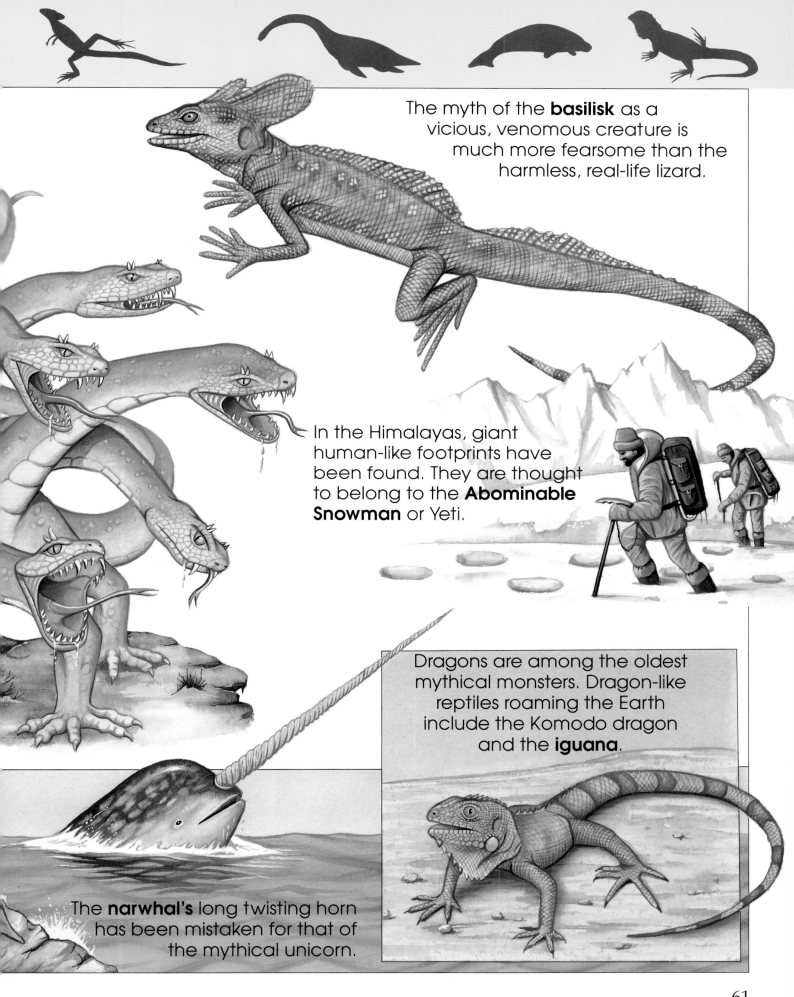

The myth of the **basilisk** as a vicious, venomous creature is much more fearsome than the harmless, real-life lizard.

In the Himalayas, giant human-like footprints have been found. They are thought to belong to the **Abominable Snowman** or Yeti.

Dragons are among the oldest mythical monsters. Dragon-like reptiles roaming the Earth include the Komodo dragon and the **iguana**.

The **narwhal's** long twisting horn has been mistaken for that of the mythical unicorn.

61

Millions of years ago, all kinds of strange monstrous animals roamed the Earth.

There were no people around when the dinosaurs ruled the world.

When people appeared they cut down forests and hunted animals. Some of the larger species were driven into extinction. Today, people still kill and threaten many animals.

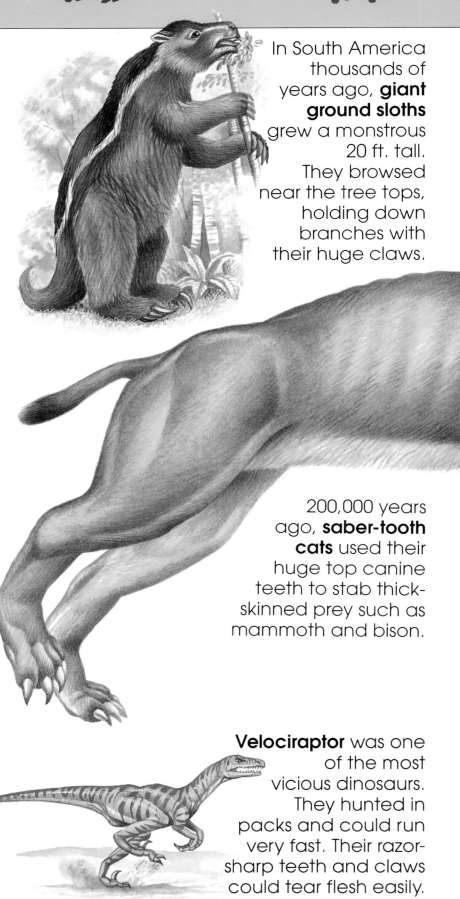

In South America thousands of years ago, **giant ground sloths** grew a monstrous 20 ft. tall. They browsed near the tree tops, holding down branches with their huge claws.

200,000 years ago, **saber-tooth cats** used their huge top canine teeth to stab thick-skinned prey such as mammoth and bison.

Velociraptor was one of the most vicious dinosaurs. They hunted in packs and could run very fast. Their razor-sharp teeth and claws could tear flesh easily.

Quetzalcoatlus' wings were made of skin like those of bats today.

97 million years ago, **quetzalcoatlus** soared through the air on wings spanning 40 feet.

Giant Irish deer grew antlers nearly 13 feet across. They died out 2,500 years ago.

Mammoths are one of the largest land mammals to have lived. They grew over 13 ft. tall and had woolly coats and huge tusks.

The giant **moa** of New Zealand was the tallest bird that ever existed. It stood over 10 feet tall.

People destroyed the moa's habitat and hunted it, so that by 1800 it was extinct.

Hyaenodon must have been a fearsome hunter and scavenger. Its skull was 26 in. long and full of needle-sharp teeth.

Coral creatures

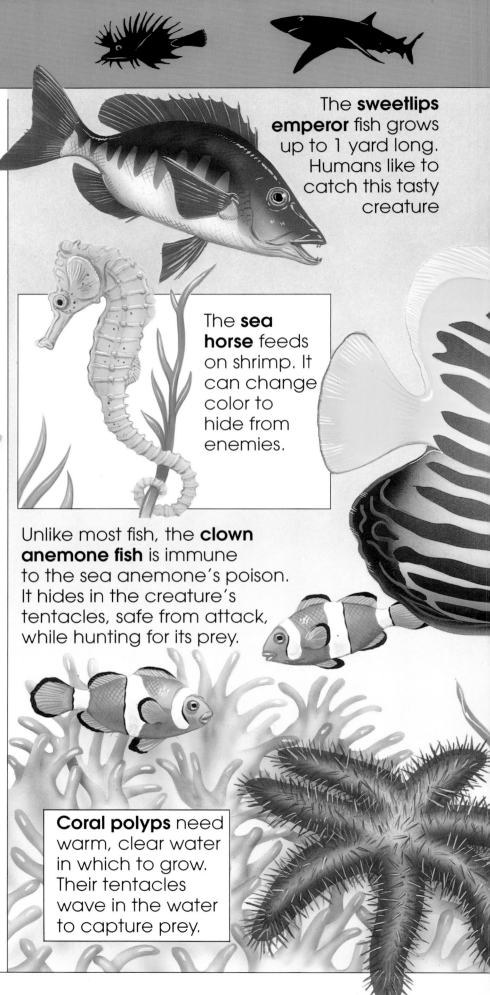

Coral reefs are made from millions of tiny creatures called coral polyps. When it dies, each polyp leaves behind a tiny limestone skeleton. There are thousands of types of polyp.

Many other creatures live on the reef. The shallow water and rocky crevices provide an ideal home.

The largest coral reef in the world is the **Great Barrier Reef** off the east coast of Queensland, Australia. It is over 1,243 mi. long.

The **sweetlips emperor** fish grows up to 1 yard long. Humans like to catch this tasty creature

The **sea horse** feeds on shrimp. It can change color to hide from enemies.

Unlike most fish, the **clown anemone fish** is immune to the sea anemone's poison. It hides in the creature's tentacles, safe from attack, while hunting for its prey.

Coral polyps need warm, clear water in which to grow. Their tentacles wave in the water to capture prey.

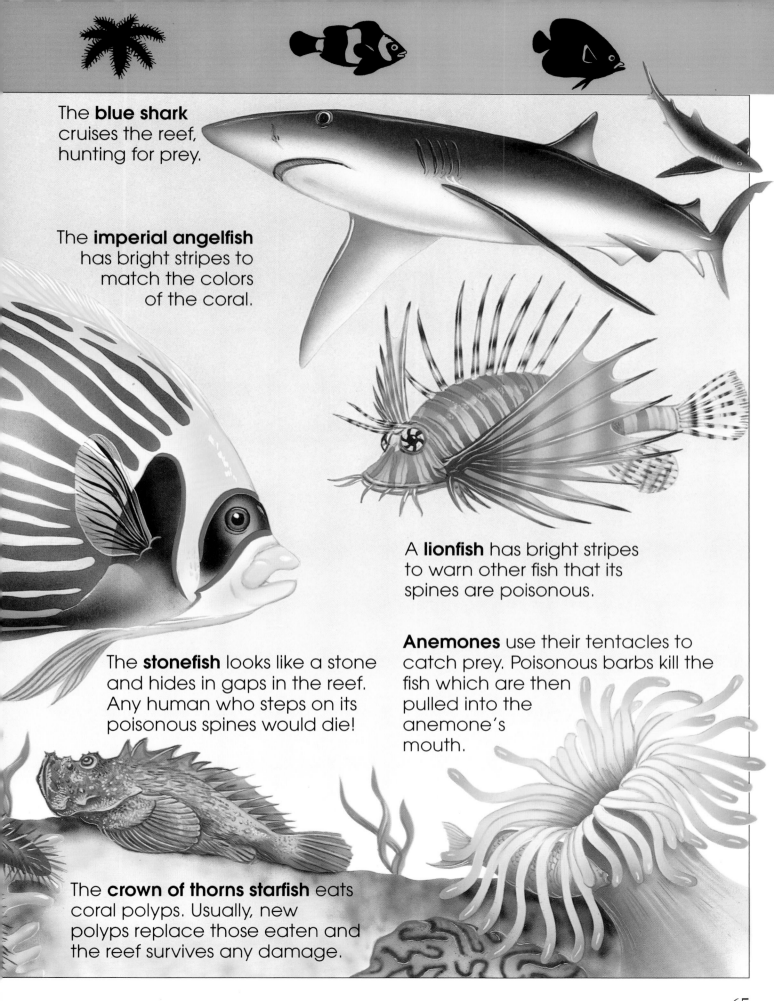

The **blue shark** cruises the reef, hunting for prey.

The **imperial angelfish** has bright stripes to match the colors of the coral.

A **lionfish** has bright stripes to warn other fish that its spines are poisonous.

The **stonefish** looks like a stone and hides in gaps in the reef. Any human who steps on its poisonous spines would die!

Anemones use their tentacles to catch prey. Poisonous barbs kill the fish which are then pulled into the anemone's mouth.

The **crown of thorns starfish** eats coral polyps. Usually, new polyps replace those eaten and the reef survives any damage.

Life on the shore can be very difficult for animals. As the tide comes in and goes out, their surroundings change from dry land to shallow sea.

Shrimp feed among the seaweed. When the tide goes out, they swim into deeper water, but sometimes they are caught in rock pools.

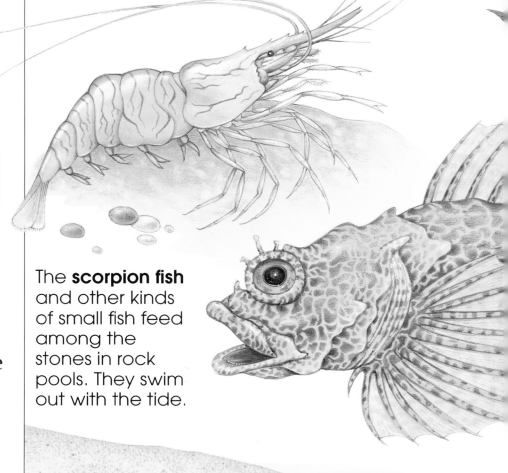

Pounding waves throw animals around. The sand is always moving as the sea pushes and pulls it around. Seashore animals must be tough to survive.

The **scorpion fish** and other kinds of small fish feed among the stones in rock pools. They swim out with the tide.

The **masked crab** lives on sandy beaches. When the tide goes out, it burrows into the sand. The tips of its two antennae poke out of the sand and act as breathing tubes.

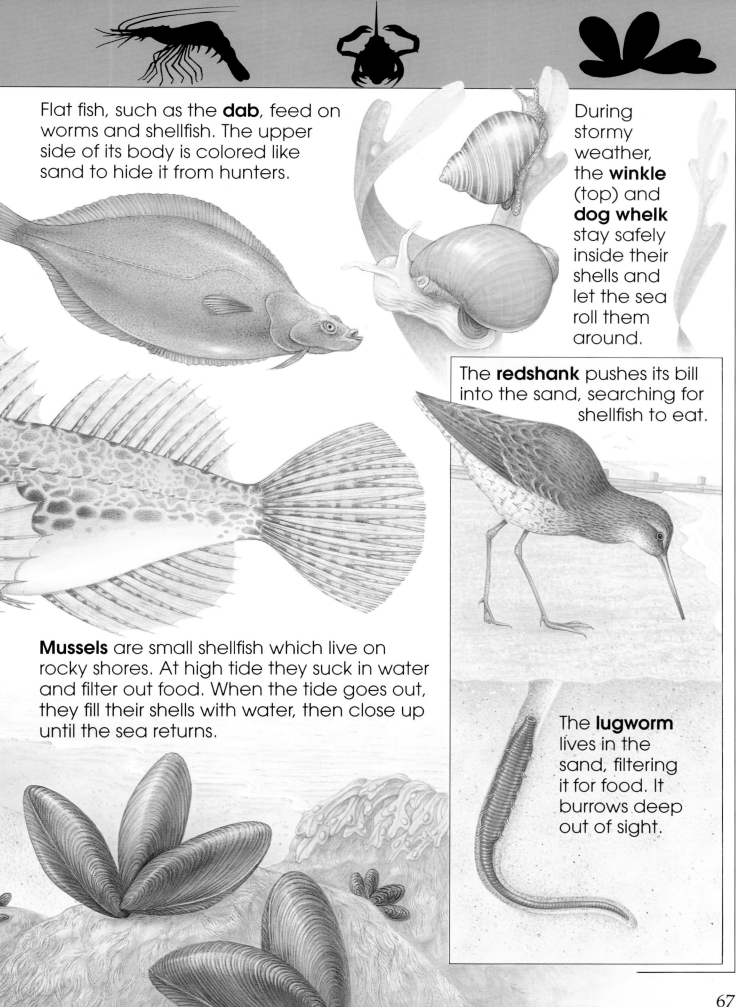

Flat fish, such as the **dab**, feed on worms and shellfish. The upper side of its body is colored like sand to hide it from hunters.

During stormy weather, the **winkle** (top) and **dog whelk** stay safely inside their shells and let the sea roll them around.

The **redshank** pushes its bill into the sand, searching for shellfish to eat.

Mussels are small shellfish which live on rocky shores. At high tide they suck in water and filter out food. When the tide goes out, they fill their shells with water, then close up until the sea returns.

The **lugworm** lives in the sand, filtering it for food. It burrows deep out of sight.

Deep-sea creatures

Most sea creatures live near the surface, where the water is warm and sunlit. The light cannot travel very deep and the sea's currents rarely move the warm surface water down to the depths of the ocean.

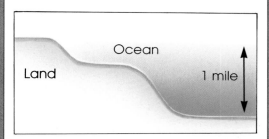

Ocean

Land

1 mile

At depths of more than 1 mile, the sea is very cold and completely dark. Some very strange creatures live here. They feed on each other and on food which drifts down from above.

Sperm whales dive down for food.

The **giant squid** can grow to 65 feet long.

Deep-sea shrimp can glow to attract a mate.

The **deep-sea angler fish** has a long growth over its mouth which glows faintly. This attracts other fish, which are then swallowed whole!

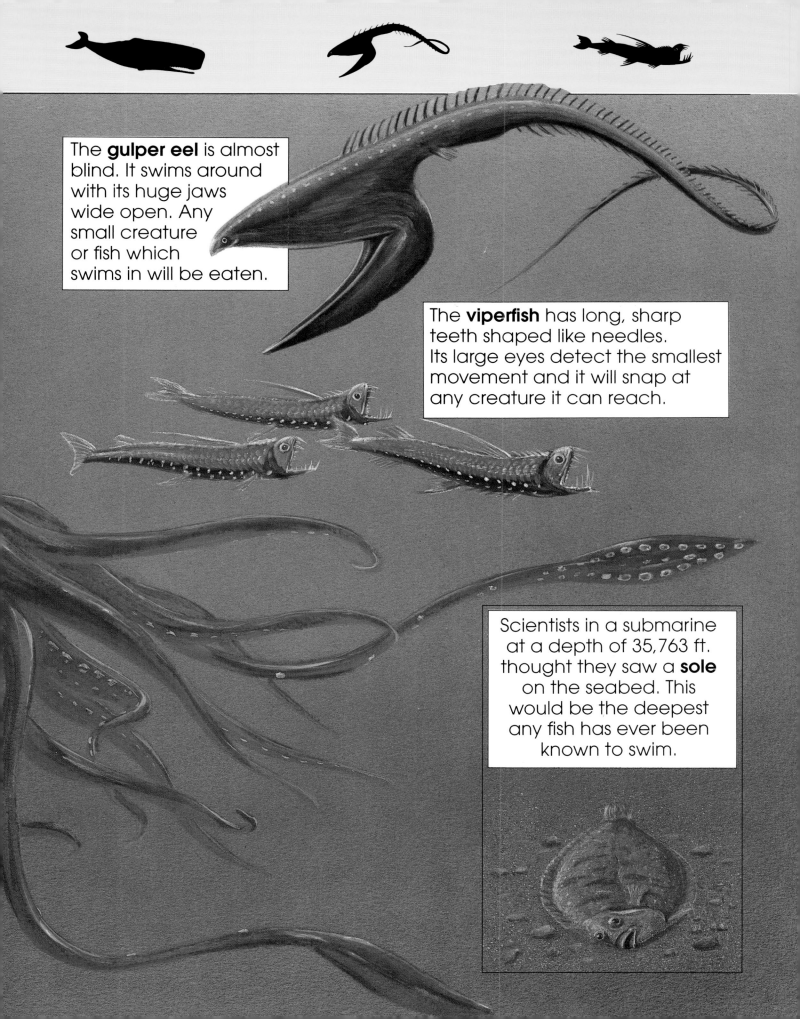

The **gulper eel** is almost blind. It swims around with its huge jaws wide open. Any small creature or fish which swims in will be eaten.

The **viperfish** has long, sharp teeth shaped like needles. Its large eyes detect the smallest movement and it will snap at any creature it can reach.

Scientists in a submarine at a depth of 35,763 ft. thought they saw a **sole** on the seabed. This would be the deepest any fish has ever been known to swim.

Around both the North and South Poles, the weather is very cold. A layer of ice floats on top of the sea all year round.

Animals which live there must be able to keep warm. They may have thick fur, like the polar bear, or layers of fat under their skin, like the common seal.

Killer whales prey on any creatures they can catch. They will even push ice from underwater to knock penguins and seals into the sea.

Penguins are birds that live around the South Pole. They lay their eggs on the ice and hunt for fish in the sea.

The largest penguin is the **Emperor penguin** which grows to over 3 feet tall.

The smallest penguin is the **fairy penguin**, which is only 16 in. tall.

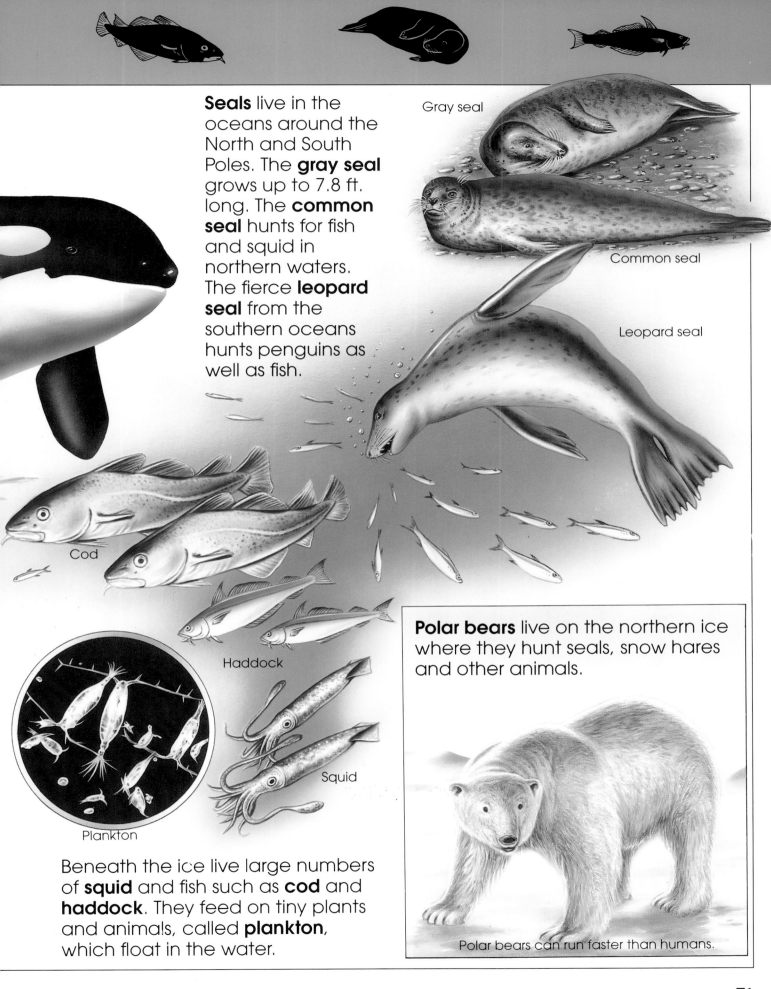

Seals live in the oceans around the North and South Poles. The **gray seal** grows up to 7.8 ft. long. The **common seal** hunts for fish and squid in northern waters. The fierce **leopard seal** from the southern oceans hunts penguins as well as fish.

Gray seal

Common seal

Leopard seal

Cod

Haddock

Plankton

Squid

Polar bears live on the northern ice where they hunt seals, snow hares and other animals.

Polar bears can run faster than humans.

Beneath the ice live large numbers of **squid** and fish such as **cod** and **haddock**. They feed on tiny plants and animals, called **plankton**, which float in the water.

71

The smallest living things in the sea are called plankton. They are so small that you could fit 40,000 of them on the end of your thumb.

Plankton can be either plants or animals. They are food for the larger sea animals.

Large clouds of plankton drift in the surface waters of all seas.

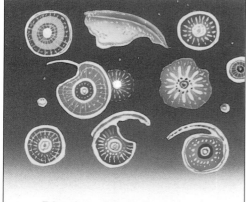

Phytoplankton are microscopic plants. They use the sunlight's energy to grow like plants on land.

The smallest animals are made of a single bodycell. **Ceratium** moves by thrashing a long, whip-like "arm." It feeds on tiny plants.

Ceratium

Radiolaria have beautiful shells. They can grow to about ¼ in. across.

Radiolaria

Tiny crustaceans, like **shrimp**, form part of the plankton cloud. They feed on other plankton.

Another name for these shrimp is **krill**.

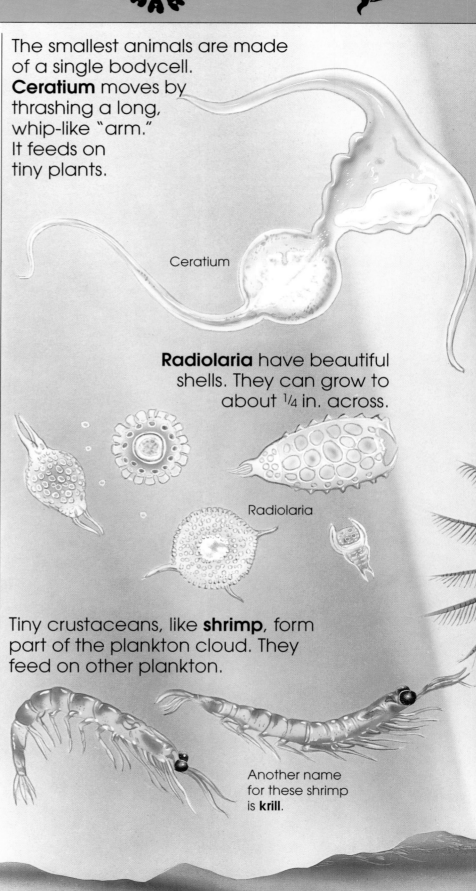

Some of the **plankton** are the young of much larger creatures. Because they drift with the ocean currents, these creatures can travel much further than they can as adults, allowing them to reach new homes.

Plankton

Ephyra

Barnacles

Jellyfish begin life as **ephyra**, small eight-armed creatures.

Adult **barnacles** and other adult shellfish cannot move at all. However, their young float in the plankton to places where they will not compete with their parents for food or space.

Whales are mammals which have evolved to live in the sea. They have fins instead of legs and a powerful tail to push them through the water.

Like all mammals, whales breathe air, so they need to come to the surface from time to time.

The **bowhead whale's** head is 20 ft. long. This is one-third of its length. The jaws are packed with baleen to filter food from the seawater.

The largest whales feed on plankton. They have special filters, called baleen, in their mouths which strain seawater and remove the tiny animals and plants to be eaten.

The earliest known whale is **basiliosaurus**, which lived about 40 million years ago.

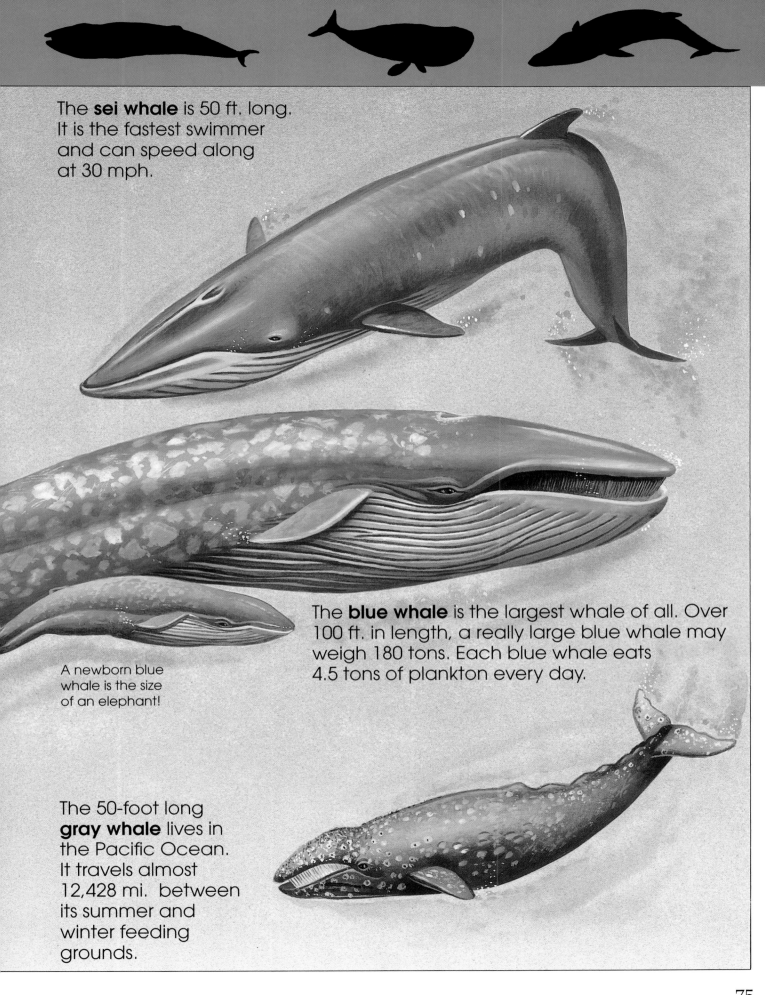

The **sei whale** is 50 ft. long. It is the fastest swimmer and can speed along at 30 mph.

A newborn blue whale is the size of an elephant!

The **blue whale** is the largest whale of all. Over 100 ft. in length, a really large blue whale may weigh 180 tons. Each blue whale eats 4.5 tons of plankton every day.

The 50-foot long **gray whale** lives in the Pacific Ocean. It travels almost 12,428 mi. between its summer and winter feeding grounds.

Coastline creatures

Seals are mammals which have evolved to live in the oceans.

Their legs have become flippers to help them swim, but they can still move on land.

Seals spend some of their time on shore, either caring for their babies or resting from hunting for fish.

Elephant seals were once hunted for the rich oil their bodies contain. At one time, only about a hundred were still alive, but today there are over 50,000 of them.

The **harp seal** hunts fish beneath the ocean surface. Thick layers of fat under its skin protect it from the icy water.

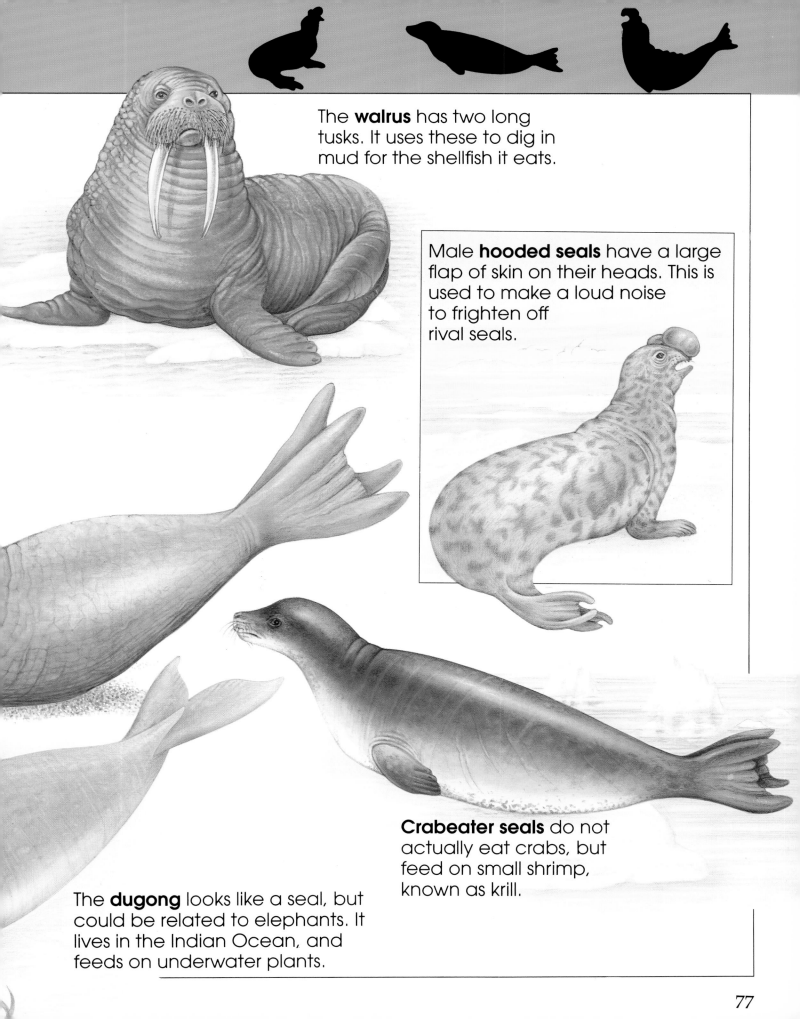

The **walrus** has two long tusks. It uses these to dig in mud for the shellfish it eats.

Male **hooded seals** have a large flap of skin on their heads. This is used to make a loud noise to frighten off rival seals.

Crabeater seals do not actually eat crabs, but feed on small shrimp, known as krill.

The **dugong** looks like a seal, but could be related to elephants. It lives in the Indian Ocean, and feeds on underwater plants.

Dolphins belong to a group of whales called toothed whales. They do not eat plankton but hunt squid and fish.

Dolphins are very intelligent creatures. They communicate with each other using different sounds arranged like words in a sentence.

Some dolphins are very rare. The **shepherd's beaked whale** is a recent discovery.

Dolphins are social animals. They live in family groups. If one dolphin is sick or injured, others will come to its rescue.

Dolphins are mammals. They breathe air and feed their babies with milk.

The **bouto** is a dolphin that lives in the Amazon River.

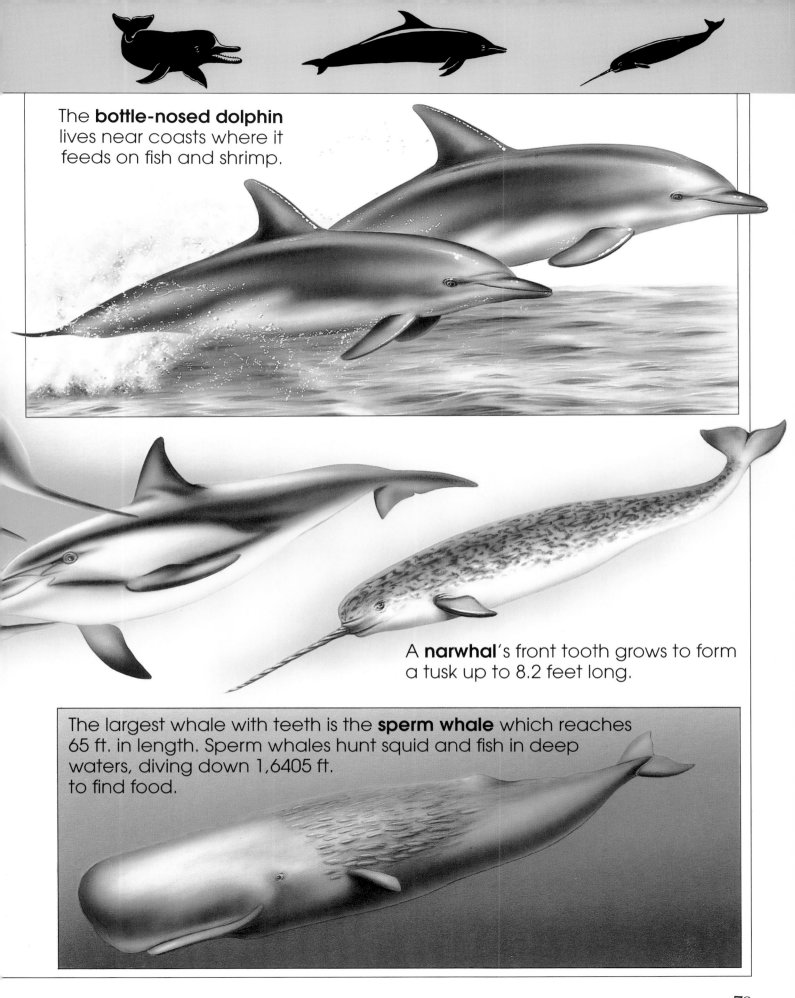

The **bottle-nosed dolphin** lives near coasts where it feeds on fish and shrimp.

A **narwhal**'s front tooth grows to form a tusk up to 8.2 feet long.

The largest whale with teeth is the **sperm whale** which reaches 65 ft. in length. Sperm whales hunt squid and fish in deep waters, diving down 1,6405 ft. to find food.

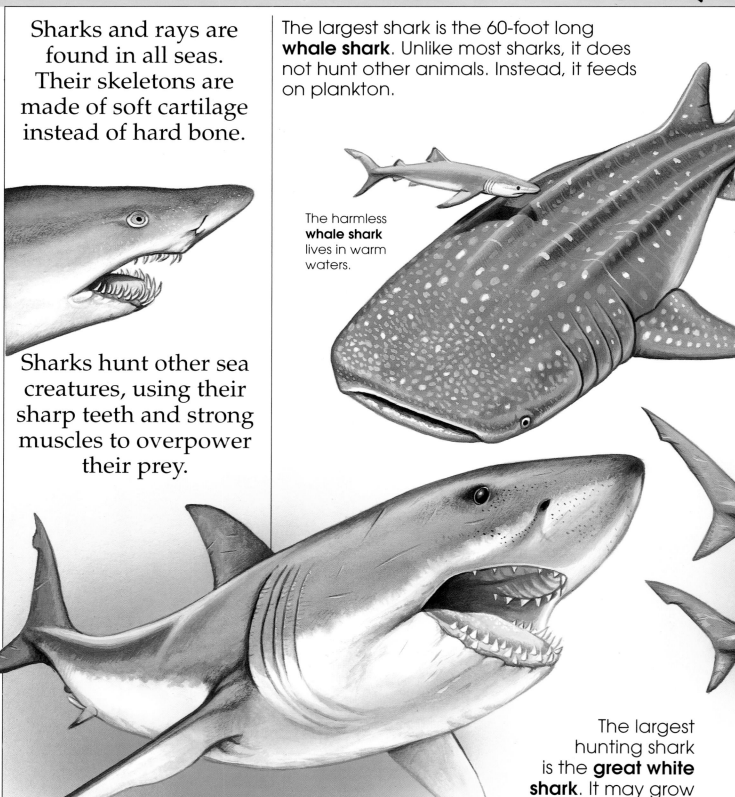

Sharks and rays are found in all seas. Their skeletons are made of soft cartilage instead of hard bone.

Sharks hunt other sea creatures, using their sharp teeth and strong muscles to overpower their prey.

The largest shark is the 60-foot long **whale shark**. Unlike most sharks, it does not hunt other animals. Instead, it feeds on plankton.

The harmless **whale shark** lives in warm waters.

The largest hunting shark is the **great white shark**. It may grow to 23 ft. long and usually feeds on larger fish and other animals.

The **great white shark** sometimes attacks people.

Receptors on the head of the **hammerhead** shark help it to detect its prey. It swings its head from side to side as it swims.

The **manta** is a giant ray. Its wings can measure 23 feet across. Sometimes it jumps out of the sea, creating a large splash when it falls back.

The **thresher shark** uses its long tail to beat the water when hunting. Experts think that this may stun fish, making them easy to catch.

The **stingray** has a large, poisonous spine on top of its tail, which it uses to fight off attackers.

Large groups, called mobs, of **blue sharks** are often found in tropical oceans. As many as a thousand blue sharks may form one mob.

Flying creatures

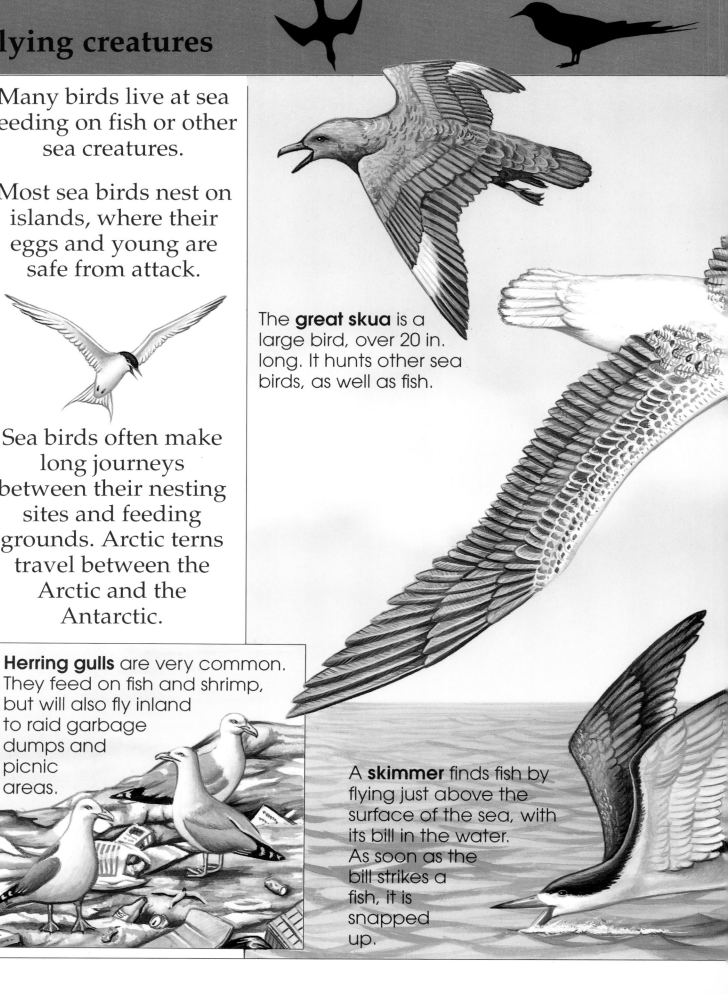

Many birds live at sea feeding on fish or other sea creatures.

Most sea birds nest on islands, where their eggs and young are safe from attack.

Sea birds often make long journeys between their nesting sites and feeding grounds. Arctic terns travel between the Arctic and the Antarctic.

The **great skua** is a large bird, over 20 in. long. It hunts other sea birds, as well as fish.

Herring gulls are very common. They feed on fish and shrimp, but will also fly inland to raid garbage dumps and picnic areas.

A **skimmer** finds fish by flying just above the surface of the sea, with its bill in the water. As soon as the bill strikes a fish, it is snapped up.

The largest sea bird is the **wandering albatross**, which has wings 11 feet across. Long ago, sailors believed it was bad luck to kill an albatross.

Steamer ducks live around the coast. They cannot fly, but swim along the shore looking for shellfish, shrimp and crabs to eat.

Puffins nest on cliffs and rocky islands. The females lay just one egg each year.

Gannet fly around searching for fish in the water. They may dive from a height of 100 ft. to catch their prey.

83

Reptiles are animals such as lizards. Most live on land.

A few types of reptile have evolved to live in the ocean, but they need to come to the surface often to breathe air.

Most sea reptiles lay their eggs on dry land. They may come ashore once a year to do this.

The **green turtle** has a tough shell to protect it from attack. It feeds on seaweed and jellyfish.

The **leatherback turtle** has no shell, but the skin on its back is very thick and tough.

Estuary crocodiles live off the coasts of northern Australia. They can grow to be over 20 ft. long and are the largest sea reptiles alive today.

Ridley turtles crunch up shellfish with their strong jaws.

The **banded sea snake** lives in the Pacific Ocean where it hunts fish. It is one of the most poisonous snakes in the world.

The **hawksbill turtle** is very rare. Not long ago, it was hunted for its shell. This was used to make things such as ornate boxes and spectacle frames.

Marine iguanas live around the remote Galapagos Islands in the Pacific Ocean. They dive into the ocean to feed on seaweed.

Marine iguanas come ashore to bask in the sun.

Strange creatures

There are many fish in the oceans that look strange to us, but they are actually very well adapted to their surroundings.

Thousands of fish have evolved to live in different places - on coral reefs, in icy waters, near the surface of the sea, or on the seabed

Flying fish are able to leap out of the water and glide through the air, using their fins as wings. It is thought that the fish "fly" in this way to escape hunters.

When danger threatens, the **porcupine fish** gulps huge amounts of water and swells up to four times its usual size. The stiff spines stick out to make the fish look like a spiky football.

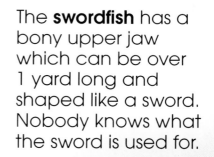

The **four-eyed fish** swims at the surface with each of its two eyes half in and half out of the water. The fish looks for insect prey on the surface, while watching for danger under the sea.

The **swordfish** has a bony upper jaw which can be over 1 yard long and shaped like a sword. Nobody knows what the sword is used for.

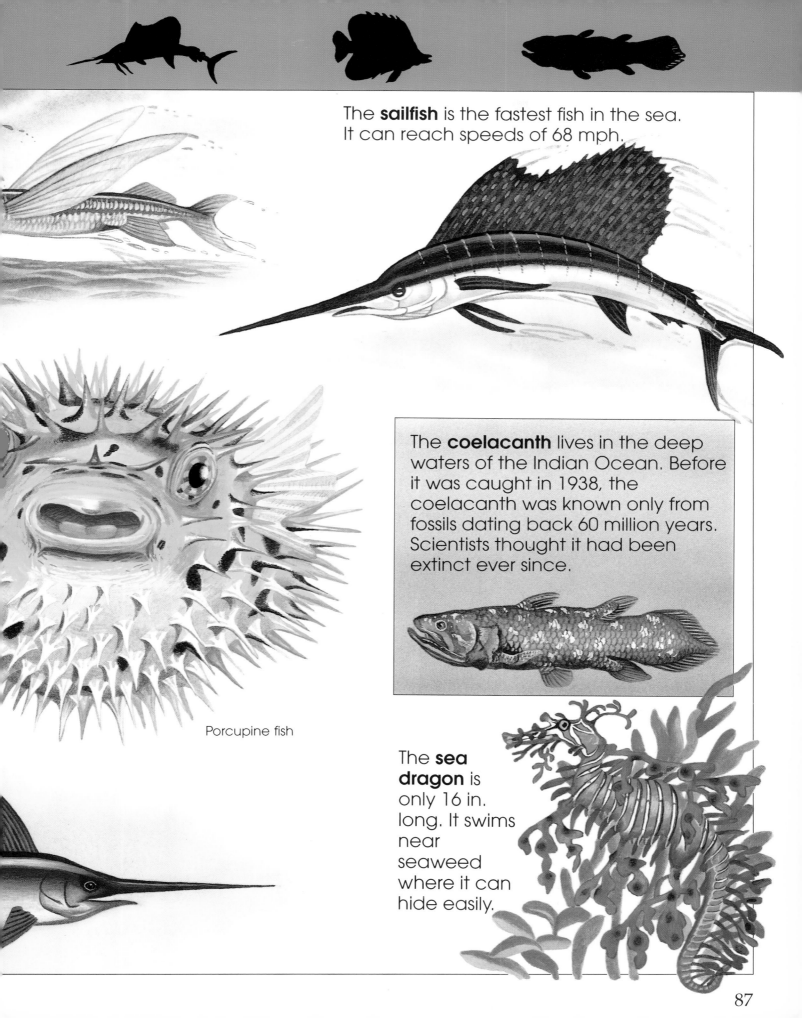

The **sailfish** is the fastest fish in the sea. It can reach speeds of 68 mph.

The **coelacanth** lives in the deep waters of the Indian Ocean. Before it was caught in 1938, the coelacanth was known only from fossils dating back 60 million years. Scientists thought it had been extinct ever since.

Porcupine fish

The **sea dragon** is only 16 in. long. It swims near seaweed where it can hide easily.

Prehistoric creatures

Millions of years ago, strange creatures lived in the oceans.

Scientists know about these creatures because they have found fossils of their bones buried in ancient rocks.

Many of these giant sea animals lived at the same time as the dinosaurs.

Kronosaurus had the largest head of any hunter in the sea. It was almost 10 ft. long and was armed with lots of sharp teeth.

Cryptocleidus had strong flippers to propel it through the water. It caught small fish in its long jaws armed with sharp teeth.

Ichthyosaurus looked like a dolphin or large fish, but was really a reptile. Ichthyosaurus could not come on shore to lay eggs like most reptiles, so it gave birth to live young.

Archelon was the largest turtle. It was nearly 13 feet long and lived about 70 million years ago.

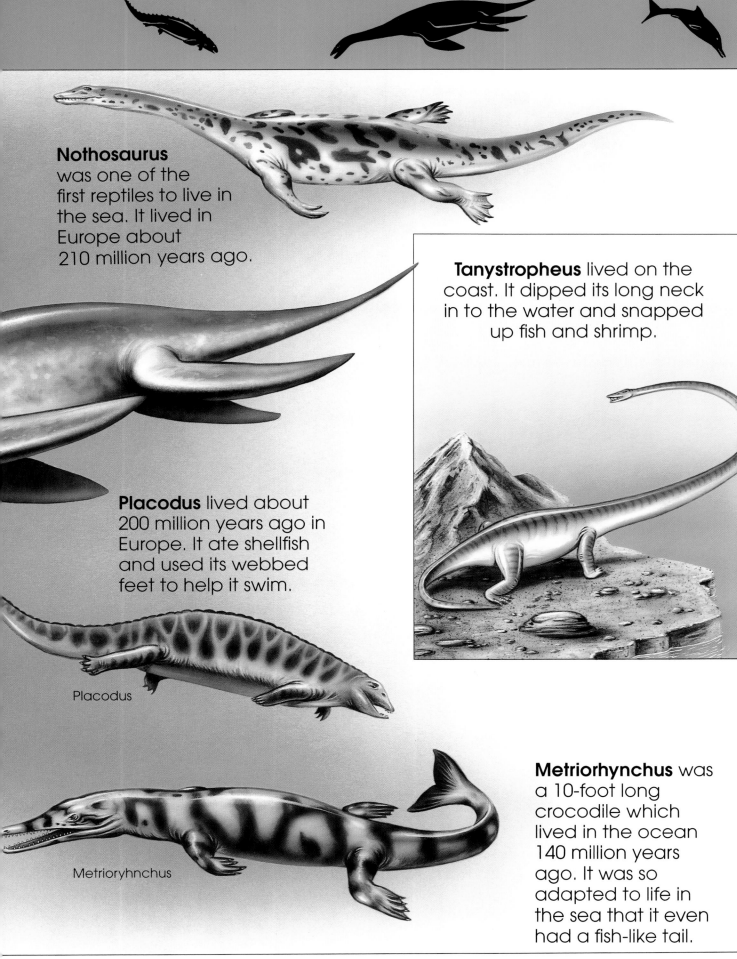

Nothosaurus was one of the first reptiles to live in the sea. It lived in Europe about 210 million years ago.

Tanystropheus lived on the coast. It dipped its long neck in to the water and snapped up fish and shrimp.

Placodus lived about 200 million years ago in Europe. It ate shellfish and used its webbed feet to help it swim.

Placodus

Metrioryhnchus

Metriorhynchus was a 10-foot long crocodile which lived in the ocean 140 million years ago. It was so adapted to life in the sea that it even had a fish-like tail.

Because the oceans are so vast, there are many areas which have never been explored properly.

Sailors who have traveled off the main shipping routes have reported seeing strange and curious creatures. As nobody has ever caught one of these mysterious creatures, scientists do not believe they really exist.

The type of **sea monster** most often seen has a small head and a long neck held upright. Witnesses say they see a large body under the water with four large fins which move the creature slowly along.

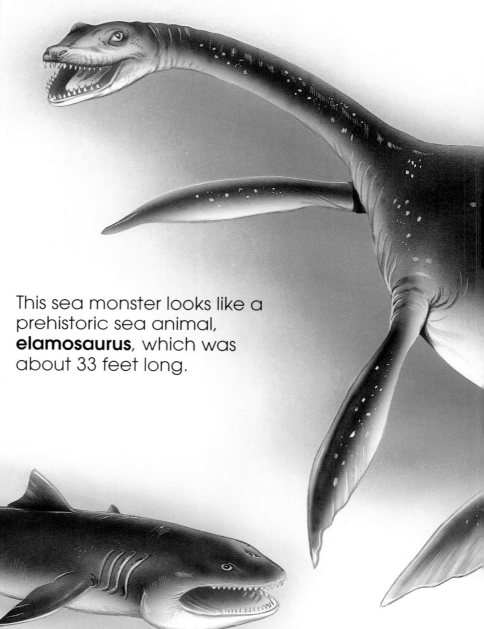

This sea monster looks like a prehistoric sea animal, **elamosaurus**, which was about 33 feet long.

The 13-foot long **megamouth shark** was not discovered until the 1980s. Nobody knew about it until one was accidentally caught in a net. This proved that large sea creatures can exist without anybody knowing about them.

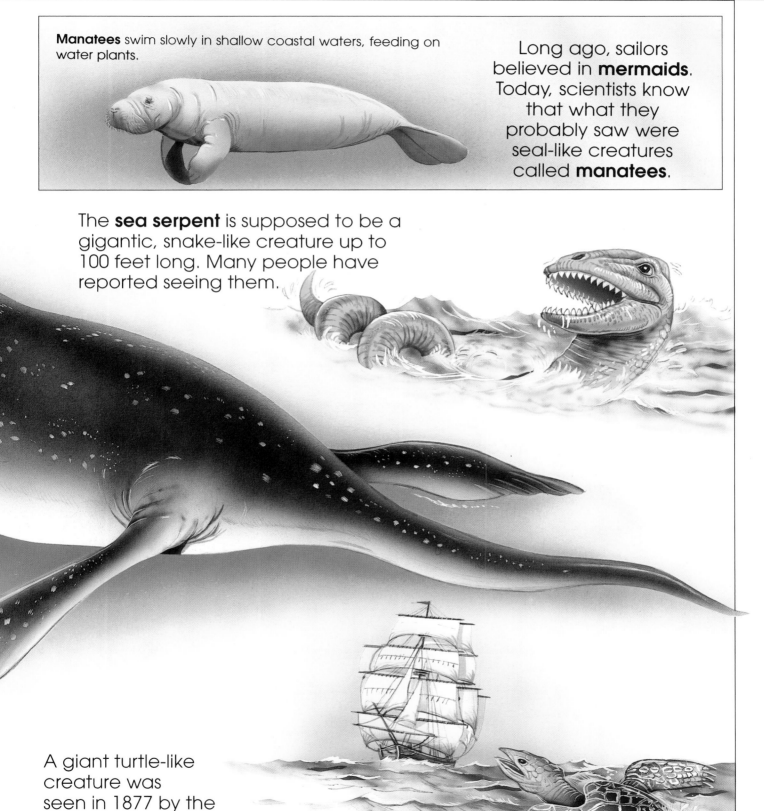

Manatees swim slowly in shallow coastal waters, feeding on water plants.

Long ago, sailors believed in **mermaids**. Today, scientists know that what they probably saw were seal-like creatures called **manatees**.

The **sea serpent** is supposed to be a gigantic, snake-like creature up to 100 feet long. Many people have reported seeing them.

A giant turtle-like creature was seen in 1877 by the crew of *HMS Osborne*. The creature was about 65 feet long and swam quickly.

Europe

Europe is the second smallest continent in the world. About 700 million people live there, so it is very crowded compared to other regions.

Europe has ocean to the north, south and west. To the east, it borders the continent of Asia.

The Ural Mountains separate Europe from Asia.

There are more than 40 countries in Europe. The continent stretches from inside the Arctic Circle down to the Mediterranean Sea. Each country has its own government, capital city, languages and customs.

Key facts

Size: 4,062,158 sq. mi. (7% of the world's land surface)

Smallest country: Vatican City (.17 sq. mi.)

Largest country: Russia (1,757,141 sq. mi. of it is in Europe)

Longest river: Volga (2,194 mi.)

Highest mountain: Mount Elbrus (18,482 ft.) in the Caucasus mountain range

Countries

Twelve European countries are members of the EC, or the European Community. The members work together to make laws in areas such as farming, industry and finance.

The flag of the EC

The group of countries in the west of the European continent is sometimes known as Western Europe.

Many countries in the east of Europe are changing. The former Soviet Union has now divided into fifteen separate republics.

Landscape

Europe's landscape is very varied. In the far north you can see lots of forests and lakes. In central parts there are meadows and low hills. The south has some high mountain ranges and wide plains.

Western Europe's highest mountain range is the Alps, which stretches across the top of Italy. Alpine peaks are snowy all year. The Alps are very popular for skiing vacations.

Economy

There are lots of industries in Europe. Goods are imported and exported through the many seaports. Farming of all kinds is also important.

Europe has many busy seaports

Main industries

Fishing — Steel

Timber — Engineering

Farming — Mining

Textiles

Weather

In Scandinavia it is cold much of the time. In Eastern Europe the winters are very cold, but the summers are warm. Over Western Europe the summers are warm, the winters are cool and rain falls throughout the year.

Map key

1 Albania
2 Andorra
3 Austria
4 Belarus
5 Belgium
6 Bosnia & Herzegovina
7 Bulgaria
8 Croatia
9 Czech Republic
10 Denmark
11 Estonia
12 Finland
13 France
14 Germany
15 Gibraltar
16 Greece
17 Hungary
18 Iceland
19 Ireland
20 Italy
21 Latvia
22 Liechtenstein
23 Lithuania
24 Luxembourg
25 Macedonia
26 Malta
27 Moldova
28 Monaco
29 Netherlands
30 Norway
31 Poland
32 Portugal
33 Romania
34 Russia
(34) Kaliningrad
35 San Marino
36 Slovakia
37 Slovenia
38 Spain
39 Sweden
40 Switzerland
41 Ukraine
42 United Kingdom
43 Vatican City
44 Yugoslavia

Map of Europe

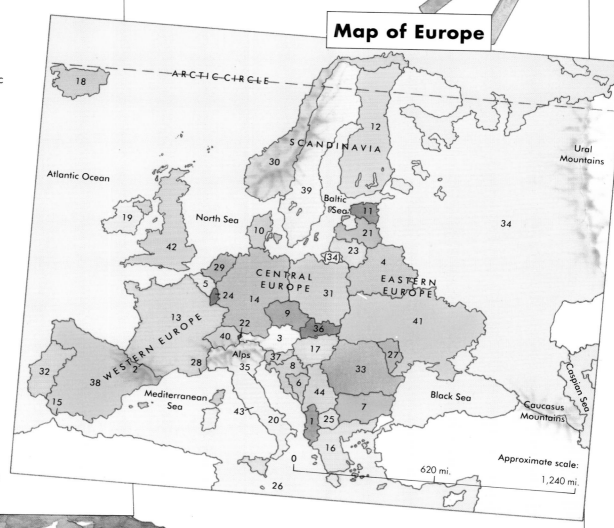

ARCTIC CIRCLE

SCANDINAVIA

Atlantic Ocean

Ural Mountains

North Sea

Baltic Sea

CENTRAL EUROPE

EASTERN EUROPE

WESTERN EUROPE

Alps

Mediterranean Sea

Black Sea

Caucasus Mountains

Caspian Sea

Approximate scale:

0   620 mi.   1,240 mi.

United Kingdom

The United Kingdom lies off Europe's north-west coast. It is made up of four countries.

Key facts

Size: 94,226 sq. mi.
Population: More than 57 million
Currency: Pound sterling
Main language: English
Also called: Britain, U.K.

England, Scotland, Northern Ireland and Wales make up the U.K.

English flag   **Scottish flag**

Welsh flag   **Northern Irish flag**

A London bus

Capital city: London. About 6.4 million people live here. London is the center of business and government.

Landscape: The highest mountains are in Wales and Scotland. The tallest is Ben Nevis (4,406 ft.) in Scotland. The longest river is the Severn (468 mi.). It flows from Wales into England.

Industries

Chemicals
Electronics
Textiles
Heavy machinery
Oil

Ben Nevis

Places to visit: There are lots of historical sites, ancient cities and towns. Britain is famous for its royal palaces and stately homes.

The Tower of London, Britain's most popular tourist attraction

France

Paris

France is one of the largest countries on the European continent.

Key facts

Size: 211,207 sq. mi.
Population: Over 56 million
Currency: French franc
Main language: French

Capital city: Paris. This is a world center of fashion and art. It has many famous art galleries and museums.

The Eiffel Tower is in Paris. It is made of iron and stands 984 ft. high. You can travel to the top by elevator.

Eiffel Tower

Landscape: France has many different kinds of scenery, with spectacular mountains, pretty river valleys and sunny beaches. Mont Blanc, on the Italian border, is the highest mountain (15,772 ft.). The longest river is the Loire (653 mi.).

Grapes are grown for wine

Industries

Farming
Wine
Tourism
Fashion
Vehicles
Chemicals

A vineyard

Places to visit: You can ski in the Alps, swim in the Mediterranean or visit many historic chateaux. EuroDisney™ is near Paris.

The royal château at Versailles

Spain

Spain is in south-west Europe. It is the third largest country on the continent.

Key facts

Size: 194,896 sq. mi.
Population: Over 38 million
Currency: Peseta
Main language: Spanish

The Royal Palace

Capital city: Madrid. This is a famous center of culture with many theaters, cinemas and opera houses.

Landscape: Spain is a mountainous country. In the center there is a vast, high plateau. The highest mountain is Mt. Mulhacen (11,440 ft.). The longest river is the Tagus (626 mi.).

The Sierra Nevada mountains

Places to visit: There are many historic cities and palaces built by the Moors, who invaded from Africa in 711. In the south there are sunny beaches.

The Alhambra, a Moorish palace near Granada

Industries

Tourism
Wine
Farming
Vehicles
Chemicals
Electronics

Germany

Germany borders nine other countries. In 1990, East and West Germany joined to become one country.

Key facts

Size: 137,743 sq. mi.
Population: About 79 million
Currency: Deutsche Mark
Main language: German
Full name: Federal Republic of Germany

Capital city: Berlin. This city was once divided by a high wall mounted with guns. Today, people can go wherever they like in the city.

The Brandenburg Gate, Berlin

Black Forest pinewoods

Landscape: There are many different kinds of scenery. The beautiful Rhine River Valley and the Black Forest are very famous. The Zugspitze (9,722 ft.) is the highest mountain. The longest river is the Elbe (724 mi.).

Neuschwanstein Castle, Bavaria

Industries

Chemicals
Vehicles
Engineering
Coal
Shipbuilding

Places to visit: There are historic cities and ancient castles in the regions of Bavaria and Saxony. In the north there are sandy beaches.

Norway

Norway lies along the coast of Scandinavia. Part of it is inside the Arctic Circle.

Oslo

Key facts

Size: 125,181 sq. mi.
Population: Over 4 million
Currency: Norwegian krone
Language: Norwegian

Capital city: Oslo. This is one of the world's largest cities, but only 500,000 people live here. You can visit many ancient Viking burial mounds and settlement sites in Norway.

Landscape: Norway has a long coastline, famous for its deep inlets called fjords. It also has over 150,000 islands. Mountains and moorland cover three-quarters of the country. Glittertind is the highest mountain (8,104 ft.). The longest river is the Glama (373 mi.).

A Norwegian fjord

Places to visit: The Norwegian mountains are famous for winter sports. There are about 10,000 ski jumps in the country, as well as lots of forest trails.

Industries

Oil
Paper-making
Timber
Fishing

Cross-country skiing in Norway

Sweden

Sweden is the largest Scandinavian country. It has a long coastline and many islands.

Stockholm

Key facts

Size: 173,731 sq. mi.
Population: Over 8 million
Currency: Swedish krona
Main language: Swedish

Capital city: Stockholm. The city is built on a string of islands. It is the home of the Royal Palace and many other historic buildings.

The Royal Palace

Landscape: Over half of Sweden is covered with forest. There are about 96,000 lakes in the south and centre of the country. Lapland (northern Sweden) is inside the Arctic Circle. Mount Kebnerkaise (6,926 ft.) is the highest peak in Sweden.

Places to visit: Sweden has thousands of islands which are ideal for boating and fishing. You can find out about Viking longboats in the Nordic Museum, Stockholm.

Industries

Timber
Vehicles
Electronics
Minerals
Chemicals

A Viking longboat

Denmark

Denmark is the smallest Scandinavian country. It is made up of a peninsula and about 400 islands.

Copenhagen

Key facts

Size: 16,629 sq. mi.
Population: Over 5 million
Currency: Danish krone
Main Language: Danish

Capital city: Copenhagen. This is a city with many old buildings, fountains and pretty squares. The well-known statue of the Little Mermaid sits on a rock in Copenhagen Harbor. The story of the mermaid was written by a famous Dane, Hans Christian Andersen.

The Little Mermaid

Landscape: Denmark has mainly low-lying countryside with forests and lakes. There are many beautiful sandy beaches and about 500 islands. Yding Skovhoj is the highest mountain (568 ft.). The longest river is the Guden (98 mi.).

Places to visit: Copenhagen has palaces, castles and a Viking museum. At Legoland™ Park everything is made of Lego™, including life-sized working trains and lots of miniature buildings.

Industries

Farming
Tourism
Textiles
Electronics
Oil

A Legoland™ train

The Netherlands

The Netherlands is one of the flattest European countries. Two-fifths is below sea level.

Amsterdam

Key facts

Size: 15,770 sq. mi.
Population: Over 15 million
Currency: Guilder
Main language: Dutch
Also called: Holland

Capital city: Amsterdam. This city is built on canals and is sometimes called "the Venice of the North." It has about a thousand bridges and many attractive seventeenth-century houses.

Amsterdam

Landscape: The Netherlands is very flat and is criss-crossed by rivers and canals. In the past, large areas of land were reclaimed from the sea. Sea-dams, called dykes, were built and the sea water was drained away. The highest point of land is only 1,056 ft.

Places to visit: The tulip fields are a world-famous sight. In the countryside there are lots of pretty old towns and villages, country houses and castles. Windmills are still used in parts of the country.

Industries

Flowers
Farming
Diamond-cutting
Electronics
Chemicals

Tulips are exported to many parts of the world

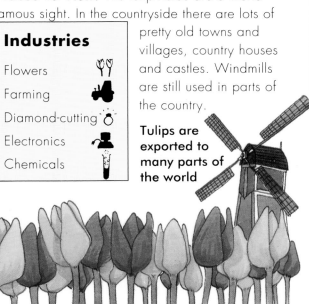

Italy

Italy is in southern Europe. The Mediterranean islands of Sicily and Sardinia are part of this country.

Key facts

Size: 116,303 sq. mi.
Population: Over 57 million
Currency: Lira
Main language: Italian

Capital city: Rome. This was once the capital of the ancient Roman empire. It has lots of Roman remains, including the ruins of the Colosseum. Here, huge audiences watched as gladiators fought and Christians were thrown to the lions.

The Colosseum

In Rome there is a tiny separate country called Vatican City. This is the home of the Pope, the head of the Roman Catholic Church.

Landscape: There are spectacular mountains and beautiful lakes in the north. In central and southern regions you can see plains and smaller mountains. Italy has several live volcanoes, including Etna, Vesuvius and Stromboli. Mont Blanc is the highest mountain (15,771 ft.). The Po is the longest river (405 mi.).

Stromboli

Industries

Farming
Vehicles
Electronics
Fashion

Places to visit: Italy has many historic cities, such as Venice, which is built on a lagoon. The easiest way to travel around Venice is by gondola. Some of the world's greatest artists have lived in Italy. You can see their work in art galleries and museums.

A Venetian gondola

Greece

Greece juts out into the Mediterranean Sea. About one-fifth of the country is made up of small islands.

Key facts

Size: 50,949 sq. mi.
Population: Over 10 million
Currency: Drachma
Main language: Greek

Capital city: Athens. This is one of the world's oldest cities. On the top of the Acropolis ridge, you can see the ruins of the Parthenon. This Greek temple is 2,400 years old.

Landscape: Mainland Greece has plains and forests in the south and is mountainous in the north. Mount Olympus is the highest mountain (9,571 ft.). The Greek islands vary in size and landscape. Crete is the largest of these. The longest river in Greece is the Aliakmon (184 mi.).

Mount Olympus, legendary home of the ancient Greek gods

Industries

Tourism
Fishing
Farming

Places to visit: There are lots of ancient sites. Many of them are linked with stories from Greek mythology. For instance, the Palace of Knossos, on Crete, is the legendary home of the Minotaur monster.

The Minotaur

Poland

Poland is in Central Europe. It shares its borders with four other countries. Its coastline is on the Baltic Sea.

Key facts

Size: 120,725 sq. mi.
Population: Over 38 million
Currency: Zloty
Main language: Polish

Capital city: Warsaw. The old city of Warsaw was destroyed in World War Two. The "Old Town" area has been rebult in the style of the old buildings.

Warsaw "Old Town"

Landscape: There are many lakes and wooded hills in northern Poland, and beach resorts along the Baltic coast. Rysy Peak (8,212 ft.) is the highest point in the mountainous south. The longest river is the Vistula (664 mi.).

Industries

Farming
Coalmining
Shipbuilding
Timber

Places to visit: There are lots of museums and art galleries in Warsaw. There are several national parks where rare forest creatures live, such as lynxes and moose.

A rare lynx

Russia

Russia is the largest country in the world. About a quarter lies in Europe. The rest is in Asia.

Key facts

Size: 6,592,812 sq. mi.
Population: About 150 million
Currency: Rouble
Main language: Russian

Capital city: Moscow. The famous Kremlin building is in the center of the city. It was once a fortress occupied by Tsars, Russian emperors, who ruled for centuries.

St. Basil's Cathedral, Moscow's famous landmark

Landscape: Russia is the world's largest country. It has some of the largest lakes and forests and longest rivers in the world. Mount Elbrus is the highest mountain (18,482 ft.). The longest river is the Volga (2,193 mi.).

Industries

Engineering
Farming
Oil
Minerals
Coal mining

Lake Baikal, is the world's deepest lake, at 6,365 ft.

Places to visit: Russia has many old cities, all with long and exciting histories. The world's longest railway, the Trans-Siberian, runs across the country from Moscow to Vladivostok.

The Trans-Siberian Railway

North America

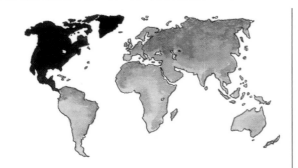

Key facts

Size: 9,035,000 sq. mi.
Largest country: Canada (second largest in the world) 3,851,787 sq. mi.
Longest river: Mississippi-Missouri (3,860 mi.)
Highest mountain: Mount McKinley (20,322 ft.)

Landscape

The North American landscape is very varied. There are huge forests, ice-covered wastelands, scorching deserts and wide grassy plains.

The Rocky Mountains

In the west, mountains run from Alaska down to Mexico. They are called the Cordillera, and include the Rocky Mountains. The Appalachian Mountains run down the eastern side.

North America is the third largest continent in the world. It stretches from the frozen Arctic Circle down to the sunny Gulf of Mexico. It is so wide that there are eight different time zones.

The frozen north

Canada, the United States of America, Mexico, Greenland and the countries of Central America are all part of this continent.

A vast plain stretches about 2,983 mi. from the Gulf of Mexico to northern Canada. The Great Plains and the Mississippi-Missouri River are in this region. Much of the world's maize is grown here.

The most northern parts of the continent border the icy Arctic Ocean. This area is called tundra. Here, the land just beneath the surface is permanently frozen.

The islands of Hawaii, Bermuda and the West Indies lie off the mainland.

The tropical south

Weather

Temperatures vary from -164°F in an Arctic winter to 137°F in summer in Death Valley, California, one of the world's hottest places. Every year in North America, there are about 550 tornadoes, mostly in the central states of the U.S. Tornado winds can spin at up to 403 mph.

A tornado

 **Chemicals**  **Farming**  **Mining**  **Oil**

People

Long ago, North America was populated only by native American people, called Native American Indiains. Over the centuries, settlers came from Europe and slaves were brought from Africa. Now, most of the population is descended from these people.

For many centuries, the Canadian Arctic has been the home of the Inuit people.

Many people from the West Indies are descended from Africans captured and brought over to the country as slaves.

Economy

The continent of North America has many natural resources, such as oil, minerals and timber.

The U.S. is the world's richest country. It has many different industries.

Timber products, such as paper, come from the northern areas

Cities

The U.S. has many cities. New York City is the largest, with a population of over 17 million.

Although Canada is the biggest country in North America, it has a small population. Its major cities are all in the south of the country, where the climate is milder than the Arctic north.

The Statue of Liberty in New York City Harbor was the first sight many immigrants had of North America

Mexico City, in Mexico, is one of the most overcrowded cities in the world.

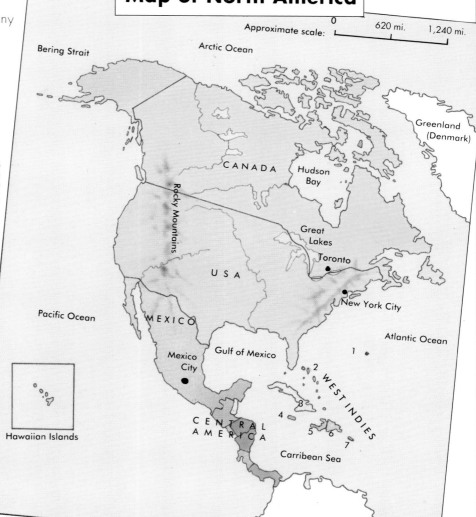

Map of North America

Map key
1 Bermuda
2 Bahamas
3 Cuba
4 Jamaica
5 Haiti
6 Dominican Republic
7 Puerto Rico

101

U.S.A.

The United States of America stretches from the Atlantic Ocean to the Pacific. It includes Alaska in the north and the Hawaiian Islands in the Pacific Ocean.

Washington D.C.

Key facts

Size: 3,618,766 sq. mi.
Population: Over 250 million
Currency: U.S. dollar
Main language: English

Capital city: Washington, D.C. This is the center of government. The President lives here in the White House.

The White House

The U.S. flag is called the "Stars and Stripes". It has thirteen red and white stripes which stand for the first thirteen states. The country now has fifty states, shown by the fifty stars on the flag.

Landscape: As well as mountain ranges, vast plains and deserts, there is the deep land gorge, the Grand Canyon, in Arizona. Mount McKinley is the highest point (20,322 ft.). The Mississippi-Missouri (3,860 mi.) is the longest river.

Grand Canyon

Industries

Farming
Oil
Steel
Vehicles
Space

Places to visit: The U.S. has many historic sites, big cities and beach resorts. Famous places include Hollywood in California, Disney World™ in Florida, and many national parks.

The famous Hollywood sign

Canada

The United States of America stretches from the Atlantic Ocean to the Pacific. It includes Alaska in the

Canada is the largest country in North America. Its northern part is inside the Arctic Circle.

Ottowa

Key facts

Size: 3,851,787 sq. mi.
Population: About 27 million
Currency: Canadian dollar
Main languages: English and French

Capital city: Ottowa. Canada is divided into ten provinces and two territories. Ottowa is in the province of Ontario.

The CN Tower, the world's tallest free-standing structure (1,814 ft. high), is in Toronto, the largest city in Canada.

CN Tower

Landscape: Nearly half of Canada is covered by forest. The Great Lakes, the world's largest group of freshwater lakes, are on the border with the U.S. The Rocky Mountains are in the west. In the center, there are vast plains, called prairies. The highest mountain is Mount Logan (19,525 ft.). The Mackenzie is the longest river (2,635 mi.).

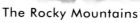

The Rocky Mountains

A totem pole

Industries

Farming
Forestry
Vehicles

Places to visit: You can see ancient totem poles in Stanley Park, Vancouver. Canada has lots of national park areas, where bears and wolves live. The world-famous Niagara Falls is a spectacular sight.

Mexico

Mexico lies south of the U.S.A. and north of South America.

Mexico City

Key facts

Size: 692,102 sq. mi.
Population: Over 80 million
Currency: Peso
Main language: Spanish

Capital city: Mexico City. Almost one-fifth of the population lives here. There are modern buildings next to ancient Aztec ruins.

Mexico once belonged to Spain. You can still see many Spanish-style buildings and churches.

A Spanish-style church

Landscape: More than half the country is over 3,200 ft. high. Central Mexico is a plateau surrounded by volcanic mountains. There are also deserts and swamps. Mount Orizaba (18,702 ft.) is the highest mountain. The longest river is the Rio Grande (1,299 mi.), which flows along the U.S. border.

Industries

Coffee
Oil
Minerals
Crafts

Places to visit: Aztec, Mayan and Toltec people once ruled Mexico. You can still see the remains of cities and temples they built.

A Mayan temple

Jamaica

Jamaica is an island in the Caribbean Sea, south of Cuba.

Kingston

Key facts

Size: 4,244 sq. mi.
Population: Over 2 million
Currency: Jamaican dollar
Main language: English

Capital city: Kingston. Built by a deep, sheltered harbor, this city was once ruled by a pirate, Captain Morgan, and his Buccaneers.

Landscape: Jamaica is a tropical island with lush rainforests, pretty waterfalls and dazzling white beaches. It is actually the tip of an undersea mountain range. Blue Mountain Peak (7,401 ft.) is the highest mountain on the island.

Captain Morgan

Places to visit: As well as beaches, there are wildlife parks and bird sanctuaries where some of the world's most exotic birds can be seen. There are working sugar and banana plantations.

Industries

Tourism
Minerals
Farming

A Jamaican beach

103

South America

South America is the world's fourth largest continent. It stretches from the border of Central America to the tip of Chile.

Early settlers came from Europe

There are 13 South American countries, each with its own distinctive type of landscape and culture.

For centuries the continent was populated only by native peoples. Europeans did not arrive until 1499. Now, many of the people are descended from these Spanish or Portuguese settlers.

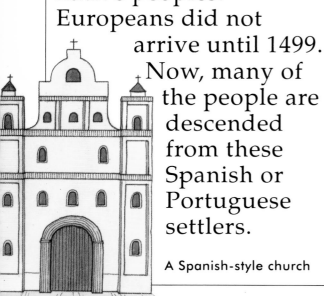

A Spanish-style church

Landscape

There are lots of different landscapes, including high mountains, hot and cold deserts, rainforests and plains.

The world's longest mountain range is the Andes, which runs all the way down the western side. Some of its mountains are live volcanoes. There are also regular earthquakes in this area.

Between the highland areas there are vast lowlands. Much of these areas are covered by dense rainforests. There are also grasslands, such as the Argentinian pampas.

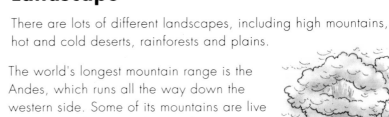

There are some live volcanoes in the Andes Mountain Range

South America has many dense rainforests

People

Many large South American cities are on the eastern coast. Outside the cities, most people live on small farms, growing just enough food to feed themselves.

There are still a few Amerindians (native Americans) living in forest settlements deep in the Amazon River Basin. They hunt animals, gather fruit and grow crops to eat.

Largest country: 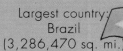 Smallest country: Highest mountain: Longest river:
Brazil   French Guiana   Mount Aconcagua   Amazon
(3,286,470 sq. mi.)   (38,749 sq. mi.)   (22,836 ft.)   (4,000 mi.)

Amazon butterflies

A jaguar

The Amazon

The Amazon River carries more fresh water than any other. It flows across South America from the Andes to the Atlantic and drains more than 2 million sq. mi. of land, much of it rainforest. It is one of the world's richest wildlife areas, with many extraordinary creatures such as hummingbirds, sloths, jaguars and piranha fish.

A hummingbird

Weather

In rainforest areas, it is warm and humid all the time and it rains almost daily.

The warmest part of South America is in northern Argentina. The coldest place is Tierra Del Fuego, which faces Antarctica at the southern tip of the continent.

The world's driest place is the Atacama Desert in Chile. Until 1971 it had not rained there for 400 years.

Industries

Coffee

Forestry

Cacao

Oil

Farming

Minerals

Map of South America

Approximate scale: 0 ... 620 mi. ... 1,240 mi.

Caracas
VENEZUELA
Orinoco River
COLOMBIA
2   3   4
1
PERU
Amazon River
EQUATOR
BRAZIL
Lima
La Paz
Brasilia
BOLIVIA
Pacific Ocean
6
Paraná River
São Paulo
Santiago
5
Buenos Aires
ARGENTINA
Atlantic Ocean
Falkland Islands (U.K.)
Tierra del Fuego
(Chile)   (Argentina)

Map key

1 Equador
2 Guyana
3 Surinam
4 French Guiana
5 Uruguay
6 Paraguay

Brazil

Brazil covers almost half of South America. It is the fifth-largest country in the world.

Brasilia

Key facts

Size: 3,286,470 sq. mi.
Population: Over 150 million
Currency: Cruzeiro
Main language: Portuguese

Capital city: Brasilia. This city was begun in the 1950s. It is famous for its futuristic architecture.

Brasilia's futuristic buildings

Landscape: Brazil has over 1 million sq. mi. of rainforest. The mighty Amazon River (4,000 mi.) runs through it, carrying more water than any other river in the world. Pica da Neblina (9,889 ft.) is the highest mountain in Brazil.

Flesh-eating piranha fish live in the Amazon River

Industries

Coffee
Sugar cane
Timber
Iron
Precious gems

Places to visit: The Amazon Rainforest has many thousands of animal and plant species. It is also the home of the Amazon Indians. Ecologists are trying to save the forest from destruction.

Rainforest birds

Argentina

Argentina lies to the east of the Andes Mountains, facing the Atlantic Ocean.

Buenos Aires

Key facts

Size: 1,068,296 sq. mi.
Population: Over 32 million
Currency: Austral
Main language: Spanish

Capital city: Buenos Aires. This is one of the largest cities in the southern half of the world. It is the birthplace of the famous tango dance.

Dancing the tango

Landscape: The scenery includes hot desert, the Andes Mountain Range and the cold wilderness of the Patagonia Desert in the south. Mount Aconcagua (22,836 ft.) is the highest point. The longest river is the Paraná (3,032 mi.).

Argentinian grassland, called pampas

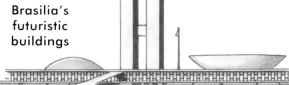

Places to visit: There are historic cities, beach resorts and wildlife parks in Argentina. The Andes is home to the spectacular and rare bird, the condor.

Industries

Farming
Textiles
Steel
Chemicals

A condor

Peru

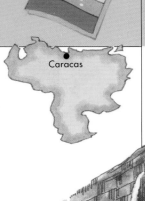

Peru is on the Pacific coast of South America. The Andes Mountains run down the center.

Lima

Key facts

Size: 496,222 sq. mi.
Population: Over 22 million
Currency: New Sol
Main languages: Spanish, Quechua

Capital city: Lima. This city was founded by the Spaniard, Francisco Pizarro, in 1535. He attacked and conquered Peru in the 1500s in search of its legendary treasure.

Francisco Pizarro

Landscape: Peru is a country of deserts, mountains and rainforests, some of it still unexplored. The source of the Amazon River is in the Peruvian Andes. The highest point is Mount Huascarán (22,206 ft.). The Ucayli is the longest river (910 mi.).

Industries

Farming
Coffee
Cotton
Fishing
Minerals

The Andes Mountains

Places to visit: Peru was once ruled by the Inca people. They built fabulous palaces, towers and temples covered in gold. You can visit the ruins of their cities, such as Cuzco and Machu Picchu.

Machu Picchu

Venezuela

Caracas

Venezuela is on the north coast of South America. This is where Christopher Columbus first set foot on the American mainland.

Key facts

Size: 352,142 sq. mi.
Population: Over 20 million
Currency: Bolívar
Main language: Spanish

Capital city: Caracas. The national hero, Simon Bolívar, is buried here. He helped to free Venezuela from the Spanish. Many buildings and streets are named after him.

Simon Bolívar

Landscape: There are lowland and highland areas. One of the lowland areas is a dense alligator-infested forest around the Orinoco River. Some of the highlands are still unexplored. Mount Bolívar is the highest point (16,428 ft.). The Orinoco (1,700 mi.) is the longest river.

Industries

Fruit
Coffee
Minerals
Tourism

The Venezuelan landscape

Places to visit: Venezuela has some of the most spectacular scenery in the world. the world's highest waterfall, Angel Falls (3,212 ft.) is in the Canaima National Park.

Angel Falls

Africa

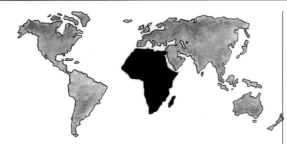

Africa is the second largest continent in the world. It is only 8 mi. to the south of Europe, across the Strait of Gibraltar. A strip of land called the Isthmus of Suez separates the continent from Asia.

There are 670 million people in Africa, but they are spread thinly throughout more than 50 countries.

Large parts of Africa are uninhabited because the climate is harsh and the terrain makes travel difficult. There are mountains, rainforests, deserts and grassland, called savannah.

Nairobi, Kenya

African desert

Key facts

Size: 11,684,158 sq. mi.
Population: 670 million
Largest country: Sudan
Smallest country: Seychelles
Highest mountain: Mount Kilimanjaro (19,341 ft.)
Longest river: Nile (4,145 mi.)

Mount Kilimanjaro

Landscape

Much of Africa is on a high plateau. Around this high, flat tableland there are narrow coastal plains. The highest mountains are in East Africa.

The Sahara Desert crosses the northern part of Africa. It is the biggest desert in the world, spreading out over a huge area almost as large as the U.S.A! Some parts of it are sandy, but much of it is rocky wasteland.

In central Africa, there are dense tropical rainforests. In southern Africa there are savannah and desert areas.

The Nile River is the longest river in the world. It flows north to the Mediterranean Sea.

The Nile River

Animals

Africa is very rich in wildlife. Many of the large mammals live on the wide grassy plains of the savannah.

Some species of animals are in danger of dying out. To save them, large areas have been made into reserves and national parks, where hunting is illegal.

African savannah

Weather

The Equator crosses Africa. Here there are hot, humid rainforests where it rains almost every day.

African rainforest

People

In the north, many people speak Arabic and follow the Muslim religion.

Pygmy people live in the rainforests of Congo and Zaïre.

In South Africa, black people make up two-thirds of the population. For many years they had few rights. This is now beginning to change.

Economy

Many Africans are farmers. They work on the land growing crops such as peanuts and cocoa beans (used for making chocolate).

A major industry is mining. Africa is rich in minerals such as gold, silver, tin and copper. It has large stores of oil and natural gas.

A farmer harvesting his crop

Map of Africa

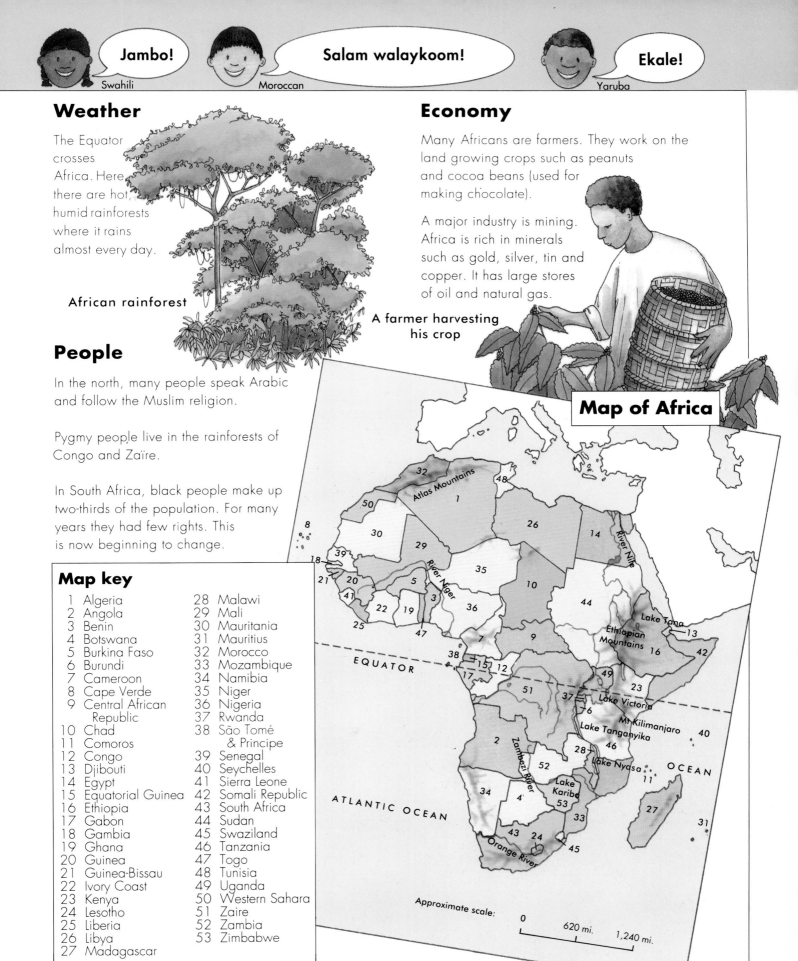

Map key

1	Algeria	28	Malawi
2	Angola	29	Mali
3	Benin	30	Mauritania
4	Botswana	31	Mauritius
5	Burkina Faso	32	Morocco
6	Burundi	33	Mozambique
7	Cameroon	34	Namibia
8	Cape Verde	35	Niger
9	Central African	36	Nigeria
	Republic	37	Rwanda
10	Chad	38	São Tomé
11	Comoros		& Principe
12	Congo	39	Senegal
13	Djibouti	40	Seychelles
14	Egypt	41	Sierra Leone
15	Equatorial Guinea	42	Somali Republic
16	Ethiopia	43	South Africa
17	Gabon	44	Sudan
18	Gambia	45	Swaziland
19	Ghana	46	Tanzania
20	Guinea	47	Togo
21	Guinea-Bissau	48	Tunisia
22	Ivory Coast	49	Uganda
23	Kenya	50	Western Sahara
24	Lesotho	51	Zaire
25	Liberia	52	Zambia
26	Libya	53	Zimbabwe
27	Madagascar		

Approximate scale:

0   620 mi.   1,240 mi.

South Africa

South Africa is at the southernmost tip of the African continent.

Key facts
Size: 471,442 sq. mi.
Population: Over 40 million
Currency: Rand
Main languages: English, Afrikaans.

Capital cities: South Africa has three capital cities called Pretoria, Bloemfontein and Cape Town. Each plays a different part in the government of the country.

Table Mountain, near Cape Town

Landscape: South Africa has a huge high plateau bordered by mountains. On the plateau there are wide grassy plains called the "veld." The long coastline has lots of beautiful beaches. The highest point is Champagne Castle in the Drakensberg (11,074 ft.). The Orange River (1,305 mi.) is the longest river.

Industries
Mining
Precious gems
Farming

South Africa is famous for its diamond mines

Places to visit: There are several famous wildlife reserves. You can see eagles, elephants, giraffes, lions and tigers living in their natural habitat.

A giraffe

Egypt

Egypt is in the north-eastern corner of Africa. Its northern shore is on the Mediterranean.

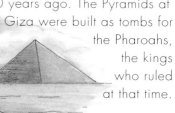

Key facts
Size: 386,659 sq. mi.
Population: Over 55 million
Currency: Egyptian pound
Main language: Arabic

Capital city: Cairo. This is a center of historic monuments and unique historical sites.

The Ancient Egyptian civilization began about 5,000 years ago. The Pyramids at Giza were built as tombs for the Pharoahs, the kings who ruled at that time.

The pyramids and Sphinx at Giza, just outside Cairo

Landscape:
The country is divided by the great Nile River. A belt of green fertile land runs along the river and spreads out around its delta (river mouth). The rest of Egypt is sandy desert. The highest mountain is Jabal Katrinah (8,652 ft.). The Nile River is the world's longest river (4,000 mi.).

Farming the Nile delta

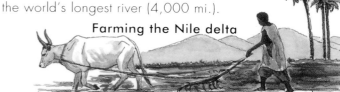

Industries
Tourism
Textiles
Oil

Places to visit: Some pharoahs were buried in the Valley of the Kings. You can see their tomb treasures on display. There are huge temples at Luxor and Abu Simbel. Around the Red Sea there are beaches and spectacular coral reefs.

The great temple of Abu Simbel

Nigeria

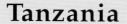

Nigeria's coast is on the Gulf of Guinea in western Africa.

● Abuja

Key facts

Size: 356,667 sq. mi.
Population: Over 88 million
Currency: Naira
Main language: The official language is English but there are over 250 local languages

Capital city: In 1991 Abuja became the new capital city, in place of Lagos.

Many people live in villages. The main groups of people are the Hausa, Ibo and Yoruba.

A village market

Landscape: There are lagoons, beaches and mangrove swamps along the coast. Inland, there are rainforests where the trees can grow as high as 100 ft. An area of grassland with scattered trees, called the savannah, lies in the south.

Coastal mangrove swamp

Industries

Oil
Cacao
Palm oil
Minerals

Places to visit: Many ancient cultures flourished in Nigeria. There are several historic cities, such as Kano, famous for its festival of horsemanship. There are wildlife parks and spectacular scenery.

A Yoruba festival mask and drummer

Tanzania

Tanzania lies in eastern Africa on the Indian Ocean. It includes the islands of Zanzibar and Pemba.

Dodoma ●

Key facts

Size: 364,896 sq. mi.
Population: About 25 million
Currency: Tanzanian shilling
Main languages: English, Swahili

Capital city: Dodoma. Dar es Salaam is the largest city and main port.

There are about 120 groups of people in Tanzania including the wandering Masai, the tallest people in the world.

Masai women

Landscape: Most of Tanzania consists of a high plateau. Savannah and bush cover about half the country. There are huge inland lakes. Mount Kilimanjaro (19,341 ft.), in Nigeria, is the highest mountain in Africa. The longest river is the Rufiji.

An inland lake

Industries

Farming
Cotton
Coffee
Minerals

Places to visit: Some of the world's finest wildlife parks are here, including the Serengeti Plain and the Ngorongoro volcano.

Lake Manyara is famous for its tree-climbing lions

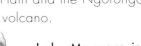

Shalom!
Hebrew

A-salam alekum!
Dhivehi (Maldives)

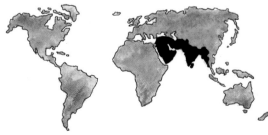

This area stretches about 3,107 mi. from the Mediterranean Sea to the Bay of Bengal. It includes Middle Eastern countries such as Saudi Arabia and the south Asian countries of Pakistan, Afghanistan, India and Bangladesh. The island of Sri Lanka and the mountainous countries of Bhutan and Nepal are also in this vast area.

The landscape varies from barren desert to the Himalayas, the highest mountains in the world.

Middle Eastern desert

The mountains of Nepal

Key facts

Size: 4,420,845 sq. mi.
Population: About 1330 million
Longest river: Ganges (2,900 mi.)
Highest mountain: Mount Everest (29,030 ft.)
Largest country: India (1,269,338 sq. mi.)
Smallest country: Maldives (115 sq. mi.)

Landscape

The landscape of Western and Southern Asia includes high mountains, wide plains, deserts and rainforests.

Mountains run all the way from Turkey to Afghanistan and dry, scrubby grassland stretches from Pakistan to Syria.

Desert covers most of Saudi Arabia and the surrounding lands.

Weather

The mountainous northern areas of the Middle East have hot summers and freezing winters. Farther south, it is hot all year round.

In India and Bangladesh, the farmers rely on the monsoon for their crops to grow. The monsoon is a season of heavy rain that falls between June and October.

Middle Eastern desert and mountains in Afghanistan

Monsoon rainfall in Southern Asia

Marhabah assalamu aleikum!
Arabic

Namaste!
Hindi

Min ga la baa!
Burmese

People

There are many different cultures in this area. Here are some examples:

In the Middle East, many people follow the Muslim faith. They pray every day facing the Holy City of Mecca, the center of their religion.

Many Indians are Hindus. They worship several gods, the chief of which is called Brahman. Some Indians follow the Sikh faith. Many Sikhs live in the Punjab region.

To Hindus, cows are sacred animals and are allowed to graze wherever they like

Economy

The countries around the Persian Gulf, in the Middle East, have vast oil reserves. They depend on the money they make from selling this oil around the world.

Throughout Southern Asia many different crops are grown, including wheat, millet, rice and cotton. India and Sri Lanka are among the world's biggest tea producers.

Tea picking

Main industries

Oil   Farming

Mining   Textiles

Map of Western & Southern Asia

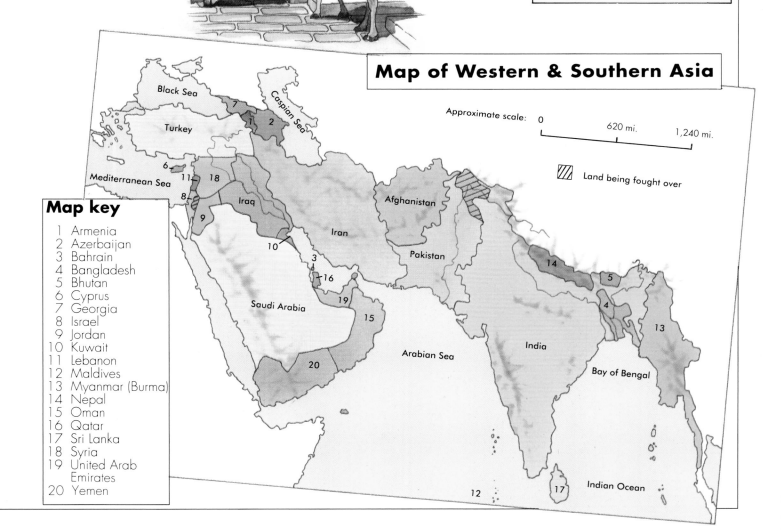

Approximate scale: 0   620 mi.   1,240 mi.

Land being fought over

Map key

1 Armenia
2 Azerbaijan
3 Bahrain
4 Bangladesh
5 Bhutan
6 Cyprus
7 Georgia
8 Israel
9 Jordan
10 Kuwait
11 Lebanon
12 Maldives
13 Myanmar (Burma)
14 Nepal
15 Oman
16 Qatar
17 Sri Lanka
18 Syria
19 United Arab Emirates
20 Yemen

Black Sea
Caspian Sea
Turkey
Mediterranean Sea
Iraq
Afghanistan
Iran
Pakistan
Saudi Arabia
Arabian Sea
India
Bay of Bengal
Indian Ocean

Israel

Israel is on the Mediterranean coast. The modern country of Israel was founded in 1948.

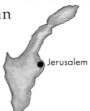
Jerusalem

Key facts

Size: 80,220 sq. mi.
Population: About 5 million
Currency: Shekel
Main languages: Hebrew, Arabic

Capital city: Jerusalem. This ancient holy city is about 4,000 years old. It is a center of Judaism, Christianity and Islam. There are many important historic sites from the Bible and the Islamic holy book, the Koran.

Jerusalem

Landscape: The hills of Galilea are in the north of Israel, and there is desert in the south. In between, there are fertile plains. The longest river is the Jordan (659 mi.), which flows into the Dead Sea. This sea is so salty that if you swim in it you cannot sink. Mount Meiron (3,963 ft.) is the highest point.

The Dead Sea

Places to visit: The history of this area goes back to about 2,000 B.C. There are many religious sites including the Wailing Wall, the Church of the Holy Sepulchre, the Mount of Olives and the Dome of the Rock. The town of Beersheba stands on the spot where Abraham is supposed to have pitched his tent 3,800 years ago.

Industries
Engineering
Electronics
Chemicals
Textiles
Fruit

The Tomb of Absalom on the Mount of Olives

Saudi Arabia

Saudi Arabia covers about four-fifths of the Arabian peninsula. It is more than four times as big as France.

Riyadh

Key facts

Size: 829,995 sq. mi.
Population: Over 14 million
Currency: Saudi Riyal
Main language: Arabic

Capital city: Riyadh. This modern city is built on an ancient site. It is the home of the ruling Royal Family.

The Bedouin people wander the desert in search of grazing for their animals

Landscape:
Much of the country is barren desert scattered with oases. The Rub Al-Khali ("Empty Quarter"), in the south, is the largest sand desert in the world. The highest point is in the Asir Range (10,279 ft.). There are no rivers in Saudi Arabia!

Giant sand dunes in the "Empty Quarter"

Industries
Oil
Natural gas
Farming

Places to visit: Only Muslims are allowed to visit the sacred cities of Mecca and Medina. The Prophet Muhammad was born in Mecca and Muslims pray toward it, wherever they are in the world. Other ancient sites include camel markets, potteries and salt mines dating back 5,000 years.

The sacred city of Mecca

Iran

Iran is in Western Asia, east of the Mediterranean Sea. It borders the Caspian Sea.

Key facts

Size: 636,293 sq. mi.
Population: About 57 million
Currency: Rial
Main language: Persian (Farsi)

Capital city: Tehran. The old city gates are in the old part of Tehran. It has one of the world's largest bazaars, where you can buy everything from carpets to silver and exotic spices.

A holy mosque

Landscape: Most of the cities are near the Caspian Sea, where the land is fertile. The rest of Iran is barren desert where much of Iran's oil is found. There are mountains in the western part of the country. The highest point is Mount Demavend (18,387 ft.).

Oil wells in the desert

Industries

Oil
Farming
Crafts

Places to visit: Iran was once called Persia. It was on the Silk Route, an important trail for merchants bringing silk and spices from the east. There are many ancient cities, museums and remains of the Roman and Persian Empires.

The Bakhtiari people spend the summer in the Zagros Mountains and the winter in the lowland areas of Iran

India

India is in Southern Asia between the Arabian Sea and the Bay of Bengal.

Key facts

Size: 1,269,338 sq. mi.
Population: Over 870 million
Currency: Rupee
Main languages: Hindi, English

Capital city: New Delhi. This modern city stands beside Old Delhi, where there are many ancient streets, temples, mosques and bazaars. The biggest city in India is Calcutta. Nine million people live there.

Old Delhi

India is the seventh largest country in the world, with the second biggest population after China.

Landscape: India is separated from the rest of Asia by the Himalayan mountain range in the north. In the north, many people live on the huge river plains of the Ganges and the Brahmaputra. Kanchenjunga (28,210 ft.) is the world's second highest mountain. The Brahmaputra (1,802 mi.) is the longest river.

Ganges

Industries

Farming
Chemicals
Electronics
Oil

Places to visit: There are many temples and palaces from the days when maharajahs ruled India. The most famous monument is the Taj Mahal.

The Taj Mahal

Ni hao! Cantonese

Haere-mai! Maori

This vast area includes China and its neighboring countries. Over one-fifth of the world's population lives in China. Asian Russia (to the east of the Ural Mountains) is in this region.

Malaysia and Indonesia (a group of thousands of islands) stretch down towards Australasia. This region includes Australia, the world's smallest continent, and New Zealand.

Chinese junks in the Pacific

Key facts about Northern & Eastern Asia

Size: About 12,399,601 sq. mi.
Largest country: Russia (about 4,835,516 sq. mi. in Asia)
Longest river: Chang (Yangtze) (3,915 mi.)
Highest mountain: Mount Everest (29,030 ft.)

Key facts about Australasia

Size: About 3,243,240 sq. mi.
Largest country: Australia (2,967,892 sq. mi.)
Longest river: Murray (1,609 mi.)
Highest mountain: Mount Wilhelm (14,794 ft.)

Landscape

Asian Russia has vast plains, with mountains in the far east and south. There is tundra in the Himalayas, with grassland and desert in central China.

Tropical rainforest stretches from southern China down through Malaysia, Indonesia and New Guinea. Some of this forest is still unexplored.

An erupting volcano

Part of this area is in the "Pacific Ring of Fire." It is called this because it has so many active volcanoes.

Much of Australia is dry grassland, with few trees. Australians call this the "outback" or "bush." There are also low mountain ranges, rainforests and deserts.

Weather

In the Himalayan mountains it is cold all year round. Farther south the weather is warm all the time. The monsoon season brings heavy rainfall to South-East Asia. Hurricanes (also called typhoons) often blow in this area. They are giant, spinning masses of wind and rain, sometimes stretching as wide as 300mi. across.

Hurricanes can blow at over 90 mph.

Selamat pagi!
Malaysian

Ohayo gozaimasu!
Japanese

G'day!
Australian

Economy

Eastern Asia is mainly farmland. Much of the world's rice is grown here. Rubber is also exported from here, all around the world. The rubber is made from milky sap, called latex, drained from trees.

Australia and New Zealand are important sheep-farming centers. In both countries, there are far more sheep than people. The sheep's wool and meat are exported to countries around the world.

Japan is one of the most powerful industrial countries in the world. It is famous for its electronic goods, such as computers and music systems. Japanese cars are exported all around the world.

Main industries

Farming

Mining

Oil

Shipbuilding

Forestry

Sheep

Map key

1 Brunei
2 Cambodia
3 Hong Kong
4 Kyrgyzstan
5 Laos
6 Macao
7 North Korea
8 Papua New Guinea
9 Singapore
10 South Korea
11 Taiwan
12 Tajikistan
13 Thailand
14 Turkmenistan
15 Uzbekistan
16 Vietnam

Map of Northern & Eastern Asia & Australasia

Japan

Japan is a chain of islands off the east coast of Asia, in the Pacific Ocean.

Tokyo

Key facts

Size: 145,833 sq. mi.
Population: About 125 million
Currency: Yen
Main language: Japanese

Capital city: Tokyo is one of the world's most crowded cities. The Imperial Palace, where the present Emperor still lives, is here.

The Imperial Palace

Japan has many islands. The four main ones are called Kyushu, Shikoku, Honshu and Hokkaido.

Landscape:

Two-thirds of Japan is mountainous. The only flat land is along the coast. There are over 200 volcanoes, half of them active. The highest point in Japan is Mount Fuji (12,389 ft.). The Shinano-gawa (228 mi.) is the longest river.

Mount Fuji

Industries

Vehicles
Electronics
Farming
Shipbuilding

Places to visit: There are many temples dedicated to the god Buddha, historic sites and ancient palaces. If you visit Japan you are likely to see traditional crafts, and rituals such as the tea ceremony.

A Japanese temple

China

China is in Eastern Asia. It is nearly as big as the whole of Europe.

Beijing

Key facts

Size: 3,705,386 sq. mi.
Population: Over 1,150 million (about one-fifth of the world's people)
Currency: Yuan
Main language: Mandarin Chinese

Capital city: Beijing. There are beautiful palaces and gardens to see. The Forbidden City is in the middle of Beijing. This was once the home of the Chinese emperors.

The Forbidden City

Landscape: There is a high plateau in the west, with flat lands in the east and several very long rivers. Mountains take up about one-third of the country. Mount Everest (29,030 ft.), on the border of China and Nepal, is the world's highest mountain. The Chang (3,436 mi.) is the longest river.

Mount Everest

Places to visit: The Great Wall of China runs from east to west for about 3,977 mi. It is the only structure on Earth visible from the Moon. The ancient tomb of emperor Quin Shihuangdi is at Xi'an. It was guarded by thousands of life-sized clay warriors, called the "terracotta army."

Industries

Farming
Minerals
Chemicals

The Great Wall of China

New Zealand

New Zealand is in the Pacific. It is made up of two main islands, North Island and South Island.

Wellington

Key facts

Size: 103,736 sq. mi.
Population: Over 3 million
Currency: New Zealand dollar
Main languages: English, Maori

Capital City: Wellington. Only about 120,000 people live here and around the magnificent harbour. Over 1 million people live in Auckland, at the northern end of North Island.

Landscape: Much of the land is mountainous, with rivers and plains. In parts of North Island there are volcanoes, hot water geysers and pools of boiling mud. The highest point is Mount Cook (12,350 ft.). The Waikato (264 mi.) is the longest river.

Industries

Minerals
Farming
Wool

A geyser spouting hot water

Places to visit: There is lots of spectacular scenery, including rainforests and glaciers. The Maoris were the first settlers in this country. Rotorua is the center of Maori culture. Many kinds of animals and birds, such as the kiwi, are found only in New Zealand.

Maori dancers

Australia

Australia lies 935 mi. north-west of New Zealand. It is the world's largest island.

Canberra

Key facts

Size: 2,967,892 sq. mi.
Population: Over 17 million
Currency: Australian dollar
Main language: English

Capital city: Canberra. Most of the population lives along the eastern and south-eastern coastline. Australia is made up of six states and two territories, each with its own capital.

Sydney Opera House

Landscape: In the middle of Australia, there are several large deserts and dry grasslands. The Great Barrier Reef stretches 1,250 mi. along the north-east coast. The highest point in Australia is Mount Kosciusko (7,317 ft.). The Murray (1,609 mi.) is the longest river.

Ayers Rock, a famous landmark near Alice Springs

Industries

Farming
Minerals
Iron
Engineering

Places to visit: The original settlers in Australia were the Aborigines. Some of their cave paintings and historic sites date back to prehistoric times. There are wildlife parks where you can see koalas, kangaroos and other animals found only in Australia. The beaches are world-famous.

The Wonders of the Ancient World

In the second century BC, a Greek man called Antipater of Sidon decided to write about seven of the most marvellous structures that existed at the time. These became known as the Seven Wonders of the Ancient World.

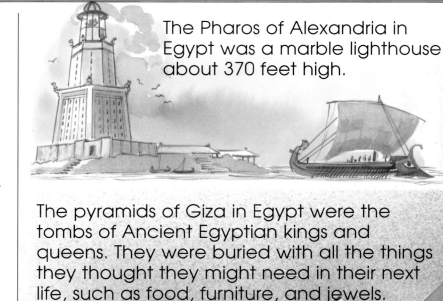

The Pharos of Alexandria in Egypt was a marble lighthouse about 370 feet high.

The pyramids of Giza in Egypt were the tombs of Ancient Egyptian kings and queens. They were buried with all the things they thought they might need in their next life, such as food, furniture, and jewels.

The statue of Zeus, King of the Greek gods, was carved from ivory and marble. It was 12 metres tall and built at Olympia, Greece.

The Ancient Greeks built temples to worship gods and goddesses. The Temple of Artemis, in Ephesus, Turkey, was built to worship the goddess of hunting and fertility.

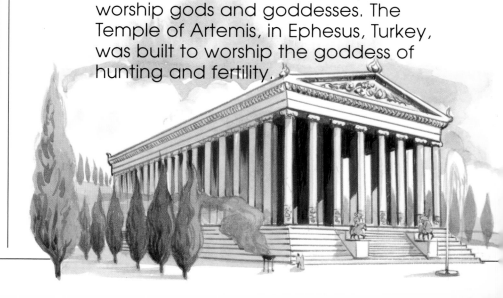

King Mausolus decided to build himself the most elaborate tomb in the world at Halicarnassus, Turkey. A new word was invented to describe the tomb – mausoleum, after Mausolus.

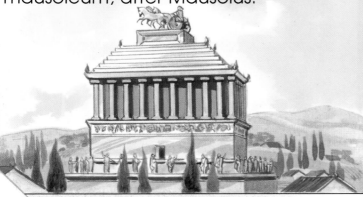

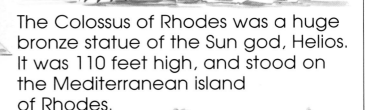

The Colossus of Rhodes was a huge bronze statue of the Sun god, Helios. It was 110 feet high, and stood on the Mediterranean island of Rhodes.

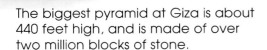

The biggest pyramid at Giza is about 440 feet high, and is made of over two million blocks of stone.

King Nebuchadnezzar built the beautiful Hanging Gardens of Babylon in Mesopotamia for his wife. Stone terraces were shaped like pyramids and filled with colorful plants.

Building Wonders

Amazing buildings are found all over the world. There are wonderful castles and palaces, strange houses, and very unusual stores!

In Houston, Texas, a store has been designed to look as though it is falling down!

Neuschwanstein Castle

In Germany in 1869, King Ludwig of Bavaria began building himself a fairytale castle with lots of towers and turrets.

Imagine a huge building made completely of glass. Crystal Palace was built in London, England, in 1851. Its great iron frame contained 300,000 pieces of glass.

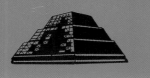

In Beijing, China, the Emperor lived in his own private city, with palaces, lakes and gardens. Ordinary people were not allowed in, so it was called the Forbidden City.

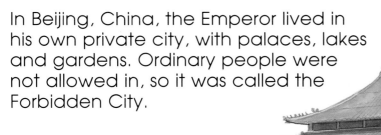

The Biosphere, in the Arizona desert, was like a huge greenhouse, containing different habitats, each with plants and animals.

The Palace of Versailles in France is 600 yards long and is the biggest palace in the world. It was built for King Louis XIV in 1682.

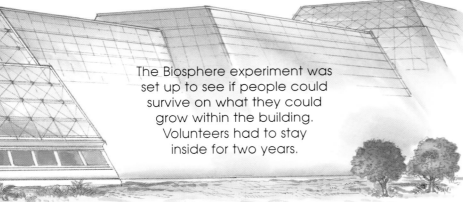

The Biosphere experiment was set up to see if people could survive on what they could grow within the building. Volunteers had to stay inside for two years.

One of the strangest houses in the world is in San José, California. Its owner, Sarah Winchester, was afraid of ghosts and believed that they would harm her unless she kept doing building work on the house. Work went on for 38 years!

It has weird features such as staircases which lead nowhere.

The house started with 18 rooms and ended with 160!

Mountains are made when rocks under the Earth's surface move. Sometimes molten rock rises up inside the Earth and pushes the land into a dome-shape.

Some mountains are volcanoes. A volcano is a hole in the Earth's surface. Hot molten rock (lava) inside the Earth shoots out of the hole when the volcano erupts.

Ayers Rock in Australia is the biggest rock in the world. It is 1½ miles long and over 1,100 feet high.

From the rocky desert of Monument Valley in Utah, strange towering pieces of rock rise to 1,000 feet. Water, wind, and temperature changes have worn away the surrounding rock to make shapes that look like ruined castles or crumbling skyscrapers.

The largest active volcano is Mauna Loa, in Hawaii. An active volcano is one that still erupts. Mauna Loa last erupted in 1984.

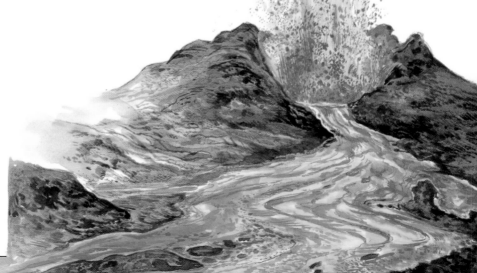

One of the biggest and most terrifying volcanic eruptions was when Krakatoa in Indonesia exploded in 1883. Rock shot 15 miles into the air, and dust fell over 3,000 miles away.

Krakatoa

When Mount Vesuvius in Italy erupted in AD 79, the Roman town of Pompeii was completely buried by volcanic ash. When archaeologists dug out the town centuries later they found that the buildings and beautiful mosaics had been preserved by the lava.

The highest mountain in the world is Mount Everest, in the Himalayan mountains. It is 29,028 feet high. The first people to climb to the top were Edmund Hillary and Sherpa Tenzing Norgay, in 1953.

The longest range of mountains is the Andes in South America. It stretches for about 4750 miles.

Towering Wonders

Many tall buildings are built with a frame made from steel and concrete. Others are built around a huge hollow concrete tube.

Builders dig deep into the ground to make a support for the building, called the foundations.

The world's most famous tower looks as if it will fall over! The Leaning Tower of Pisa, in Italy, was finished in 1350. It is 179 feet high. Because the soft ground has sunk under the tower, it leans over 12 feet to one side.

Alexandre-Gustave Eiffel built the world's tallest tower for the Paris Exhibition of 1889.

The Eiffel Tower, Paris, France is 1,050 feet high. It is made of iron girders held together by rivets.

Built in 1931, the Empire State Building in New York City, appeared in a famous movie. Using trick photography, a fierce giant ape called King Kong was shown clinging to the top of the 1,250-foot skyscraper.

Lighthouses warn ships where there is danger from underwater rocks. The tallest lighthouse in Great Britain is Bishop Rock, near the Scilly Isles. It is 150 feet high.

The tallest tower in the world today is the CN Tower in Toronto, Canada. It is 1,815 feet high. From its revolving restaurant you can see for 75 miles.

More than 62,000 tonnes of earth was excavated for the CN Tower's foundations.

The Chrysler Building, New York City, is one of the world's most beautiful skyscrapers. Some of its design was based on a rising sun and parts of a Chrysler automobile!

Superhuman Wonders

Since ancient times, people have sculpted images of humans and gods. Some are carved from stone or wood, or cast from metal. Many of them are enormous.

In Ancient Britain, people carved giant figures and animals into chalky hillsides. The "Long Man" at Wilmington, East Sussex is 205 feet long – the largest hill carving in Britain.

An enormous statue of Jesus overlooks Rio de Janeiro in Brazil. The sculptor, Paul Landowski, built the 120-foot tall concrete statue in 1931.

On Easter Island in the South Pacific Ocean, hundreds of strange stone figures were discovered. Archaeologists think they were carved some time between AD 1000 and 1600.

In 1257 BC, an Egyptian pharaoh decided to build a great temple at Abu Simbel. It had four 60-foot tall statues of the pharaoh, Rameses II, at the entrance.

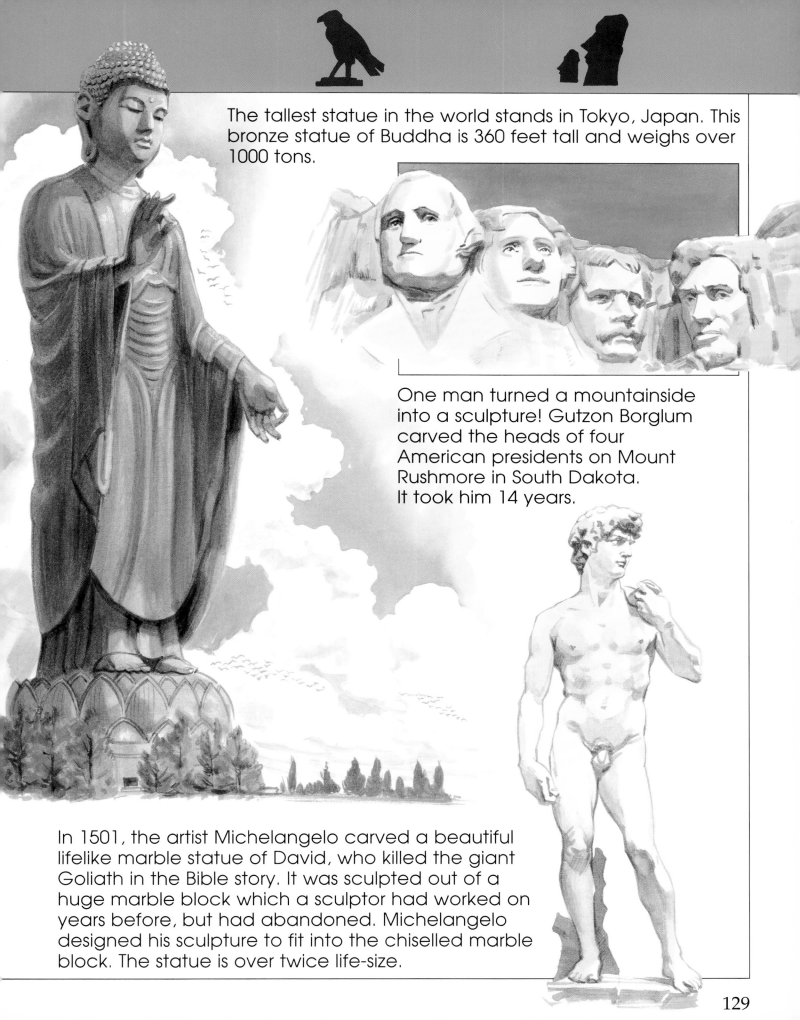

The tallest statue in the world stands in Tokyo, Japan. This bronze statue of Buddha is 360 feet tall and weighs over 1000 tons.

One man turned a mountainside into a sculpture! Gutzon Borglum carved the heads of four American presidents on Mount Rushmore in South Dakota. It took him 14 years.

In 1501, the artist Michelangelo carved a beautiful lifelike marble statue of David, who killed the giant Goliath in the Bible story. It was sculpted out of a huge marble block which a sculptor had worked on years before, but had abandoned. Michelangelo designed his sculpture to fit into the chiselled marble block. The statue is over twice life-size.

129

A waterfall is formed when a river wears away the soft rock beneath a layer of hard rock to form a step.

Geysers are caused when water is heated by hot rocks under the ground. Steam pressure builds up and forces a jet of hot water out of a hole in the ground.

The highest waterfall in the world is the Angel Falls in Venezuela. It drops 3,212 feet.

One of the most famous waterfalls in the world is the Victoria Falls on the River Zambezi in Africa. Visitors have a great view of the Falls from cliffs just 250 feet away.

The Great Barrier Reef off Queensland in Australia is the biggest coral reef in the world. It is a rock-like mass built up from tiny sea creatures called corals and their skeletons.

Many sea urchins, oysters, and colorful fish live on the Reef.

On his way to California, in 1933, a sailor saw the highest ever recorded wave during a hurricane. It was just over 100 feet tall.

The tallest ever geyser shot out hot, black water and huge rocks to a height of 1,400 feet. The Waimangu Geyser in New Zealand used to erupt about every three days, but has been quiet since 1904.

Today, the tallest geyser is in Yellowstone National Park, Wyoming. Known as the Steamboat Geyser, its eruptions reach heights of up to 350 feet.

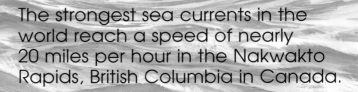

The strongest sea currents in the world reach a speed of nearly 20 miles per hour in the Nakwakto Rapids, British Columbia in Canada.

Tunneling Wonders

Tunnels carry roads and railways beneath cities, through mountains and under the sea. Some tunnels supply water, and others take away sewage.

Tunnels may be cut out of rock by huge boring machines. Some tunnels are built in sections and then buried.

Tunnels allow canals to pass through hills. Up until the mid-1900s, canal boats were guided through tunnels by men called 'leggers'.

The Channel Tunnel is the world's longest tunnel under the sea. It travels 30 miles under the English Channel between England and France.

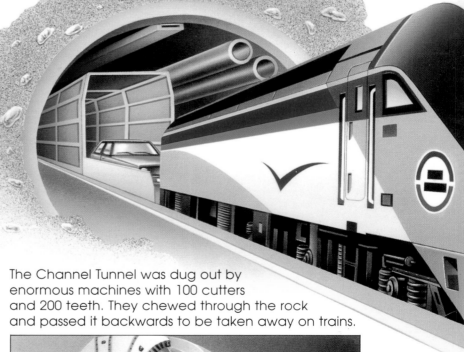

The Channel Tunnel was dug out by enormous machines with 100 cutters and 200 teeth. They chewed through the rock and passed it backwards to be taken away on trains.

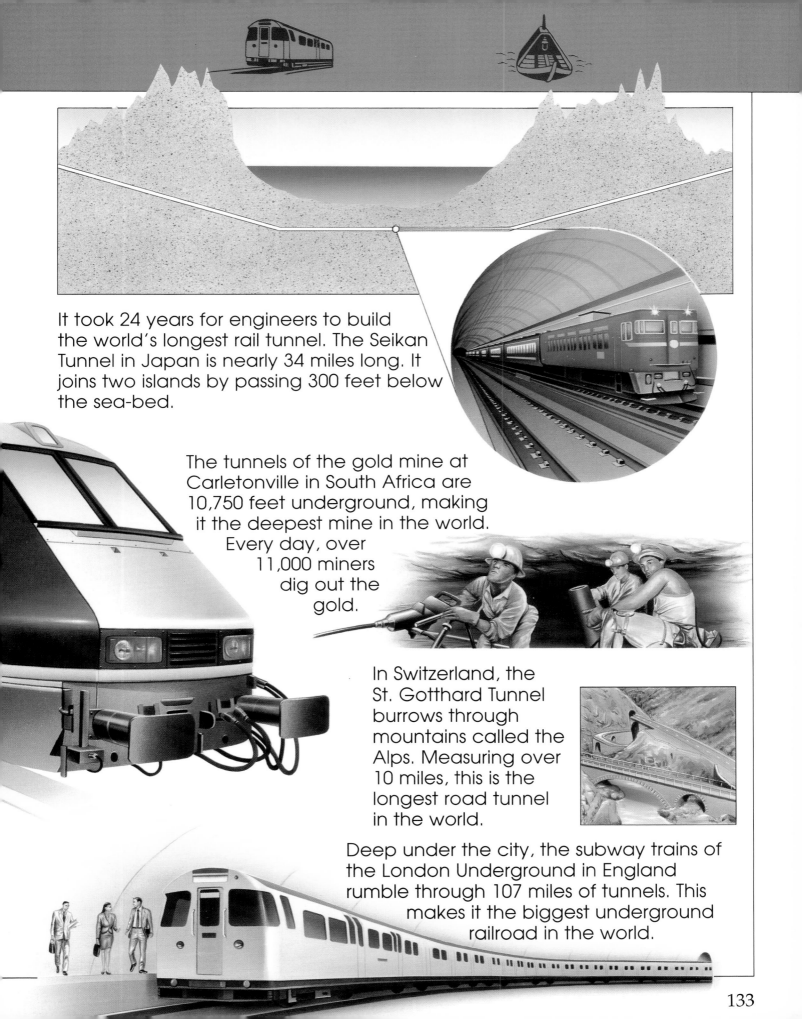

It took 24 years for engineers to build the world's longest rail tunnel. The Seikan Tunnel in Japan is nearly 34 miles long. It joins two islands by passing 300 feet below the sea-bed.

The tunnels of the gold mine at Carletonville in South Africa are 10,750 feet underground, making it the deepest mine in the world. Every day, over 11,000 miners dig out the gold.

In Switzerland, the St. Gotthard Tunnel burrows through mountains called the Alps. Measuring over 10 miles, this is the longest road tunnel in the world.

Deep under the city, the subway trains of the London Underground in England rumble through 107 miles of tunnels. This makes it the biggest underground railroad in the world.

Entertaining Wonders

Throughout history, people have created magnificent structures for entertainments.

Sydney Opera House overlooks Sydney harbor in Australia. It is shaped like a series of shells and is covered in tiles which catch the light. There are five separate halls inside.

Las Vegas, Nevada, has many buildings lit with neon lights.

The Romans built the Colosseum in Rome, Italy. It was a huge sporting arena. Up to 50,000 people would come to watch gladiators fight.

Walt Disney World in Florida, is the biggest amusement park in the world. It takes five days to look round all of it!

The longest roller coaster ride in the world is at Lightwater Valley Theme Park in Yorkshire, England. It is over 1¼ miles long.

In Ancient Greece, open-air theaters were very popular. At the Epidaurus theater, 14,000 people could watch a play. Actors on stage could be heard even if you sat right at the top.

The four-story Colosseum can still be seen in Rome. It is 160 feet high, and measures 1,600 feet round.

The biggest football stadium in the world is in Rio de Janeiro in Brazil. It can hold a crowd of 205,000 people.

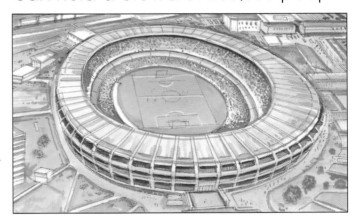

The Superdome in New Orleans, Louisiana, is the largest indoor stadium in the world. In Toronto, Canada, SkyDome Stadium, shown below, has the biggest moving roof in the world. It is rolled back in summer.

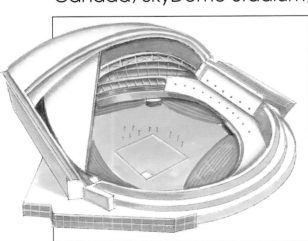

Southend Pier in Essex, England, is the longest pier in the world. The stroll along it is nearly 1½ miles. Since it was built in 1830, 14 ships have crashed into it!

Caves are formed when rainwater gradually wears away rock, and streams work their way underground. The streams form tunnels which slowly grow into caves.

In the Cueva de Nerja, Málaga, Spain, hangs a 180-foot stalactite – the longest in the world. The tallest stalagmite in the world is in the Krásnohorská cave in Slovakia. It is 100 feet tall.

In Kentucky, explorers have found the biggest collection of connected caves in the world. The Mammoth Cave system covers 350 miles.

The deepest cave in the world is at Réseau Jean Bernard in France. It is nearly 5,000 feet deep.

Stalagmites and stalactites are formed in limestone caves by continually dripping water containing calcite, which gradually collects on the rock. Stalactites grow downward from the roof, like icicles. The water which drips off them forms stalagmites which build upward. Eventually, the two may meet!

Since the sixteenth century, people in Knaresborough, England, have hung objects at the Dropping Well. Dripping water gradually turns the objects to stone. This happens in the same way as stalactites are formed.

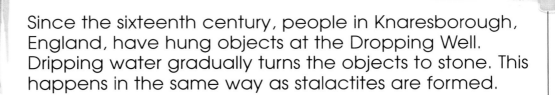

The biggest underwater cave is in Mexico. Divers have explored 25 miles of passages in the Nohoch Na Chich caves.

At 2,500 feet long and 1,000 feet wide, with a roof at least 250 feet high, the biggest cave in the world is the Sarawak Chamber, Lubang Nasib Bagus, in Sarawak, Malaysia.

137

Religious Wonders

There have been many religions in the history of the world. Since ancient times people have believed in one or many gods.

Often impressive structures have been built as places of worship.

In the Far East, Buddhists build tower-shaped temples called pagodas. This wooden Japanese pagoda in Kyoto was built in the seventh century.

In Wiltshire, England, the massive stones of ancient Stonehenge stand in a circle. Nobody really knows what they were for, but they may have been used for religious ceremonies. Stonehenge could be over 4,000 years old.

The Buddhist Temple of Borobudur in Indonesia is built in huge layers of steps. There are 72 bell-shaped shrines on them, each containing a statue of the Buddha. It is the largest Buddhist temple in the world.

Angkor Wat is the biggest place of worship in the world. It is a Hindu temple in Cambodia built in the twelfth century. The carved stone towers and passageways cover more than one square mile.

The architect Antoni Gaudí started work on the Cathedral of the Sagrada Familia (Barcelona, Spain) in 1883, but it remains unfinished. Its fantastic spires are over 320 feet tall.

In Moscow, Russia, the towers of St. Basil's Cathedral look as though they are topped with many different colored candies!

The Great Mosque at Mecca in Saudi Arabia is visited by many Muslim pilgrims. This vast mosque was built in the seventh century. At the centre of its huge open courtyard is a holy shrine.

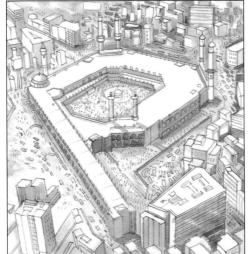

The Golden Temple at Amritsar in India is the most holy shrine of the Sikh religion. This beautiful golden building glistens in the sunlight. Inside, it is richly decorated with elaborate paintings and gold.

Artists have created exciting works of art in many different forms, from painting and sculpture to textiles and glass.

One of the earliest ways to decorate walls was by mosaic. Using tiny pieces of glass, stone, or marble, artists put together colorful pictures like amazing jigsaw puzzles.

The oldest artistic wonders date back to 30,000 BC, when Palaeolithic people created cave pictures using mineral powder.

The first cartoon strip in the world was embroidered in wool in the eleventh century! The Bayeux Tapestry tells the story of how the French conquered England in 1066. It is 231 feet long.

A battle scene from the Bayeux Tapestry.

This mosaic of the Empress Theodora is in a church in Ravenna, Italy. It was made in the sixth century AD.

Pablo Picasso produced more works of art during his life than any other artist. When Picasso died at the age of 78 in 1973, he had created around 148,000 pieces. His cubist paintings show several views of an object at the same time.

Stained glass windows in Christian churches were used to teach people about the Bible. This window in Cologne Cathedral in Germany tells the story of Jonah and the whale.

The most famous painting in the world is probably the *Mona Lisa*, which was painted by the Italian artist, Leonardo da Vinci, in about 1503.

It is said that music was played at every sitting for the portrait, so that the mysterious smile would not fade from the model's face.

141

Wherever the weather is very hot, dry, or cold, the landscape displays incredible features. Canyons or gorges are valleys with steep rock walls.

The biggest glacier in the world is the Lambert Glacier in Antarctica, which is over 440 miles long. The fastest-moving glacier is in Alaska, and can move about 70 feet a day.

The Vicos Gorge in Greece is 3,500 feet wide and 3,000 feet deep.

A glacier is a huge, slow-moving river of ice.

The biggest gorge in the world is the Grand Canyon, Arizona. It is between 4 and 18 miles wide and 278 miles long.

Visitors to Death Valley in California, must be careful of the extreme heat. Sometimes it gets as hot as 126°F.

The shores of the Dead Sea in Israel are 1,292 feet below sea-level. This is the lowest point on land in the world. The Dead Sea is the saltiest lake in the world. It has so much salt that you can't sink in it.

The largest desert in the world is the Sahara in North Africa. It spreads over 3,500,000 square miles. The biggest sand dunes can be found in the Sahara. They rise to 1,500 feet.

In 1956, a survey ship sighted the biggest ever iceberg in the South Pacific Ocean. It was 210 miles long and over 60 miles wide. Icebergs are huge chunks of ice which have broken off glaciers or ice sheets and entered the sea.

Engineering Wonders

Engineering is work that uses scientific knowledge for designing and building machines, vehicles, buildings, roads and structures such as bridges, dams and walls.

Aqueducts were first built in ancient times to carry water over a distance into cities. The Romans built the longest, which ran to the city of Carthage in Tunisia from springs 90 miles away.

Work on Britain's longest wall was started by the Romans in AD 122. Hadrian's Wall took only four years to build, and snaked nearly 74 miles across northern England.

The most concrete ever used to build a dam was poured into the huge Grand Coulee Dam in Washington State. It is 3,850 feet long and 551 feet high.

In the US, trains trundle 12 miles along the longest railway viaduct in the world. The viaduct crosses the Great Salt Lake in Utah.

Suspension bridges hang from cables between two towers. The Humber Estuary Bridge over the River Humber, England, is the longest in the world. The distance between its towers is 4,250 feet.

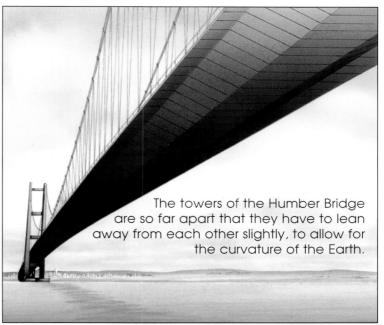

The towers of the Humber Bridge are so far apart that they have to lean away from each other slightly, to allow for the curvature of the Earth.

Sydney Harbor Bridge in Australia is the widest bridge in the world. At 150 feet wide, it carries two railway tracks, an eight-lane highway, a cycle path, and a footpath.

The longest wall in the world can be seen from Space! The Great Wall of China stretches 2,165 miles along a mountain range. The wall was built to keep invaders out of China. Builders worked for over a hundred years to finish it in about 210 BC.

Phenomenal Wonders

A phenomenon is any remarkable occurrence. Natural phenomena are those which occur in nature.

A tornado looks like a tube reaching out of a cloud. Its spiralling winds may reach over 300 miles per hour.

A comet is a rocky object which travels around the Sun and can periodically be seen from Earth. Halley's Comet was first recorded in 240 BC.

A waterspout is a tornado which has formed over water, and created a tall spinning column of watery mist. The highest waterspout reached 4,600 feet off New South Wales, Australia, in 1898.

A mirage is the illusion of a distant object or a sheet of water. It is caused by atmospheric conditions in hot weather.

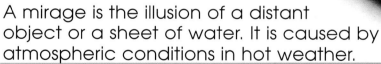

A solar eclipse is when the Moon passes between the Sun and the Earth. The longest solar eclipse in recent times was in 1715, and lasted four minutes.

Meteorites are broken bits of comets or asteroids which fall to Earth. The biggest one ever found was 9 feet long and weighed 60 tons. It was found in Namibia, Africa, in 1920.

Hailstones form when water droplets in storm clouds freeze and fall to Earth. The heaviest hailstones fell in Bangladesh in 1986. They weighed 2.2 pounds and killed 92 people.

The northern lights, or aurora borealis, are different coloured bands of light that move across the sky in the polar region. They are caused by particles from the Sun reaching the Earth's magnetic field.

St. Elmo's fire is a luminous area which may appear around objects such as church spires, ships' masts, or aircraft wings. It is caused by electricity in the atmosphere.

Earthquakes

An earthquake happens when the surface of the Earth moves. It can strike suddenly and without warning. Buildings collapse and people are often buried alive.

We live on the Earth's crust. This is divided into huge plates that glide around very slowly. The most severe earthquakes take place near the edges of these plates.

The size of an earthquake depends on the amount of **pressure** that has been built up along the plates. It can be a small rumble or be so strong it brings down buildings, bridges, and roads.

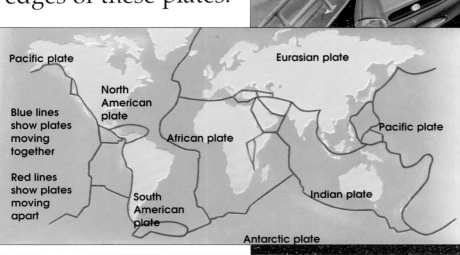

Pacific plate

North American plate

Blue lines show plates moving together

Red lines show plates moving apart

Eurasian plate

African plate

Pacific plate

South American plate

Indian plate

Antarctic plate

In the middle of the oceans, **plates** move apart and new rock is formed to fill the gaps. This movement causes earthquakes, but we do not feel these because they are so far from land.

If a plate is forced down beneath another plate in a sudden movement there will be a huge earthquake. This happened in 1923, in **Japan**. The city of Tokyo had the world's most terrible earthquake. About 300,000 buildings were destroyed and approximately 100,000 people were killed.

In January 1995, Japan suffered its worst earthquake since 1923. In the city of Kobe and the surrounding region over 5,000 people were killed when more than 1,200 buildings were destroyed, highways collapsed, and fires raged throughout the area.

A **fault** is a huge crack that runs across the land where plates move alongside each other.

A fault

A man called **Dr. Charles Richter** devised a scale to measure the force of earthquakes. This is measured on a scale of 1–10.

The Richter Scale is still used today.

Famous Earthquakes		Richter
Date	Place	value
1906	San Francisco	8.6
1923	Sagami Bay, Japan	8.2
1955	North Assam, India	8.6
1988	Armenia	6.9
1989	San Francisco	6.9

The **San Andreas Fault** in California, is where the Pacific plate and the North American plate slide past each other. The cities of San Francisco and Los Angeles are in this earthquake zone.

There was a massive earthquake in **San Francisco** in 1906 and another smaller one in 1989. In January 1994, an earthquake in **Los Angeles** killed more than 50 people.

Volcanoes

A volcano is a hole in the Earth's crust. When a volcano erupts, hot molten rocks from inside the Earth pour out of the hole onto the surface.

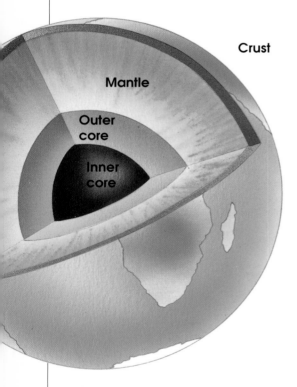

Crust

Mantle

Outer core

Inner core

There are two kinds of volcanic eruptions. Some volcanoes explode without warning, and others erupt slowly and quietly, usually allowing time for people to escape.

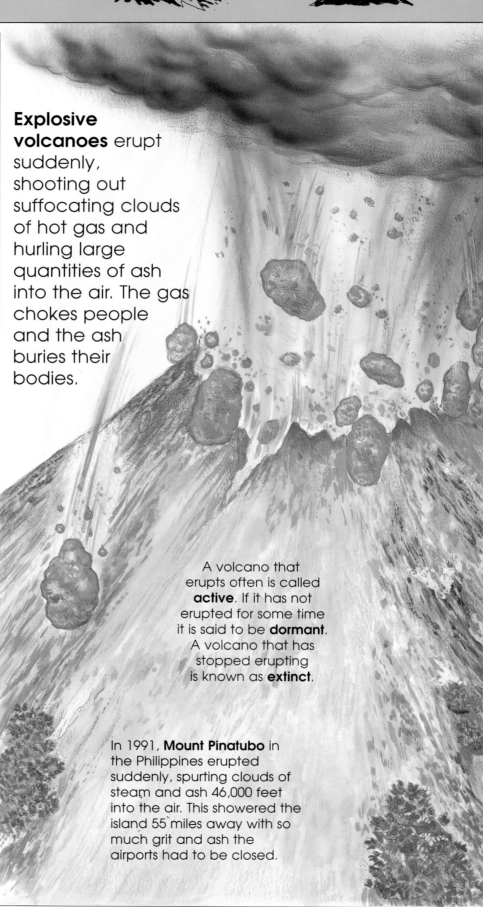

Explosive volcanoes erupt suddenly, shooting out suffocating clouds of hot gas and hurling large quantities of ash into the air. The gas chokes people and the ash buries their bodies.

A volcano that erupts often is called **active**. If it has not erupted for some time it is said to be **dormant**. A volcano that has stopped erupting is known as **extinct**.

In 1991, **Mount Pinatubo** in the Philippines erupted suddenly, spurting clouds of steam and ash 46,000 feet into the air. This showered the island 55 miles away with so much grit and ash the airports had to be closed.

In the Pacific Ocean there is a string of volcanic islands that form the state of **Hawaii**. The volcanoes were caused by a hot spot just below the Earth's crust.

In 1883 the volcanic island of **Krakatoa** erupted with such force that a pillar of steam 36,080 feet high shot up into the sky. The air was filled with fumes, hot cinders, and black dust that blotted out the sun. The heat from the island could be felt almost 2 miles away.

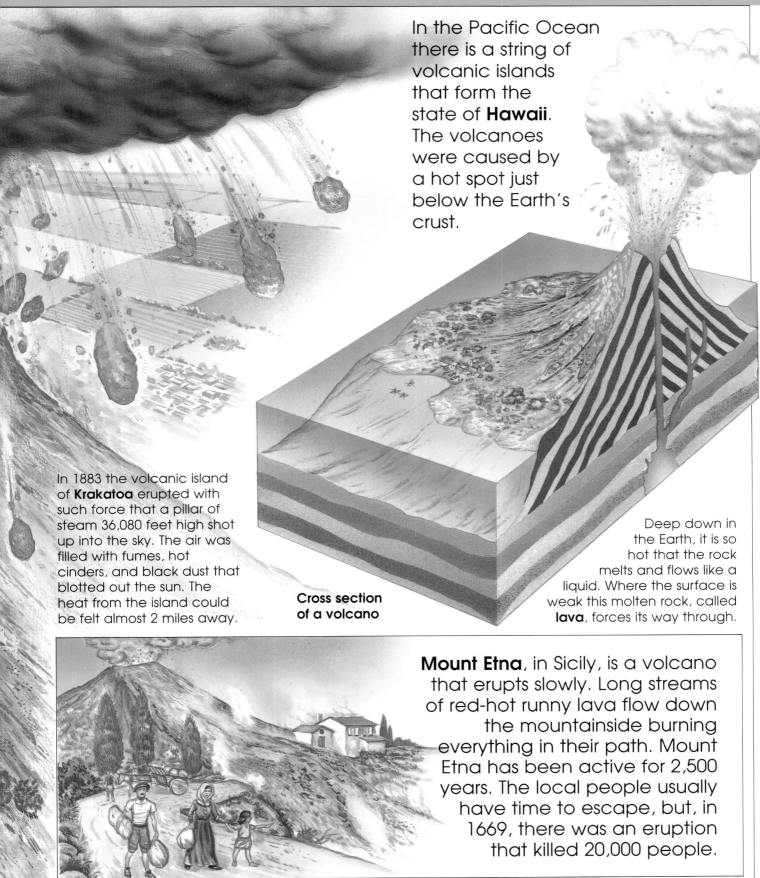

Cross section of a volcano

Deep down in the Earth, it is so hot that the rock melts and flows like a liquid. Where the surface is weak this molten rock, called **lava**, forces its way through.

Mount Etna, in Sicily, is a volcano that erupts slowly. Long streams of red-hot runny lava flow down the mountainside burning everything in their path. Mount Etna has been active for 2,500 years. The local people usually have time to escape, but, in 1669, there was an eruption that killed 20,000 people.

151

Many natural disasters are caused by weather, especially storms. Every day about 45,000 thunderstorms happen somewhere in the world.

A thunderstorm is caused when warm, moist air rises very quickly, forming thunderclouds.

Electrical charges build up inside the clouds. These charges cause flashes inside the clouds, between one cloud and another, or between a cloud and the ground as lightning.

Light travels nearly one million times faster than sound so lightning is seen before thunder is heard.

A flash of **lightning** carries enough electrical energy to light a small city for several weeks. It causes heat five times that of the sun. This makes the air expand and makes a crash of **thunder**.

The safest place to be in a thunderstorm is inside a car or in a building. Never stand under a tree or hold a metal umbrella.

Thunderstorms sometimes contain **hailstones**. In April 1986, hailstones weighing up to 2 pounds killed 92 people in Bangladesh.

In 1959, **Colonel William Rankin** bailed out of his aircraft, which had been battered by a thunderstorm in Virginia. As he parachuted down, he was sucked into the heart of the storm.
For 40 minutes he was pelted by hailstones, deafened by thunder, and blinded by lightning, but he survived.

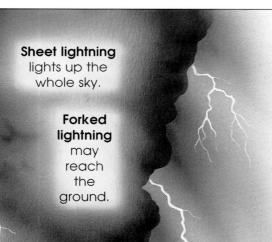

Sheet lightning lights up the whole sky.

Forked lightning may reach the ground.

Many buildings have **lightning conductors**. These carry the electricity down into the ground so the building is not damaged. The **Empire State Building** in New York City gets struck by lightning 500 times a year but is protected by a conductor.

In December 1963, 81 people were killed when a **Boeing 707 jet airliner** was struck by lightning in Maryland.

Hurricanes and tornadoes

Hurricanes are the most violent large storms. They form over the warm oceans during the hottest months of the year.

The high winds of a hurricane become more powerful as they reach land. Some can release the same energy as a volcanic eruption and cause terrible destruction.

A tornado is a smaller storm than a hurricane, but it can have even stronger winds.

In the Atlantic Ocean the storms are called **hurricanes**; in the Indian Ocean they are known as **cyclones**, and in the western Pacific they have the name **typhoon**.

In 1992, **Hurricane Andrew** swept across southern United States. Winds of over 125 miles per hour made 200,000 people homeless and caused $20 billion worth of damage in Florida, alone. It was the costliest natural disaster in the history of the United States.

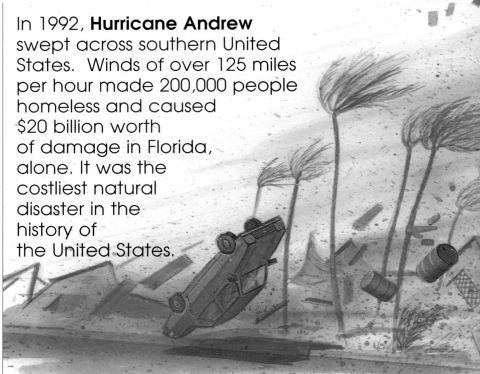

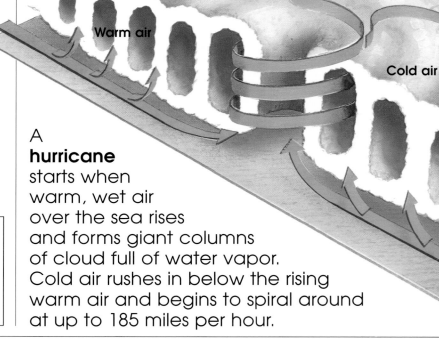

Warm air

Cold air

A **hurricane** starts when warm, wet air over the sea rises and forms giant columns of cloud full of water vapor. Cold air rushes in below the rising warm air and begins to spiral around at up to 185 miles per hour.

Every hurricane is given a **name** to identify it. The names are chosen in alphabetical order, alternating between male and female names for each new storm. **Hurricane Gilbert** was the most powerful hurricane this century.

In 1991, a cyclone disaster killed almost 139,000 people in **Bangladesh**. Winds of 140 miles per hour caused floods over 500 square miles making ten million people homeless. Four million faced death from starvation.

A **tornado** is a funnel-shaped cloud that descends from storm clouds to the ground, sucking up dust and debris as it moves. Tornadoes can tear trees out of the ground and cause buildings to explode.

About 200 tornadoes a year are recorded across the United States. They are a major hazard in the Mississippi Valley, which is sometimes known as **Tornado Alley**.

Tornado Alley

Mexico

Caribbean

In May 1986, in **China**, it was reported that 13 schoolchildren had been sucked up into a tornado and carried 12 miles before being dropped gently to the ground again.

155

Floods

A flood is too much water. This can come from heavy rainfall, overflowing rivers, sudden melting of snow and ice, or high tides.

Throughout history floods have caused more death and destruction than any other natural disaster on this planet.

The Bible story of **Noah** tells of a great flood that destroyed every living thing, except the family and animals on the ark.

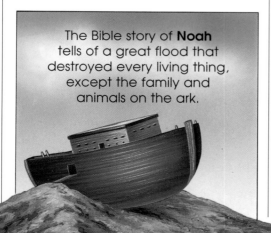

In 1993, there was severe flooding in the **mid west**. The Mississippi and Missouri rivers broke their banks along a stretch of 500 miles, killing over 40 people and submerging 15,000 square miles of land. The president announced it to be a major disaster area.

In **1994-5**, there were more floods across the world than there have been for many years.

Northern Italy had the most ferocious rainstorms of the century. Over 100 people died.

In **northern Spain** houses were flooded and a bridge collapsed.

Greece suffered from heavy flooding.

In **Egypt**, floods killed hundreds and caused damage of $2.7 billion.

In **Africa**, flash floods hit drought areas. The cocoa crops of West and central Africa were destroyed.

In **Germany**, the Rhine River became three times deeper than normal and flooded the city of Cologne.

In **China**, freak rainstorms made thousands of people homeless.

Huge seas washed away roads in Victoria, **Australia**.

In **India**, 192 people died and 40,000 people were made homeless after rainfall caused by a cyclone.

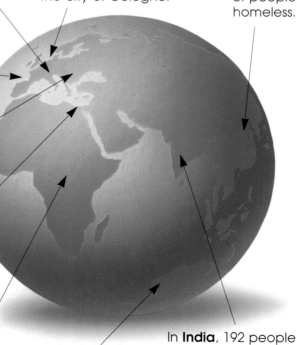

The Huang River is known as "China's Sorrow" because it has caused the world's worst floods. In 1887, in the city of **Zhengzhou**, over one million people died, either by drowning or from the terrible disease and starvation which followed.

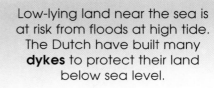

Low-lying land near the sea is at risk from floods at high tide. The Dutch have built many **dykes** to protect their land below sea level.

In January 1995, 250,000 people fled their homes in the Netherlands as the worst floods in nearly sixty years swept across large areas of Europe. The country's dykes were threatened and some were close to collapse.

Bangladesh, in Asia, suffers from terrible floods when cyclones sweep in from the Bay of Bengal, causing high tides and heavy rain. Nearly all of Bangladesh is on the floodplain of the Ganges and Brahmaputra rivers.

The **Thames Barrier** was built across the Thames River in London, England, to prevent the surges of the tide from flooding the city.

Avalanches and landslides

Torrential rainfall and earthquakes can trigger landslides, which cause terrible destruction.

Avalanches often happen after prolonged snowfalls. They can be caused by the slightest noise.

During **World War 1**, 10,000 soldiers lost their lives on one day in a series of snowslides.

An **avalanche** is a mass of loosened snow and earth that slips down a mountainside, growing in size as it travels.

In January 1718 the village of **Leukerbad**, in Switzerland was engulfed by a massive avalanche. Over 50 houses disappeared, and 52 villagers were buried under a blanket of snow.

Avalanches are a danger in any mountainous area with bare slopes and heavy snow. Where slopes have been cleared of trees for skiing or farming, walls and snow fences are built to break up any avalanche that might develop.

In **winter sports areas**, snow patrols keep a special watch and give warnings of possible avalanches to ski resorts. All roads and ski slopes are closed at any sign of danger.

In 1970, on **Mount Huascaran**, Peru, an earthquake caused a gigantic rock and **mud slide**. It covered 9 miles in less than four minutes and wiped out towns and villages in its path. A dam burst, rivers flooded, and 186,000 buildings were destroyed. It was estimated that over 20,000 people died and 200,000 were left homeless.

Soil and rock on mountains and hills can creep, slide, flow, and fall. **Creeps** happen on hillsides, usually very slowly. **Slides** can travel between 2 inches a year and 10 feet a second. Slides on mountains can remove large sections of rock.

Rock slide

Earth flow

Soil creep

Rock fall

Mud flow

159

Drought

A drought is a shortage of rain. In parts of the world where there are long periods of dry weather, droughts are common.

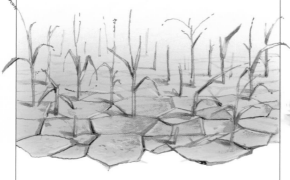

This means that trees and crops die, and so there is a shortage of food.

If the drought continues for a long time there is a famine in the land and many people die of starvation.

In 1770 millions of Indians died of hunger when **drought** ruined their harvests. In 1877 nearly 10 million Chinese were lost in a famine. In the twentieth century, thousands of Africans have died of starvation when crops were ruined and cattle starved to death.

The plains of Oklahoma and Texas were once covered in lush grass. Then the farmers plowed them up to plant wheat. In 1930 a drought killed all the crops, and strong winds blew away the top soil. Nothing could be grown there, and the area was called **The Dust Bowl**. Later the land was reclaimed and today it is no longer a desert.

During droughts 39 square miles of the Earth's surface may become desert every day.

When plants die the soil is exposed to the wind and may easily be blown away. Green grasslands can soon turn into deserts. This is called **desertification**. It is worst in areas where people overgraze land with their large herds of cattle, or cut down trees and shrubs.

The Sahel

AFRICA

To bring water to land devastated by drought people dig **irrigation channels**. These bring water to the land so that crops can grow.

When droughts cause plants to dry up, they can catch fire easily.

Lightning from a storm or a careless cigarette can start a fire that destroys thousands of square miles of forest.

In the fall of 1993, a series of bushfires raged across **California**. Many rich and famous Hollywood stars watched as their homes went up in flames.

In January 1994, high temperatures and hot winds fanned the worst **bushfires** ever known in **Australia**. Over 130 fires raged around Sydney and the coast of New South Wales, destroying hundreds of homes. The heat was so intense it caused windows to melt and houses to explode. Over 7,500 fire fighters battled with the blaze which stretched for 600 miles and burned over 988,000 acres of land. Miraculously, only four people died.

In some large forests there are tall **lookout towers** where foresters can spot the first signs of fire. Observers in helicopters fly over the fire and note its size. Then they quickly transport fire fighters and equipment to the scene of the fire to fight the blaze.

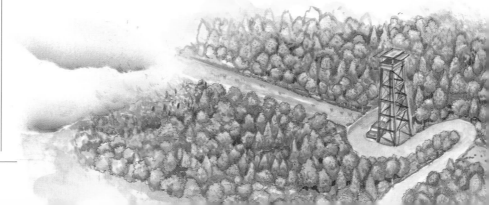

During the 1994 bushfires in Australia, most of the wildlife that lived in the surrounding national parks was wiped out, including entire colonies of koalas. The animals that did manage to flee had no food or shelter.

Some scientists feel that fire is nature's way of renewing the land. In 1988 fires raged through **Yellowstone Park**. Many people wanted the fires put out, but as there was no property in danger they were allowed to burn. After the fires were over, the vegetation grew again very quickly.

The main tree in Yellowstone Park is the **lodgepole pine**. The cones on this tree depend on fire because they need a minimum temperature of 113° F to open and release their seeds.

Ice ages are periods when great sheets of ice extend far beyond the land and sea they cover today.

The Earth has experienced many ice ages, some lasting for over 100 million years.

During an ice age, sheets of ice cover large parts of the world and the level of the sea is much lower than it is now.

Ice sheets and **glaciers** erode or wear away the land they move over. The ice pulls pieces of rock from the land beneath it. These rocks can be carried for miles before they are dropped.

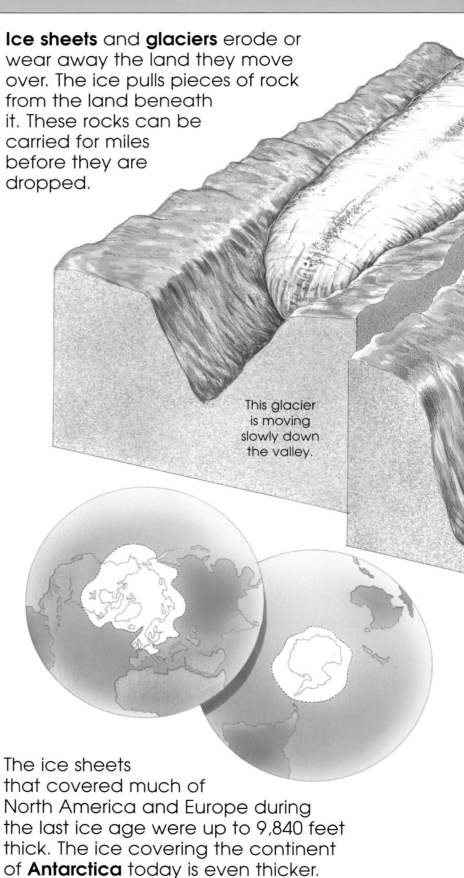

This glacier is moving slowly down the valley.

The ice sheets that covered much of North America and Europe during the last ice age were up to 9,840 feet thick. The ice covering the continent of **Antarctica** today is even thicker.

The most recent ice age started two million years ago. During that time there were periods called **glacials** when the ice sheets were expanding, and times called **interglacials** when they became smaller. We may now be living in an interglacial period. If world temperatures fall, the ice sheets could grow again.

Woolly mammoths lived on Earth during the recent Ice age and became extinct about 10,000 years ago.

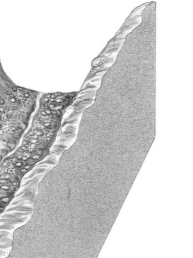

When the glacier melts it leaves a valley in the land.

The **fjords**, or deep sea inlets, along the coast of Scandinavia were made by glaciers during the last ice age.

Approximately 18,000 years ago, toward the end of the **last ice age**, the world's climate changed dramatically. The Earth became drier, deserts grew larger, and tropical rain forests shrank. Parts of South America that now have rain forests were covered in moving sand dunes.

The sea has always held many dangers for sailors and other voyagers. High winds during storms create huge waves in mid-ocean. These can drive ships off their course, or wreck them on rocks and seashores.

In April 1912, the **Titanic**, the newest and most luxurious liner ever built, set sail on her maiden voyage to New York City. One dark night the ship collided with an enormous **iceberg**, which ripped a hole in her side 295 feet long. About 1,500 people were left stranded on the liner, which quickly sank beneath the waves. It was the worst shipping disaster of all time.

Waterspouts, tidal waves, icebergs, and pack ice are hazards that can cause great loss of life.

Icebergs from **Antarctica** are low, flat-topped and cover a large area.

Icebergs in the **North Atlantic** are tall and jagged, but mostly hidden beneath the waves.

A **waterspout** is a column of rising water that forms when a tornado descends over the sea. Waterspouts are often seen off the coast of the Gulf of Mexico and over the Atlantic Ocean, near Florida. They suck up huge amounts of seawater into a great black cloud. Boats floating on the sea can be sucked up too.

Pack ice in the Arctic Ocean and around Antarctica can trap or crush ships. Some of the vessels used by the polar explorers were lost in this way. Nowadays, specially built **icebreakers** can force their way through.

160 feet

The **biggest wave** ever recorded in the open sea was seen from a ship during a storm in 1933. It was 112 feet high.

112 feet

The huge volcanic eruption of **Krakatoa**, in August 1883, caused enormous waves, called **tsunamis**, to form in the sea. These swept toward the shores of Java and Sumatra, sucking up more water as they traveled. The gigantic waves, more than 160 feet high, crashed down on the coast, destroying 300 villages and drowning 36,000 people.

167

Plagues

A plague is a very contagious disease that spreads quickly, killing many people.

Many diseases can spread rapidly if people do not take special care to stop this happening. Any illness that causes many members of a community to be ill at the same time is called an epidemic.

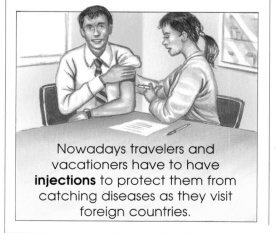

Nowadays travelers and vacationers have to have **injections** to protect them from catching diseases as they visit foreign countries.

Between 1334 and 1351, a terrible epidemic, **the Black Death**, swept across Asia and Europe, killing millions of people. The disease was a form of **bubonic plague** and was spread by black rats that boarded trading ships. It was the fleas that lived on the rats that carried the plague, but unfortunately no one realized this at the time.

Another insect that carries disease is the mosquito. **Malaria** is passed on by the bite of a mosquito that lives in tropical and subtropical areas.

Although there are medicines that can keep this sickness at bay, no one has found a cure for it. Millions still die from malaria each year.

Leprosy is a disease that can be infectious. It occurs mainly in tropical and subtropical regions. It is a terrible disease that causes disfigurement.

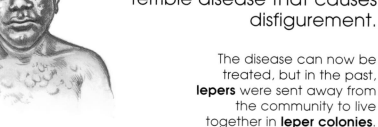

The disease can now be treated, but in the past, **lepers** were sent away from the community to live together in **leper colonies**.

In 1994, **plague** broke out in **India**. This, too, was spread by fleas, carried by rats. Nowadays, the disease can be treated with medicine called **antibiotics** if it is detected early enough.

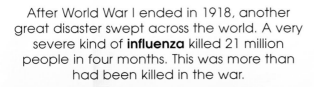

After World War I ended in 1918, another great disaster swept across the world. A very severe kind of **influenza** killed 21 million people in four months. This was more than had been killed in the war.

Epidemics of **cholera** are common in Asia. Between 1898 and 1907, 370,000 people in India died of this disease, which is often caused by drinking dirty water.

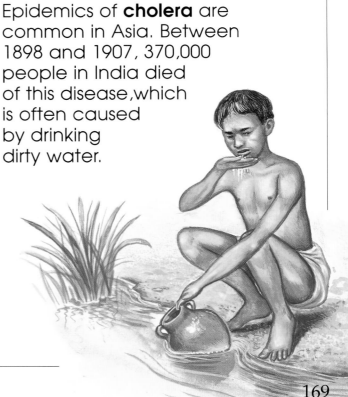

169

Plant and animal pests

Throughout history natural disasters have been caused by insect or animal pests, that destroy the crops on which humans live.

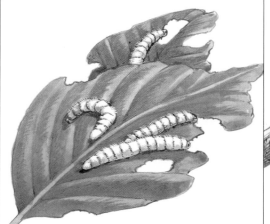

Some of these disasters are caused by people changing the creatures' habitats, by farming the land, or by introducing new animals into areas where they were previously unknown.

One of the worst pests in Africa is the **quelea bird**. These small brown birds live together in huge flocks and can destroy crops. Sometimes two million pairs can be found in an area of about 120 acres.

In 1889, a swarm of locusts seen flying over the **Red Sea** was roughly 1,900 square miles in size.

Locusts are giant grasshoppers that can fly long distances and travel in vast swarms. When they land, they devour the crops for miles around, causing great destruction and often widespread famine.

In the 1840s, there was a terrible disease, or **blight**, on the potato crops in Ireland. As many people lived only on these vegetables, there was a terrible shortage of food, known as the **Potato Famine**.

Dutch elm disease has killed thousands of elm trees throughout the world. It is spread by the **European elm bark beetle**. Young trees can die within two months.

The Colorado potato beetle, or potato bug, is an insect pest that feeds on the leaves of potato plants in western North America. Originally, the insect fed on a wild plant that grows in the Rocky Mountains.But since potato plants were introduced into the United States, it has preferred to eat those instead.

In the 1800's, English settlers took **rabbits** to Australia with them. Some of these eventually escaped to the outback, where they started a colony of wild rabbits which was to become one of Australia's greatest pests. They ate farmers' crops, turned grassland into desert, and their warrens caused the ground to collapse.

In the 1930s, the **cane toad** was introduced into Queensland, Australia, in order to control beetles. Now the toads are a pest!

171

World pollution

Over the past hundred years, industry and modern technology have changed the world. Because of these changes, many new forms of pollution now affect our planet.

Many nations have begun to act to combat pollution. But we still need stricter laws to stop any further damage.

Oil tankers spill vast amounts of crude oil into the sea, poisoning everything that lives there. These are called **oil slicks**.

Many factories and power plants produce **toxic waste**. This is released into the environment and poisons rivers and lakes. The creatures that live in and around these waterways die or grow deformed.

The burning of forests increases the carbon dioxide in the air, and means that there are fewer trees to absorb this gas.

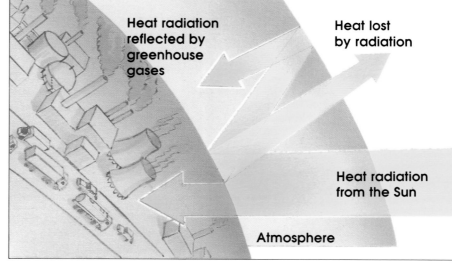

Heat radiation reflected by greenhouse gases

Heat lost by radiation

Heat radiation from the Sun

Atmosphere

As we pollute the atmosphere by burning fossil fuels, we also poison our rain, sleet, and snow. **Acid rain** has killed forests and freshwater fish in many parts of the world. It also eats away at stone buildings and corrodes anything made of steel.

If we do not stop pollution, scientists think the average world **temperature** will rise dramatically over the next 50 years. This could cause the polar **ice caps** to melt, flooding large areas of the world. Other areas would have terrible droughts.

Low-lying parts of London could be flooded if the average world temperature rose.

We burn the **fossil fuels** in factories, cars, and power plants. These cause pollution and increase the amount of **carbon dioxide** in the air. This gas keeps heat in the **atmosphere** around the Earth. We call this **global warming**. The Sun's rays are trapped within the atmosphere just as they are in a greenhouse. So, the warming of the planet is called the **greenhouse effect**.

Some aerosols and refrigerators give off chemicals called CFCs into the atmosphere. These are damaging the **ozone layer**, which protects us from the Sun's dangerous **ultraviolet** rays. The use of CFCs has now been banned.

Some scientist believe that 65 million years ago, a meteorite fell to Earth from space.

Every year the Earth attracts more than a million tons of new material from space. These are called **meteors**. Most meteors disintegrate before they reach the ground, but sometimes the core survives and is called a **meteorite**.

They think that the effects of the crash damaged our planet so badly that the dinosaurs became extinct.

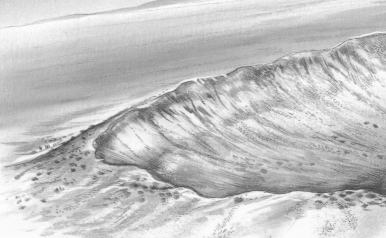

If, as some scientists think, a large meteorite did hit the Earth millions of years ago, it would have thrown up a huge cloud of dust. This would have lowered the temperature and eventually killed most of the plant and animal life.

If a similar collision happened today, it could threaten the human race.

In **Arizona**, there is a gigantic crater in the ground, caused by a meteor measuring about 100 feet across. It must have been traveling at a speed of about 31,000 miles per hour because the meteor struck the ground with such force it made a crater nearly 650 feet deep and 1 mile wide.

Small meteors often break up into fragments as they travel through the atmosphere, causing streaks of light that flash across the sky. We call these **shooting stars**.

In July 1994, 21 giant particles of rock and ice from the comet **Shoemaker-Levy 9**, collided with the planet **Jupiter**. One of the fragments created a giant fireball and Earth-sized hole in the planet's atmosphere. The U.S. government has given scientists $ 50 million to create an early warning system to predict such a thing happening to the Earth.

175

What is a warrior?

Warriors were men or women who fought bravely. Often they were not paid to fight, but fought because they believed they were right.

Warriors did not win all of the time. Some of the most famous warriors are those who lost, but who fought with great courage.

Byrhtnoth was an English earl. In 991, he and all his men died fighting a Viking force near Maldon in Essex. They fought so bravely that a poem, called "The Battle of Maldon," was written about their heroic struggle.

Shaka was the king of the Zulu, a large tribe in South Africa. In 1816, Shaka trained the Zulu warriors in new battle tactics. By 1850 the Zulus had defeated all neighboring tribes. In 1879 the Zulus wiped out a British regiment before being defeated by the British at Rorke's Drift and Kambula.

Warriors used different types of **weapons**. Early warriors used clubs and rocks, while more modern warriors used rifles and cannons.

The Assyrians conquered a large empire in the Near East about 3,000 years ago

Ashanti warriors fought in the dense forests of West Africa about 100 years ago.

The **Maori** live in New Zealand. They used to live in great tribes which fought wars with each other, and later, with European settlers. Sometimes whole tribes were killed in battle as they refused to surrender. Although the Europeans accepted the Maori as equals in 1840, wars continued for many years.

Alexander the Great

In 336 B.C. Alexander the Great became King of Macedonia (in northern Greece). He was only 20 years old. Within 13 years he had become the most powerful ruler in the world.

He defeated armies larger than his own using clever new tactics and weapons.

Alexander's horse was called **Bucephalus**. According to legend, Alexander, who was only 12 years old at the time, was the only person who could control him. When Bucephalus died Alexander named a town in India, Bucephala, in honor of him.

The Battle of Gaugamela in 331 B.C. was Alexander's greatest victory. He defeated a Persian army of 150,000 men with his army of only 35,000 Macedonians. The battle was won when Alexander led a cavalry charge which scattered the Persian infantry.

The cavalry led the attacks in battle. They were used to open gaps in the enemy army. The horsemen would charge forward, followed by the infantry.

King Darius, was Alexander's biggest enemy. He became ruler of the Persian Empire in 336 B.C. after murdering the previous three rulers. Darius was a successful warrior who defeated many enemies, but he lost two major battles to Alexander. In 330 B.C. Darius was murdered by his cousin.

Infantry in Alexander's army used a very long spear called a **sarissa**. Each sarissa was 15 feet long.

By 323 B.C. Alexander's Empire was the largest in the world at that time. He wanted to join all the kingdoms he had conquered to form one country. After Alexander died, his generals divided the empire between themselves. Within 150 years the empire no longer existed.

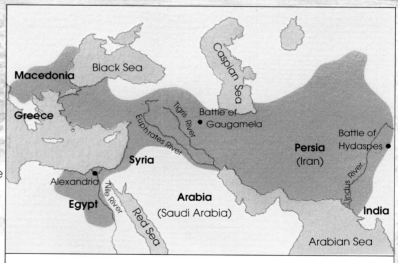

Macedonia
Black Sea
Greece
Caspian Sea
Euphrates River
Tigris River
Battle of Gaugamela
Persia (Iran)
Battle of Hydaspes
Syria
Alexandria
Nile River
Indus River
Egypt
Arabia (Saudi Arabia)
India
Red Sea
Arabian Sea

The Empire of Alexander the Great

Alexander reached **India** in 326 B.C. He defeated a local king, Porus, at the Battle of the Hydaspes (modern-day Jhelum) and added new territories to his empire.

Attila the Hun

Attila was the king of the Huns, a warlike tribe feared in Europe and Asia. He became sole King in 444 after murdering his elder brother, Breda, who was joint King at the time.

Attila organized the Huns into a powerful army. By conquering neighboring kingdoms he built up a large empire. Soon, he became known as "the scourge of God."

In 453 Attila died suddenly after a feast on his wedding day. He was buried with his treasure. The slaves who buried him were all killed to keep the location secret. Without Attila's leadership, the Huns were easily defeated by their enemies.

The Huns came from central Asia in about 370 and settled in what is now Hungary. Attila led his tribe in wars that ranged across Greece, southern Russia, Germany and France.

The Huns loved gold - during one raid into Greece they stole over 2,000 lbs!

Attila arrived in Italy in 452 and captured many cities. Pope Leo I persuaded him to spare Rome from attack.

Venice is a city in northern Italy surrounded by the sea. It was founded by Romans fleeing from Attila. The escaping Romans were safe on the islands of Venice as the Huns did not have a navy.

Horses were the Huns' most important possession. They used them to look after their large herds of cattle and sheep. They also fought on horseback, using spears and bows to attack their enemies.

Hun warriors scarred their faces with knives to make themselves look fierce to frighten their enemies.

The Huns used the **lasso** as a weapon. One Hun would catch an enemy with a lasso, allowing another warrior to kill the captive.

Romans

The Roman Empire began around 753 B.C. and lasted over 1,000 years until A.D. 476. It covered all the lands around the Mediterranean, and much of Europe.

These lands were conquered and policed by the Roman Army. The Romans defeated many enemies because of their superior weapons and tactics.

The Romans were excellent builders as well as warriors. They made roads to move their armies from one place to another, and built forts and walls to keep out invaders. **Hadrian's Wall**, in northern England, was built to keep enemies from invading England from Scotland.

The legionary was the most important type of Roman warrior. Legionaries wore strong suits of armor and fought on foot. They were grouped together in a century, made up of 80 legionaries led by an officer known as a centurion.

Roman legionaries marched and fought together in a large group of 5,200 legionaries, called a **legion**.

Horatius was a legendary early Roman warrior. In about 670 B.C. a large Etruscan army (from northern Italy) attacked Rome. The bridge leading to Rome across the Tiber River had to be cut down to stop the Etruscan invasion. Horatius fought the Etruscans single-handedly to give the Romans time to cut down the bridge. Rome was saved and Horatius survived to be declared a hero.

Mark Antony was a famous general. He fell in love with Cleopatra, the Queen of Egypt, and gave her land belonging to Rome. This led to a civil war with the Roman authorities which Mark Antony lost. Later, he took his own life.

Legionaries arranged themselves in special formations when attacking the enemy. The "tortoise" protected legionaries from arrows and spears. The "wedge" was used to smash through enemy ranks.

A bronze eagle was the symbol of a legion and it was carried into battle. Romans thought it was an insult to the gods if the eagle were captured by the enemy.

Enemies of Rome

The Roman Empire was very large and had many enemies. There were tribes fighting their Roman conquerors, and armies from other empires trying to invade Rome.

The **Celts** were divided into many different tribes, who lived right across Europe from Scotland to Serbia. They were often a war-like people, who rode chariots into battle and sometimes sang as they fought. After a battle, the Celts would cut off the heads of their dead enemies and hold a feast to celebrate.

Vercingetorix was the Celtic leader of Gaul (modern-day France). He fought against the Roman general Julius Caesar in 52 B.C. After several battles, Vercingetorix was captured and beheaded.

Hannibal was a famous nobleman from Carthage (in modern-day Tunisia). He was one of Rome's most dangeous enemies. In 218 B.C. he led his army, along with 38 elephants, from Spain through France and across the Alps into Italy. He won many battles there, including the defeat of 50,000 Romans at Cannae. He never reached Rome and was forced to return to Carthage.

Spartacus was a slave who escaped from a gladiator school in 73 B.C. Thousands of other slaves ran away to join him. Spartacus led them through Italy stealing and burning everything they could find. He was defeated and died in battle at Lucania in 71 B.C. The 6,000 prisoners captured by the Romans were all crucified.

Boudicca was Queen of the Iceni, a tribe from East Anglia, in England. In A.D. 61 she led her tribe in revolt after she and her daughters had been ill-treated by the Romans, who had also increased the taxes. Boudicca's Celtic warriors destroyed Colchester, London and St. Albans before being beaten by the Romans. Rather than surrender, she poisoned herself.

Arminius was a German chief. In A.D. 9 he and his warriors trapped three Roman legions in a swampy forest and killed them all.

Masada was a fortress in Palestine held by 1,000 Jewish rebels in A.D. 72-73. After a two-year siege by 15,000 Romans, all but seven of the Jews, including the children, committed suicide rather than surrender.

Ireland was never conquered by the Romans. Instead, Ireland remained a land ruled by Celtic chiefs.

Although there was a High King of Ireland most tribes continued to fight each other.

Irish kings and chiefs often lived in well defended **strongholds**. The remains of the Rock of Cashel in Tipperary County are a good example of an ancient Irish stronghold. The rock was home to the kings of Munster.

Cuchulainn was the great warrior hero of Ulster. His story is told in a poem called "The Cattle Raid of Cooley" which was written around the year 500. In the poem Cuchulainn is described as being very strong and having a terrible temper.

Brian Boru was the greatest High King of Ireland, reigning from 1002 to 1014. He fought to free Ireland from Viking invaders. He was murdered by a fleeing band of Vikings after finally defeating the Viking army at Clontarf.

Women are important characters in Irish mythology. The legendary **Queen Maeve** of Connaught led an army against Ulster, and fought against Cuchulainn.

Fionn mac Cumhaill was the legendary hero of Leinster. According to the stories told about him, he led a band of brave young warriors who loved to hunt. These warriors were known as the Fianna. The Fianna rebelled against Cairbre, High King of Ireland, in an argument about hunting lands. The Fianna were destroyed in the following battle.

Strongbow was the nickname of Richard Fitzgilbert, a Norman lord. He came to Ireland in 1170 to help Dermot MacMurrogh, King of Leinster, become High King. After Dermot's death, Strongbow grabbed his lands for himself. Soon, other Norman and English knights came to Ireland and took over much of the country.

Vikings

The Vikings came from Norway, Denmark and Sweden. They raided northern Europe and even traveled to North America and Italy.

A carved head from a Viking ship

The Vikings were also merchants, trading with Arabs and people from Asia. They sold furs, ivory and slaves and bought silk, spices and gold.

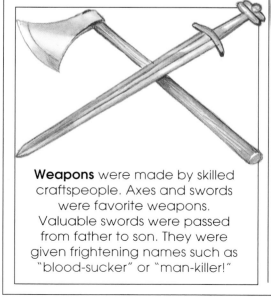

Weapons were made by skilled craftspeople. Axes and swords were favorite weapons. Valuable swords were passed from father to son. They were given frightening names such as "blood-sucker" or "man-killer!"

Raids were carried out by warriors in longships. As many as 100 longships would take part in a single raid. The Vikings would land, capture as much money, food, cattle and valuables as possible and sail away again.

Longships were narrow boats which could be up to 100 feet in length. They were not very heavy and were very quick through the water as they had oars as well as a large sail. Some longships had dragon heads carved on to them to make them look fiercer.

Sweyn Forkbeard was the greatest Viking of his time. He built a large empire based around the North Sea. He was King of Denmark and Norway, and in 1013 he became King of England.

The Vikings started to settle in the places that they had raided in the past. There were **settlements** in northern England, northern France and southern Ireland. Remains of these settlements can still be seen in York, in England, and Dublin, in Ireland.

Eric Bloodaxe became King of Northumberland, in England, in 948. He had been forced to flee from Norway after murdering two of his brothers to become sole King of Norway. Eric was driven out of England in 948, and again in 954. He was killed later that year on returning to England.

Viking warriors believed that when they died they would go to **Valhalla**, the banquet hall of the gods. Viking chiefs and famous warriors would often be buried with their boats and their favorite possessions when they died. Sometimes the body would be placed on the deck of the boat and burned.

Genghis Khan

Genghis Khan united all the Mongol tribes of central Asia and created the largest land empire the world has ever seen.

His empire relied upon ferocious mounted warriors and a reign of terror, which left cities burnt to the ground and millions of people dead.

Each warrior had two bows, 100 arrows, a lance and a sword. Arrows came in several designs. Some were specially shaped to travel long distances, others to pierce metal armor. One type of arrow was fitted with a whistle to frighten enemy troops.

Genghis Khan's real name was **Temujin**. He was born in 1167, the son of a minor tribal chief. His father was poisoned by a neighboring tribe, but Temujin became leader himself. He acted very bravely in battle and at a meeting of the Mongol tribes in 1206 he was given the title "Genghis Khan," which means "Great Ruler."

Genghis Khan was also the ruler of the **Merkit, Tartar, Kirghiz** and **Naiman** tribes.

The Mongols were a very ruthless tribe. When they captured a city they would put women, young children and the craftsmen who made weapons to one side. Then they would kill everybody else. When the city of **Merv** was captured, about 700,000 people were killed.

The invasion of **China** began in 1211 when the Mongols broke through the Great Wall. In 1215, Peking was captured and northern China was conquered.

The Mongols fought on horseback. Their horses were small and strong. They were bred to withstand the cold and heat and were trained to keep calm in battle.

The **Mongol Empire** was the largest land empire ever known. By 1279 it stretched from Hungary to Korea and included most of Asia.

Russia

Arabia

India

Arabian Sea

China

Pacific Ocean

The Mongol Empire

Crusaders

The Crusades were wars between Christians and Muslims. There were seven Crusades between the years 1095 and 1300.

The name "Crusader" comes from the Latin word for cross. The Christian warriors were called Crusaders because they wore a cross as their badge.

Richard the Lionheart was a King of England who led the Third Crusade in 1190. At the battle of Arsouf, in 1191, Richard defeated a large Muslim army and in the following year, he defeated another Muslim army at Jaffa. He led the Christian attack himself and acted with great bravery. Richard forced the Muslims to agree to a truce that allowed Christians to visit Jerusalem.

Assassins were sent into Crusader camps by the Muslims to murder important leaders.

Warrior monks fought in the Crusades. These were special monks who made promises to God to fight against the Muslims. The Templar Order was the most famous group of warrior monks. The order was founded in 1118 to protect pilgrims going to Jerusalem. Other orders included the Hospitallers, the Trufac and the Teutonic.

Saladin was the great Muslim leader of the 1100s. In 1175 he became Sultan (ruler) of Damascus and went on to unite the Muslims. He defeated the Crusaders in many important battles and stopped them from taking over Jerusalem.

El Cid was the nickname given to Rodrigo di Vivar. He was a great Spanish warrior who fought against the Muslims. El Cid means "The Champion." In 1094 he defeated the Muslims and captured the city of Valencia. He ruled it until his death in battle in 1099.

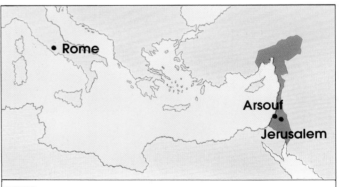

The Kingdom of Outremer

The Crusaders set up their own kingdom in Palestine called **Outremer**. The name means "Beyond the Sea," because Palestine is across the Mediterranean Ocean from Rome, the Christians' headquarters.

193

Aztecs and Incas

The Aztecs were a warlike people who lived in Mexico. By 1450, they had formed a large empire stretching from the Pacific Ocean to the Caribbean.

Aztec Empire

Inca Empire

The Incas came from Peru. Their empire covered an area four times as large as France. The Incas believed it was their holy duty to conquer other tribes and make them worship the Sun God.

The Aztecs and Incas used weapons made from wood with sharp polished pieces of a rock called **obsidian** set in them to make a cutting edge.

In 1423 Pachacuti, the Inca ruler, ordered work to start on the fortress of **Sacasahuaman**. The fortress had three massive towers and three walls made of stone. The walls were in a zigzag shape. The stones were specially shaped to fit into each other like pieces in a jigsaw.

Every Aztec man joined the **army** at the age of 17. If he had not performed a brave act by the age of 23, he had to leave the army to become a farmer or merchant. Very brave warriors were allowed to wear special animal skins.

Spanish troops, known as **Conquistadors** (meaning conquerors), attacked the Aztecs in 1519, and the Incas in 1532. The Conquistadors rode horses into battle and were armed with steel swords and guns. These modern weapons were too powerful for the Aztecs and Incas, and both their empires were conquered.

Prisoners captured by the Aztecs were taken to the temples in Tenochtitlán, the capital city. Priests killed the prisoners as a sacrifice to the gods. At least one person was killed each day. On special holy days, over a thousand people might be sacrificed at a time. Sometimes, wars were fought simply to capture prisoners.

Sitting Bull

Sitting Bull was the greatest leader of the Sioux people. He united the Sioux tribes.

With the help of the Blackfeet, Cheyenne and Arapahoe tribes, he led a war against the American settlers.

Warriors like the Sioux fought on horseback. They were armed with spears, bows and arrows, or guns bought from the white settlers.

The **first Indian War** began in 1608 when English settlers fought the Powhatan tribe in Virginia. The war ended in 1613 when the Indian princess Pocahontas married an Englishman.

Red Cloud was chief of one of the Sioux tribes. He fought against the American army to stop them from building forts and a road across land belonging to the Sioux and Cheyenne tribes. The war lasted for two years, from 1865 until 1867, when the government was forced to leave the tribes' land. Red Cloud made peace with the settlers, but continued to defend the rights of his people with many visits to the government in Washington.

When **gold** was found on Sioux land, the American government ordered Sitting Bull to move his people to a new reservation 235 mi. away. Sitting Bull refused to move and war broke out between the government and the Sioux.

In 1876, General Custer was sent with the 7th Cavalry to attack the Indian camp at **Little Big Horn**. Custer sent part of his troops to attack the Indian rear, and charged forward with the remaining troops. He rode straight into a trap set by Sitting Bull and another chief, called Crazy Horse. Custer and all his men were killed.

Geronimo was the leader of the Apache, who lived in the deserts of the U.S.-Mexico border. In 1859, the Apache were attacked by Mexicans. After this the Apache fought a war against all whites. For many years Geronimo led his warriors in a brutal conflict until he surrendered in 1886.

Warriors of the Orient

The Orient is the name given to the lands to the east of the Mediterranean Sea, especially those in eastern Asia, such as China or Japan.

Many ruthless warriors have fought each other across this vast area of land.

Samurai warriors came from Japan. They were highly trained fighters who were loyal to their local lord. All Samurai followed a strict set of rules, known as Bushido. These rules encouraged the Samurai to be brave, honest and live a simple life. If a Samurai broke the rules of Bushido or lost a batle, he had to kill himself. This was known as seppuku.

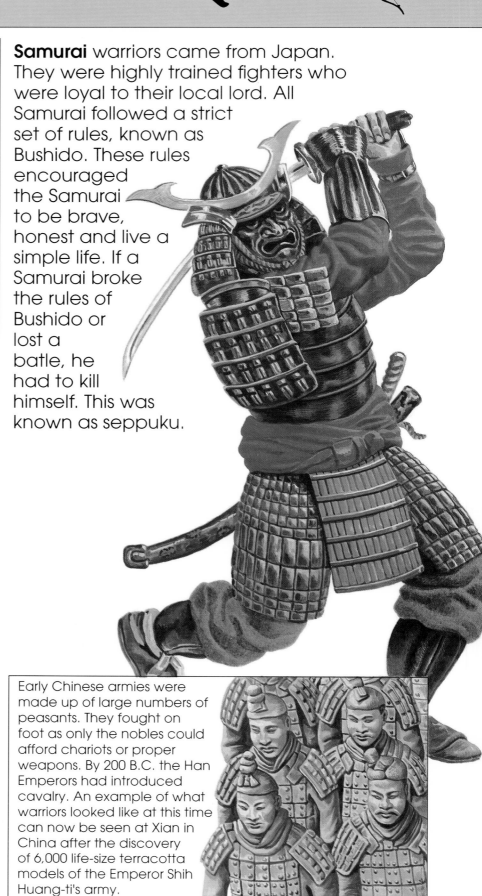

The **Great Wall of China** was built by the Emperor Shih Huang-ti around 220 B.C. It was designed to protect China from invasions from the north. It is over 3,728 mi. long and wide enough to drive a chariot along the top. Today it is a major tourist attraction.

Early Chinese armies were made up of large numbers of peasants. They fought on foot as only the nobles could afford chariots or proper weapons. By 200 B.C. the Han Emperors had introduced cavalry. An example of what warriors looked like at this time can now be seen at Xian in China after the discovery of 6,000 life-size terracotta models of the Emperor Shih Huang-ti's army.

Timur the Lame, or Tamerlane as he was known in Europe, was the ruthless leader of the Tartar warriors from southern Asia. He was born in 1336 in Samarkand, which is in modern-day Tajikistan. By 1399, he had conquered or made treaties with all of central Asia, and invaded Russia and India. Timur was a cruel person who slaughtered thousands of people. He would build great pyramids of skulls from the people he killed before taking their treasure back to Samarkand.

An Lu-Shan was a Turkish warrior who became ruler of China. As a young man, he was a cavalry commander in the Chinese army. He won many victories against the enemies of China and was soon commander of the entire northern army. In 756, thinking the Emperor had ordered his death, An Lu-Shan attacked China. He overthrew the Emperor and became ruler of China. He was murdered one year later by a servant.

Freedom fighters

Freedom fighters are warriors who try to free their country from the rule of a foreign nation.

Most freedom fighters work in small groups rather than with a large army. Sometimes they win and their country is freed. Other freedom fighters fail but they become heroes and inspire others to follow their ideas.

Joan of Arc led the French in a war against the English. In 1429 England ruled most of France. Joan, a young farmer's daughter, persuaded the Dauphin (the French heir to the throne) to let her fight with a small army. Joan amazed the troops with her bravery and leadership. She was captured and executed by the English in 1431. Thousands of French people were inspired by Joan and within a few years France was free.

Simon Bolívar fought to free South Americans from the Spanish Empire. In 1810 Venezuela threw out the Spanish governor. Bolivar took command of the rebel army and won many victories. In 1821 Spain accepted defeat. Bolívar then went on to lead rebels in Colombia, Peru, Ecuador and Bolivia.

Francois Toussaint L'Ouverture was a black slave who led the slaves of Haiti to freedom. In 1791 he led a slave revolt against the foreign rulers of the island and by 1797 he was ruler of Haiti. Toussant outlawed slavery and brought in many humane laws.

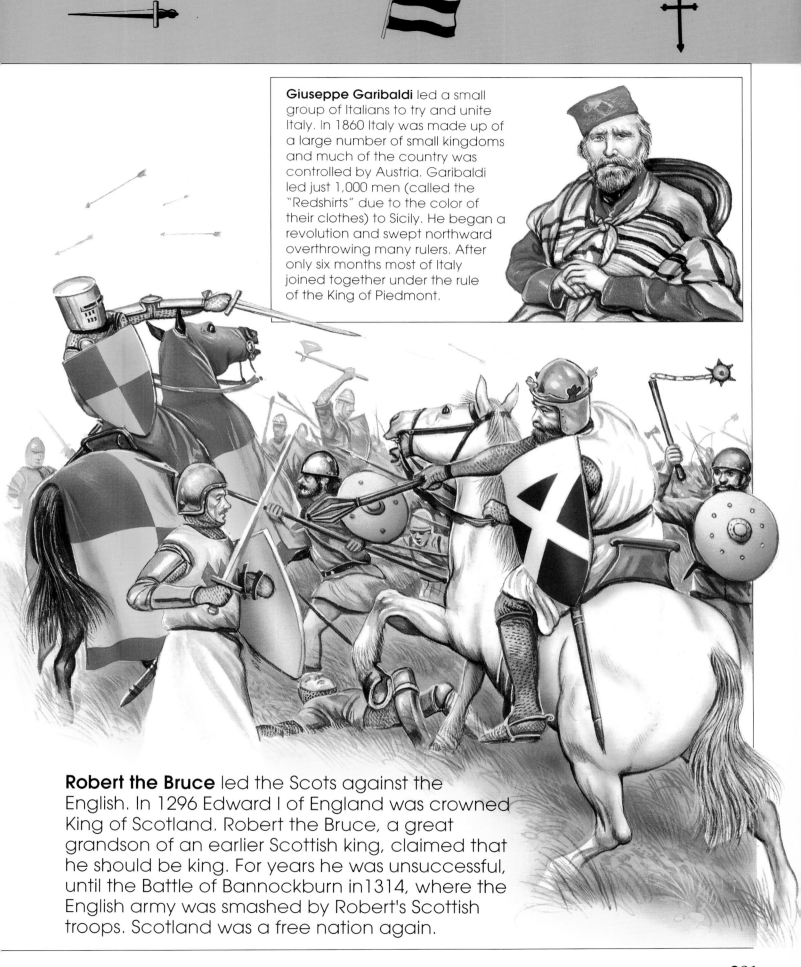

Giuseppe Garibaldi led a small group of Italians to try and unite Italy. In 1860 Italy was made up of a large number of small kingdoms and much of the country was controlled by Austria. Garibaldi led just 1,000 men (called the "Redshirts" due to the color of their clothes) to Sicily. He began a revolution and swept northward overthrowing many rulers. After only six months most of Italy joined together under the rule of the King of Piedmont.

Robert the Bruce led the Scots against the English. In 1296 Edward I of England was crowned King of Scotland. Robert the Bruce, a great grandson of an earlier Scottish king, claimed that he should be king. For years he was unsuccessful, until the Battle of Bannockburn in 1314, where the English army was smashed by Robert's Scottish troops. Scotland was a free nation again.

Mythical warriors appear in legends from many countries.

Although fantastic stories are told about these warriors, the legends are often based upon the lives of real people.

Gilgamesh was a legendary hero of Ancient Persia in about 2000 B.C. In the legend, Gilgamesh was a king who goes on a long journey to try to discover the meaning of life. It is thought that Gilgamesh was a famous warrior-king of Uruk in about 2500 B.C.

Horus was an Ancient Egyptian god. It is thought that the many stories told about his conflict with the god Seth refer to ancient tribal conflicts before the first pharaoh united Egypt in about 2800 B.C.

The Ancient Greeks and Persians told stories of female warriors called **Amazons**. The Amazons were a race of war-like women who raided other countries to capture gold and men. In fact, the Amazon legend was probably based on a real-life tribe called Sarmatians, who lived near the Black Sea between 800 B.C. and 300 B.C. Sarmatian women had equal rights with men and fought in battles. This seemed very strange to the Greeks and Persians of the time and led to the stories about the Amazons.

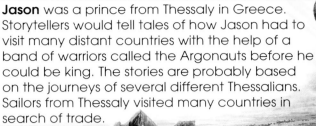

Jason was a prince from Thessaly in Greece. Storytellers would tell tales of how Jason had to visit many distant countries with the help of a band of warriors called the Argonauts before he could be king. The stories are probably based on the journeys of several different Thessalians. Sailors from Thessaly visited many countries in search of trade.

King Arthur is a legendary warrior of Britain. According to legend, Arthur was a great king who led a band of noble and gentle knights. The knights sat around a round table so that no one would appear to be more important than any of the others by sitting at the head of the table. In fact, Arthur was probably a Celtic warrior who fought against the Anglo-Saxons (who invaded Britain after the Romans left). He is thought to have been killed at the Battle of Camlann in about 515.

Sigurd was a great hero warrior of the Vikings. He was the last of the Volsung tribe and had many adventures, like fighting a dragon and finding treasure. Nobody has been able to discover who the character of Sigurd was based upon.

Sources of power

Before engines were invented nature was the only source of power available. Animals pulled carts, and the wind and running water moved windmills and water wheels. Water, wind and animal power are still important today.

However, engines are an important source of power. Cars, trucks, trains, aircraft and ships all have their own special engines to power them along.

The first **steam machine** was made before A.D. 100 by a Greek engineer, called Hero. It spun around as steam shot out of the pipes.

Over 2,000 years ago the Ancient Greeks were using **water wheels** for grinding flour. Water was the main source of power for industry until steam engines were invented.

The weight of water falling into the buckets turned the wheel.

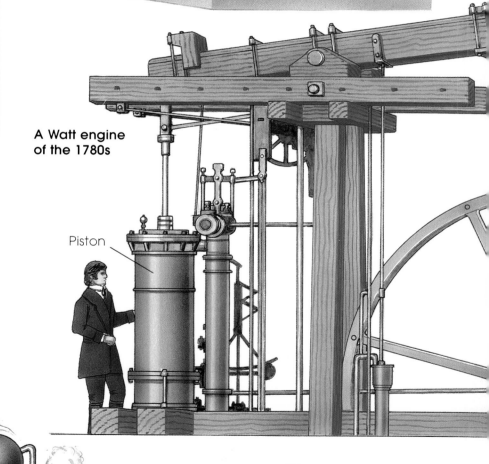

A Watt engine of the 1780s

Piston

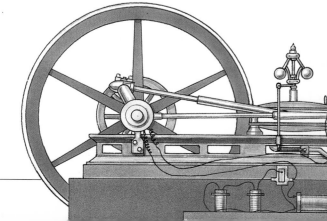

A **turbine** spins very fast when water flows through it. The turbine was invented in 1827. It soon replaced the water wheel.

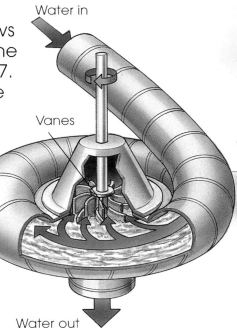

Water in

Vanes

Water out

Water pours into the turbine through a narrow pipe. It pushes the vanes round.

Windmills were first used around 650. They turned huge millstones which ground grain to make flour. They also pumped water and worked machinery.

In 1776 James Watt built a **steam engine** for pumping water out of coal and tin mines. Steam from boiling water moved a piston in and out. The moving piston worked the water pump.

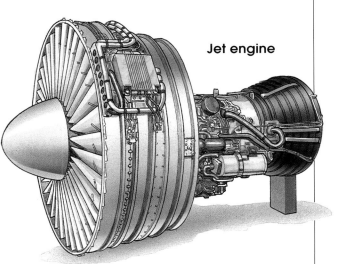

Jet engine

The sort of engine used in most modern cars is called an **internal combustion engine**. The first of these engines was built in 1860.

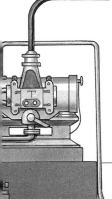

An internal combustion engine has cylinders and pistons like a steam engine. The first one used gas for fuel.

In 1939 the first aircraft with a **jet engine** took off. It was called the Heinkel He 178. Jet engines meant that aircraft could fly much faster than before.

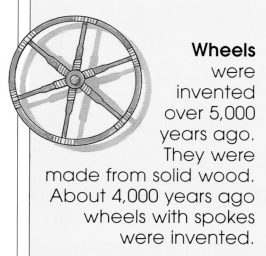

The wheel was one of the most important inventions in history. Think how difficult it would be to get around without it. Cars, bicycles, trains and carts use wheels.

For thousands of years carriages and carts were pulled by horses. But as soon as engines were invented people began making powered vehicles.

Wheels were invented over 5,000 years ago. They were made from solid wood. About 4,000 years ago wheels with spokes were invented.

Trevithick's locomotive

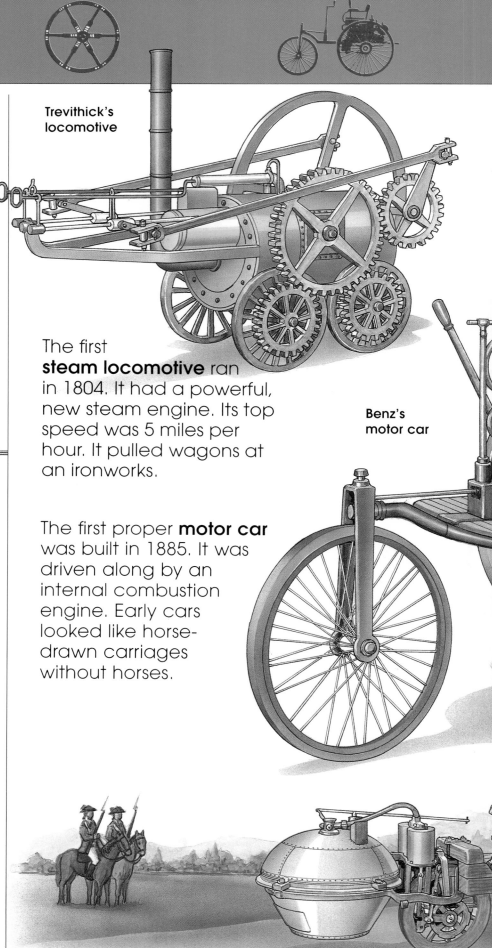

The first **steam locomotive** ran in 1804. It had a powerful, new steam engine. Its top speed was 5 miles per hour. It pulled wagons at an ironworks.

The first proper **motor car** was built in 1885. It was driven along by an internal combustion engine. Early cars looked like horse-drawn carriages without horses.

Benz's motor car

The first **electric locomotive** was demonstrated in 1879 in Berlin.

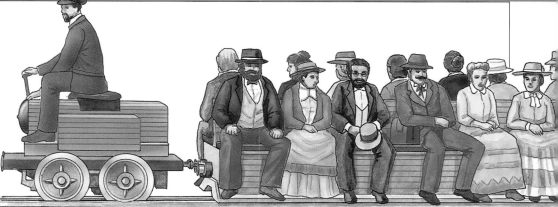

The pedal **bicycle** was invented in 1839 by a Scottish blacksmith, called Kirkpatrick Macmillan. He only built one machine, which he rode himself.

To make the bicycle go, the rider pushed the pedals backward and forward.

The first **motorcycle** was simply a bicycle fitted with a steam engine. It was built in 1868. The engine was under the saddle.

Steam engines powered tractors, trucks and buses. The first **steam vehicle** was designed to pull military cannons.

Cugnot built his steam tractor in 1769 or 1770. It was slow and quickly ran out of steam.

Sea and sailing

Ships and boats are very old inventions. Archaeologists think that people first made journeys in small boats 50,000 years ago. The boats were very simple canoes carved from tree trunks.

Ships and boats are not only used for transporting people, but for trade, too. Today, most of the goods traded between different countries are sent by ship.

A triangular sail, called a **lateen sail,** was invented around 300 B.C. Boats with lateen sails could sail where their crews wanted them to.

A type of boat called a dhow has a lateen sail.

In the 1400s **full rigging** was developed. Full-rigged ships had two or three masts with square and triangular sails.

In the 1400s and 1500s European explorers, such as Christopher Columbus, sailed small full-rigged ships across the oceans.

Archaeologists don't really know when **sailboats** were invented. However, the Ancient Egyptians sailed boats made of reeds along the Nile River over 5,000 years ago.

These reed boats had square sails.

Soon after small portable steam engines were invented engineers built **steam-powered boats**. The *Charlotte Dundas* was built in 1801.

The engine turned large paddle wheels which pushed the boat through the water.

For thousands of years sailors steered using large oars attached to the side of their ship. The **rudder** was invented in China around 700.

Most modern ships are pushed along by a **propeller**. It was patented in 1836 and soon replaced paddle wheels.

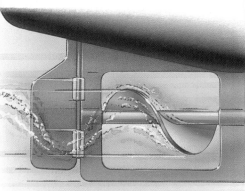

A hydrofoil has wings which lift it out of the water. This means it can go much faster than ordinary boats.

Forlanini hydrofoil

The idea for the **hydrofoil** was thought of in 1881. However, the first hydrofoil was not tested until 1905.

A **Hovercraft** is half boat, half airplane. It skims across sea or land on a cushion of air. The first practical Hovercraft was launched in 1959.

Flying machines

People dreamed of flying like birds for thousands of years before flying machines were made. Many people tried to copy the way birds flew. They tied wings to their arms, but with little success.

Today, there are many different types of aircraft. Every day, millions of people travel around the world in airliners and private aircraft. War planes include small fighters, bombers and huge transport planes.

The first aircraft with wings were **gliders**. Otto Lilienthal made many short glider flights in the 1890s.

The first machine to carry a person into the air was a **hot-air balloon**. It was built by the French Montgolfier brothers in 1783.

The balloon flew 5 miles on its first flight.

The first successful **airship** was built in 1852. In the early twentieth century, airships were popular for transport.

Airships were pushed along by propellers and steered by a rudder.

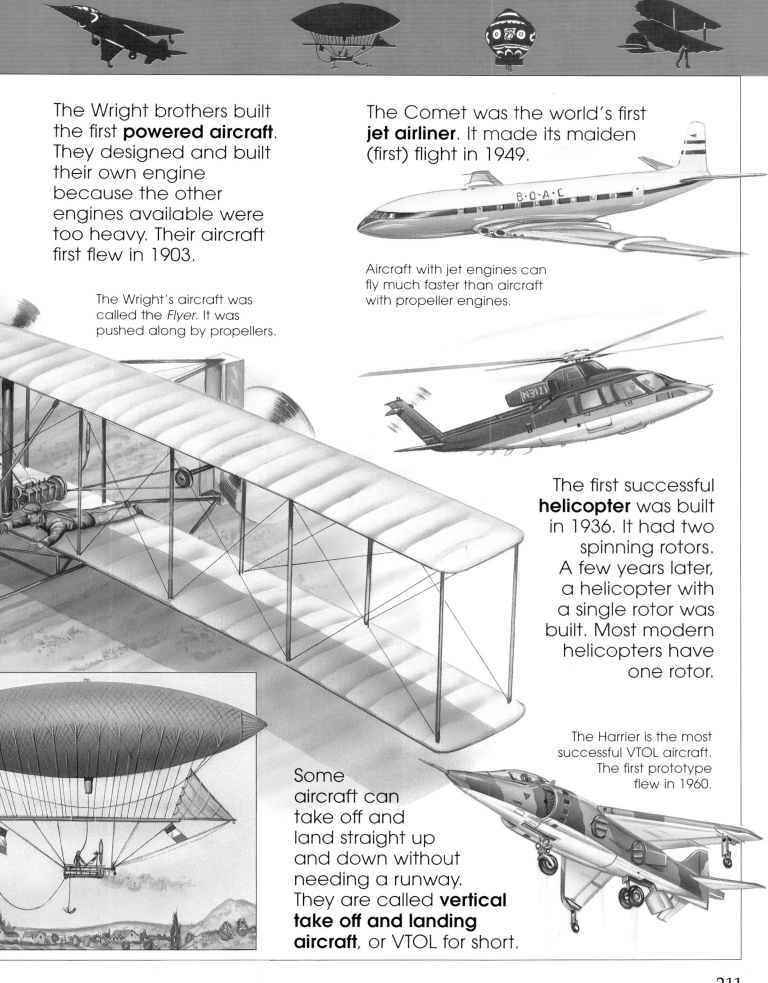

The Wright brothers built the first **powered aircraft**. They designed and built their own engine because the other engines available were too heavy. Their aircraft first flew in 1903.

The Wright's aircraft was called the *Flyer*. It was pushed along by propellers.

The Comet was the world's first **jet airliner**. It made its maiden (first) flight in 1949.

Aircraft with jet engines can fly much faster than aircraft with propeller engines.

The first successful **helicopter** was built in 1936. It had two spinning rotors. A few years later, a helicopter with a single rotor was built. Most modern helicopters have one rotor.

The Harrier is the most successful VTOL aircraft. The first prototype flew in 1960.

Some aircraft can take off and land straight up and down without needing a runway. They are called **vertical take off and landing aircraft,** or VTOL for short.

Five hundred years ago people could see only what was visible with their own eyes. Nobody knew how their bodies worked or what was out in space.

When the microscope and the telescope were invented, scientists and astronomers began to discover microscopic cells and millions of new stars.

In 1931, the first **electron microscope** was built. The picture of the object being studied appears on a screen.

An ordinary microscope can only make things look about 2,000 times bigger. An electron microscope can make things look millions of times bigger.

The first **microscope** was probably made in about 1590. In the 1650s, Robert Hooke used his microscopes to study plants. He drew sketches of what he saw.

Hooke's microscope was made from three lenses inside a cardboard tube.

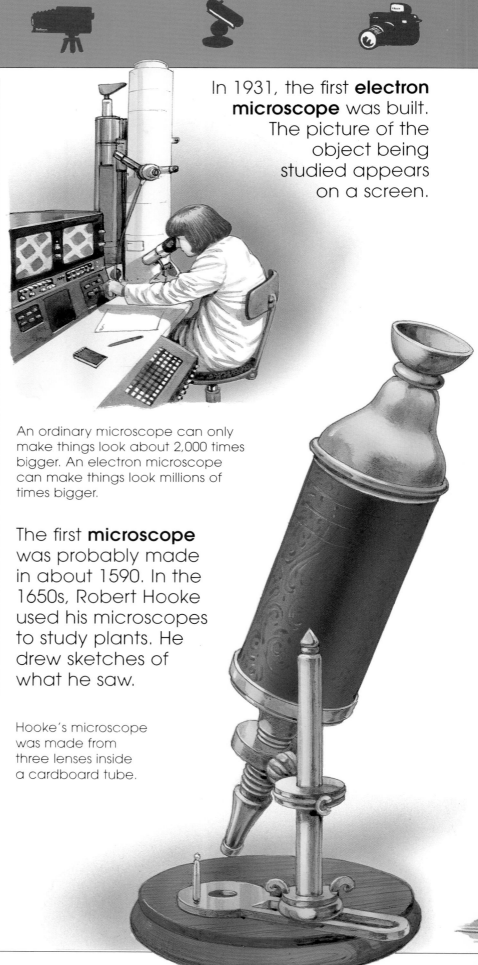

The first **telescope** was probably made in 1608. The next year Galileo Galilei built his own telescope and used it to study the stars.

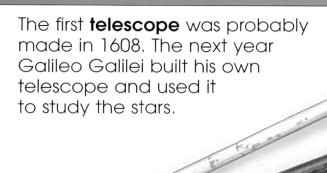

Using his telescopes, Galileo discovered that the Moon's surface is covered in craters.

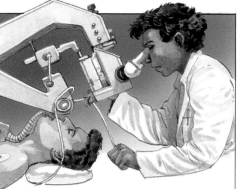

An **endoscope** is a long tube for seeing inside the human body. The first flexible one was built in 1956.

A **reflecting telescope** uses mirrors instead of lenses. It was first made in 1668. Most telescopes used by astronomers are reflecting telescopes.

Isaac Newton's reflecting telescope

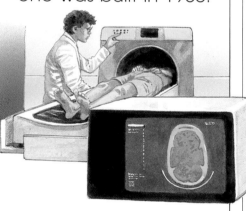

The first **medical scanner** was built in 1971 for looking inside the brain. Scanners for looking at the whole body soon followed.

Radio telescopes collect radio waves coming from outer space.

Radio waves from space were first detected in 1931.

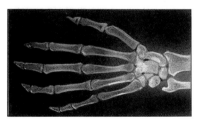

X-rays were discovered in 1895 by Wilhelm Röntgen. They were soon being used to take pictures of human bones.

Weaving a fabric

The first clothes worn by human beings were made from animal skins and fur. Later, people learned to make cloth from other natural materials, such as plants, and still later, from artificial fibers.

Most types of cloth are made on a loom. The loom weaves threads together. Modern looms work automatically. Some weaving is still done on traditional hand looms.

Some materials, such as cotton and wool, have to be spun before they are woven. Spinning makes short fibers into long thread.

People started to spin wool and cotton fibers into thread many thousands of years ago. The first **spinning machine** was like a long spinning top.

The **spinning wheel** was probably invented in India. People started using it in Europe around the year 1300.

A spinning wheel spins and collects thread at the same time.

Around 1767 James Hargreaves invented a machine that he called the **spinning jenny**. It spun thread automatically and made spinning much quicker.

The **loom** appeared around 5000 B.C. The first looms were very simple.

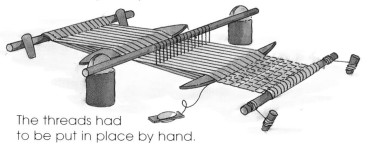

The threads had to be put in place by hand.

Weaving by hand was very slow. The **flying shuttle** was invented in 1733. It carried the thread from side to side automatically. Before this, it was passed through by hand.

The **Jacquard loom** was invented in 1801. It could weave complicated patterns into the cloth.

The loom was controlled by rows of holes in a long strip of card. Early computers used the same idea.

Rayon fibers, as seen under a powerful microscope.

The first **artificial fiber** was patented in 1892. It was an artificial silk, called rayon.

Thousands of years ago, people did not need to tell the time. They got up when the Sun rose and went to bed when it set. Gradually, as life became more complicated, clocks began to play a larger part in people's lives.

The first clocks were used for waking priests and monks in time for their nightly prayers. Today, clocks seem to rule our lives.

The first clocks were **shadow clocks**. The shadow moved as the Sun moved across the sky. They were invented around 3,500 years ago.

Mechanical clocks were probably developed in Europe during the 1200s. They did not have a face or hands, but rang bells.

The speed of the clock was controlled by a mechanism called an escapement, but it was not very accurate.

In a **water clock**, water drips out of a container so that the level of water inside gradually falls. The Ancient Egyptians were using water clocks about 1500 B.C.

The **pendulum clock** was invented in 1657. It was much more accurate than the clocks before it.

Each swing of the pendulum takes the same amount of time. This keeps the clock running at the same speed all the time.

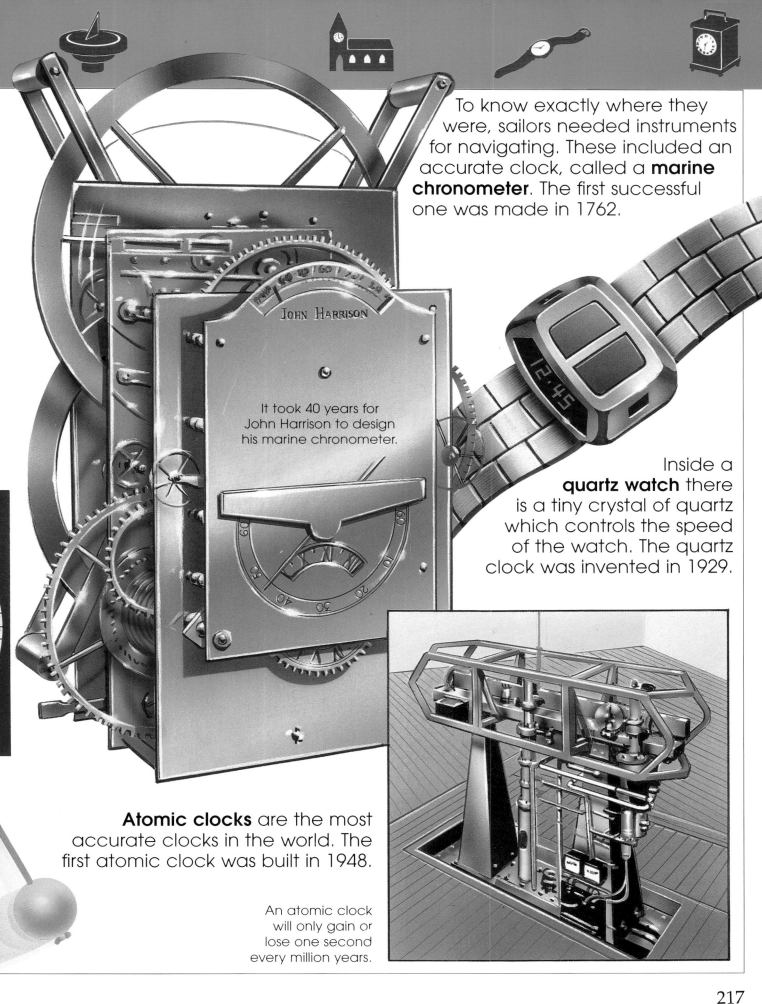

To know exactly where they were, sailors needed instruments for navigating. These included an accurate clock, called a **marine chronometer**. The first successful one was made in 1762.

JOHN HARRISON

It took 40 years for John Harrison to design his marine chronometer.

Inside a **quartz watch** there is a tiny crystal of quartz which controls the speed of the watch. The quartz clock was invented in 1929.

Atomic clocks are the most accurate clocks in the world. The first atomic clock was built in 1948.

An atomic clock will only gain or lose one second every million years.

For thousands of years, people did not write anything down. Instead, they passed on information and stories by word of mouth. Shapes and pictures were the first sort of writing.

The books that we know today were not made until printing was invented. Until then, every book was copied by hand by people called scribes. Long books took months to copy.

The Ancient Egyptians used **picture writing**. Each small picture stood for a word or sound. These pictures, or symbols, are called hieroglyphics.

The first simple **pens** were brushes, or hollow reeds, dipped in ink. The Ancient Greeks used a metal, or bone, stylus to write on soft wax tablets. Later, people used quill pens made from goose feathers.

The end of a goose feather was sharpened and then cut to make a nib shape. To write with a quill, you have to keep dipping the nib in ink.

The first **ballpoint pens** were made in 1938 by Lazlo Biro. When a cheap ballpoint pen runs out, you throw it away. For other pens, you can buy an ink refill with a new ball.

Inside the tip of a ballpoint pen is a tiny steel ball. It rolls around as you write, spreading ink on to the paper.

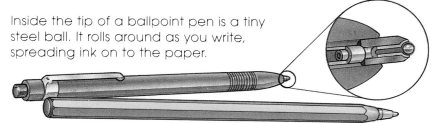

The first **printed book** that still exists was made in China in 868. It is a long roll of paper, and is called the *Diamond Sutra*.

The *Diamond Sutra* was printed by pressing carved, wooden blocks covered with ink on to the paper.

Around 1450, Johannes Gutenberg built the first **printing press**. It could print about sixteen pages of a book every hour.

In 1939, **phototypesetting** was invented. It has now replaced metal type. The words are now typed onto a computer and printed out on photographic paper.

Gutenburg made up words by putting metal letters, called type, together.

Newspapers were first printed in Europe at the beginning of the 1600s. Before then, newspapers were only printed when there was a lot of news.

Listening to recorded music is something most people do every day. However, when sound recording was first invented it was a novelty, and nobody took it seriously.

Every so often, a new way of recording sound is invented. Recordings of speech and sounds are also important historical records.

The first machine to record sound and play it back was the **phonograph**. It was invented in 1877 by the American inventor Thomas Edison.

Speaking into the phonograph made a needle move up and down. As the drum went around, the needle made a groove in the tin foil.

A **tape recorder** records sound as a magnetic pattern on a long strand of tape. The first tape recorder used iron wire. Plastic tape coated with magnetic material appeared in 1935.

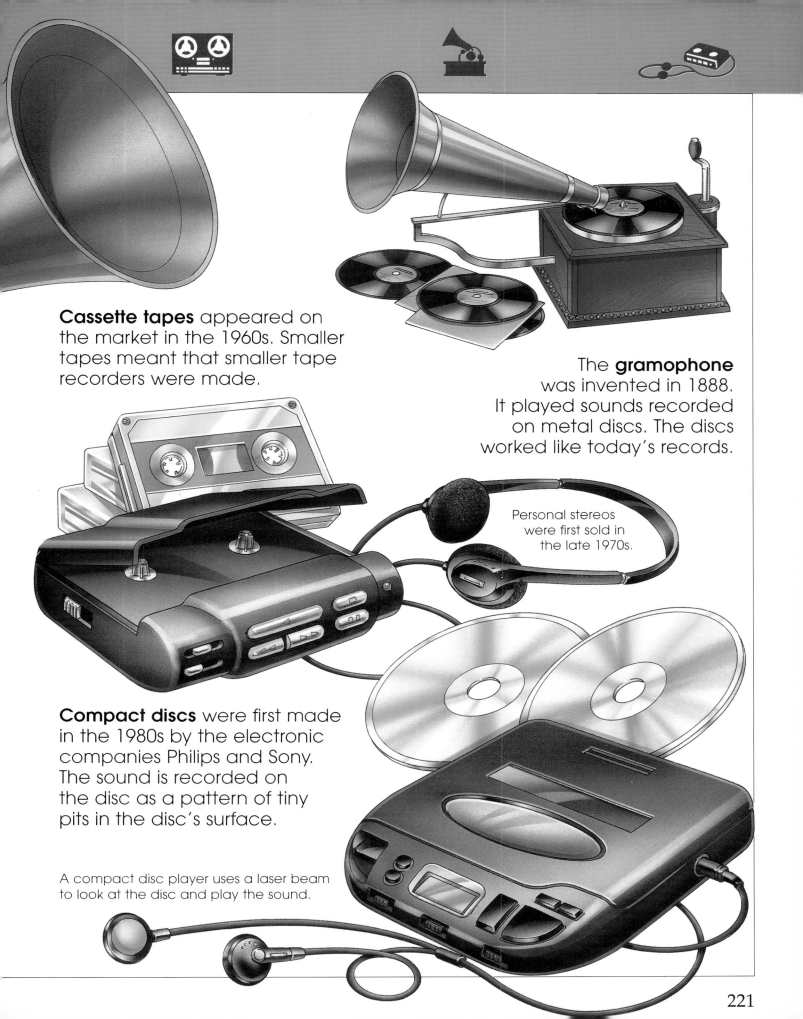

Cassette tapes appeared on the market in the 1960s. Smaller tapes meant that smaller tape recorders were made.

The **gramophone** was invented in 1888. It played sounds recorded on metal discs. The discs worked like today's records.

Personal stereos were first sold in the late 1970s.

Compact discs were first made in the 1980s by the electronic companies Philips and Sony. The sound is recorded on the disc as a pattern of tiny pits in the disc's surface.

A compact disc player uses a laser beam to look at the disc and play the sound.

221

Until about 200 years ago the only way to send a message was by messenger or by mail. Sometimes, hilltop bonfires were used to send emergency signals.

Today, you can talk on the telephone to friends and relations in almost any part of the world. It takes just a few seconds to dial. Your call might even travel via a satellite in space on the way.

Many telephone calls go along **optical fibers**. Your voice is turned into flashes of light which travel along the fibers.

The **semaphore** system was the first way of communicating over long distances. Semaphore stations were positioned on hilltops, and the message was passed from one station to the next. The system was first used in France in 1794.

The message was shown by moving the arms on top of the semaphore station to different positions.

Messages were tapped with the key as dots and dashes.

The first simple electric **telegraph** was built in 1804. In 1837, Samuel Morse invented **Morse Code**. It was used to send messages by telegraph.

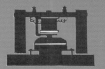

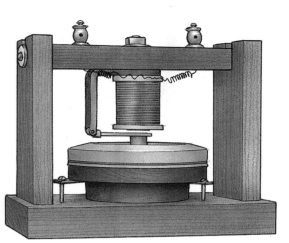

In 1876, Alexander Graham Bell patented the **telephone**. It converted sound into electrical signals. The signals were sent down a wire to another phone and turned back into sound.

Radio was first used in the 1890s. Sailors used it to send signals to the shore by Morse Code. The first radio program was broadcast in 1906.

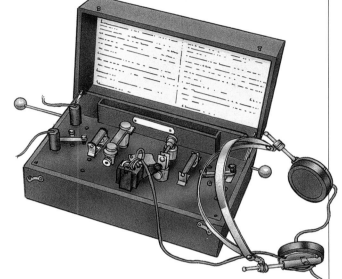

An automatic telephone exchange was in operation in 1897. **Electronic telephone exchanges** were built In the 1960s.

The first **telephone exchange** was built in 1878. Only a few people could use it, and it needed a person to operate it.

Facsimile machines (fax machines for short) send words and pictures along telephone lines. The idea for fax was first thought of in 1843, but it took until the 1980s for faxes to become common.

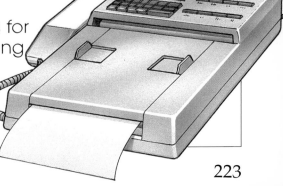

Until the 1820s there were no photographs or films. To make pictures of anything, people had to draw or paint them. Taking photographs is a much easier process.

When moving pictures first appeared nobody took them seriously. The machines that made the pictures move were thought of as toys.

Television is part of our everyday lives. We can watch soap operas, films, the news and sports. Thanks to satellites, we can even watch events happening live around the world.

The first **camera** of the type we use today was made by the Eastman company in 1888. It had film that you could send away for processing.

The **kinetoscope** was invented in 1891 by Thomas Edison. You had to look through the top and wind a handle. The film inside lasted only about 15 seconds.

Inside the kinetoscope was a long strip of film with hundreds of pictures on it. Each picture was slightly different from the one before to make an action sequence.

The first **cinema** opened in Paris in 1895. The film was projected on to a screen. The projector worked like the kinetoscope.

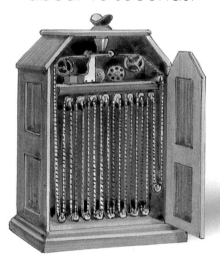

The first time **television** pictures were transmitted by electricity was in 1926. The pictures weren't very good - they were in black and white, wobbly and blurred.

The pattern of light and dark on the picture was made by a spinning disc with holes in it.

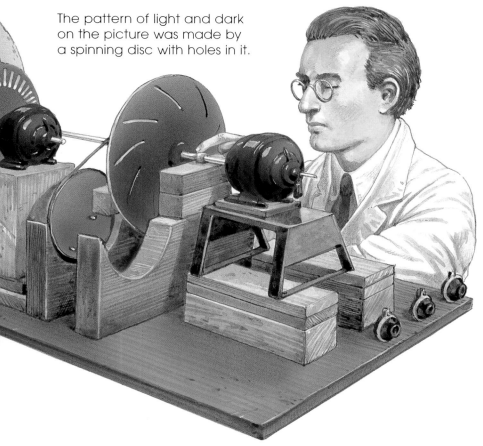

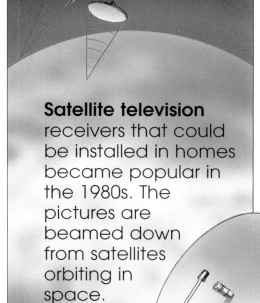

Satellite television receivers that could be installed in homes became popular in the 1980s. The pictures are beamed down from satellites orbiting in space.

In 1928, the first television program was broadcast In America. It was used to test a new **television transmitter**. The pictures were of Felix the Cat™

Color television pictures were first broadcast in 1953.

Video tape and **video recorders** were invented in 1956. Pictures are recorded on videotape just as sounds are recorded on audio tape.

Electronic circuits are often used to control and work machines. Computers, televisions and telephones all use electronics. So do some simpler machines, such as washing machines and alarm clocks.

Electronic circuits are made up of electronic components. There are many different sorts of components. One of the most important is the transistor. Its invention meant that electronic circuits could be made much smaller than before.

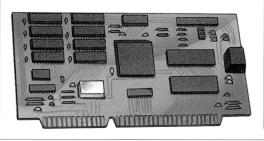

In the 1830s, years before electronics were possible, British scientist Charles Babbage designed a mechanical computer. He called it an **analytical engine**. It was never finished.

The first electronic device was called the **thermionic valve**. It was first made in 1904.

Thermionic valves were used in early radios and televisions.

The first general-purpose electronic **computer** was called ENIAC, which stands for Electronic Numerical Integrator and Calculator. It was built in 1946.

ENIAC used over 18,000 valves and filled a whole room.

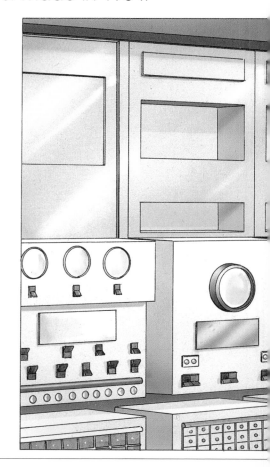

The **transistor** was invented in 1948 by a team of scientists in America. Transistors took over from valves, but were much smaller and cheaper.

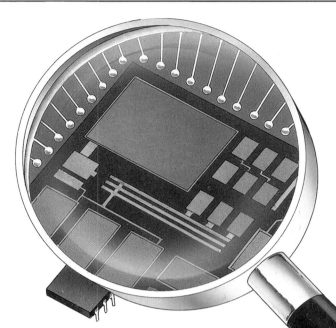

A **silicon chip**, or microchip, as small as a fingernail can contain many thousands of transistors and other electronic components. The first silicon chip was made in 1959.

A silicon chip in a plastic casing

Engineers began to fit more and more components on to a silicon chip. Eventually engineers at Intel built a complete computer on a single chip. This is called a **microprocessor**.

Every personal computer has a microprocessor "brain."

Until the eighteenth century people did all their household chores by hand. There were no washing machines or vacuum cleaners. No one had running water or a flushing toilet either.

The first domestic appliances were mechanical. It was still hard work to operate them. Things really changed when electric motors became cheap to make. Imagine what life today would be like without electricity!

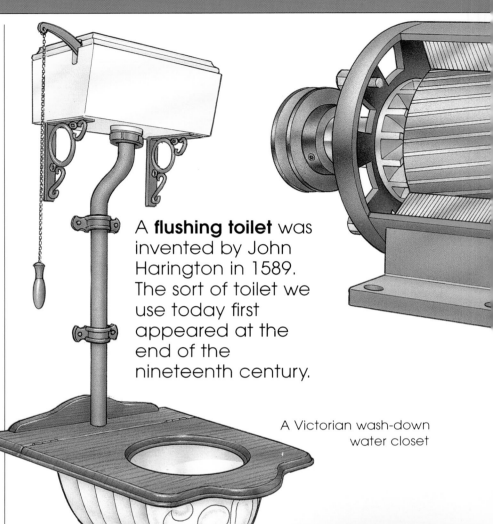

A **flushing toilet** was invented by John Harington in 1589. The sort of toilet we use today first appeared at the end of the nineteenth century.

A Victorian wash-down water closet

Englishman Joseph Swan made a long-lasting **light bulb** in 1878. The next year, Thomas Edison made a similar bulb.

In Edison's light bulb, the electricity flowed through a piece of carbonized bamboo, making it glow.

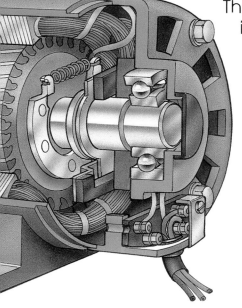

The first **electric motor** was made in 1835. Its power came from a battery because there was no mains electricity at the time.

Before refrigerators, food was kept fresh in a cool place or boxes lined with ice. The ice had to be replaced as it melted.

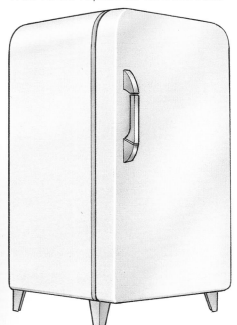

The **vacuum cleaner** was patented by Englishman Hubert Booth in 1901. Booth's first machine had to be hired, together with people to operate it.

Microwave ovens appeared in the 1950s. They were used by catering companies.

Refrigerating machines were developed at the end of the nineteenth century. It was not until the 1950s, however, that domestic refrigerators became popular.

Microwave ovens cook most foods many times faster than electric or gas ovens.

Weird and wonderful inventions

For every invention that has been a success, there are many more that have been failures. The great age of crazy inventions was the nineteenth century when inventing things became many people's favorite hobby.

Some inventions have no chance of success because their inventor has not understood the scientific principles behind them. Others are simply flights of fancy, designed for fun.

In the fifteenth century, the artist **Leonardo da Vinci** made drawings of many machines, including tanks and flying machines, long before they were actually invented.

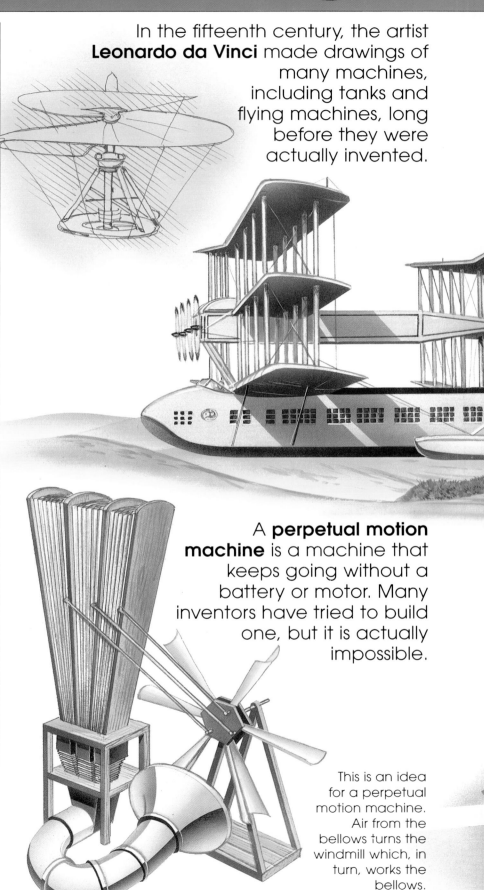

A **perpetual motion machine** is a machine that keeps going without a battery or motor. Many inventors have tried to build one, but it is actually impossible.

This is an idea for a perpetual motion machine. Air from the bellows turns the windmill which, in turn, works the bellows.

The Italian Count Caproni built several huge airplanes. The largest was the **Ca 60**, which had nine wings and eight engines.

The Ca 60 crashed just after take-off on its first flight in 1921.

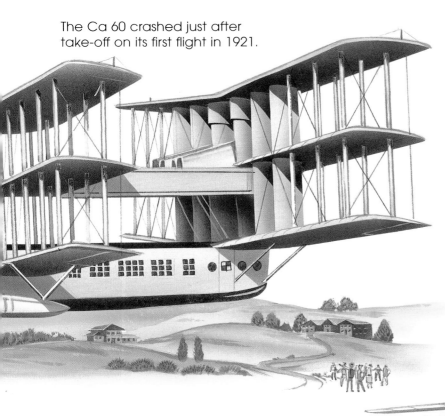

Rube Goldberg was a cartoonist who drew very complicated machines that were completely useless.

The airstrip was never built because it was too expensive.

The *Sinclair C5* was a tiny electric car. It was designed in the 1980s for cheap travel around town. However, most people thought it was too dangerous to drive.

Sir Clive Sinclair

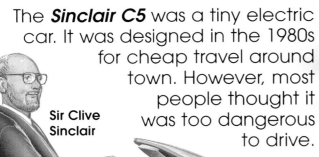

In 1942, English inventor Geoffrey Pyke designed an **iceberg airstrip** on which aircraft could refuel in the Atlantic Ocean.

The existence of ghosts has never been proved scientifically. However throughout history many people have reported sightings of ghosts.

Ghosts are believed to be the spirits of people who have died, but sometimes they seem to resemble living people. There are animal ghosts and even ghostly ships, cars, planes and trains.

It is said that there have been many appearances of **royal ghosts.** King Henry VIII's beheaded wife, Anne Boleyn, is said to haunt the Tower of London, England. Two of his other wives roam the corridors at Hampton Court Palace.

In 1962, English brothers, Derek and Norman Ferguson claimed to have seen lots of **ghostly animals** while driving their car along a highway in Scotland.

A **bizarre bat** with a human head is a ghostly legend of Northern American Indians.

Haunted computers have been reported in many parts of the world.

Glamis Castle, the birthplace of Princess Margaret, is believed to be the most haunted royal building in Scotland. This 14th-century castle is said to be the home of a monster, a vampire and a whole host of ghosts.

Some people believe that ghosts like to haunt houses as well as ancient castles. In 1966, a British family had to be rehoused by their local government because they thought their house had been haunted for two years.

FOR SALE

Ghosts around the world

There have been hundreds of ghostly sightings. Such stories have been reported from many countries around the globe.

Often these stories reflect the legends and traditions of the country in which the hauntings occur.

One of the best known English ghosts is that of **Dick Turpin** who was famous for robbing travelers. He was a hero of the poor people because he stole from the wealthy. Turpin was hanged in 1739. It is widely believed that his ghost still appears on Hounslow Heath – now known as **Heathrow Airport**!

Abraham Lincoln was one of the most influential presidents of the United States. He was assassinated in April, 1865. It is said that every year during the month of April, the President's funeral train appears. It can be seen traveling along a stretch of track in New York State.

Over 150 years ago, a **Danish** man was wrongfully hanged for stealing. It is claimed that a shadowy outline of a body, hanging from a gallows, still appears today, just before the death of a family member.

It is said that whenever the President's ghostly train appears, a complete military band can be heard blasting away.

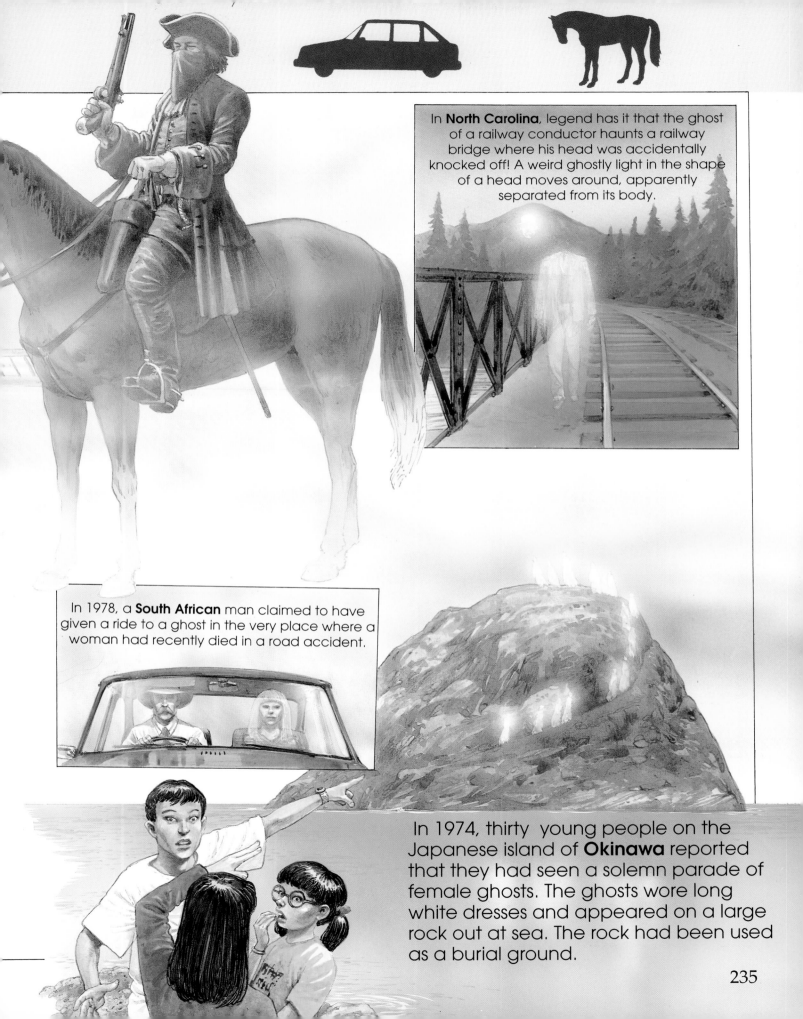

In **North Carolina**, legend has it that the ghost of a railway conductor haunts a railway bridge where his head was accidentally knocked off! A weird ghostly light in the shape of a head moves around, apparently separated from its body.

In 1978, a **South African** man claimed to have given a ride to a ghost in the very place where a woman had recently died in a road accident.

In 1974, thirty young people on the Japanese island of **Okinawa** reported that they had seen a solemn parade of female ghosts. The ghosts wore long white dresses and appeared on a large rock out at sea. The rock had been used as a burial ground.

Poltergeists

A poltergeist is described as an invisible and noisy ghost. It is said that when a poltergeist is present people hear scratching, banging and mysterious voices. Sometimes fires start and strange smells fill the air.

Often poltergeists throw things around, smash ornaments and move heavy furniture. They are said to be invisible vandals!

In 1661, a magistrate confiscated a drum from a local beggar in **Tedworth**, England. Legend has it that a phantom drum could be heard frequently and lit candles floated up the chimney. The magistrate's horse was even found with its hind leg stuck in its mouth!

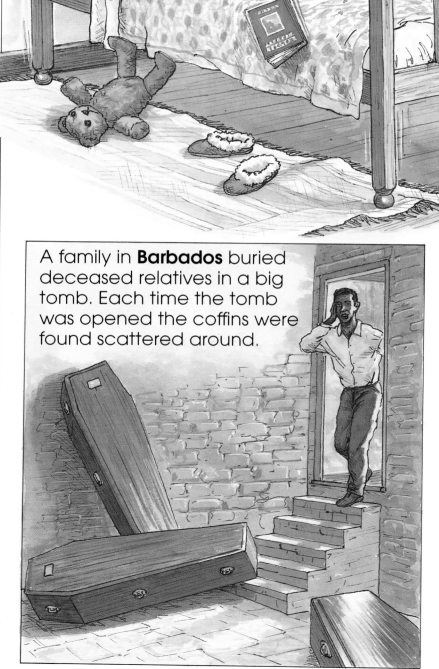

A family in **Barbados** buried deceased relatives in a big tomb. Each time the tomb was opened the coffins were found scattered around.

In 1960, an 11-year-old Scottish girl, **Virginia Campbell**, claimed she was being aggravated by a poltergeist for two months. It followed her wherever she went. One night her bed started shaking as if there was an earthquake. The haunting stopped once her parents held prayer meetings in their house.

Objects were said to fly around when a poltergeist made its home on a farm in **Lancashire**, England. A cow was even lifted to a hay loft. How it got there nobody knows – it certainly could not have climbed up the rickety ladder.

In 1951, a family reported strange happenings in their **London** home. A policeman found furniture being thrown across a room. Strangely, the violent activity stopped instantly once a light was turned on.

During 1967, a poltergeist started creating a disruption around 11-year-old **Matthew Manning** from Cambridge, England. Furniture began to move all over the family home and strange scratching noises could be heard. The haunting ended when Matthew began to create strange and beautiful drawings.

Funny ghosts

It is said that ghosts like playing tricks. But ghosts and people seem to have a very different sense of humor. Often people do not find what ghosts do very funny. Ghosts are more likely to terrify people than make them laugh.

Over 60 years ago, on the Isle of Man in the Irish Sea, a ghostly **mongoose** was said to haunt an old farmhouse by the sea. It told jokes, sang songs and even swore. It told everyone its name was Gef. When the farmhouse was sold the new owner shot an unusual little furry animal. Gef has never been seen since.

Over 25 years ago, a derelict hotel in Wales was being demolished. Even though the electricity to the building had been cut off, the **elevator** kept on working.

Twelve-year-old English boy, **Michael Collingridge**, was recovering from tonsillitis when a walking stick in his bedroom appeared to dance. It jumped all around the room and began to tap out well-known tunes!

When the Pritchard family from **Pontefract** in Wales was plagued by a ghost, a woman from a Christian charity tried to drive the ghost away by singing *Onward Christian Soldiers*. The ghost responded by picking up her gloves and conducting her as she sang!

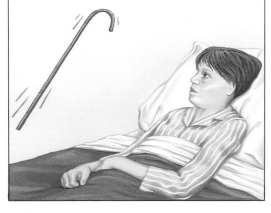

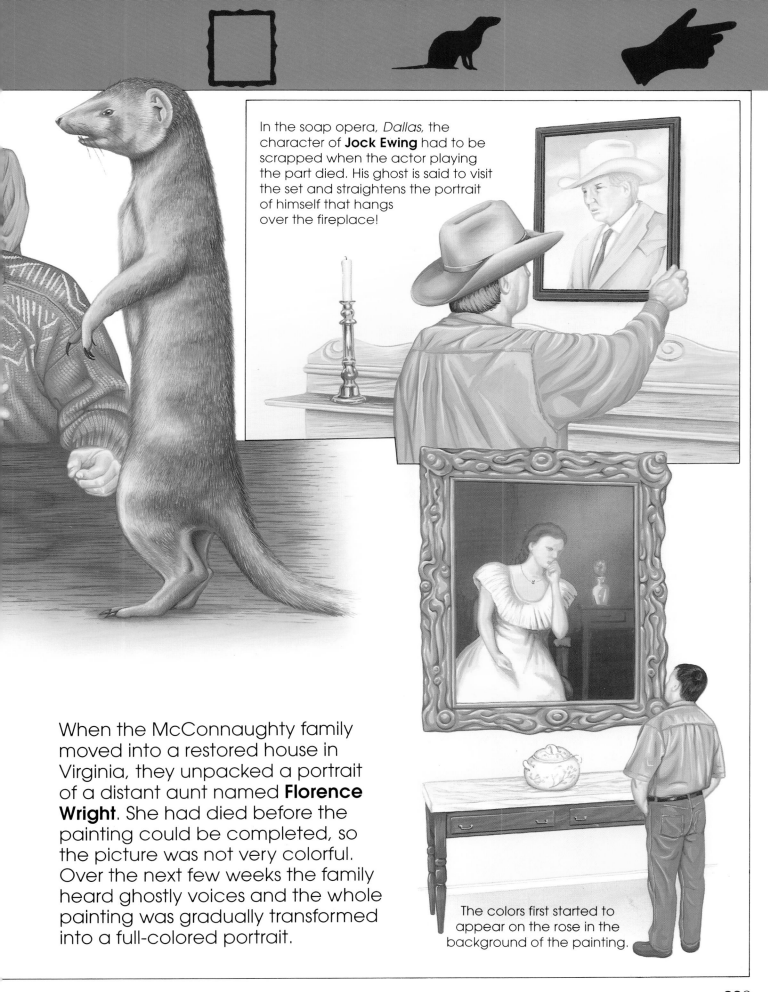

In the soap opera, *Dallas,* the character of **Jock Ewing** had to be scrapped when the actor playing the part died. His ghost is said to visit the set and straightens the portrait of himself that hangs over the fireplace!

When the McConnaughty family moved into a restored house in Virginia, they unpacked a portrait of a distant aunt named **Florence Wright**. She had died before the painting could be completed, so the picture was not very colorful. Over the next few weeks the family heard ghostly voices and the whole painting was gradually transformed into a full-colored portrait.

The colors first started to appear on the rose in the background of the painting.

239

Haunted houses

It is said that haunted houses creak and ghosts glide through the walls.

It is believed that ghosts haunt places where they once lived, but no one knows if hauntings really happen!

Legend has it that **Ballechin House** in Scotland is haunted by invisible dogs who hit guests with their tails. It is also said to be home to ghostly nuns and a disembodied hand!

Raynham Hall in Norfolk, England, is thought to be haunted by the ghost of Dorothy Walpole who died there. In 1936, a photograph of a ghostly woman in a veil was snapped by a professional photographer visiting the hall.

After studying the picture, some experts believe that it is genuine.

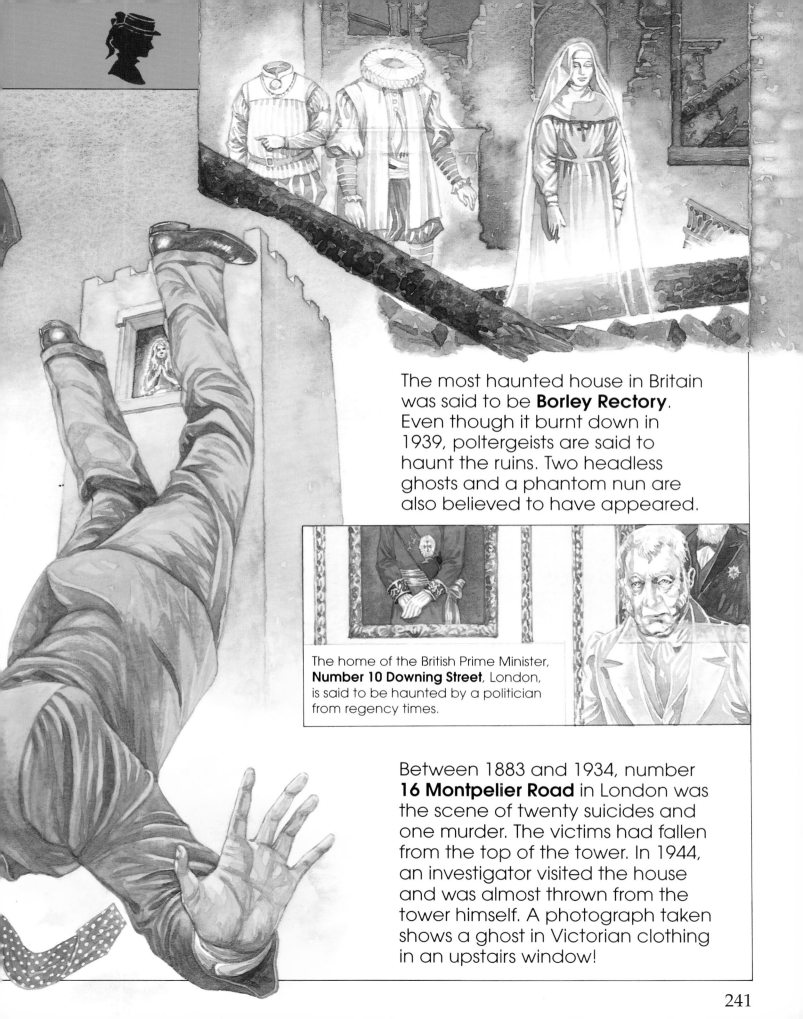

The most haunted house in Britain was said to be **Borley Rectory**. Even though it burnt down in 1939, poltergeists are said to haunt the ruins. Two headless ghosts and a phantom nun are also believed to have appeared.

The home of the British Prime Minister, **Number 10 Downing Street**, London, is said to be haunted by a politician from regency times.

Between 1883 and 1934, number **16 Montpelier Road** in London was the scene of twenty suicides and one murder. The victims had fallen from the top of the tower. In 1944, an investigator visited the house and was almost thrown from the tower himself. A photograph taken shows a ghost in Victorian clothing in an upstairs window!

Scaring away ghosts

People have invented all kinds of weird ways to ward off ghosts. Good luck charms and complicated rituals are used to scare ghosts away.

Inuits never remove someone who has died in an **igloo** through the front door. It is thought the spirit of the dead person would return if it knew where the front door was!

In China, the burning of **joss sticks** is thought to ward off unwanted spirits. Loud drums are beaten and noisy fireworks are set off at funerals to frighten away evil spirits.

Some people wear **amulets** and **talismans** (good luck charms) around their necks to scare off evil spirits and bring good fortune.

Some Asian communities will demolish the house someone has died in and then build a new home. It is believed that this gives the dead a resting place before finding **eternal peace**.

Many societies believe everyone has a **guardian spirit**. Mohammedans believe that we have four – two for the day and two for the night!

In many parts of the world it is still the custom to cover all the **mirrors** in a house until after a funeral. This protects against a spirit stealing the reflection of a living person and taking them off to the spirit world.

243

Mysteries in the sky

Thousands of people have reported strange sights in the sky, from frogs to unidentified flying objects (UFOs).

There have even been stories of close encounters with aliens. As a result, many people are convinced that there is life beyond planet Earth.

The first reported sighting of a **UFO** was during the 1200s, long before the invention of the airplane!

In 1975, a farmer in Switzerland sighted a **flying saucer**. Over the years he said he was visited by its three passengers called Somjasc, Ptaah and Asket. They told him that they were from the planet Erra, about 400 light years away.

In 1985, writer Whitley Strieber claimed that he had been abducted by **aliens** who gave him a thorough scientific examination. So disturbed was he by the experience that he sought the help of a hypnotist. Hypnosis revealed that he believed that aliens had been visiting him since childhood!

Numerous sightings of aliens have been reported in the **Broadhaven Triangle** in Wales. A luminous ball chased one car for miles. The occupants reached home to find a burnt-out television in their living room and a glowing figure in a silver suit in their garden.

In 1954, shoppers in Birmingham, England, were rained on by hundreds of tiny **frogs**! Many similar instances have been reported. Sometimes these are believed to be caused by supernatural forces.

In 1948, a **spacecraft** was reported to have crash-landed in New Mexico, United States. Eye-witnesses claimed that fourteen aliens were discovered on board the spacecraft. It has been said that the aliens were three feet tall and looked like humans with green, webbed feet.

Throughout history there have been reports of people vanishing without trace. Ships and airplanes seem to have disappeared into thin air! Some of these cases are still shrouded in mystery.

Sometimes stories have been made up to explain disappearances. When famous band leader, **Glenn Miller**, vanished in 1944, some people believed that his face had been so disfigured in a plane crash that he had decided to hide away for the rest of his life.

The crew's meal was found half-eaten on the table.

In 1872, the entire crew of the merchant ship, the **Marie Celeste**, vanished. The ship was completely undamaged but no one aboard was ever seen again.

Often disappearances are hoaxes. In 1880, the story of a farmer who had apparently vanished hit the headlines in **Tennessee**. It turned out that a hardware salesman, who had been snowed into his house, had invented the whole story out of boredom!

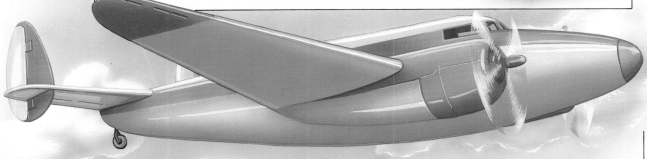

In 1937, **Amelia Earhart**, a record-breaking pilot, disappeared en route to an island in the Pacific Ocean. No one has ever been able to explain this mysterious disappearance.

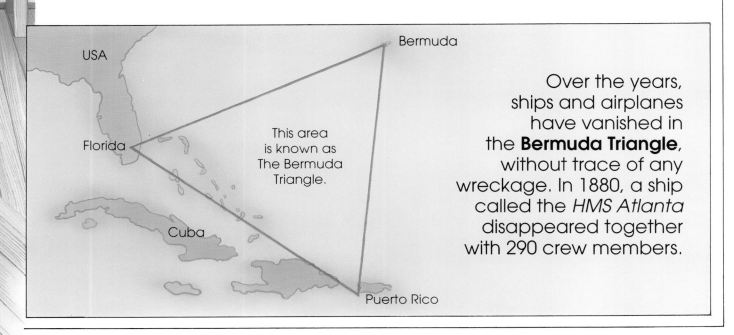

USA

Bermuda

Florida

This area is known as The Bermuda Triangle.

Cuba

Puerto Rico

Over the years, ships and airplanes have vanished in the **Bermuda Triangle**, without trace of any wreckage. In 1880, a ship called the *HMS Atlanta* disappeared together with 290 crew members.

Witchcraft

Witchcraft comes from two old English words, *wita* and *craeft* which means craft of the wise. Some witches are thought to have special knowledge of the plants and herbs used to cure sickness.

In the past witches were thought to use their powers in an evil way.

In the past, anybody accused of **witchcraft** could be brought to trial. They were sometimes tortured until they had no option but to "confess."

Witchcraft was outlawed in the United Kingdom until 1951, when the old law was overturned. Today, it is quite legal to be a witch and join a **coven** or group of witches.

During 1692, in **Salem**, Massachusetts, a group of children accused 200 residents of being witches. The "witches" were brought to trial and 20 were executed. It was later agreed it had all been a terrible mistake.

At the time of the **winter solstice**, in December, witches perform "The Dance of the Wheel," a special ceremony to coax back the sun. They dance and leap around a boiling cauldron to represent the spring.

Traditional doctors in Africa used to be referred to as **witch doctors.** These doctors are expert herbalists and they sometimes call upon spirit powers to help cure their patients.

During the 1300s, the **Christian Church** formed a group called the **Inquisition** to find people who disagreed with the church, including witches. They falsely believed that "witches" made pacts with the devil, flew on broomsticks and even ate babies!

249

Many people believe that fortunetellers can look into the future. Some of them look at cards or tea leaves. Others look to the stars to see what lies ahead.

Rune stones are a set of 25 small tablets or stones which are believed to have special meaning. A rune reader can recognize what the stones represent according to the way they are laid out.

Most fortune telling methods originated in China. **I Ching** is an ancient Chinese book of knowledge which is believed to have the answer to everything!

No two hands are the same. **Palmists** read people's hands to predict how long they will live and even how many children they will have.

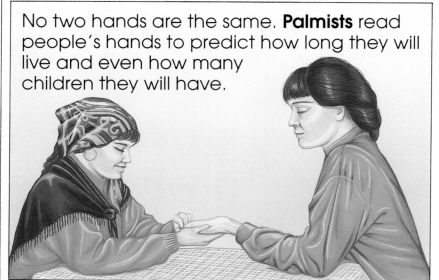

Astrology places people into twelve different groups which correspond with their birth dates. Maps of the stars and planets are consulted to forecast what the future holds.

Phrenology is the art of telling a fortune by feeling the bumps on a person's head.

Some people read their **horoscope** to predict what will happen during a day, week or month.

The Chinese invented **dominoes** as a method of predicting the future. The dominoes are put in a pouch, shaken and removed. Fortunes are read according to the position in which the dominoes are laid out.

Second sight

Some people claim to have second sight. They believe that they see or sense things which are invisible to other people. Sometimes they even say that they can tell when a terrible event is about to happen.

In 1889, **Morgan Roberts** wrote *The Wreck of the Titan*. It tells the story of a massive luxury liner, called the *Titan*, which hit an iceberg and sank. The ***Titanic*** did exactly that 14 years later and hundreds of the passengers were drowned.

In 1925, a famous palmist predicted that **Edward, Prince of Wales** would be forced to abdicate soon after he became King. Amazingly, 11 years later this premonition became fact!

In May 1979, an American called **David Booth** dreamed of a terrible air crash. He informed the airline but they took no notice of him. The next day an airplane crashed at the Chicago airport killing 273 people.

Jeane Dixon, an American who claims to have powers of second sight, warned that the President would be assassinated. Eventually, on November 23, 1963, she told friends that the day had come. **John F. Kennedy** was shot dead that afternoon.

The police have often been helped by people with second sight. **Gerald Croiset** spent his life helping Danish police to find murderers and to locate missing people and buried bodies.

253

It is said that some people are gifted with bizarre powers. They claim to be able to make things rise above the ground and objects change shape all by themselves.

Astral projection is when a person feels that their spirit is rising out of their actual body. Such people claim that while sleeping they can sit on the end of their bed and watch themselves.

Many people believe that **dowsers** can sense where gold and oil are hidden in the ground. They use instruments, such as bent metal rods or forked twigs, which tremble or rotate when they have found the hidden treasure.

Levitation is said to defy the law of gravity by making bodies or objects rise and float in the air. Some eastern holy men are supposed to be able to levitate themselves at will.

Experts are unable to explain the strange pictures created by psychic photography.

It is claimed that **psychic photography** is the ability to take photographs of thoughts. Ted Serios from Chicago believed that when he took a photograph of his face an image in his thoughts would appear on the film!

Psychokinesis is the ability to affect objects by mental means alone. **Uri Geller** from Israel, for example, is famous for bending keys. He has even claimed to be able to stop a cable car in midair. Many magicians believe he is a fraud.

Strange and bizarre

For hundreds of years sightings of strange creatures, mysterious monsters and bizarre landmarks have been reported all over the world. Even today experts are unable to find scientific explanations for many of these mysteries.

Bigfoot – or **Sasquatch** -- is described as a tall, hairy monster that lives in Washington State. A Bigfoot sighting is reported regularly so there must be lots of these monsters!

Yeti, or the **Abominable Snowman** is thought to be a tall, white, furry monster. The first sighting was reported in Tibet in 1921 and there have been numerous reports of appearances ever since.

Enormous, elaborate shapes known as **crop circles** have appeared in the crop fields of Hampshire and Wiltshire, England. No one is sure how they are formed or where they came from although many explanations have been suggested.

It is said that the **Pyramids** in Egypt are surrounded by strange powers. Plants apparently grow faster and it is even claimed that people are filled with amazing energy around the Pyramids!

Nowadays modern technology, from radar to the latest computers, is used to investigate sightings of unknown creatures.

The **Loch Ness Monster** is believed to be a gigantic prehistoric reptile which still survives in Loch Ness, Scotland. Sightings of it have been reported as long ago as 565 B.C. Although there are numerous photographs, the existence of this "monster" has never really been proved.

257

More spooky cases

Tradition has it that when a dramatic event has occurred, ghostly phantoms will return to haunt the place where the disturbing incident happened.

Here are two especially chilling phantom stories.

During the 1600s, the owner of **Bettiscombe Manor** in Dorset, England cruelly enslaved an African man and brought him back to England. The slave said that if he was not buried in his homeland he would return to haunt the manor. The slave's request was ignored and he was buried in the local churchyard.

It is said that such terrible screaming could be heard in the churchyard that the owner was forced to dig up the coffin and put it in the loft of Bettiscombe Manor.

The skull remains at Bettiscombe Manor and seems to guard it. If the skull is taken outside, it is said that screams shake the house.

The Flying Dutchman was a ship which sank in the 1600s. Its ghost is said to haunt the oceans. In 1881 the crew of *HMS Inconstant* thought they saw the ship.

In 1939, over 100 people claimed to have seen the ship as they sunbathed on a beach near Cape Town, South Africa.

During World War II, a German admiral reported that the crew of his U-Boat submarine had seen the phantom ship.

In 1911, the crew of the steamer, *Orkney Belle*, encountered **The Flying Dutchman**. It was totally deserted. It is said that three bells were heard and the ghost ship vanished into the fog.

The eye and the brain

When your eyes are open light travels into them from the world outside. The source of the light could be the Sun, or a light bulb.

As it enters your eyes, light reflects off objects that are in your **field of vision** – the things you can see.

Sometimes there is not much information for the brain to work with. It must use other information to understand what it is seeing. If you cover up the second of the two words below it is not so easy to see that the first word is FISH. Your brain fills in the gaps by using any other available information.

FISH FINGERS

There is a **blind spot** at the back of your eye where the optic nerve connects to the brain. It is an area which is insensitive to light.

The image on the **retina** is actually upside-down but your brain flips the image allowing you to see it the right way up.

The eye

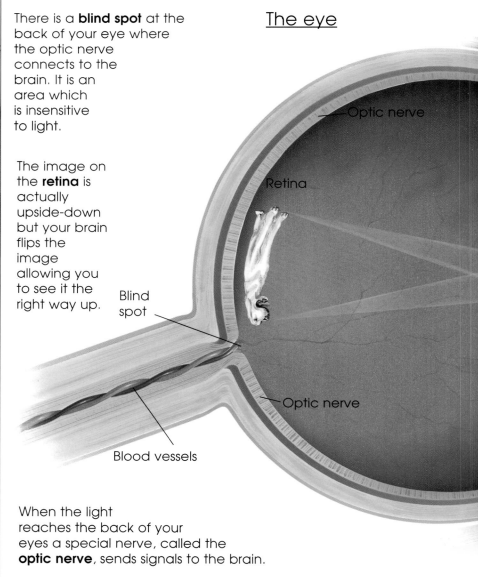

Optic nerve

Retina

Blind spot

Optic nerve

Blood vessels

When the light reaches the back of your eyes a special nerve, called the **optic nerve**, sends signals to the brain.

Even when your eyes are shut your brain still thinks it sees. When your eyes have been looking at a bright light or you have been staring hard at something, an **after-image** can stay on the back of your eye for some time. Try staring for a minute or two at the black cat, then close your eyes. You should see an image of the cat even though your eyes are closed.

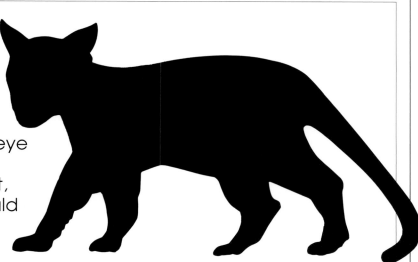

Eyelid

Pupil

Iris

Light passes through the pupil which can get bigger (dilate) in dim light and smaller (contract) in bright light. This is to allow varying amounts of light into your eye.

Iris

Pupil

Lens

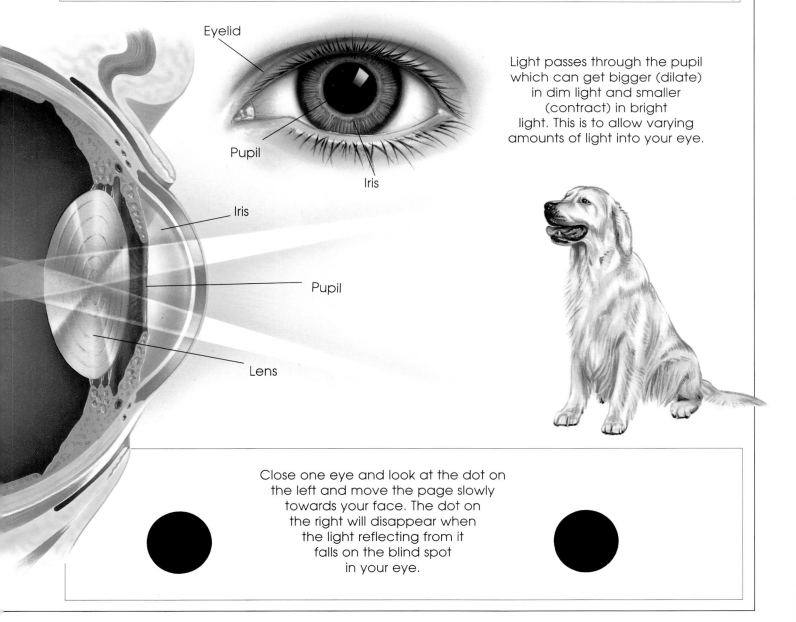

Close one eye and look at the dot on the left and move the page slowly towards your face. The dot on the right will disappear when the light reflecting from it falls on the blind spot in your eye.

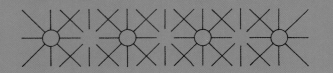

Lines and shapes

Simple lines and shapes can fool your brain. Phantom blobs can appear from nowhere and straight lines can seem to bend.

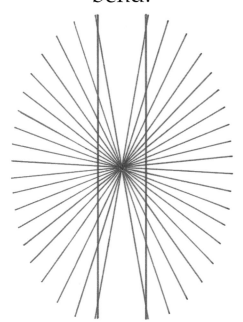

Here are some diagrams that will trick your eyes.

Try staring at the circle. You will find it hard to see a steady picture. Your eyes are being drawn to the centre of the circle where the black stripes get closer and closer together. The lines appear to 'interfere' with each other, producing a shadow effect around the circle. This is known as the **Mackay Effect**.

The unenclosed circles at the centers of the crossed lines seem to be brighter than the enclosed outlined circles.

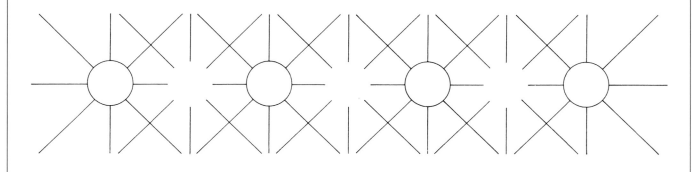

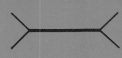

Stare at the black squares and you will see faint shaded blobs at the corners.

Stare at the white squares and pale blobs appear, again at the corners.

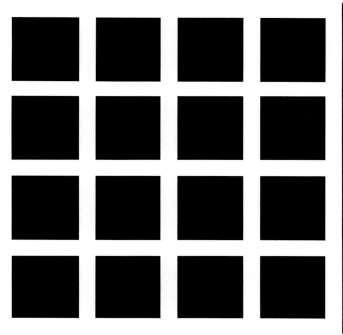

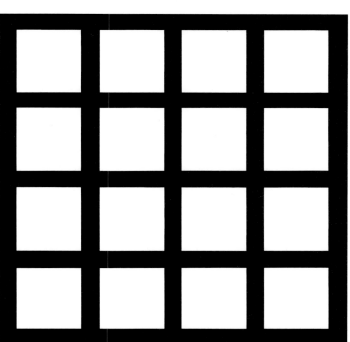

Which of these lines do you think is longest? A or B? In fact they are both the same length. Your eyes follow the direction of the arrows which makes your brain think one line is shorter than the other.

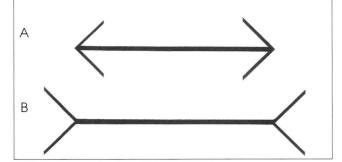

Parallel lines are lines that are the same distance apart, however long they are. Here, the parallel lines seem to curve away from each other.

The diagonal lines draw your eyes away from the horizontal lines, making them appear to bend.

The bricks in this wall look as if they are being partly squashed. Although they are, in fact, all rectangles, they appear to be wedge-shaped. This interesting optical illusion only works when the lines between the bricks are brighter than the dark bricks and darker than the light bricks.

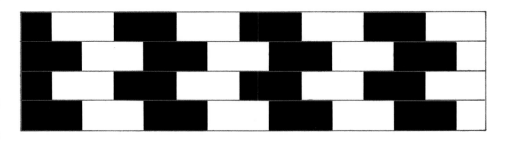

We live in three-dimensional space. This means we can move from side to side (one dimension), forwards and backwards (the second dimension) and we can jump up and down (the third dimension).

A flat sheet of paper has only two dimensions, but an object can be drawn so it looks three-dimensional.

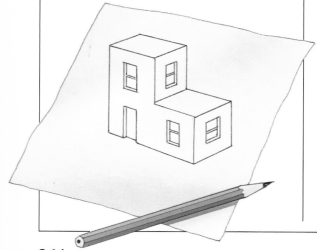

This drawing of a cube appears to be a three-dimensional (3-D) shape, even though the paper it is printed on is only two-dimensional (2-D). The brain is being tricked into believing the lines form a 3-D figure.

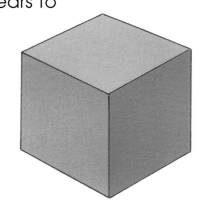

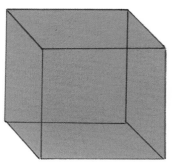

This type of cube is known as the **Necker cube**, named after the man who first drew it.

There is no way of knowing which is the front or back of the cube.

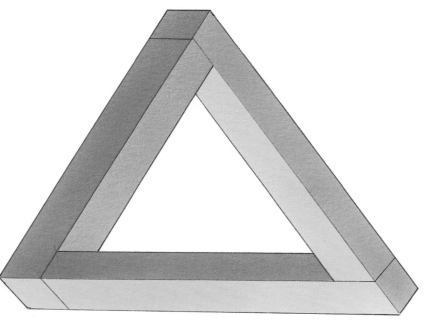

This 3-D triangle, sometimes called a **tribar**, appears to be a picture of a simple 3-D shape. However, on closer inspection it is clear that it could not exist in a real three-dimensional space!

Railroad lines are parallel lines. However, a picture of a railroad track disappearing into the distance shows the lines getting closer and closer together. This is called **perspective**. Perspective is used to show 3-D pictures in 2-D.

To learn the rules of perspective, artists sometimes paint what they see through a window on to the glass itself!

The Dutch artist **Maurits C Escher** produced amazing geometric drawings. Some are of buildings that at first glance appear quite normal, but would be quite impossible to build in real life.

A mouse looks tiny when compared to a human, but compared to a flea it looks huge.

The brain always compares one thing with another to decide their size or position. However, these comparisons can often confuse the brain!

Clouds are a **scaled** phenomenon. This means it is impossible to tell how near or far away they are, as there is nothing to compare the clouds to in order to guess their size.

At a reading distance of 12 inches, the mouse and the elephant appear to be the same size. In real life, if the mouse (2 1/2 inches high) were in the foreground, the elephant (10 feet high) would have to be 100 feet behind the mouse to appear to be the same size.

A **constellation** is a group, or pattern, of stars. The Big Dipper, part of the Ursa Major constellation, is made up of seven bright stars. When viewed from Earth, they all appear to be the same distance away, but in fact some are much closer than others.

A light year is the distance light travels in a year. Light travels at 180,000 miles per second, so a light year is around 5,878,000,000,000 miles!

The closest star in the Big Dipper to Earth is 60 light years away, the furthest is an amazing 110 light years away!

As the light from the furthest star in the Big Dipper takes 110 years to reach us, it may not even be there anymore and we would not realize. If the star had burned out five years ago we would not be able to tell for another 105 years!

Which is the largest of the centre circles? They are both the same size! Your brain compared them with the circles that are surrounding them and decided that one was 'small' in comparison with other circles and the other was 'big'.

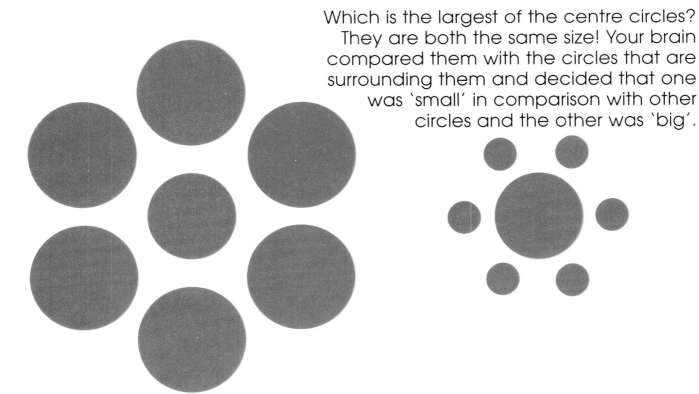

Color tricks

Light can be split into different colors. These colors are red, orange, yellow, green, blue, and violet, and are called the spectrum.

Rainbows are a natural example of how sunlight can be split into the colors of the spectrum (see page 28).

You can try a simple experiment to see how the colors of the spectrum combine to make white light. Divide a card circle into six sections and color the segments the colors of the spectrum. Push a pencil through the center of the card. When you spin the pencil fast, the colors will blend together until they look white.

There are two sorts of cell in the human eye which are sensitive to light. They are shaped like **cones** and **rods**. The cones are sensitive to bright light and the colors red, blue, and green. The rods are sensitive to dim light, but not to color.

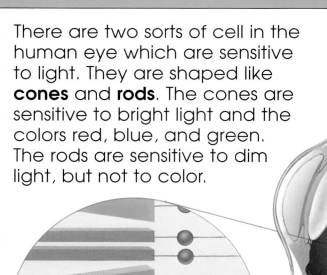

The eye

Cone

Rod

Sometimes photographers use colored **filters** on the camera lens. The filter blocks some of the colors in the spectrum and can make photographs look very dramatic.

Using a yellow filter makes blue sky look darker and makes white clouds stand out more.

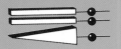 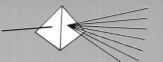

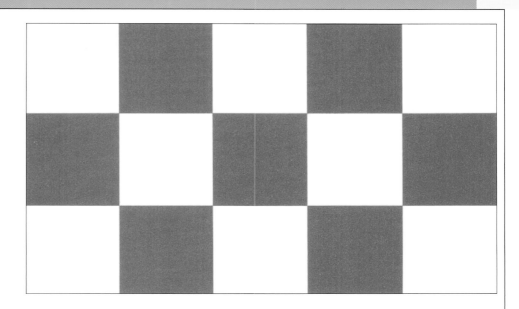

Stare at the red square in the centre of the red and white checkered pattern for about a minute. Now stare at the white square to its right. The white square will seem to change to a faint cyan (a shade of blue).

When two colors can combine to produce white light, they are said to be **complementary** colors.

The cones in your retinas have become tired of taking in the red light. So, for a while, your eyes will ignore it. The color produced by the rest of the light is cyan. Cyan is the complementary color to red.

If a person cannot see some colors, they are called **color blind**. Color blindness is 20 times more common in men than in women.

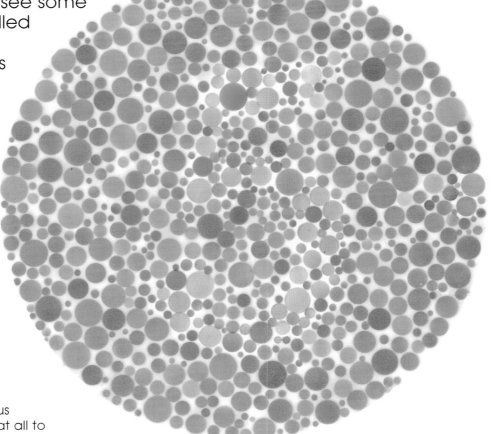

Tests like this are used to see if people are red-green color blind.

Color blindness is not serious and makes no difference at all to the day-to-day lives of most people.

269

Motion pictures are often called "movies." However, when you watch a "movie" you simply see a series of still pictures shown quickly, one after another. Each picture or **frame,** is slightly different from the previous one so an illusion of movement is created.

A technique often used in nature films is **time-lapse photography**.

Individual pictures are taken of an object every day, and are then joined in sequence to make a film. In this way, a week in the life of a plant can be seen in a matter of seconds. This is an extreme form of fast-motion.

In the 19th century, before motion pictures were invented, you could have seen simple animation, using a toy called a **zoetrope**.

Sometimes when watching a film or the television you might see a car wheel apparently spinning the wrong way. This happens when the position of the wheel's spokes in each frame makes it easier for the brain to think that the wheel is moving slowly backwards than very fast forwards.

The spinning drum had evenly spaced slits cut into it. Through each slit you could see a small image that was drawn slightly differently to the one next to it. Spinning the drum let you see one image after another, creating the illusion of movement.

Television pictures are made up of many tiny luminescent dots that form hundreds of lines across the screen. The dots are constantly changed from top to bottom, producing 25 frames every second. As the images change so quickly, they appear to be moving.

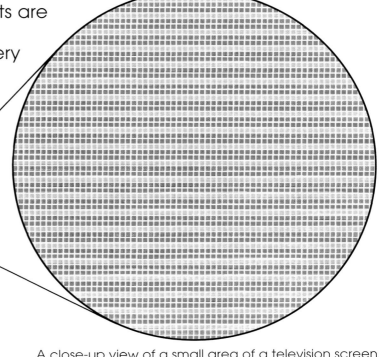

A close-up view of a small area of a television screen.

Animated films or **cartoons** work like normal movies, except that between each frame the picture, or model, is changed slightly, either by hand or on a computer.

Some animated films use models made from modeling clay. The models must be changed slightly between each frame. It can take up to two years to make a 30-minute movie using animated models.

271

As your eyes are about two inches apart, you see things from two slightly different angles. This is called **binocular vision**.

Your brain has two views of the same thing to deal with, but it cleverly combines the two views so that your mind sees in 3-D. This is **stereo vision**.

The field of vision is the area in which you can see things without moving your eyes. A fly has hundreds of eyes, giving it a very wide field of vision. This makes it very difficult for a predator to sneak up on it, or a human to swat it!

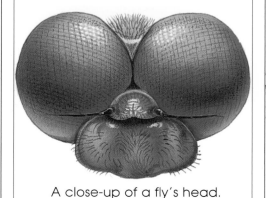

A close-up of a fly's head.

Stereo vision allows people to judge how far away an object is. This is called **spatial awareness**. It is much harder for your brain to judge the position of an object when it only sees the object through one eye (from one angle). You can try this yourself by throwing and catching a ball, or picking a ball up off the floor, when you have one eye closed.

Put the tips of your index fingers together and hold them about 8 inches away from your eyes. Relax your eyes or look at something a few feet in front of you. You will see that the ends of your fingers appear to overlap. A finger-like object appears between your fingers.

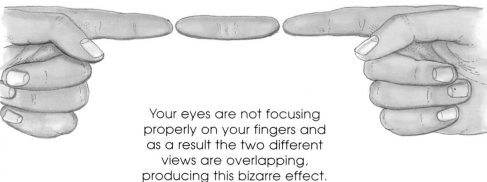

Your eyes are not focusing properly on your fingers and as a result the two different views are overlapping, producing this bizarre effect.

Each eye has a different view of the same object. If you close your left eye and point at a small object in the distance, and then close your right eye and look with the left, you will no longer be pointing at the object.

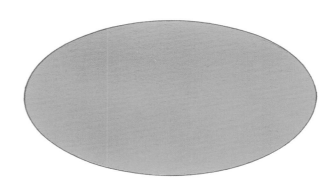

You can see 3-D pictures and 3-D movies by wearing special glasses with one red and one green lens.

Two slightly different views of the picture are drawn on top of each other. Each view can only be seen through one lens of the colored glasses. As each eye has a different picture, your brain then combines them to produce a 3-dimensional picture.

Holograms and stereograms are two ways of representing a 3-D image.

When lit correctly, a hologram can make a 2-D image appear to be in 3-D.

They are both created using technology developed in the last few decades.

The first laser beam was generated by **Theodore Maiman** in 1960 using a flash tube and a ruby crystal.

A hologram is created using **laser light**. The laser beam is split in two. One half of it is reflected from the object on to the film material. The other half is directed straight on to the film without reflecting from the object. When the hologram film is lit in a certain way, a 3-dimensional picture can be seen.

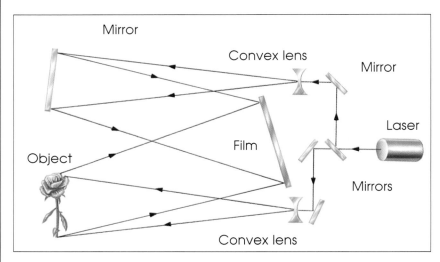

Laser light waves are coherent - they are the same length and go up and down together. Holograms can only be made using laser light, as the process requires regular light waves. Unlike laser light, ordinary light waves are highly irregular, and therefore useless for the job.

A **stereogram** is a computer-generated picture that seems, at first, to be a random pattern of colored dots and squiggles. But if you look at a stereogram in a particular way, a seemingly 3-D image emerges from within the pattern.

To see the stereogram try focusing on a point beyond the stereogram. It is not as easy as it sounds. Focus and then relax your eyes.

A 3-D picture is hidden in the scattered dots of a stereogram.
A computer is used to work out where the dots should be positioned.
The dots make up two images of the same shapes – one for each eye.
When you stare at the stereogram in the right way, your brain mixes
the two images and magically recognizes the shapes in the picture.

Stage and screen

These days many movies are full of incredible special effects, which can be created using computers.

Movie-makers have always used visual illusions, even in the early days of movies, over 100 years ago. Then illusions were based upon the successful techniques used on the stage.

In the 1902 film, *A Trip to the Moon*, film makers used trick photography to show a rocket crashing into the moon.

Early comedy movie-makers like **Mack Sennett** and **Charlie Chaplin** used simple filming techniques to produce hilarious results. Although their special effects do not seem very convincing compared with modern techniques, they were revolutionary at the time.

One of the earliest special effects used in the theatre was **Pepper's Ghost**. A large mirror, hidden beneath the stage, reflected the figure of an actor on to a large piece of glass at the front of the stage. As the glass was invisible on the darkened stage, the audience saw a transparent phantom appearing in front of them!

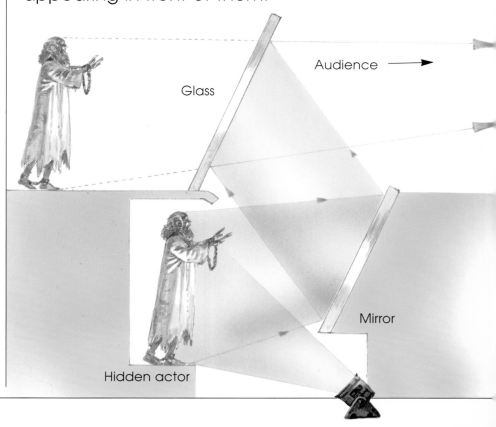

Audience

Glass

Mirror

Hidden actor

A technique that is used a lot in movies and television is **superimposition**. Two film sequences are shown at the same time. This gives the illusion that the actor is appearing twice in the same shot.

In television, superimposition is often done using **Color Separation Overlay**. Two videos, or the pictures from two cameras, are shown at the same time. Wherever the color blue appears on the first picture, the second picture shows through.

With the help of computers it is possible to create almost any visual effect you could wish for on television or film. A picture can be stored **digitally** as trillions of binary numbers (ones and zeros). Computer software can perform complicated calculations with the stored numbers to produce spectacular effects.

Morphing is an effect where one object can appear to be smoothly transformed into another.

Most magic tricks are optical illusions that require years of practice. Magicians, or illusionists as they are sometimes known, are skilled at deceiving the eye.

To aid sleight of hand and palming, magicians try to distract the audience's attention, often by waving a 'magic' **wand.**

Magicians use **sleight of hand** to deceive their audience. This means they can cleverly move a small object, such as a coin, without anyone noticing.

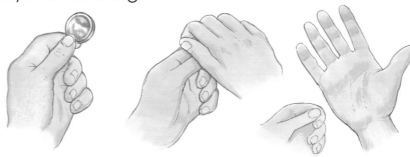

Palming is a method of holding playing cards or coins, without the audience seeing. It takes a lot of practice to make hand movements look natural whilst concealing an object.

David Copperfield is one of the most famous magicians in the world today. One of his most successful illusions is when he appears to fly around the stage.

Drop a one penny coin into an empty drinking glass. Pour water into the glass and the coin will appear to become a two pence coin!

Make sure your audience only sees the coin through the side of the glass by holding your hand around the rim.

The water distorts the audience's view of the coin making it appear larger than it really is.

Hold two coins between your index fingers. Rub the two coins quickly together and it will appear that there are now three coins.

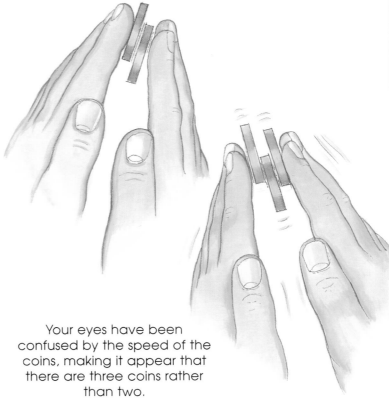

Your eyes have been confused by the speed of the coins, making it appear that there are three coins rather than two.

Light can bounce and bend. This is known as reflection (bouncing) and refraction (bending).

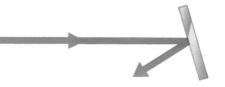

Light reflects from a mirror and refracts on entering and leaving water, sometimes producing amazing effects.

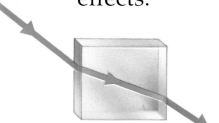

When light passes from air to water, it refracts. **Refracted light** distorts images. If you stand in the shallow end of a swimming pool and look down at your legs, they appear to be much shorter and stubbier than when you are out of the water. This is not because they have shrunk, it is because light is bent, or refracted.

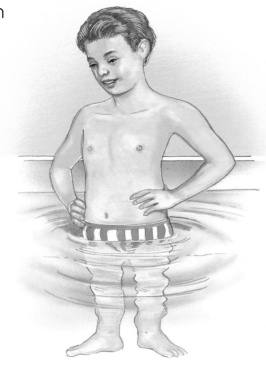

A simple experiment to see how light refracts can be tried using a straw and a glass of water. Dip the straw in the glass of water and view it from different angles. The light bends on contact with the water, distorting the image of the straw.

The famous artist Leonardo da Vinci did not want other people to copy his ideas. So he sometimes used **mirror writing** when making his notes. Mirror writing can only be read if it is held up to a mirror.

A **concave** mirror curves inward, like the bowl of a spoon. Light that reflects off it **converges** (comes together). The light focuses at a point in front of the mirror. After it has focused, the light **diverges** (separates).

The reflection in a concave mirror is upside down.

A **convex** mirror curves outwards, like the back of a spoon. It produces a small upright image, but also has a wide field of view. This means it shows things to the sides which a normal mirror would not reflect.

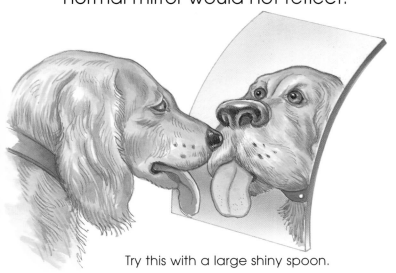

Try this with a large shiny spoon.

You may have seen weird images of yourself in a **Hall of Mirrors** at a fairground. The mirrors are curved so that some parts are concave and some are convex.

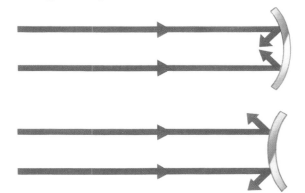

If the light meets your eye before it focuses, you see a magnified image of your face. If the light meets your eye after the focal point, you see an upside down image of your face.

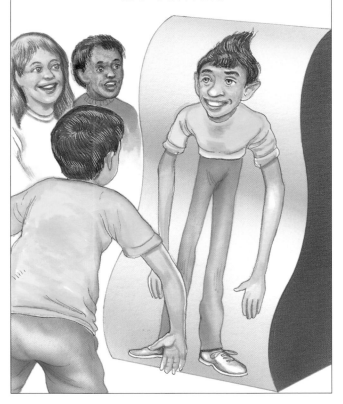

281

Optical illusions are often entertaining, but they can also be very useful.

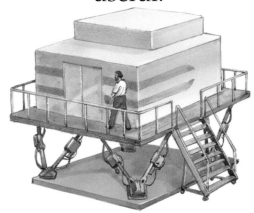

Deceiving our eyes can allow us to practise dangerous activities – but without the danger.

Pilots who fly large modern airplanes have to be very well trained, in order to prevent accidents. Pilots can practice their skills using specially built machines called **flight simulators**.

Simulators are built to be exactly like the cockpit of the plane. Large computer screens display a realistic moving picture of what the pilots would see if they were really flying the plane. The computer-generated pictures respond to the controls as the pilot manipulates them.

Fashion designers use optical illusions when designing clothes.

Wearing clothes with vertical stripes makes you look taller and slimmer.

Horizontally-striped clothing (hoops) can make you look shorter and fatter.

Wearing all black can also make you appear slimmer.

Using a design method called **Computer-aided design (CAD)**, architects can design a house, and see inside the rooms using the 3-D image on the computer screen. House-buyers can be shown around the new house as if it had already been built.

Landscape architects can design a garden to make it look bigger than it really is. If a path gradually becomes narrower as it gets further away, the garden will look longer.

If you looked down the garden your brain would assume that the path was the same width from one end to the other and, therefore, that the end of the garden was further away.

In some countries, a stretch of road approaching a traffic circle is striped with **yellow lines**, which get closer and closer together as they near the traffic circle. This creates the illusion that vehicles are traveling very quickly and encourages drivers to brake earlier to reach a safer speed.

Some optical illusions occur naturally. They are all around us.

Strange illusions appear in the sky, certain animals can blend into their surroundings, or look like something completely different.

On some clear days at sunset the sun will appear to turn bright green for a few seconds. This is called the **green flash**.

WARNING:
NEVER LOOK DIRECTLY AT THE SUN!

A **rainbow** is a natural optical illusion that can appear when sunlight reflects off raindrops.

The light from the sun is bent as it travels through the drops. The different colors that make up white light do not bend at the same angle, so they are split into the six colors of the spectrum. Although it can appear as if there are seven colors in a rainbow, most experts agree there are only six.

On sunny days, pools of water seem to appear on the road. This is known as a **mirage**. The light has been refracted by the rising hot air close to the ground. The expanding hot air also makes the light shimmer, giving an overall effect of blue rippling water.

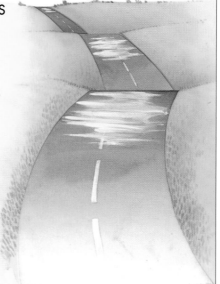

Peacock butterflies scare off predators with the vividly-colored circles on each wing. These look like a pair of ferocious eyes.

Some animals have evolved ways of hiding themselves from other creatures. They use **camouflage.** A lion has sand-colored fur to make it hard to see in the long dry grass of the African plains.

Zebra, which might be a lion's prey, are marked with irregular black and white stripes. The stripes make it hard for the lions to tell one zebra from another in a large herd.

The **stick insect**, as its name suggests, has evolved to look exactly like a small twig.

Imagine wandering through a world that does not exist, or catching a ball that is not there. It is all possible with virtual reality.

Virtual Reality is anything that seems to exist but does not. A painting you might do of an imaginary house is virtual reality! The house only exists in the painting. With modern computers we can experience **Interactive Virtual Reality**. Interactive means it responds to things that you do.

Virtual Reality computer programs can create imaginary landscapes that seem as real as the view you might see from the window of a train. Computer programmers use mathematical formulae to generate very realistic landscapes that move with you through this virtual world.

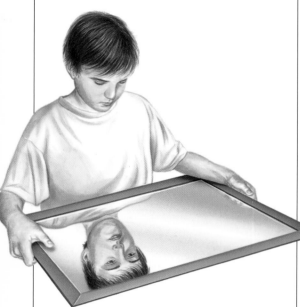

If you look into a **mirror**, you can see a virtual world behind your reflection. Try holding a mirror horizontally in front of you while you walk from room to room. It seems like you are walking on the ceiling.

WARNING:
BE VERY CAREFUL IF YOU DO THIS, AS IT COULD BE VERY DANGEROUS

There are various items of equipment that can be used for exploring virtual reality. The best known is the **headset.** In front of your eyes are two tiny TV screens that give you a 3-D view of the computer-generated landscape. Some more expensive headsets change the view as you move your head up and down or from side to side.

A **VR glove** contains sensors that can detect the movements of your fingers. Soon gloves will have sensors that make it seem as if you can actually feel virtual objects, objects that do not really exist.

287

The history of ballet

The tradition of dance dates back thousands of years. People danced to worship their gods, to bring good fortune, and to celebrate festivals.

The true origins of ballet, however, date back to Italy, 500 years ago.

Today, ballet is full of variety because of its rich history. Movies and television have made it more popular than ever.

During a period in history known as the **Renaissance**, wealthy Italian families entertained visitors at exciting parties with poetry, music, mime, and dancing.

Catherine de Médici, an Italian courtier, became queen of France in 1547. She introduced spectacular dance pageants. They were known as *ballet de cour* since they were danced by the courtiers themselves.

King Louis XIV of France was an enthusiastic dancer. In 1661, he set up a school for dance where the five basic ballet positions were first written down.

Louis XIV as the Sun in the *Ballet de La Nuit.*

In 1760, **Jean Georges Noverre** introduced story ballets or *ballet d'action*. An early story ballet was *La Fille Mal Gardée*, which is still danced today.

A French dancer named **Marius Petipa** joined **The Imperial Ballet** in Russia in 1847. He created famous ballets, such as *The Sleeping Beauty*.

In 1909, **Serge Diaghilev** formed **Les Ballets Russes** with the most talented dancers he could find. Diaghilev brought audiences ballets such as *The Firebird* and *Rite of Spring*.

Modern dance began in the United States with **Isadora Duncan**. She danced barefoot in flowing tunics inspired by ancient Greece.

Martha Graham in *Night Journey*.

In the 1930s, a new dance technique, with awkward, angular movements, was developed by **Martha Graham**.

289

Popular ballets

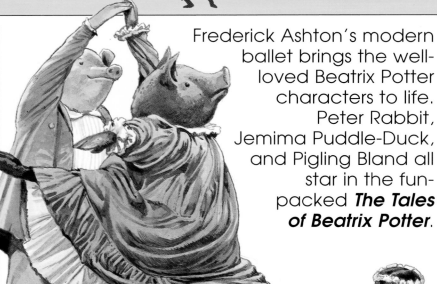

Frederick Ashton's modern ballet brings the well-loved Beatrix Potter characters to life. Peter Rabbit, Jemima Puddle-Duck, and Pigling Bland all star in the fun-packed *The Tales of Beatrix Potter*.

Ballets old and new entertain audiences with stories of love, magic, and faraway places.

Some ballets are long, with three or four acts, while others last for just one act.

Not all contemporary ballet and dance tells a story. Sometimes just music and movement alone are fun to watch.

In the romantic ballet *La Sylphide*, James falls in love with a forest sprite (a *sylphide*) on the eve of his wedding. He is tricked by a witch and kills the sprite by accident.

The Nutcracker story is set at a Christmas Party. Little Clara dreams that she and her toys are attacked by a mouse king. She defeats him and her favorite toy, the Nutcracker, becomes a handsome prince.

Appalachian Spring is a famous ballet choreographed by Martha Graham. It tells the story of a newly married pioneering couple starting their life on the prairies of America.

Set in a crowded fairground, Fokine's ***Petrushka*** captures all the excitement of the fair. A magician makes three dolls dance and, when night falls, they secretly come to life on their own.

In ***Coppélia***, Dr. Coppelius, a toymaker, is tricked into believing that his beautiful doll has come to life!

Unforgettable dancers

Ballet moved to the theater from the royal palaces over 200 years ago. Ballerinas and male dancers have been popular ever since.

Taglioni was perfect in the role of the forest sprite in *La Sylphide*.

In the 1830s, **Marie Taglioni** was the first great ballerina. Her lightness and poise brought beauty to every performance. People had never seen such graceful jumps and landings.

While many dancers are famous for their incredible technique, others have brought something new and exciting to the world of dance.

One of the most famous male dancers of all time was **Vaslav Nijinsky**. He brought dramatic skill and physical presence to ballet. His amazing leaps and expressive movement gave a special quality to every role he played.

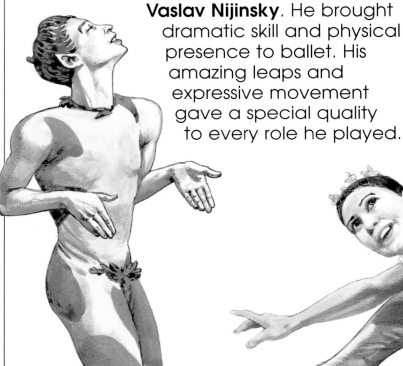

Nijinsky caused a sensation in *L'Après-midi d'un Faune*.

Anna Pavlova was one of the world's greatest dancers. She devoted her whole life to dance. Every role she played seemed magical. She could transform herself into many graceful images.

Pavlova as *The Dying Swan.*

After defecting from Russia in 1961, **Rudolf Nureyev** danced with the Royal Ballet in London. He was an exciting, dynamic, and strong performer. Male dancing became very popular because of him.

Isadora Duncan is famous for beginning the modern dance movement. She danced freely, wearing a simple tunic.

The choreographer Kenneth MacMillan created *The Prince of the Pagodas* specially for Darcey Bussell.

Isadora's movements were inspired by nature.

Margot Fonteyn was a leading ballerina of this century. Her partnership with Rudolph Nureyev was very famous.

Trained at the Royal Ballet School in London, **Darcey Bussell** is one of today's leading ballerinas.

Ballet around the world

Ballet is performed and enjoyed throughout the world.

The **Royal Danish Ballet Company** is the world's oldest ballet company. Founded by **August Bournonville**, this company is famous for its powerful male roles and enchanting female stars.

Each country and culture brings something different and new to ballet.

The Australian Ballet is internationally renowned for performances of classical and modern ballets.

From the English classical style to Cunningham's technique, there is a rich variety of work that celebrates people's love of dance.

Edward Borovansky from the famous Ballet Russes started the Barovansky Ballet in 1939. When he died, the company was renamed **The Australian Ballet**.

Arthur Mitchell formed the first black classical ballet company in the United States, in 1971. It is called **The Dance Theater of Harlem**.

The Royal Ballet was originally called the Vic-Wells Ballet. It is now one of the great British ballet companies.

The **Merce Cunningham Dance Company** from the United States, is at the forefront of modern dance. Many of the dancers are classically trained.

Merce Cunningham mixes ballet steps with everyday movements.

One of the largest and best-known companies is the **Bolshoi Ballet** from Russia. Its colorful and dramatic story ballets are seen all over the world.

You can start dancing from the age of three. In your first lesson you will learn basic steps and exercises.

Stepping, jumping, walking, and running will all help to strengthen your muscles, give you better coordination, and help you dance in time to the music.

Dance classes are held at local dance schools in the evenings and on weekends. If you want to be a professional dancer you can join a dance academy when you are about eleven years old, or later at sixteen or eighteen years old.

Clothes for dance classes must be light and simple, to allow you to move easily.

Boys dance in leotards or T-shirts and tights.

Girls usually wear leotards and tights.

For other dance forms, bare feet, jazz shoes, and tap shoes are used.

In a **dance studio** there are usually mirrors on the walls so that you can see that you are moving correctly. The floor is made of wood or vinyl and can be built to help you jump.

Ballet shoes are soft and flat, and made from satin, canvas, or leather.

The **barre** is a wooden rail attached to the wall that is used to give the dancer support while exercising.

All dance classes are accompanied by **music**. As a dancer you learn to feel and express the music in the way you move.

To become a strong, expressive dancer you must **practice**. Even the most famous dancers go to class every day to stay strong and supple.

When you have learned the basic ballet steps and can put them together, you are ready to start taking **ballet exams**. Exams test how much you know and show that you are ready to learn more.

Ballet steps

The first ballet school was founded by King Louis XIV of France. It was here, in Paris, that the first ballet steps were set and written down. Ever since, the language of ballet has been French.

In a ballet class, you learn each position, or exercise, by its French name.

Before making any shape or position you must have the correct **posture**. This means standing tall with your hips directly over your feet. The back must be straight to give the body a slim line.

En seconde
Second position

En première
First position

En troisième
Third position

It is important to keep the neck relaxed, the head poised, and the shoulders open and low.

The first exercise in any ballet class is the **plié**, which means "to bend." *Pliés* give the legs strength and suppleness.

298

Turn out is the amount you can turn your feet sideways in any position. Your legs must be turned outward from the hip.

The way you carry your arms is called *ports de bras*. Arms should make a gentle curve and move gracefully.

Fingers should always be slightly curved and soft.

En quatrième
Fourth position

En cinquième
Fifth position

There are **five basic positions** for the feet and arms. They are used at the beginning and end of movements and in passing from one movement to another.

The order of exercises in a ballet class has been developed over hundreds of years. Each class starts at the **barre**.

After exercising at the *barre*, dancers move to the center of the room for **center practice**. Here the *barre* exercises are practiced without support.

Pointing the toes correctly is an important part of ballet. Your foot should be pointed from the ankle with the leg turned out. This way your foot should make a straight line with your leg.

299

To become a professional dancer takes a great deal of dedication and hard work.

There are many complicated movements to learn and master.

Ballerinas and leading male dancers have studied, practiced, and performed for many years before gaining world fame.

Girls start to learn **pointe work** at about age eleven. This means dancing on the tips of their toes, wearing special **pointe shoes**.

The toe of a **pointe shoe** is hardened with layers of satin, paper, and coarse material called **burlap**.

A series of exercise positions and movements performed together is called an **enchaînement**.

Many dancers join a ballet company as a member of the **corps de ballet** or chorus. Performing as a group of dancers, they learn to work together and to play a character on stage.

You can start training to become a professional ballet dancer at age sixteen. This takes at least two years, working and dancing for many hours a day.

The **arabesque** is one of the most beautiful ballet positions. It requires perfect balance while standing on one leg, with the other stretched out behind.

As dancers complete their training, they start to look for jobs. To become a member of a **dance company** they must **audition**. This means taking part in a class and performing a solo in front of a panel of experts.

A **pirouette** is an exciting and difficult step where the dancer spins on one leg. This needs balance and strength.

The **pas de deux** is a partnership between two dancers. The male dancer lifts and supports his partner.

Modern dance

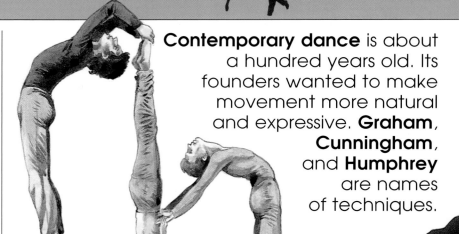

Ballet is the oldest dance technique in the Western world, but many other dance forms are taught at schools throughout the world. These include contemporary dance, tap, and jazz.

Contemporary dance is about a hundred years old. Its founders wanted to make movement more natural and expressive. **Graham**, **Cunningham**, and **Humphrey** are names of techniques.

Contemporary dancers usually dance barefoot.

Contemporary dance has different sets of positions to ballet. There may be **floor movements** and dancers can use their breathing to help form the different positions.

These techniques are very different from ballet, but a knowledge of ballet can help when learning them.

Tap dancing was started by African slaves in the United States. Traditional African dances were mixed with those of white people. Over the years, tap steps have been made into the method that is taught in schools today.

Fred Astaire was one of the most famous tap dancers. He was both a talented dancer and choreographer.
Today, dancers such as **Savion Glover** continue to make tap dancing very popular.

Tap dancing is very fast and rhythmic. In **musicals** there are often as many as thirty dancers all tap dancing at the same time. The sound they make is very exciting.

Jazz dancing started in the United States. It developed from a mixture of African and European dances. Like tap dance, it is used in musicals and is also known as **show dancing**.

Tap shoes have metal toe and heel plates fitted to make a special sound on the floor.

Dancers who work in musicals are trained in many dance techniques. They are adaptable and perform ballet, tap, and jazz.

Costumes and makeup

Ballet does not use speech, so dancers must use all their expressive skills to convey their mood and character.

Early ballet dancers started to wear shorter and looser clothes as they began to perform more complicated steps.

Costumes, makeup, and mime are all important for telling a ballet story and setting the scene.

Dancing tights were invented by Maillot at the Paris Opera in the early 1800s. They allowed dancers to wear shorter dresses without showing their bare legs!

Early ballet masters created **mime gestures** that have become part of today's choreography. Using movements of the eyes, arms, and head, dancers can convey the emotions and intentions of the characters they play.

Some costumes look as if they are very hard to dance in but they are made of very lightweight materials.

Theater lights are so bright, dancers wear makeup to stop their skin from looking pale and shiny.

A dancer's hair is usually tied back from her face so that her eyes and mouth can be clearly seen.

Hair is often decorated with a **headdress** or flowers.

Costumes must be strong and easy to move in. They can be made from silk, velvet, chiffon, or lycra and decorated with beads, braid, and ribbons.

Tutus have short, stiff skirts that stick out from the waist.

The **classical tutu** was designed so that dancers could perform difficult turns, such as *fouèttés*, for which their legs needed to move freely.

Stage makeup is bright and heavy. It has to be applied boldly so that it can be seen from a distance.

Some dances look so natural and spontaneous it seems as though the dancers are making up the steps.

The **choreographer** chooses the story, selects the music, and arranges the steps for a ballet. The ideas may come from a fairy tale, a painting, or a poem.

Movements from *Square Dance* by Balanchine.

Every dance has been carefully worked out and set to music by the choreographer.

George Balanchine was a famous choreographer who created over a hundred ballets. He made dances that were both graceful and athletic.

Modern choreographers often create abstract dances with no story.

Twyla Tharp is a contemporary choreographer who uses movement of all kinds. Her work includes ballet and jazz dance.

Igor Stravinsky was one of the most distinguished composers to write ballet music. He worked with famous choreographers such as **Fokine** and **Balanchine**.

A scene from Petipa's staging of *Swan Lake*.

Keeping a written record of dance pieces is called **notation** or **choreology.** This means ballets can be accurately recreated. The **Benesh** system is most commonly used to write down movements in classical ballet. **Labanotation** is used to record contemporary dance.

Music is a basic ingredient of nearly all dance. Choreographers sometimes ask a composer to write new music for a ballet. **Marius Petipa** worked with the famous ballet composer, **Pyotr Ilyich Tchaikovsky**. He wrote the magical music for *The Sleeping Beauty*, *The Nutcracker*, and *Swan Lake*.

Benesh notation from *Les Sylphides*.

On with the show

Everyone in a ballet company has a part to play in putting on a successful show.

The dance is choreographed, or designed, to fit the theater. The stage is carefully lit and the scenery painted.

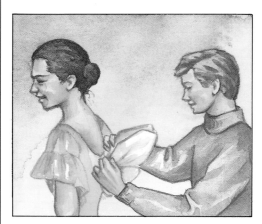

There must be rehearsals and time for costumes to be made or repaired.

Stagehands or **dressers** must check where to stand backstage to help a dancer with a quick costume change.

The **stage manager** and **technical crew** check that all the scenery and props are safe and in place.

The **dress rehearsal**, when costumes are first worn, is the last chance to practice before **opening night**.

A good **lighting designer** can transform the stage and create a magical atmosphere by the way the lights are positioned.

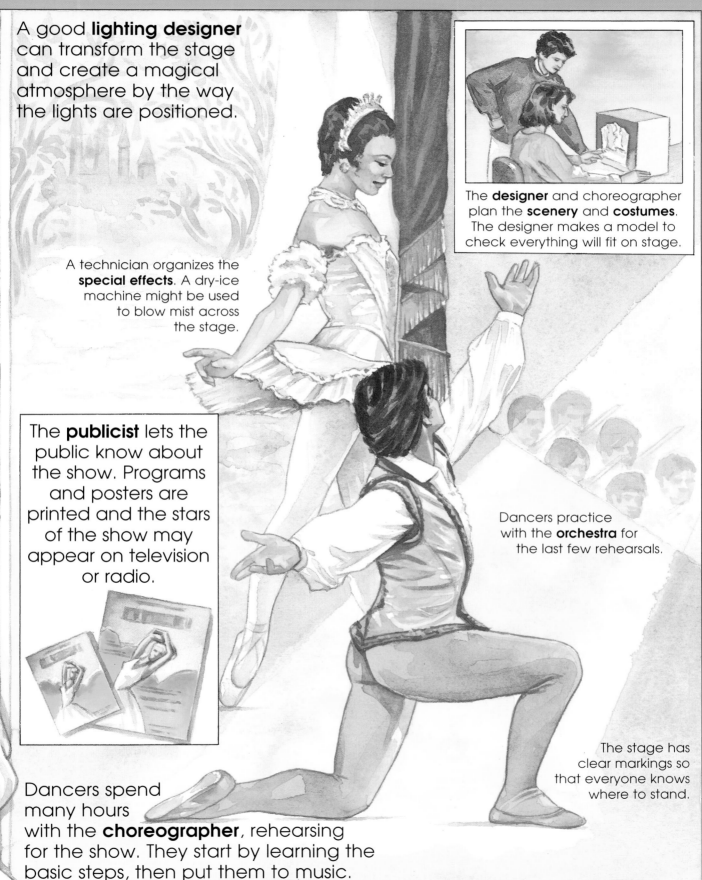

The **designer** and choreographer plan the **scenery** and **costumes**. The designer makes a model to check everything will fit on stage.

A technician organizes the **special effects**. A dry-ice machine might be used to blow mist across the stage.

The **publicist** lets the public know about the show. Programs and posters are printed and the stars of the show may appear on television or radio.

Dancers practice with the **orchestra** for the last few rehearsals.

The stage has clear markings so that everyone knows where to stand.

Dancers spend many hours with the **choreographer**, rehearsing for the show. They start by learning the basic steps, then put them to music.

Dance for fun

People all over the world get together to dance for fun and to meet people.

Ceroc is a new and exciting form of modern jive based on French rock 'n' roll. There are steps to learn but you can dance to almost any kind of music.

Social dance is affected by fashion and is often inspired by movies and music.

Rap, **rave**, and **cult dance** all rely on the beat and sound of the loud music. The DJ plays the music the dancers want to hear!

The Waltz is perhaps one of the most famous social dances. It was first danced in Germany in 1780 when the swinging turns and the close contact between partners were considered shocking!

Johann Strauss wrote the music that made the waltz popular.

Ballroom dancers often take part in competitions.

Ballroom dancing is very popular. **Old-time**, **Modern**, and **Latin American** are all types of ballroom dancing.

Latin dance came from South America, with lively dances such as the Rumba, Samba, and Mambo.

Latin music is very rhythmic and noisy!

The **Jitterbug** and **Boogie-Woogie** were thrilling new dances in the 1940s. American and Canadian soldiers took them to Britain during World War II. These dances are now known as **jive**.

Rock 'n' roll became popular in the 1950s when records became cheap enough for young people to buy. Dancers jumped, turned, and twisted to music by popular singers such as Bill Haley and Elvis Presley.

The **Alligator** and **The Monkey** were fashionable 1960s dances.

Dances like **The Twist** and **The Mashed Potato** were invented in the 1960s when people began to dance on their own.

Disco dancing began in the 1970s. You do not have to dance in pairs and there are no set steps. The way you look and move are more important.

National dance

Every country has its own dance form. National dances grow from religion, folk tales, and even the weather.

Colorful costumes and decorations are part of each country's national dance.

India has a tremendous diversity of peoples, climates, languages, and dances. One of the most popular is **Bharata Natyam**, which started as part of religious worship 2,000 years ago. A story is told using hand movements and facial expressions.

The dancer's bare feet tap out complex rhythmic patterns.

In England, **Morris dancing** is traditionally danced by men. They wear bells and ribbons and dance in lines facing each other. A man called the "fool" carries a colorful stick and hits anyone who misses a step!

The Polish **Mazurka** is danced by eight or sixteen couples in a circle.

The main Spanish dancing styles are regional dances like the **fandango** and **flamenco**. Flamenco has developed from Asian, Arabic, and gypsy dancing.

Settlers in the United States have created many country dances. At a **Square Dance** the "caller" tells the dancers what to do. Dancers swing their partners as the banjo and fiddle play.

Flamenco is often danced to the music of guitars and castanets.

Irish dancers' costumes are embroidered with Celtic designs.

In **Irish dancing**, the upper body is kept straight and stiff while the legs and feet kick and step.

The **Scottish Reel** is a gliding and springing dance performed by couples. Music is played on the bagpipes. The men wear a pleated, tartan kilt that is like a skirt.

The **Maoris** of New Zealand use dance to communicate. As they dance they chant, quiver their hands, and use facial expressions. The dancing is often accompanied by a sung poem.

Women wear a white dress with a tartan sash for dancing.

Ballet school life

Anyone who wants to become a professional ballet dancer will need to train hard for many years.

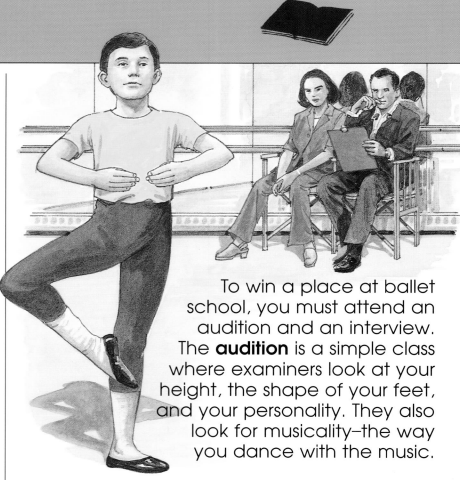

To win a place at ballet school, you must attend an audition and an interview. The **audition** is a simple class where examiners look at your height, the shape of your feet, and your personality. They also look for musicality–the way you dance with the music.

Ballet schools give every student the chance to dance the best they can, to discover their talents, and perhaps, become a famous dancer.

Ballet schools are much like any other schools. Pupils study for exams and learn the usual subjects, such as English, Math, and Biology. They also have special lessons including Music, Drama, History of Dance, Singing, and Contemporary Dance.

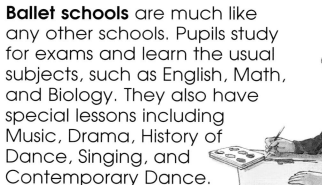

When pupils reach the age of sixteen, they begin to learn **ballet repertory** and **classical pas de deux**.

Regularly, students at **The School of American Ballet** put on performances at Lincoln Center in New York City.

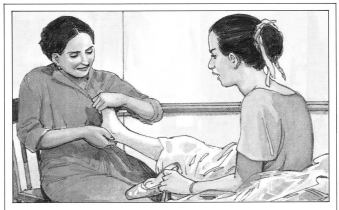

A thorough training in dance opens up many career opportunities. Dancers can become choreographers, stage managers, administrators, teachers, and **physiotherapists**.

Being involved in a performance is excellent practice for the future. Not only do dancers learn about the art of performing but also the demands of **rehearsals** and the many jobs involved in producing a show.

Days are long and demanding but dancers must have a good all-around education as not every student will take up a career as a dancer.

A career as a dancer is not easy or secure. Not everyone will grow to the right height and there is always the risk of injury. Dancing is not just a career—it is a way of life that can be very exciting and rewarding.

Factfinder

INDEX

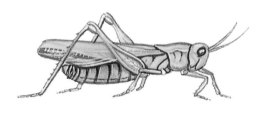

D

da Vinci, Leonardo 230, 280
Dab 67
Damselfly 9, 18
Dance classes 296
Dance companies 294-295, 301
Dance Theatre of Harlem, The 295
Darius, King 179
David, statue of 129
Dead Sea 114, 143
Death Valley 100, 143
Death's head hawkmoth 44
Death-watch beetle 33
Deep-sea angler fish 68
Deep-sea fish 39
Deep-sea shrimps 68
Demavend, Mount 115
Denmark 97, 234
Dermistid beetle 15
Desert 161
Desertification 161
Diadem butterfly 28-29
Diaghilev, Serge 289
Dinosaurs 173
Disco 311
Disease 168-169
Diverging light 281
Dixon, Jeane 253
Dodoma 111
Dogwhelk 67
Dolphins 78, 79
Dominoes 251
Dormant 150
Downing Street 241
Dowsing 254
Dr. Charles Richter 148
Dragonfly 18
Drakensburg Mountains 110
Dropping Well 137
Drought 160-160, 162

Dugong 60
Duncan, Isadora 289, 293
Dung beetle 46
Dust Bowl 160
Dutch elm disease 171
Dyke 157

E

Earhart, Amelia 247
Earth 174
Earthquake 148-149, 158
Earthworm 9, 24
Earwig 34
East Germany 95
Easter Island 128
Eclipses 147
Ecuadorian erenus butterfly 28
Edison, Thomas 220, 224, 228
Edward I, King 201
Edward, Prince of Wales 252
Egypt 110
Eiffel Tower 126
Eiffel, Alexandre-Gustave 126
El Cid 193
Elasmosaurus 90
Elbe River 95
Elbrus, Mount 92, 99
Electric lift 238
Electric locomotive 207
Electric motor 229
Electron microscope 212
Electronic telephone exchanges 223
Elephant 36-37
Elephant seal 50-51, 76
Elm bark beetle 34
Emperor dragonfly 18
Emperor penguin 70
Empire State Building 127, 153
Enchaînement 300
Endoscope 213

I

N

Rock 'n' Roll 311
Rock of Cashel 186
Rockpools 66, 67
Rocky Mountains 100, 102
Rods 268
Romans 182-186
Rome 98
Röntgen, Wilhelm 213
Rorke's Drift, Battle of 176
Royal Ballet School, The 315
Royal Ballet, The 295
Royal Danish Ballet Company, The 294
Royal ghosts 232
Rub Al-Khali (desert) 114
Rudder 209
Rufiji River 111
Runes stones 250
Russia 92, 99
Rysy Peak 99

S

Sabretooth cat 62-63
Sacasahuaman 194
Sagrada Familia 139
Sahara Desert 108, 143
Sahel, the 161
Sailfish 87
Sailing boats 208
Saladin 193
Salem 248
Samarkand, City of 199
Samurai 198
San Andreas fault 149
San Francisco 149
Sandwasp 35
Sarawak Chamber 137
Sardinia 98
Sarmatians 202
Satellite television 225

Saudi Arabia 112, 114
Sawfish 53
Scandinavia 93, 96, 97
Scarab beetle 14
Scorpion 8, 48
Scorpion fish 66
Scottish Reel 313
Scottish warriors 201
Sea anemone 43, 64, 65
Sea birds 82, 83
Sea dangers 166-167
Sea dragon 87
Sea horse 64
Sea reptiles 84
Sea serpent 91
Sea urchin 54
Seals 70, 71, 76, 77
Seashore 66, 67
Sei whale 74
Seikan Tunnel 133
Semaphore 222
Sennet, Max 276
Serengeti Plain 111
Serios, Ted 255

T

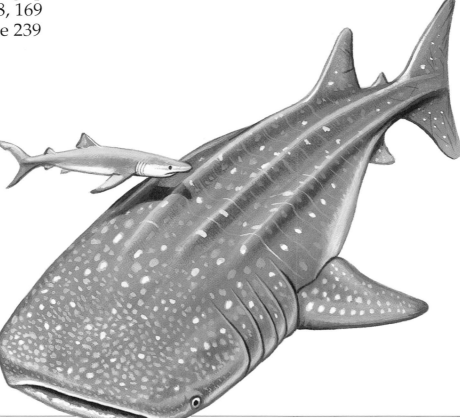

This book was created by Zigzag Publishing,
a division of Quadrillion Publishing Ltd., Godalming Business Centre,
Woolsack Way, Godalming, Surrey GU7 1XW England

Written by
Moira Butterfield, Fiona Corbridge, Jon Day, Gerald Legg, Rupert Matthews,
Duncan Muir, Maggie Tucker, Chris Oxlade, and Carol Watson

Consultants:
Keith Lye, John Becklake, Richard Thames, Laura Wade

Editors:
Kay Barnham, Helen Burnford, Paul Harrison,
Fiona Mitchell, Philippa Moyle,
Hazel Songhurst, and Nicola Wright

Originally published in eleven separate volumes from the Zigzag Factfinder series:
*Minibeasts, Monster Animals, Fantastic Sea Creatures, Countries, Wonders of the World,
Natural Disasters, Warriors, Inventions, Supernatural, Optical Illusions, Ballet and Dance.*
Copyright © 1997 Zigzag Publishing.

This edition published in 1997 by Zigzag Publishing

Distributed in the U.S. by SMITHMARK PUBLISHERS
a division of U.S. Media Holdings, Inc.
115 West 18th Street, New York, NY 10011

Color separations: RCS Graphics Ltd, Leeds and
Sussex Repro, Portslade, England and Proost, Belgium
Printed in Singapore

ISBN 0-7651-9273-X
8503